Y0-AAG-582

Personnel Administration and Human Resources Management

Dedicated to the memory of
Gerald John Sikula, Cathleen Ann Casey
and Virginia Grace Curran.

ANDREW F. SIKULA

Department of Management

University of Illinois at Chicago Circle

Personnel Administration and Human Resources Management

A Wiley/Hamilton Publication

JOHN WILEY & SONS, INC.

Santa Barbara / New York / London / Sydney / Toronto

Library of Congress Cataloging in Publication Data

Sikula, Andrew F
  Personnel administration and human resources
management.

    Includes bibliographies and indexes.
    1. Personnel management. I. Title.

HF5549.S5894 1976   658.3   75-8691
ISBN 0-471-79140-7

Printed in the United States of America

10-9 8 7 6 5 4 3 2 1

Preface

The personnel or human resources of an organization are its most important and valuable assets. Therefore, the management of human beings is fundamental to all administrative activities. The student of introductory personnel management will find here a summary of the best and most current thinking related to the management of people in their work environments. The book's unique features are its brevity and my desire to give an all-encompassing overview of the personnel administration function instead of dealing with organization theories, human relation concepts, and supervisory principles. To help the student to understand the personnel function, an outline and learning objectives are included for each chapter. Numerous illustrations point out important personnel concepts.

I am grateful to my academic colleagues and the Wiley staff who helped me to prepare this textbook. I especially thank my wife, Celeste, who was coauthor, editor, artist, typist, proofreader, critic, and friend.

ANDREW F. SIKULA

Contents

PART ONE

Background and Setting of Personnel Administration

contents

learning objectives

1. To understand the general evolution of the personnel function from a historical perspective.

2. To become aware of definitional and semantic problems within the field of personnel administration.

3. To be able to identify the major modern movements affecting personnel administration.

4. To envision personnel administration as a partial composite of "career," "professional," and academic "disciplinary" elements.

One cannot thoroughly understand the present or the future without adequate knowledge of the past.

1

The Evolution Of Personnel Administration

1. Terminology and Definitional Problems

Various problems of terminology must be dealt with before a comprehendible discussion of personnel administration can take place. Several semantic and definitional complications are encountered when attempting to identify the discipline and practice of personnel administration. Many of these definitional difficulties are due to the failure to distinguish general management and administration from personnel management and administration.

Definition of Management

Management in general refers to the planning, organizing, controlling, staffing, leading, motivating, communicating, and decision-making activities performed by any organization in order to coordinate the varied resources of the enterprise so as to bring about an efficient creation of some product or service. The exact activities or functions performed by managers are subject to debate and conjecture, but traditionally the processes of planning, organizing, and controlling are among the most frequently cited and identified activities. Management is concerned with various organizational resources

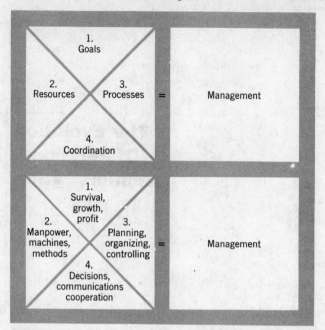

FIGURE 1-1   Four elements of a good definition of management.

or inputs. Men, money, methods, materials, and machinery are examples of such inputs. Land, labor, capital, buildings, and equipment are also organizational resources of general management concern. Although many definitions of general management can be proposed, any adequate definition should contain four elements: (1) an identification of general management activities or processes; (2) an identification of organizational resources or inputs; (3) a predetermined enterprise goal or objective; and (4) a means of total organizational coordination. Figure 1-1 summarizes these key elements.

Additional semantic issues related to the concept of general management can be observed when it is recognized that the term "management" is used grammatically in a variety of ways. The word "management" or one of its many derivatives is frequently used in grammatical forms such as a noun, an adjective, a verb, or a participle. In terms of context, however, the concept of "management" is usually used as (1) a set of processes, (2) a group of people, (3) a discipline or area of study, or (4) a career. As a set of processes, management refers to the planning, organizing, and controlling activities of an organization. For example, to say that "the management of the organization is inefficient" may mean that the organization has poor planning, organizing, and controlling techniques or procedures. Or this statement may mean that the people running the organization are inefficient — in which case management now refers to a group of people instead of to a set of processes. If a student is taking a management course, however, management now refers to an academic discipline or area of study. In addition, to say that you have "a position in management" may imply that you have a job, occupation, or career in this field. Closely related to the concept of management as a career is the idea of management as a profession. The preceding discussion indicates that the word "management" is used in a variety of ways, and the individual must ascertain its intended meaning.

Personnel Subarea

Personnel management is a subarea of general management. Personnel concentrates on the human activities element of general management; that is, personnel management is concerned basically with the manpower or "people" organizational resource or input. Figure 1-2 illustrates how personnel management can be conceived of as a subarea of general management.

Personnel Terminology

Many concepts and phrases in the personnel field are closely related and, to some degree, represent interchangeable terminology. For example, personnel, personnel administration, personnel management, employee relations, and industrial relations all have only shades of difference in meaning. Personnel administration is usually the preferred identification, since it is the most comprehensive. The term personnel administration was used initially to describe the staffing activities taking place within a nonprofit, public institution, and the phrase personnel management or industrial relations was reserved to identify staffing activities occurring in the private, profit-oriented

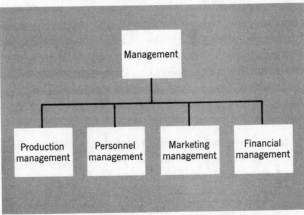

FIGURE 1-2 Personnel management as a subarea of general management.

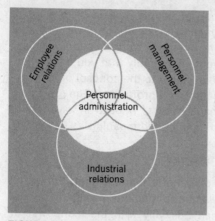

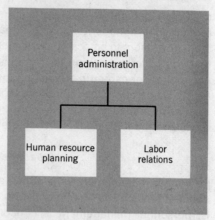

FIGURE 1-3 Interrelated "personnel" terminology.

FIGURE 1-4 Human resource planning and labor relations as subareas of personnel administration.

sector of the economy. Today, however, the phrase personnel administration is usually preferred because of its greater scope. In this broadened capacity, personnel administration applies to both the private-industrial and the public-nonindustrial institutional sectors of the economy. The phrase employee relations, however, is still preferred by some authors when identifying global personnel matters taking place within various organizations (Sokolik). "Human resource planning" and "labor relations" are also sometimes used in reference to personnel staffing matters; they are, however, best thought of as subareas of personnel administration. Human resource planning concentrates on forecasting future personnel requirements of an organization, while labor relations concentrates on contract negotiation and collective bargaining activities between organizational labor and management entities. Figure 1-3 illustrates that the phrases "personnel administration," "personnel management," "industrial relations," and "employee relations" are commonly thought of as highly interrelated and interchangeable concepts. However, Figure 1-4 shows that human resource planning and labor relations are best pictured as unit subareas of global personnel administration activities.

Definition of Personnel Administration

It is difficult to arrive at a universally accepted definition of personnel administration from the many that are available (Kimmerly). However, the following is my preferred definition: personnel administration is the implementation of human resources (manpower) by and within an enterprise. The key word is "implementation." Differing definitions replace or expand the idea of personnel implementation. For example, a more comprehensive

Human resource planning
+ Staffing and appraisal
+ Training and development
+ Compensation: Wage and salary administration
+ Compensation: Benefits and services
+ Health and safety
+ Labor relations-collective bargaining
+ Personnel research

TOTAL PERSONNEL ADMINISTRATION

FIGURE 1-5 Personnel administration equation.

definition is outlined by the Table of Contents of this textbook. Such a definition would indicate that personnel administration concerns the human resource areas of human resource planning; staffing and appraisal; training and development; compensation: wage and salary administration; compensation: benefits and services; health and safety; labor relations-collective bargaining; and personnel research. This more comprehensive personnel definition is shown in Figure 1-5 as a "personnel administration equation."

Another definition with a staffing emphasis is that personnel administration is the recruitment, selection, placement, indoctrination, training, and development of human resources (manpower) by and within an enterprise. Figure 1-6 shows that these six subareas are part of the larger idea of manpower or human resource implementation.

2. Evolution of the Personnel Function

The historical evolution of the personnel function is inseparable from the historical evolution of mankind. All the events that make up history have had at least some impact on the evolving nature of employee relationships. A

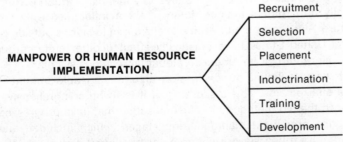

FIGURE 1-6 Manpower or human resource "implementation."

global and comprehensive study of personnel and human relations must initially begin with the study of human beings.

The study of the historical evolution of the personnel function began with the occurrence of interpersonal relationships (Singer). Nevertheless, it is impossible to trace through such developments thoroughly without considerable time and space allowances. Because this chapter is to merely present a cursive introductory background of personnel administration, only major variables and factors affecting the development of personnel administration will be discussed in the remainder of this chapter.

A Historical Viewpoint

Before we proceed, preliminary cautions and observations must be noted. First, the evolution of the personnel function is historical in that it is intimately intertwined and associated with the times and events of history. The social, economic, political, technological, and cultural occurrences that have left their marks on history in general have also influenced at least indirectly the developing nature and scope of personnel administration. Second, the historical evolution of the personnel function is evolutionary, not revolutionary. That is, the changes that have occurred in the personnel field have been caused mostly by gradual cultural changes, not by drastic happenings. Some events, of course, have taken place in history that have had an immediate and significant impact on societies and cultures within a relatively short time. However, such incidents are relatively rare compared to the normal pace of change.

American — Post 1900

In narrowing down the scope of the evolutionary history of personnel administration, I will discuss only the historical events that have had their major impact since the turn of the century and those that have had a decided influence on the evolving nature of uniquely American employee relations. "The turn of the century" refers to the years since 1900. Uniquely "American" employee relations refers generally to North America, but "American" specifically means in reference to the United States of America. Although world events generally have global impact, some of them influenced only the American culture. Also, some major events occurring in locations outside of the continental United States have drastically affected other cultures but have had only minor impact on American industrial relations systems.

Even though we have limited our discussion, an unmanageable amount of historical data still remains. This discussion, if it is to be comprehensive, must still refer to the old methods of industrialization that have progressed through the once prominent manufacturing stages, which included and made use of primitive tribes, slavery, serfdom, the handicraft system, and the putting out or cottage arrangement. The introduction of factory methods and modern industrial relations systems featuring division and specialization of labor, mass production, interchangeable parts, the assembly line, and other relatively recent phenomena would also still have to be explained in detail. In addition, comprehensive coverage of this era should trace the major acts of legislation, especially at the national level, that have affected modern American personnel practices. Although this period requires an extensive discussion of the previously mentioned materials, I will highlight other major occurrences during this era that have drastically affected modern American personnel practices. Students who desire more detailed information should refer to the bibliography at the end of this chapter (especially Eilbirt).

3. Major Modern Movements Affecting Personnel Administration

Different authors and historians may identify different events when they determine the major modern movements that have affected American personnel administration practicies. Neither the exact number nor the specific instances involved can be universally agreed on because of varying interpretations of the terms "major," "modern," and "movements." "Major" is a scope measure that differs in magnitude when perceived by various authors. For some, major represents an event of colossal impact, while for others it identifies a dimension of much less significance. An added complication is that even if scholars agree on the scope of the label major, they still may not agree on how important a historical event may be. The problems associated with the term "modern" have already been mentioned. Some writers use modern for current events only. Many historians do not consider events that are dated by more than a decade or two to be modern. Much of this issue depends on the time span or time period of reference used. In my opinion, since it has been recognized that the historical evolution of personnel administration began with the introduction of man onto this planet, it does not seem unreasonable to label events of the last seventy-five years modern. Another controversy or difficulty is vested in the concept of a "movement." Although some author disagreement tends to exist, the concept of a movement generally is used to identify not an isolated event, but a sequence of interrelated events that often seem to have occurred in a chain-reaction or multiplier-effect fashion. Usually such movements are initially begun by one or a few specific events or occurrences, but the total, final impact of such a movement is caused by a synergistic linking together in cluster fashion of initial events and later related occurrences.

The major modern movements affecting American personnel administration practices, as I envision them, include (1) the industrial revolution; (2) the growth of unionism; (3) the scientific management era; (4) the paternalistic era; (5) the industrial psychology era; (6) the human relations era; (7) the behavioral era; (8) the emergence of personnel specialists; and (9) the welfare era.

A. INDUSTRIAL REVOLUTION

It is difficult to date the era collectively identified as the industrial revolution. This movement seems to have occurred at different times in different cultures. Even within the American culture there is no general consensus as to when this period begins and ends. However, most historians admit that the major impact of this force began around the turn of the century (Eilbirt). The question of when, if ever, this movement officially ended is another issue of unresolved debate. Instead of arguing the dates of its existence, it is more important to identify key characteristics of the period. This era has been labeled an "industrial" revolution because the changes that took place at this time and had such an impact on society in general were found within the industrial and economic sectors of the economy. New factory methods and techniques were introduced that drastically changed how products were produced. This industrial era has also been labeled as a "revolution." Many historians prefer the term "evolution," instead of revolution. The controversy is semantic. Because there were many rapid changes in industry at this time compared to the prior normal progression and advancement of industrial methodologies, history refers to these years as an industrial revolution, not as an industrial evolution.

Characteristics of the Industrial Revolution

In essence the industrial revolution describes a period that saw the rise of the factory system and the substitution of machine for human power. Industrial work was no longer done in the home; instead, many people worked in one factory. This made it possible to supervise and control employees more closely. Now it was also possible to handle the production processes much more efficiently. The invention and manufacture of power-driven machinery occurred with the development of the factory system. As a consequence, employees were brought together basically to serve in primarily machine-operating and parts-assembling jobs.

Modern industrialized society has greatly expanded and developed the original factory system of production (Dunlop). Science and technology have been applied to all facets of the modern industrial corporation. This expanded revolution features many characteristics that were relatively nonexistent before the turn of the century. The most important of these industrial revolution features are division and specialization of labor, mass production and assembly, automation, elimination of heavy physical labor, emergence of scientists and engineers, and development of computerized control systems.

Interrelated Characteristics

All of these developments are intimately interrelated and have evolved collectively. Division and specialization of labor allowed a worker to become an expert in some minor area of production. This expertise led to the development of specific skills which, in turn, led to both a large quantity and a greater quality of product. Large quantities became part of the philosophy of mass production and, after mass production, came the natural aftermath of mass assembly. It had by this time become apparent that mass production and mass assembly could be enhanced by automation, that is, by the control and regulation of machines by machines. Automation, in essence, involves the use of machines and substitutes for human tenders or operators. Using machine power made it possible to a great extent to eliminate heavy physical labor from most jobs. With this increased use of specialized labor and machinery came the emergence of key types of personnel. Especially important during the industrial revolution era were the developing roles of the scientist and engineer. Science and technology advanced to new levels of sophistication during this time. Undoubtedly, the most significant scientific and technological development of this period was the introduction of computers. Computers made it possible to efficiently control various aspects of industrial behavior. Production control, methods control, inventory control, financial control, and manpower control have all been enhanced immeasurably by the introduction of computerized techniques and procedures.

Implications

Of course, not all of the implications and ramifications of the industrial revolution have been positive in nature. Increased industrialization also brought new and increased human problems. Materialism, discipline, monotony, boredom, job displacement, impersonality, worker interdependence, and related behavioral phenomena also resulted from this new industrial era. Although not all historians agree, most observers believe that the benefits of the industrial revolution universally have far outweighed the costs of increased industrialization (Perline and Tull).

B. GROWTH IN UNIONISM

Shortly after the advent of the factory system, groups of employees began to get together to discuss mutual employer problems and concerns. Initially, they discussed child abuse, long hours, and poor working conditions. Over time, however, economic conditions became the focal point. The important matter was the wage level paid to the employees. Later economic issues dealing with employee benefits and services were of major emphasis. Workers joined together collectively over matters of common interest to improve their lot.

Strength in Numbers

Initial employer-employee relationships served as examples to later workers that employees could do little, if anything, when they tried individually to confront management about certain issues. The basic philosophy underlying unionism is simply that there is strength in numbers. That is, if enough people could collectively support a certain position, management would more or less be forced to listen to a complaint, even though the complaint was initiated by a group of nonsupervisory working personnel. The type of force used by employees took a variety of forms; the most feared was the strike. Slowdowns, walkouts, pickets, boycotts, sabotage, and actual physical force were also frequently used employee group power tactics during this unionism period, which began to grow rapidly during the early 1900s.

Unionism efforts by American workers first emerged as trade unions. Workers performing the same type of jobs joined together to promote their general trade interests. Cobblers, printers, carpenters, meat cutters, coal miners, and others began to form groups and unions devoted to the security and the advancement of their particular job interests. Eventually the concept of unionism spread to include even the positions that were unskilled in nature. While some unions were formed to protect particular skills and trades, others were started to protect the general interests of unskilled workers.

Through the years and even up to the present time, employers often have not taken kindly to the unionization of their workers. The general feeling expressed by management was initially that "we own the facilities so we alone have the right to direct how such facilities are to be used." When corporations, instead of sole proprietorships and partnerships, became the most common legal form of organization within American industry, such a rationale became even harder for workers to accept since, in a corporation, the owners and managers are often not the same people. Even within corporations, however, many managers still do not like to have their authority challenged by organized workers.

Legislation

In addition, groups of workers pressured elected officials and campaigned for politicians who supported their causes. Particularly as a result of such efforts, numerous legislative statutes were passed at the federal and state levels to enhance the rights of organizational employees. Such laws were enacted especially during the 1930s and the 1940s. The most influential of these laws were the Wagner and Taft-Hartley Acts. The Fair Labor Standards Act, the Social Security Act, the Civil Rights Act, and President John F. Kennedy's Executive Order 10988 have also had a tremendous impact on the growth of American unionism.

Nonunionized

Although unionism has grown tremendously in America over the last century, still well over half of the workers in this country are not unionized. In general, unionism prevails within large corporations in key industries that utilize semiskilled and skilled workers. Service and professional employees in white collar jobs still remain largely unorganized, although many of these groups have recently decided to involve themselves in unionization activities and movements. Today, many nonunionized settings resemble unionized environments. Benefits won in unionized shops frequently transfer to nonunionized shops in the same industry or geographical location. Wage rates, grievance systems, holidays, disciplinary procedures, pension plans, and the like are common examples of benefits existing in nonunionized settings as a result of the mimicking of similar unionized work settings and conditions.

Unionization Impact

There is disagreement in this country about what impact, if any, the labor movement in general and unionism efforts in particular have had on corporate activities. Although there is a debate about what the economic level of wages currently would be if unionism had not arrived on the scene, there is less questioning of other implications and ramifications of American unionism. Unionism has had tangible influence on the management of personnel, such as the adoption of employee grievance handling systems, almost universal acceptance of arbitration to resolve conflicts of rights, due process discipline practices, expansion of employee benefit programs, liberalization of holiday and vacation time off, clear definition of job duties, job rights through seniority, and the installation of rational and defensible wage structures (Eilbirt).

C. SCIENTIFIC MANAGEMENT ERA

The scientific management era began in 1900, reached its peak approximately in 1930, and then dwindled in relative importance but remained somewhat alive, even up to the present. The term "scientific" is used to describe this period because emphasis was and is given to the systematic study of management techniques and procedures. This era features an engineering perspective of studying managerial duties, activities, and responsibilities. Technical analysis of machine operations was initiated in extensive fashion during the early years of this historical period.

Frederick Taylor

The scientific management movement is usually associated with the works of Frederick W. Taylor. Taylor, who has been labeled the father of scientific management, popularized important shop management techniques such as time study, methods study, functional foremanship, standardization of tools, a differential piece-rate system, instructional cards for workmen, and a cost control system. Taylor basically performed his experiments and studies in the coal mining and steel industries, but other researchers spread his ideas throughout various American industries (Eilbirt).

There is considerable controversy over the question of what role Taylor should be credited with historically in the development of the American industrial system. Originally Taylor was believed to have been responsible for the creation of many new and, until his time, unheard of management techniques. Advocates and followers of Taylor formed Taylor Societies to promote and advance these ideas and techniques. Many later historians, however, when analyzing Taylor's academic training and work background, revealed that many of the management concepts originally credited to Taylor actually were not new ideas but management techniques that had been practiced in other European countries for some time and were yet still unknown to the American culture. With this frame of reference, some modern historians are much less willing to credit Taylor with much in the way of original creativity. Instead, such observers point out that Taylor did not create but, instead, he introduced and popularized certain managerial techniques within this country.

One Best Way

Taylor believed strongly in the philosophy of the "one best method." Unquestionably, there are almost an infinite number of ways to perform any job or task. But Taylor explained that some methods of performing a task are much more efficient and effective than others. Furthermore, if there are several possible efficient ways to perform any task, one of these alternatives must be "the one best method" in terms of economic feasibility and practicality. Taylor's works are devoted to this idea of finding the one most economically efficient method of performing a job. Until his insistence, relatively few managers within American industrial organizations gave much emphasis to discovering "the one best way" to accomplish their objectives.

Time and Motion Studies

The methodology used to discover this "one best way" featured time and motion studies. Worker body movements were timed with a stopwatch and recorded on charts. Attempts were then made to eliminate unnecessary motions. Alternative shapes and sizes of hand tools were also studied in an effort to discover the elusive one best method. Later versions of time and motion studies introduced the movie camera as an additional technique of this type of scientific analysis.

Many individuals in addition to Frederick Taylor are associated with the scientific management era. Some of the more frequently cited personalities are Frank and Lillian Gilbreth, Henry L. Gantt, Morris L. Cook, and Harrington Emerson. It is believed that such persons exerted a profound effect on management thought and practice throughout the world.

Scientific Management Impact

The scientific management movement has had a great impact on employee-employer relationships and on management in general. It elevated management by plan, system, and design while causing management by hunch and intuition to decline. In so doing, this movement contributed greatly to the professionalization of management. It also brought the engineer into a more active management role.

After two or three decades of extreme popularity, however, the scientific management movement, featuring its exclusive engineering philosophy, began to lose some of its prestige and glamour because of its failure to solve certain types of managerial problems. It later became apparent that many, if not most, of management's problems were the result of human, not mechanical phenomena. Such reasoning and insight gave impetus to the development of the welfare era, the industrial psychology era, and the human relations era.

D. PATERNALISTIC ERA

The paternalistic era is a philosophical movement that appeared sporadically throughout the nineteenth century. The paternalistic philosophy identifies a humanistic and altruistic attitude that seemed to exist within the hearts and minds of some of the upper-level officers of many industrial enterprises. There is uncertainty about why and how such a philosophy initially got started. Some historians attribute this movement largely to unionism activities. The fear of unionism unquestionably led to this enlightened philosophy in some instances. Other observers believe that federal and state laws and directives provided the initial impetus for this era. Some laws directly called for certain improved employee conditions, while other informal directives, rulings, and suggestions indirectly brought about other environmental improvements for industrial workers. The fear of additional mandatory legislative requirements stimulated the development and protection of many employee rights. Although laws and unionism did affect the paternalism movement, it is still generally believed that enlightened humanitarian and altruistic concerns sincerely expressed and exhibited by certain management personnel had at least some impact on the evolution of this era (Williams).

Paternalism Backlash

Not all employees were particularly happy about this paternalistic movement. Overall working conditions were improved, but sometimes at the expense of employee individualism and pride. Some aspects of the paternalistic era were identified in philosophy as being "fatherly." All workers did not particularly enjoy a family relationship, where "daddy" was always supplying his "children" with the economic necessities of life while in return requiring, if not demanding, respect, admiration, and loyalty. The company town situation, where workers lived in company housing, bought their food and clothing from company owned stores, and even utilized company owned recreational facilities, was initially gladly accepted by workers, but they later developed an intolerance for this life-style. Paternalism seemed to fulfill the economic and security needs of workers, but it did so at the expense of human freedom and dignity. Some employees became so disheartened with this employer-employee relationship that they compared it to slavery or serfdom.

The paternalistic movement reached its peak from 1900 to 1920. This movement attempted to uplift the physical, hygienic, social, and educational conditions of working-class people. Early paternalistic programs included health facilities, wash-up and locker room arrangements, lunch rooms, recreational equipment, schools and libraries, group insurance and pension programs, and savings and legal aid provisions. Unfortunately, some employers offered these benefits to their employees to placate them into accepting long hours, low wages, and bad working conditions. Opportunism and expediency were the motives of some businessmen. Eventually managers became disillusioned when baseball and horseshoe-pitching leagues, company picnics, reading rooms, savings associations, and company housing did not increase productive efficiency. On the other hand, employees became equally disillusioned when they sensed that employer interest in them was not always genuine.

Although the paternalistic aspect of this era seemed to die out during the 1920s, the philosophy still lingered. The general well-being and living conditions of employees have remained vital issues over the years. The New Deal legislation and other federal and state laws were at least in part developments of this continued paternalistic philosophy and movement. The protection of worker rights and the enhancement of the economic and social status of employees are still major societal concerns today. These concerns had their beginnings in the original paternalistic era.

Impact

Over the last forty years we have seen a larger and larger proportion of the total employee compensation package in the form of various company benefits and services. This proportion or percentage of total compensation started out from zero and has risen to 25-35 percent for the typical industrial employee. There are even some examples currently available where benefits and services today comprise 40 percent of an employee's total compensation package. This increased concern over worker benefits and services had its roots in the paternalistic era. Thus, the paternalistic philosophy and movement is still with us even today, but its basic nature has changed and its existence is largely evidenced only within rising indirect compensation percentages.

E. INDUSTRIAL PSYCHOLOGY ERA

Industrial psychology is another general movement or philosophy that started during the twentieth century and seemed to develop, grow, and mature into its present form. This period identifies a time when psychologists were introduced into the field of industrial management to study systematically many of the prevailing personnel problems being experienced by various industrial organizations. This movement is usually associated with Hugo Musterberg, "the father of industrial psychology." This movement began around 1913.

The scientific management and the industrial psychology eras are similar in that they each began to investigate systematically the procedures and methods used within industrial organizations. The main difference, however, is that the scientific management movement stressed the role of the engineer and the study of production methods, while the industrial psychology movement stressed the role of the psychologist and the study of personnel practices.

Selection, Matching, and Testing

Many personnel practices were significantly improved because of the work of industrial psychologists. Advancements were made in selection, placement, testing, training, and research practices. Before the 1900s employee selection and placement almost appeared to be chance events. Worker qualifications and job requirements were of little concern in the hiring process. No disciplined attempts were made to try to coordinate the jobs to be done with the skills and abilities of the available manpower. Industrial psychology introduced the "matching" or "fitting" concept into the areas of employee selection and placement. The underlying rationale for the "matching" concept is simply that both jobs and employees exhibit unique individualized characteristics, and that needed job qualifications and requirements and displayed employee traits should be matched, fitted, or paired together in as compatible a manner as possible. Without doubt, different jobs require different skills and abilities. Also, different individuals possess different aptitudes and talents. The matching or fitting concept merely attempts to link together the right person and the right job. Although this is a relatively simplistic idea, it was, nevertheless, largely unrecognized and unpracticed until the turn of the century. Even though the concept is easy to understand, the techniques and methods of analysis needed to implement it are difficult to develop. Industrial psychologists were the first researchers to measure individual job and employee differences. Perhaps the most significant change that industrial psychologists brought about was the introduction of testing into the normal routine of industrial personnel practices. The analysis of job requirements and worker qualifications also led to the study of employee training procedures. If job needs and worker skills were not in balance, engineers attempted to restructure the job, while psychologists attempted to train or retrain the worker so as to bring these two organizational elements and resources into proper alignment. Employee training, management development, and other educational matters were the later results of the pioneering work done by the earliest industrial psychologists. These same industrial psychologists also did much to advance the general acceptance of the statistical research method as a frequently used managerial tool and technique of analysis.

The major contributions of industrial psychology to the professional practice of personnel have been in personnel testing, interviewing, attitude measurement, learning theory, training, fatigue and monotony studies, safety, job analysis, and human engineering. Of these, the major applications of the knowledge and techniques of industrial psychology have been in testing for employment, job placement, promotion, and training. Psychologists over the years have made major contributions to the practice of personnel basically because of their adherence to careful experimentation, their rigorous research designs, and their use of sophisticated statistical methods.

Industrial Psychology Impact

Usually only the largest corporations employ professionally trained industrial psychologists full time. Nevertheless, the impact of the industrial psychology movement is widespread because of the numerous current publications and consulting services that concentrate on such activities. The popularity of industrial psychology concepts and techniques rises and falls over the decades, often in direct relationship to the introduction of and later the disenchantment with new ideas created by personalities working within this field.

F. HUMAN RELATIONS ERA

The human relations movement peaked between the 1920s and the 1950s, although aspects of this era appeared before and after these dates. Much of the early basis for this period was due to a research program conducted at the Hawthorne Works plants of the Western Electric Company in Chicago during the late 1920s and early 1930s. This research study was headed by Elton Mayo, Fritz Roethlisberger, and W. J. Dickson of the Harvard University Graduate School of Business Administration. The study was originally an engineering type of experiment typical of the scientific management era. Physical and technical variables were manipulated to determine their effects on productivity. The experiment was abandoned because of the inconsistent relationships found between such physical factors and employee productivity. Temperatures, illumination, rest pauses, work period lengths, and other variables were changed and corresponding production effects were measured. It was found that within reasonable limits of intensity, it did not matter whether such factors were increased or decreased. Every change that was made led to increased productivity. Of course, if the changes were of extreme variation (e.g., if it became so dark that one could not see or so hot that physical exhaustion and fainting occurred), then obviously production would decrease. Nevertheless, the direction of the physical change, whether increased or decreased, usually led to increased productivity. The original researchers eventually abandoned this experiment, and Mayo and his colleagues later were called in to examine the situation. They concluded that human and social factors, not physical variables, accounted for the productivity phenomenon. The workers being studied felt privileged to be having their activities analyzed. They participated together as a group and developed a measure of rapport and teamwork. As a result of this experiment, employee productivity began to be analyzed in behavioral terms such as teamwork, participation, cohesiveness, loyalty, and *esprit de corps* instead of in terms of engineering alternatives. The basic conclusion of the Hawthorne Works experiments was that sociological and psychological phenomena often exerted even greater influence on output than physical, measurable conditions of work did. Accordingly, concepts such as social system, informal organization, group control of behavior, equilibrium, and logical and nonlogical behavior entered the language of human relations writers and personnel management specialists.

Human Emphasis

The human relations movement grew out of a reaction against the impersonality of the scientific management era. As management matured and became more professional, there was a growing realization that human resources were the most valuable asset that any organization possessed. An enterprise can have a great deal of money, machinery, methods, and equipment but, without competent manpower resources, such physical resources are useless. Management officials believing this were quick to accept behavioral research studies, which challenged the previously popular engineering philosophy. Since 1950, however, attempts have been made to repeat the types of experiments done at the Hawthorne Works plants. Many of these studies have reached differing conclusions. Although the exact relationships among behavioral phenomena and organizational productivity are still not known, it is generally believed that such human factors have a tremendous impact on total corporate operations.

Connotations in Meanings

The phrase "human relations" has acquired a variety of meanings. It commonly refers globally to interpersonal dealings and relationships between and among persons and groups. Sometimes the phrase exhibits an ethical connotation and dimension. For example, to say that a manager practices good human relations in the plant may mean that he respects the worth and dignity of his individual employees. Human relations now also refers to a discipline of study and a set of research experiments. Readers must interpret this phrase depending on the context in which it is used.

Impact

Just as the scientific management period exhibited extreme popularity for a couple of decades and then began to fade, so also did the influence of the human relations era reach a peak and then diminish. During the 1950s it became apparent that neither the scientific management era nor the human relations movement could, by itself, provide all the answers to all the numerous and complex organizational problems and dilemmas. Engineers, psychologists, and other professionals in recent years have been requested to work together to analyze and explain organizational activities (Domm and Stafford).

G. BEHAVIORAL ERA

Some observers believe that a separate movement, usually identified as the behavioral era, developed from the human relations era. This period begins around 1955, and its major impact lasts some ten to fifteen years. These years saw a blending of many of the features of previous eras. Human and behavioral factors were studied and emphasized, but the importance of scientific research and empirical data verification were also stressed. The term "revisionists" is also sometimes used to describe the philosophy of this era. Revisionists avoided the extreme engineering or scientific management approach, but did not entirely advocate the other extreme, which saw human relations factors as the only major variables affecting institutional life and organizational performances. Some management historians believe that even the present time period is highly indicative of the behavioral era and the revisionistic philosophy. Other reporters, however, do not distinguish between the human relations and the behavioral eras. Because the identification and importance of this era has not yet been universally agreed on, no further elaboration of this philosophy will be presented.

H. EMERGENCE OF PERSONNEL SPECIALISTS

Once the factory system began and the economy grew to a certain level of industrialization, the size of organizations made it mandatory for companies to devote at least some of their time and effort toward the accomplishment of certain specialized tasks. As soon as an organization grew to a magnitude of several hundred employees, numerous sets of activities which, in the past, did not take much time now began to require full-time efforts. One of the first of these specialized positions was the employment clerk, who was initially responsible for hiring a company's personnel. Later this role expanded into the recruitment and placement as well as the selection of personnel. When a company has several hundred employees, the recruiting, selection, and placement activities and responsibilities are usually significant enough to warrant a full-time manager.

Wage and salary administration also became a full-time job once a company reached a certain size. This subfunction began as a payroll activity, but later was also responsible for developing systematic methods of determining wage rates, usually through the development of job descriptions and job specifications. Later, when fringe benefits became an employee interest and concern, either the wage and salary manager took on this additional responsibility or, more commonly, another personnel specialist, the benefits and services manager, began performing these duties.

Training was another specialty area that became necessary as an organization grew. Someone had to be responsible for seeing that workers acquired the skills necessary for the performance of their jobs. This responsibility began as a part-time obligation of some company officer, but later became a full-time job. Eventually the job grew beyond merely the training of non-supervisory personnel to do manual types of jobs. Later management development programs emphasizing the learning of broader conceptual concerns by supervisory personnel were also incorporated into the duties of such a specialist.

Other types of personnel specialists also began to arrive on the scene. Safety experts, physicians, security guards, behavioral researchers, labor relations specialists, and others seemed to emerge from organizations that grew very large. Eventually, for organizational and administrative purposes, all of these diverse activities were collected together and put under the responsibility of some main manager, who was usually identified as a personnel manager, since all of these specialty areas involved unique problems associated with the human resources or manpower inputs employed by organizations.

Structural Implications

Unlike the other major modern movements that have affected personnel administration, the emergence of personnel specialists does not represent a philosophical movement; instead, it is best thought of as a physical or structural movement. The growing size of organizations forced these personnel specialists into existence. Their occurrence did not come about basically because of attitudinal or philosophical changes, although such considerations may have later indirectly affected the evolution of the personnel specialists.

It is hard to say which type of personnel specialist will be the first, second, or third to arrive on the scene once an organization begins to grow. This is determined largely by the nature of the company, the type of product it produces, the leadership styles and managerial philosophies of the officers of the company, the peculiar and unique working conditions existing within the organization, and other related factors. It is, nevertheless, quite common to find the employment, wage and salary, and training personnel subfunctions as specialty areas that quickly become necessary in any organization employing over a few hundred employees.

Professionalization of Roles

Initially these personnel specialists were not specialists; they had no special training or study in their job areas. They were specialists only in that their activities and efforts concentrated on a limited scope of duties and responsibilities. However, after decades of practicing this narrowly defined job area, such specialists did, in fact, become specialists or experts in these areas. Eventually this expertise was incorporated into specialized training programs and educational curriculums. Graduates of such programs may be called specialists in the sense that this term commonly is interpreted today.

Impact

Today personnel departments are formed in growing organizations in much the same manner as they have always been formed (Kramer). Specialists dealing with unique manpower problems met under the auspices of a central personnel officer to deal with personnel and personnel-related problems and issues.

I. WELFARE ERA

Some historians refer to the period we are now living in as a welfare era. This period of philosophy has developed over the last forty years. The welfare label is used because the concern now seems to be for the general well-being of all humans. This sentiment started in the paternalistic era of the early 1900s and gained impetus with the federal welfare legislation of the 1930s.

Over the years concern for employee welfare has taken other significant additional steps. Indirect compensation is now 30 percent of an employee's total compensation. Affirmative action, EEOC, and OSHA have enhanced the well-being of all workers. Soon to come will be national health insurance benefits to assist all persons in the payment of major medical expenses. These and other activities, combined with women's liberation, black pride, and an emphasis on equality, honesty, and justice have led to the development of the welfare era.

The welfare label is not always used to describe the present attitudes of the country. Some critics object to the term "welfare" because it connotes being "on welfare," that is, accepting money from the government but not providing any useful service for society in return. ADC (aid to dependent children) and social security benefits are examples of such government payments. The real problem with such benefits is not with their rationale, but with their administration. The ideas behind such forms of payment are laudable, but the inefficient bureaucratic organizations set up to distribute these benefits leave much to be desired.

Historical Synthesis

The study of the historical evolution of personnel administration is inseparable from the study of culture in its broadest context. Nevertheless, certain key eras or movements (discussed in sections A to I) have had a profound influence on the development of modern personnel practices in the United States since the turn of the century. These periods or movements represent applied operational philosophies and progressive sequences of events. The time frames of these movements overlap, as do many of the concepts characteristic of each major era. Figure 1-7 illustrates that these nine major

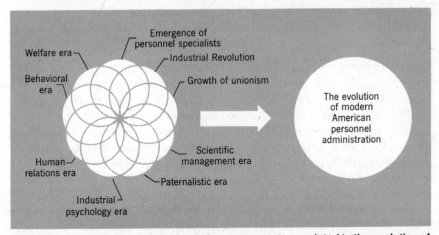

FIGURE 1-7 Interdependencies in modern movements as related to the evolution of the personnel function.

movements should best be envisioned as interrelated events and applied philosophies, instead of as totally distinct or completely synonymous movements, and that the study of the historical evolution of modern American personnel administration practices can be explained in terms of the development over time of these interrelated movements. Controversy remains, however, over the relative degree of interrelationship.

4. Personnel Administration as a Career

The personnel function is a sequence of jobs that deal with the handling of people in work settings. Personnel administration is a recognized vocation, although this field has not achieved the degree of specialized professionalism that medicine and law have. Nearly all universities and many colleges offer courses and integrated programs of study in personnel management, industrial relations, organizational behavior, and related areas.

Education

There is no single educational pattern that is required for entry into a career in personnel administration. Today, however, it is strongly recommended that those desiring to pursue careers in personnel and industrial relations should obtain at least an undergraduate college education with a background in the social sciences (specializing in the behavior sciences: sociology, psychology, and anthropology). A major should be taken in applied business administration, featuring general courses in statistics, data processing, finance, production, business policy, and the social and legal environment of business. Specific courses in personnel administration, labor relations, compensation, motivation, and communication should also be taken if available.

Positions

Beginning positions in personnel administration are usually jobs such as job analyst, employment interviewer, personnel trainee, training specialist, and labor relations specialist (Bernthal). In large companies three personnel position levels usually exist. The specialist level includes entry jobs such as those described previously. The next level consists of managers in charge of various personnel subfunctions, such as the managers of labor relations, employment, training, and compensation. The final level is the vice-president or director of personnel (or some comparable title). This represents top-level management, and such a person usually reports directly to the president. Of course, in smaller companies, there are fewer jobs and fewer levels in the personnel department and, in the really small organization, the personnel function might consist of only one part-time manager.

Salaries

Salaries for beginning positions are generally a little lower than the beginning pay for engineers, accountants, and computer programmers. Although there is as much as a several hundred dollar variation from one company to another, data are available to indicate that entry level personnel jobs paid approximately $750 per month to college graduates as of 1971. (U.S. Dept. of Labor, "book" reference citation, 1971). Supervisory and executive jobs in personnel command pay that is essentially equivalent to that paid similar managerial positions within the organization. Salaries for these managerial jobs, however, depend on company size. In general, larger companies pay higher salaries. For example, during the early 1970s the top personnel executive in a small company received $15,000 to $20,000 annually, while large corporations often pay top level personnel managers incomes of $20,000 to $40,000. Although these data refer only to industrial personnel positions, many lucrative personnel jobs are also available in the public sector of the economy.

Status

In terms of status, the personnel-industrial relations director today often serves as a key member of the top management team (Isaack). A vice-presidential ranking is usually assigned to the top personnel man in a large corporation. He has ultimate responsibility for all personnel and labor policies. In the past, personnel departments were often staffed with individuals of only modest capabilities and skills. The typical stereotype of the company personnel manager was that of an old, loyal, well-liked individual who was very familiar with all organizational traditions and practices. Such a person usually envisioned his job as one of hiring and firing workers, keeping records, and administering the cafeteria, charity drives, company parties, and picnics. This image has vanished to a great extent, especially in larger organizations. The best run companies today display a strong personnel unit. The top director of personnel in such a company plays a key role in personnel and labor policy, but also serves as a counsel in making decisions about company expansion or contraction, new facilities, plant relocation, organization planning, executive development, and community relations policy.

Numerous surveys tell us something about the typical personnel director. For example, in a National Industrial Conference Board study of large enterprises, 126 of the 249 top personnel executives surveyed carried the title of vice-president (Stieglitz and Janger, "book" reference citation). Director was the second most frequently occurring title (92 times). In another study of 132 personnel directors, about 90 percent reported that they had attended a college or university. Of these, 71 percent had earned a bachelor's degree, 21 percent a master's degree, and 8 percent a law degree. Half of the degrees had been earned in areas directly related to business administration. Almost all these personnel directors had taken courses in industrial psychology, personnel management, and labor relations. In the nonbusiness fields, courses and degrees in psychology were common. Over one-third of these personnel directors had been in personnel work for their entire careers. These employee directors averaged almost fifteen years of experience in personnel work.

Job Opportunities

There are numerous personnel jobs available in the public sector of the economy. Many opportunities in federal, state, and local governments are currently available. There are also various opportunities for those who desire to go into business for themselves as management or labor relations consultants. Trained personnel workers are also employed by universities, hospitals, labor organizations, and social work agencies. Job opportunities for blacks and women are especially plentiful in such organizations. Expectations are that excellent personnel jobs will be available for many years to come. One source, for example, projects the demand for personnel workers as providing for a 43 percent increase from 1968 to 1980 with about 6900 annual openings (U.S. Dept. of Labor, "book" reference citation, 1973).

The types of personnel jobs currently available for those who are qualified include systems and procedures analyst, job analyst, organizational planning manager, employment interviewer, employment manager, research psychologist, assessment manager, training director, employee opinion analyst, safety director, employee counselor, labor relations manager, wage and salary administrator, employee benefits and service manager, recreation director, and personnel research manager

5. Personnel Administration as a Profession

Personnel administration as a practicing field is rapidly approaching the status of a profession. A profession, by definition, is an occupation that involves a liberal education or its equivalent, and mental instead of manual labor. Law, medicine, and theology are normally considered to be among the oldest professions. Sometimes the term profession is interpreted more loosely in reference to any calling or occupation (other than those that are commercial or manual) that requires special attainments or training. Professions are also advanced to a point where they are considered to be an academic discipline or area of study as well as being a set of practicing activities.

There is much controversy about whether or not personnel administration can properly be called a profession. The majority of this debate centers around the definition of the term profession.

Criteria of a Profession

Attempts have been made to identify the features or criteria of a profession. Usually requirements such as the following are mentioned during such endeavors: (1) a recognized body of knowledge; (2) the existence of societies for career practitioners; (3) a service instead of a profit motive; (4) formalized training and educational programs; (5) the creation of an ethical code; and (6) the licensing or accreditation of members joining the occupation.

Body of Knowledge

Personnel administration does possess a recognized body of knowledge. There is much literature available about the concepts, procedures, and methodologies involved in attempting to coordinate personnel matters within an organization. Theories and techniques in all of the personnel subfunctions have been widely researched and written about. Methods of properly handling labor relations, wage and salary, training, safety, employment, and other personnel problems can easily be found in numerous textbooks on these subjects. The development of college and university curriculums dealing with these areas is also ample evidence of the fact that personnel administration today possesses a recognized body of knowledge. This point will be expanded in the next section, which discusses personnel administration as a discipline.

Professional Societies

There are a number of national personnel administration societies and associations. Some of the most well known are the Industrial Relations Research Association, the International Personnel Management Association, the American Society of Personnel Administrators, the American Society for Training and Development, the Personnel Division of the American Management Association, and the Manpower and Personnel Subdivision of the National Academy of Management. There are also several international personnel societies and many regional and local personnel managers' associations.

Service Motive

Professions are allegedly service instead of profit based. Such a mission represents an ideal, not a practicality. Few, if any, lawyers, doctors, and other professionals will work for extended periods of time without financial remuneration. The same phenomenon exists among personnel administrators. To say that service takes precedence over a profit motive indicates that professionals ideally are or should be devoted basically to the societal advancement of their work and expertise instead of being concerned largely with the issue of how much money they personally are accumulating. This service-profit option is not an either-or question. It is simply a matter of relative emphasis. Most professionals are concerned about both these incentives, especially a professional in business for himself who must weigh and balance these concerns, since they determine to a great degree whether or not his general business and his individual livelihood will thrive or cease to exist.

Training Programs

Formalized training and educational programs for personnel trainees also exist today. This issue has already been discussed in reference to personnel administration as a career and as a recognized body of knowledge, and it will be explained in greater detail in the next section, which describes personnel administration as a discipline.

Ethical Code

Professional societies frequently adopt ethical codes to be used as guides of behavior within their profession. Some of the above mentioned personnel associations have attempted to develop such guidelines. Similar to the service mission phenomenon, however, this criterion of a profession often represents an ideal, not a strict actuality. Ethical behavior is often a matter of personal opinion. What one person considers right may be considered wrong by someone else, even if they are noted professionals in the same practicing area.

Licensing

Licensing or accreditation is often also identified as a characteristic of a profession. Usually such licensing is done by one central accrediting organization. For example, doctors and lawyers are so accredited. Personnel administration does not meet this criterion of a profession. There are certificates saying that you are a recognized personnel administrator. To some degree, however, professional societies and colleges of business administration are sanctioning entities for personnel administrators because they provide educational programs for personnel trainees, and they also grant certificates and diplomas indicating a member's or graduate's achieved status in personnel administration.

Conclusion

Personnel administration at least partially fulfills all of the professionalization criteria with the possible exception of the licensing condition. The central question of whether or not personnel administration is a profession boils down to a semantic issue centered around the precise definition of the term profession. Unquestionably, if personnel administration has not yet achieved this status, it has nevertheless made significant advances over the years toward the attainment of such a goal and undoubtedly it will continue to move in this direction.

The issue of professionalism is important to personnel managers because it directly affects their status within organizations. The solid identification of personnel administration as a profession will enhance the image of the personnel director as a key executive. As discussed earlier, this enlightened image does not, in fact, exist in all organizations today, especially in the smaller and medium-sized companies. Thus this issue of professionalism is central to both the individual and collective status and advancement of all personnel administrators whether they are working in private or public organizations or especially if they are self-employed personnel specialists and consultants.

6. PERSONNEL ADMINISTRATION AS A DISCIPLINE

Personnel administration is recognized today as an academic discipline or area of study. As mentioned previously, college and university curriculum programs in which personnel management and related courses are offered are common. A body of theoretical and practical knowledge concerning personnel subfunctions has accumulated over the years. The major subject matter areas of personnel administration include employment, training and development, wage and salary administration, benefits and services, health and safety, labor relations, and behavioral research. Methods, techniques, and procedures in each subfunction are available separately; collectively they constitute the discipline of personnel administration.

Literature

Numerous textbooks and journals devoted to personnel administration are currently available. There are twenty well-known, popular, general introductory personnel management texts. Many books are available that concentrate on specific personnel subfunctions. Also, many journals are devoted almost exclusively to current personnel administration topics, including *Personnel, Personnel Psychology, Personnel Administration, Personnel Administrator, Personnel Journal, Management of Personnel Quarterly, Public Personnel Review,* and *Public Personnel Management.* Most of these journals are published by or affiliated with personnel associations and societies, such as those mentioned in the previous section of this chapter.

Academic Affiliation

Personnel administration is a subarea of a larger discipline usually identified as management or business administration. Personnel administration courses in colleges and universities are usually offered by departments of business administration in smaller colleges and by departments of management within colleges of business administration in larger universities. Usually only larger universities are able to offer a variety of course work in this area. Courses related to personnel are usually called "Introductory Personnel Administration," "Wage and Salary Administration," "Selection Techniques and Employment," "Industrial Training and Development," "Indirect Compensation Systems," "Health and Safety Management," "Labor Relations," and other related titles.

Teaching the Discipline

Controversy exists about the best way to teach personnel administration. Some educators concentrate on economic concepts, while others believe that psychological, sociological, or other matters are more important. The necessity of a background in mathematics, statistics, computer programming, data processing, finance, marketing, production, accounting, and quantitative methods is also being debated. At least beginning expertise in each of these business subareas should be acquired by personnel trainees. Advanced knowledge, however, is usually not needed by a personnel specialist.

There is no agreement about what subject areas should be taught to personnel students, and *how* such materials should be introduced to trainees is also a pedagogically raised question that is largely a matter of personal opinion. Some teachers prefer a lecture format to convey personnel concepts; others prefer case studies, films, guest speakers, field trips, internships, term papers, library readings, research, or self-study. Although personnel administration is a recognized discipline and body of knowledge, the elements that make up this body of knowledge and the pedagogical approaches and methodologies that are best suited to instill such knowledge are still being debated.

Personnel Administration as a Science

To say that personnel administration is a discipline with a recognized body of knowledge is to imply that personnel is a science. A science, by definition, is an exact and systematic statement or classification of knowledge concerning some subject or group of subjects. Personnel principles, laws, rules, procedures, methodologies, techniques, and concepts all have been presented and expounded by various authors. One viewpoint envisions such principles and concepts as strict laws dictating the most efficient methods of handling personnel matters. This is a strict and, fortunately, rare interpretation. Most observers see more flexibility with the recommended personnel practices. Such an interpretation views personnel principles as flexible guidelines, not as strict laws. This is, of course, more realistic. Personnel administration is a science, but it is an applied rather than a pure science; that is, it is flexible and adaptive, not rigid and strict.

Personnel Administration as an Art

Personnel administration as a career was previously presented in this chapter. To identify personnel management as a career implies that artistic qualities are associated with the practice of personnel. This viewpoint sees personnel not so much as a science or discipline, but as an art or practice. An art, by definition, is the application or skill or knowledge in a unique and creative manner. Such a perspective portrays the personnel manager as one who picks and chooses what personnel principles to believe in and how such concepts can best be introduced into his work setting. This viewpoint recognizes that personnel practices are more a result of unique creative individual management styles than a result of set personnel rules and procedures.

Personnel Administration as an Attitude

As previously discussed, personnel administration is seen by many as a profession. This professionalism is usually best thought of as an attitude or a state of mind. The argument is often presented that if a person thinks he is a professional, he acts accordingly, regardless of what his actual occupation is. On the other hand, if a person does not consider himself to be a professional, he typically does not act in a professional manner. Professionalism is an attitude held by a person, not a discipline of knowledge learned by a trainee (Megginson and Sanford). With this interpretation, a personnel manager could be a professional, while some lawyer or doctor hypothetically may not rightfully be so identified.

Personnel administration as a composite of the career, profession, and discipline subsets is portrayed in Figure 1-8, Figure 1-9 shows that the career, profession, and discipline aspects of personnel administration properly

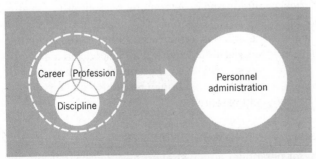

FIGURE 1-8 Personnel administration as a composite set of career, profession, and discipline subsets.

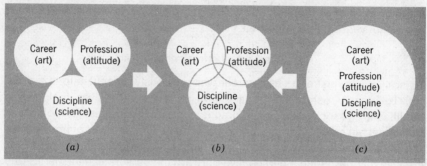

FIGURE 1-9 Career (artistic), profession (attitudinal), and discipline (scientific) dimensions of personnel administration as distinct, interrelated, and synonymous set entities. (*a*) Distinct. (*b*) Interrelated. (*c*) Synonymous.

should be interpreted as interrelated phenomena (Figure 1-9b) instead of distinct (Figure 1-9a) or synonymous (Figure 1-9c) set entities. Figure 1-9 also shows that the artistic, scientific, and attitudinal natures of personnel administration are associated with personnel management respectively being described as a career, discipline and profession.

7. Summary

Numerous terminology, definitional, and semantic problems are encountered when discussing the historical evolution of personnel administration. In its broadest context, the study of the evolution of personnel administration is inseparable from the study of culture. However, the development of modern personnel practices within the United States can be associated with: (1) the industrial revolution; (2) the growth of unionism; (3) scientific management; (4) the paternalistic era; (5) industrial psychology; (6) the human relations era; (7) the behavioral era; (8) the emergence of personnel specialists; and (9) the welfare era. The time frames and some of the ideas and concepts characteristic of each of these major eras overlap.

Because of its historical evolution and development, personnel administration can be considered a career, a profession, and an academic discipline. A modern personnel manager combines artistic, attitudinal, and scientific parameters and qualities in an individualized, personalized manner when carrying out his duties and responsibilities. Personnel administration is collectively considered as a practicing vocation, a respected calling, and an acknowledged area of study and research.

DISCUSSION QUESTIONS AND ASSIGNMENTS

1. How can the study of personnel administration be fitted or tied into the broader field of general management or administration?

2. Identify and briefly explain the major modern movements that have affected personnel practices.
3. Is personnel administration a profession, a career, or an academic discipline? Defend your answer.
4. Design a code-of-ethics statement for personnel managers. Incorporate your views as to what constitutes ethical and unethical behavior in personnel practices.
5. Cite historical events other than those mentioned in the chapter that you feel had an influence on the evolution of personnel administration.
6. Present your definition of personnel administration.

REFERENCES

General Book References

Beach, Dale S., *Personnel: The Management of People at Work.* New York: Macmillan, 1970, pp. 3–38.

Chruden, Herbert J., and Arthur W. Sherman, Jr., *Personnel Management.* Cincinnati: South-Western, 1972, pp. 2–29.

Dunn, J. D., and Elvis C. Stephens, *Management of Personnel: Manpower Management and Organizational Behavior.* New York: McGraw-Hill, 1972, pp. 4–18.

Flippo, Edwin B., *Principles of Personnel Management.* New York: McGraw-Hill, 1971, pp. 3–17.

French, Wendell, *The Personnel Management Process: Human Resources Administration.* Boston: Houghton Mifflin, 1970, pp. 3–30.

Jucius, Michael J., *Personnel Management.* Homewood, Ill.: Irwin, 1971, pp. 1–35.

Ling, Cyril Curtis, *The Management of Personnel Relations: History and Origins.* Homewood, Ill.: Irwin, 1965, pp. 3–24.

McFarland, Dalton E., *Personnel Management: Theory and Practice.* New York: Macmillan, 1968, pp. 63–95.

Megginson, Leon C., *Personnel: A Behavioral Approach to Administration.* Homewood, Ill.: Irwin, 1972, pp. 77–98.

Miner, John B., and Mary Green Miner, *Personnel and Industrial Relations: A Managerial Approach.* New York: Macmillan, 1973, pp. 17–34.

Odiorne, George S., *Personnel Administration by Objectives.* Homewood, Ill.: Irwin, 1971, pp. 17–50.

Stieglitz, Harold, and Allen R. Janger, *Top Management Organization in Divisionalized Companies.* New York: National Industrial Conference Board, Studies in Personnel Policy, No. 195, 1965, pp. 10–20.

United States Department of Labor, *Occupational Outlook Handbook* (1970-1971 Edition). Washington, D.C.: U.S. Department of Labor, Bulletin No. 1965, 1971, pp. 30–40.

United States Department of Labor, *Occupational Manpower and Training Needs.* Washington, D.C.: U.S. Department of Labor, Bulletin No. 1701, 1973, pp. 1–40.

Specific Journal References

Bernthal, Wilmar, "New Challenges Demand That We Change Roles," *The Personnel Administrator, 13* (6), 1968, pp. 33–38.

Domm, Donald R., and James E. Stafford, "Personnel: Behind the Times," *Personnel Journal, 49* (7), 1970, pp. 563–568.

Dunlop, John T., "The Nation's Manpower Arrangements," *The Conference Board Review, 7* (3), 1970, pp. 25–30.

Eilbirt, Henry, "The Development of Personnel Management in the United States," *Business History Review, 33* (3), 1959, pp. 345–364.

Isaack, Thomas S., "Perceiving Personnel Management," *Personnel Journal, 46* (11), 1967, pp. 733–737.

Kimmerly, Dean, "What is Personnel?" *The Personnel Administrator, 22* (5), 1969, pp. 46–47.

Kramer, Charles, "The Personnel Function Today and Tomorrow," *Management International Review, 7* (6), 1967, pp. 34–43.

Megginson, Leon C., and Aubrey Sanford, "A Reevaluation of the Human Resources Philosophy," *Personnel Journal, 48* (1), 1969, pp. 52–57.

Perline, Martin M., and Kurtis L. Tull, "Automation: Its Impact on Organized Labor," *Personnel Journal, 48* (5), 1969, pp. 340–344.

Singer, Henry A., "The Impact of Human Resources on Business," *Business Horizons, 12* (2), 1969, pp. 53–58.

Sokolik, Stanley L., "Reorganize the Personnel Department?" *California Management Review, 11* (3), 1969, pp. 43–52.

contents

learning objectives

1. To envision the personnel function in its entirety and to understand how personnel work relates to total organizational operations.

2. To become aware of some of the fallacies or falsehoods associated with the personnel function.

3. To learn of the changing nature and scope of personnel administration.

4. To understand the various roles performed by the personnel manager.

2

The Personnel Function
and Its Relationship to
the Total Organization Structure

1. The Personnel Function

In Chapter 1 personnel administration was defined as the implementation of human resources by and within an enterprise. Personnel collectively refers to the people or manpower that staff an organization. Personnel function refers globally to all of the activities performed by a personnel unit or department that pertain directly to the coordination of human effort within the company. These functions describe all of the duties, practices, and processes exhibited by a personnel manager each day. These functions comprise the implementation concept within the definition of personnel administration. Such functions are commonly identified as staffing (recruiting, selecting, placement, and indoctrination) and appraisal; training and development; compensation: wage and salary administration; compensation: benefits and services; health and safety; labor relations-collective bargaining; manpower planning; and personnel research.

Size and Philosophy Factors

The relationship of the personnel function to the total corporation depends largely on the size of the organization. In a small organization (under 200 employees), the personnel function may be handled on a part-time basis by one of the organization officers. In medium and large companies, personnel usually becomes its own department. In organizations of 1000 or more, the personnel department commonly will additionally be broken down into several subdivisions. Along with company size, the managerial philosophy and leadership style of the top corporate official(s) will also partly determine the relationship of the personnel function to the rest of the corporate structure. Executives who believe in the professionalism of the personnel discipline are most likely to give the personnel department a key role to perform in the total operation of enterprise activities (Rabe).

The personnel function will be discussed first in reference to numerous personnel fallacies associated with the personnel management discipline. Second, the subject matter subareas of personnel administration will be broken up into eight subfunctions, and each subunit will be briefly discussed. Third, the changing scope of personnel administration will be presented in a format analyzing the old, new, and changing emphasis areas of the personnel function. Fourth, the roles of a personnel manager will be analyzed in a manner that both reviews traditional interpretations and presents modern interpretations of the roles exhibited by personnel officers. The relationship of the personnel function to the total corporate structure will then be presented in a discussion of the personnel ratio concept, an explanation of personnel being a staff position or staff function, and a presentation of the personnel shared responsibility concept.

2. Personnel Fallacies

A. WORKING WITH PEOPLE

One misconception associated with personnel administration is that personnel work involves working directly with people most of the time. Personnel trainees and students often initially state an interest in the personnel discipline because they believe that such work involves interpersonal relationships with many people. This assumption is not supported by fact. There is nothing particularly "personal" about personnel work. Personnel managers do not work directly with people any more. If an individual enjoys a great deal of direct worker contact he should be in a first-line supervisory position. In an industrial setting, the foreman or superintendent is the one most involved with daily interpersonal relationships. The personnel manager does not, except in a few instances (such as labor relations problems), deal with people in his normal daily activities. Factual data information about absenteeism, wages, benefits, contract agreements, corporate policies, legislative statutes, safety requirements, employment surveys and the like, instead of human

FIGURE 2-1 "Personnel" not "personal" manager.

beings, are the main variables and factors with which the typical personnel manager works. To accomplish objectives, a personnel manager must also work with people, he does not spend more time at this than any other organizational supervisor. Most of the people a personnel manager deals with are his own staff, the people within his department. Although the personnel department generally and the personnel manager specifically may be involved with the initial hiring and the terminal retirement or firing of many employees, most workers do not have any other direct contact with the personnel function. Figure 2-1 indicates that it is a misconception to think of a "personnel" manager as a "personal" manager.

B. WELFARE WORK

Many laymen wrongly believe that personnel work is welfare or social work. This misconception has some historical evidence related to its existence, but such a viewpoint is currently only partially true. A small portion of a personnel manager's job may be related to welfare and social issues, but normally such matters do not occupy the bulk of any personnel administrator's job unless the corporation is extremely large and a full-time employee for such matters perhaps may be justified. It is true that personnel managers spend some of their time with company benefits and services issues. But, after the establishment of these benefits and services, this activity becomes a record-keeping function for the personnel department. Although benefit and services matters are dealt with, a welfare philosophy does not prevail within the typical modern personnel department. Personnel managers are not "do-gooders" who go around trying to find ways to make employees happy. Benefit and service provisions when provided for within company policies and contracts are done so on an economic-rational basis, not on a "give me" premise. The typical industrial personnel manager is a businessman, not a philanthropist. His duties and responsibilities are predominantly related to total organizational effectiveness, not to individual humanistic concerns. In addition, although some specific programs may be designed for certain disadvantaged and culturally deprived individuals and groups, the personnel department generally should not be confused with a social work agency. The unique programs designed for disadvantaged groups are only a small part of total organizational personnel matters. The persons administering such programs also do not necessarily have a special dedication or allegiance to these projects. If one's calling and mission in life is to alleviate the misery and suffering of societal indigents and outcasts, he should become a social worker, not a personnel manager. Too often novice personnel students and apprentice personnel trainees are unduly optimistic and idealistic about the misconceived and alleged (but not acknowledged) degree of altruism associated with the practice of personnel administration. Personnel work is not social work nor welfare work; personnel administration is the administration of personnel. Although the personnel function may vary among profit and nonprofit organizations, the belief that personnel activities constitute welfare work should be avoided.

C. LABOR RELATIONS

A third illusion is that personnel deals basically only with labor relations problems and issues. These are labor-management interactions that pertain specifically to the negotiation and administration of an employer-employee contract or agreement. The negotiation of the actual agreement involves the area usually identified as collective bargaining, while the day-to-day administration of such a contract commonly is referred to as labor relations. Labor relations and collective bargaining are part of the personnel manager's responsibilities, but often such duties require little time compared to the other duties of a personnel administrator. This is especially true of small- and medium-sized companies. In addition, not all organizations are unionized. Typically, the labor relations personnel function, even though it still would exist, would be less important in an unorganized labor setting. Also, when contracts are negotiated only once a year, or once every three years, as the current trend seems to be, labor relations aspects of personnel often seem to take a backseat to other more pressing personnel problems. In larger organizations the labor relations function breaks away from the personnel domain and becomes its own department (Wood, 1967a). But such a division only occurs when companies grow well over 1000 employees (Spencer and Singer).

Perhaps this labor relations misconception is due to the semantics and terminology associated with the definition of personnel administration. Personnel administration and labor relations are not synonymous and interchangeable concepts. The general interpretation of labor relations envisions personnel administration as the larger set and labor relations as a minor subset of overall personnel activities. This particular personnel subset deals only with contract negotiation and collective bargaining matters. The remaining personnel activities, such as employment, training, development, compensation, health, safety, research, and other matters, are also subset areas of the larger set known and identified as personnel administration. As shown in Figure 2-2, labor relations-collective bargaining is one of several personnel administration subsets.

D. COMMON SENSE

The final fallacy commonly associated with the personnel discipline is that personnel administration is nothing but common sense. This error is made generally in connection with business administration practices and specifically in connection with personnel management activities. Because many managers become effective administrators without the aid of a formal education (i.e., without graduate or undergraduate university and college degrees), the myth that management is nothing more than applied common sense

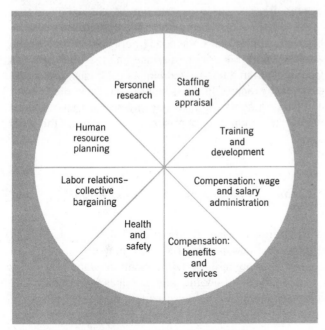

FIGURE 2-2 Personnel administration subsets.

exists. All successful managers have received a tremendous amount of training and experience from formal classroom instruction, self-instruction, or the involvement and evolvement of a management trainee through a training program made up of a progressive sequence of administrative posts. Chapter 1 stated that management and personnel administration are partially an art, a science, and a profession. The scientific portion of administration includes hundreds of management principles, concepts, policies, laws, procedures, rules, and guidelines. Theoretically and empirically based superior methods of effective enterprise operation exist. Such methods have painstakingly been arrived at after years of sophisticated research. In personnel administration, for example, numerous specific methodologies have been discovered in the areas of wage and salary administration and employment practices. A unique creative blending of management principles and concepts still is displayed by any manager in conjunction with an attitudinal frame of reference. However, these two phenomena are best envisioned respectively, as the artistic and professional dimensions of administration, instead of something as nebulous and ambiguous as common sense.

There is nothing common or sensical about common sense. It is a phrase used by laymen to explain matters that they do not understand. If a person claims that a decision is based on common sense, he really means that the decision is a result of intuition and judgment derived from past experiences. Superior judgment or intuition displayed by managers is not "common." In addition, the concept of common sense is not "sensical" or rational; it is a catchall that nonacademic people use to explain identifiable variables that they have not been able to understand. If the person who explains management activities by the concept of common sense is honest with himself, he can usually cite examples where his common sense has led him astray as frequently or more frequently than it has served him as the basis for a sound decision. Most of us can easily recall situations where our first impression or decision, which was based on some intuitive gut feeling, was later proved inaccurate to the extent of being the opposite conclusion to the final decision.

3. Subject Matter Subareas of Personnel Administration

I will use the following format to discuss the subject matter subareas of personnel administration: (1) human resource planning; (2) staffing and appraisal; (3) training and development; (4) compensation: wage and salary administration; (5) compensation: benefits and services; (6) health and safety; (7) labor relations-collective bargaining; and (8) personnel research.

A. HUMAN RESOURCE PLANNING

Human resource planning is the process of determining manpower requirements and the means for meeting those requirements in order to carry out the integrated plans of an organization. This process involves determining the required capabilities and the needed number of people. The location and timing of manpower needs is also important. Human resource planning involves having the right number and the right kinds of people at the right places, at the right times, doing the right kind of things, which result in both long-run maximum individual and organizational benefits.

Emphasis on the Future

·Human resource planning involves projecting and forecasting present personnel functions into the future. Setting up a man-plan involves anticipating the future patterns of an organization and of the business environment and then relating manpower requirements to these conditions. Both internal organizational and external environmental factors must be taken into account during human resource planning endeavors.

Systems Perspective

The application and implementation of human resource planning requires a systems approach, since several interrelated and interacting stages of activities are involved. Such an integrated view of the personnel system of an organization allows individual managers to make improved day-to-day decisions that can be consistent with total organizational long-run needs.

Human Resource Planning Components

Human resource planning is a systematic procedure featuring a planned sequence of events or a series of chronological steps. These steps or events are the components of the manpower planning process. Human resource planning components include: (1) objectives; (2) organization planning; (3) human resource auditing; (4) human resource forecasting; and (5) action programs, including affirmative action and EEOC. These human resource planning components will be explained in detail in Chapter 5.

B. STAFFING AND APPRAISAL

Traditionally the staffing function has been the core of personnel administration. The staffing function involves engaging the services of human beings for the operations of a company. The staffing function in reference to personnel work means only the use or employment of people or human beings. Of course, other types of resources besides human beings are employed or used by organizations. But such resource uses are not considered to be within the province of the personnel employment or staffing function. The employment of raw materials is the concern of the production department, the use of capital is the responsibility of the finance department, the utilizaiton of advertising techniques is the province of the marketing department, and the engagement of manpower is the job of the personnel department.

Staffing Concept

The traditional personnel function of employment is commonly referred to today as the staffing function. Staffing in this regard means to provide with a staff. The staff is the general body of persons responsible for carrying out the purposes of the organization. The concept of a staff in this format is different from the concept of a staff in reference to line and staff positions. The staff in "staffing" refers to the employment of all personnel, while the staff in reference to line and staff positions identifies only certain specific organizational personnel, specifically, those involved with work that is of an advisory, service, administrative, or control nature instead of work that directly relates to either the production or sales of the company product or service. Staffing involves the employment of all company personnel, not just the employment of personnel in organizational "staff" positions.

Selection and Placement

Traditionally, the employment function was seen as only a hiring function. This interpretation has expanded greatly over the years to the point where hiring is considered only a minor aspect of the total personnel employment function. Employee selection and placement matters became part of the employment function over the years. Selection is the act of choosing some employees in preference to others. This process has changed over the years from a subjective to an objective procedure. In the past, selection was done on a personality or nepotism basis. A person got a job because he knew or was related to someone in an authority position or because his personality gained favor with the company representative responsible for hiring new employees. This subjective approach has been replaced today by more objective selection criteria in most instances. Now tests, interviews, reference checks, physical examinations, and other factors are used to assess employee potential. The selection process has become more and more scientific over the years. Once an employee has been selected, he must then be placed in the proper organizational slot. Employee placement involves matching an employee with his unique qualifications to a job with its unique requirements. This placement function is an ongoing process. A proper match initially may become imbalanced later on because of human and technological changes. As a consequence, employees must be placed within an organization many times over the years.

Recruitment, Indoctrination, and Appraisal

The employment or staffing function has expanded also to include the areas of recruitment, indoctrination, and appraisal. (Recruitment involves the attraction and tentative supplying of new personnel to an organization. Recruitment precedes selection, since it is intended to gather an interested pool of potential employees, while selection involves the actual choosing of those from this pool who will be offered jobs within an organization) Indoctrination, which is sometimes also referred to as induction or orientation, refers to the initial instructions and training an employee receives while on the job. The type of information conveyed during orientation procedures refers to overall company policies and procedures instead of to specific instruction related to a particular job or position. Performance and personnel appraisals now are also considered part of the total employment function. Formal appraisals using specific techniques and methodologies often take place semiannually within organizations, but informal evaluations and assessments through general observation occur continuously. Performance appraisals for company personnel are necessary to determine promotions, salary increases, and related staffing procedures.

The personnel employment or staffing function includes aspects of recruitment, selection, hiring, placement, appraisal, and other issues that, because of their individual and collective importance, will be discussed more thoroughly in Chapter 6. The effect of "affirmative action and EEOC programs as they relate to staffing activities will be discussed more thoroughly in Chapter 5.

C. TRAINING AND DEVELOPMENT

Employee training and manager development are other subject matter areas of traditional personnel administration. Training company employees in order for them to do a better job has always been a main concern of the personnel manager. Training is, by definition, a short-run educational process involving systematic instruction and drill that emphasize learning manual and operative skills by nonsupervisory employees. Training is a learning process for its participants. The instruction involved is systematic, rational, and organized. The type of activity to be taught or conveyed involves some manual or operative skill such as the proper techniques of running some piece of machinery. The concept of training is intended to describe this learning process as viewed and experienced from the perspective of a nonsupervisory employee.

Training Methods

Various methods have been used over the years to bring about employee training. The most popular and commonly used training technique has been on-the-job training, that is, learning by doing or actual practice and experience. Traditional classroom devices including the lecture, conference, case study, role playing, and programmed instruction methodologies are also frequently used training techniques. Vestibule training, demonstration, simulation, and other approaches have, on occasion, also been included in typical employee training programs.

Training Importance

Employee training is important for a number of reasons. Training reduces the amount of learning time necessary for an employee to reach an acceptable level or standard of performance on a new job. Training also improves performance on present jobs and aids in the solution of everyday operational problems. Training benefits individual employees by allowing them to acquire new knowledge and job skills and perhaps even by permitting the formation of new worker attitudes. For the organization as a whole, employee training better enables a company to fulfill its manpower needs and requirements. Employee training, like employee placement, should properly be envisioned as a continuous process, not as a one shot affair. In his lifetime, a typical employee will be trained and retrained numerous times.

Development Defined

Development is a long-term educational process involving systematic instruction and practice that emphasize learning abstract and theoretical concepts by supervisory employees. Systematic instruction and practice are a part of both training and development but, in the former, the emphasis is on manual and operative skills, whereas in the latter, educational process, the emphasis is on abstract and theoretical concepts. The training and development audiences are different, also. Training focuses on nonsupervisory personnel, while development concentrates on managerial clientele. It is often difficult to tell a training technique from a development device. Nevertheless, training and development are somewhat different concepts, the major differences being the subject matter taught, the time periods involved, and the audiences to which the instruction is directed.

Development Methods

Many of the methods used in managerial development programs are identical to those used in employee training courses. Traditional classroom methodologies such as lecture, conference, case study, role playing, and programmed instruction are commonly used instructional techniques. Demonstration and simulation approaches are also frequently used. However, there are some additional educational procedures used in development programs that are not typically found within employee training programs. Some examples of such educational procedures include the use of understudies, job rotation, coaching, multiple management, management games, the managerial grid, and sensitivity training.

In contrast to the training function, the importance of managerial development has only relatively recently been widely accepted. The reasons why managerial development is important are similar to the previously mentioned reasons of why training is important. If a person accepts the idea of continuous training and retraining, then he must rationally also accept the idea of continuous development; all managers have evolved through a series of nonsupervisory positions.

This training and development discussion is introductory. Because of the importance of employee training and managerial development, I will present a more comprehensive coverage of these educational concepts and personnel subfunctions in Chapter 7.

D. COMPENSATION: WAGE AND SALARY ADMINISTRATION

Wage and salary administration involves seeing to it that employees are systematically paid for their efforts. This wage and salary objective is readily accepted, but there is considerably less argeement about the manner of accomplishing this goal. This disagreement is the result of numerous complex and interrelated problems and issues that constitute the body of the wage and salary administration personnel subfunction. These issues include the problems of wage and salary "levels," wage and salary "structures," "individual" wage and salary determination, payment method, indirect compensation, exempt employees, and wage and salary control. Wage and salary administration is the organizational process involved with analyzing these problems and providing workable solutions to them. Of course, all of these problems are highly interrelated and are, in fact, inseparable in practice from one another.

Wage Criteria

Additional wage and salary administration problems are encountered when it is recognized that various criteria can be used to determine wage and salary rates. The most common criteria are the economic concepts of prevailing wages, cost of living, living wage, ability to pay, productivity, labor supplies, bargaining power, and purchasing power. Because different employee and employer constituencies stress one or the other of these criteria, additional problems for the wage and salary administrator often result.

Job Evaluation

A number of techniques, methodologies, and procedures in wage and salary administration have been developed over the years in an attempt to solve these types of problems. Job evaluation, job analysis, job descriptions, and job specifications are examples of such methods. Specific job evaluation procedures include nonquantitative methods, such as ranking and grade classification, and quantitative techniques, such as factor comparison and the point method. In addition, internal and external wage and salary surveys enable a company to cope better with compensation issues and problems. Wage incentives, nonfinancial rewards, indirect compensation, and the remuneration of special employment groups are other examples of where both unique wage and salary problems exist and where unique methodological techniques are used to resolve these problems.

Wage Versus Salary

Wage administration and salary administration are normally considered to be one collective subarea of personnel. However, wage and salary are not identical. A wage is received by labor for services rendered, especially the pay of laborers who receive a fixed sum, depending on an hourly or daily rate. A salary is received by a manager or clerical worker for services rendered, especially the pay of professionals receiving a fixed sum, depending on a weekly, monthly, or annual rate. A wage earner can increase his compensation by working more hours per week, but an employee on salary is usually not paid a bonus for overtime work. A wage earner is said to belong to the nonexempt group, while a person on salary is exempt. Exemption refers to whether or not the Fair Labor Standards Act requires an employer to pay a premium rate to an employee for overtime. Workers paid a wage (i.e., an hourly rate), are nonexempt, since they must be paid time and a half for overtime. Employees on salary (i.e., paid by a weekly or monthly rate), are exempt, since this law does not apply to nor affect their rate of compensation regardless of the total number of hours they work. The exempt and nonexempt classifications are much more complicated than the above explanation indicates; however, wage earners generally make up the nonexempt group, and salary recipients constitute the exempt classification.

Compensation

Many authors prefer today the term compensation to wage and salary problems and issues. The term compensation is broader than wage and salary, since it adds the dimensions of indirect and nonfinancial rewards to the overall remuneration concept. Because overall remuneration patterns of modern corporations today include a significant percentage of fringe benefits, indirect rewards, and other quasifinancial services, the concept of compensation is commonly preferred by current personnel administrators over the older idea of wage and salary administration, since the compensation concept is more global and all inclusive in interpretation. Chapters 8 and 9 will elaborate on financial and quasifinancial remuneration issues and problems.

E. COMPENSATION: BENEFITS AND SERVICES

Company benefits and services to employees are of major concern to any personnel manager. Benefits and services are usually considered synonymous and interchangeable personnel concepts. However, some authors prefer to apply the term benefits to items for which a direct monetary value to the individual employee can be easily ascertained; they reserve the term services to describe items for which a direct money value for the individual employee cannot be readily established. Using such a distinction, a benefit would be similar to a pension, separation pay, paid sick leave, or accident insurance; a service would be similar to a company newsletter, athletic field, Christmas party, or some other social or quasisocial program or function.

Semantics

Many phrases heard today refer to the general area of company benefits and services. Such phrases include fringe benefits, employee services, supplementary compensation, bonus remuneration, indirect compensation, and supplementary pay. These phrases are synonymous and interchangeable.

Beyond Base Pay

All organizations today provide their employees with certain benefits and services over and above the basic paycheck. These company benefits and services fulfill several important functions. They may supply financial protection against risks such as illness, accident, or unemployment; others may attempt to fulfill the social and recreational needs of employees. Although benefits and services are not directly related to the productive effort of the workers, management often expects to aid its recruitment effort, raise morale, create greater company loyalty, reduce turnover and absenteeism, and generally improve the strength of the organization by instituting a well-conceived program in this area.

Thirty Percent and Rising

Benefits and services as a part of an employee's total compensation package have grown and increased tremendously over the last fifty years. Starting from nothing, they have increased to a point where they constitute just under 30 percent of the average employee's total compensation and remuneration package. There are many reasons for this phenomenal growth and increase. Public policy is perhaps one of the most fundamental reasons. The Social Security Act of 1935 requires employers to share equally with employees the cost of Old Age, Survivors and Disability Insurance. In addition, employers pay the full cost of unemployment insurance. Other factors affecting the growth of company benefit and service programs have been the growth of unionism; National Labor Relations Board rulings; court interpretations of the Wagner and Taft-Hartley Acts; wage stabilization directives from the federal government; labor scarcity; shifting tax laws; and the increasing societal emphasis on employee security.

The preceding factors identify the major general environmental forces that cause companies to establish and expand their benefit and service programs. Management must consider other factors when establishing particular kinds of employee benefits and services, such as union power, costs, the company's ability to pay, tax considerations, employee needs, and various organizational long-run consequences. Such considerations have major impact on the ultimate design of any employee benefit and service program.

Types of Benefits and Services

Although it is impossible to identify all the possible benefits and services a company might offer to its employees, these supplements usually fall into one of four broad classifications: (1) employee security; (2) pay for time not worked; (3) bonuses and awards; and (4) service programs. Employee security includes items such as pensions, life insurance, hospitalization, medical, and surgical payments, paid sick leave, supplemental unemployment benefits, severance pay, accident insurance, and contributions to savings plans. Pay for time not worked might include holiday pay, vacation pay, military service allowance, jury duty pay, and voting time pay. A bonus or award may be a profit-sharing bonus, or Christmas bonus, or an anniversary award. Service programs include social and recreational events such as parties, picnics, athletic facilities, clubs, and dances, and special company services, such as savings plans, credit unions, loan funds, employee scholarships, product discounts, company purchasing services, medical services, and food services. Company benefit and service programs will be discussed in Chapter 9.

F. HEALTH AND SAFETY

Organizational health and safety matters are additional concerns of the personnel administrator. Although these matters are highly interrelated and overlapping in content, most authors treat the two as separate concerns. Organizational health, or industrial hygiene, as it is commonly called today, concerns itself with the prevention of occupational diseases. The goal of industrial hygiene is to create and maintain a work environment that is conducive to good health, good morale, and high production.

Occupational Diseases

Industrial safety concerns itself with injuries caused by accidents; occupational health or industrial hygiene concerns itself with occupational diseases. Although the affected worker suffers in either case, and the difference is immaterial to him, such a distinction is nevertheless important under state workmen's compensation laws, because many states grant only limited coverage and benefits for occupational diseases. An injury caused by an accident usually occurs at a specific point in time and place and is ordinarily unexpected or unforeseen; an occupational disease usually develops gradually over an extended period of time as a result of repeated or continuous exposure to toxic substances, microorganisms, airborne contaminants, or stress-producing elements. Occupational diseases are caused by hazards and conditions found within organizations, especially industrial organizations, such as unsafe thermal conditions, atmospheric pressures, mechanical vibrations, radiation, noise, air contamination, and skin diseases.

"Whole Man" Concept

Historically, company health programs were inaugurated as a result of the passage of workmen's compensation laws. Industrial hygiene has grown, however, to the point where, in many companies, an employee's health problems are viewed from not only an on-the-job, but also from an off-the-job perspective. The concept of the "whole man" is supported within companies that exhibit a progressive personnel philosophy. Such a philosophy often today goes beyond the mere concept of physical health and extends the overall health concept to include mental health.

Safety and Accidents

Safety concerns itself with accidents and injuries. Not all accidents, however, result in injuries. An accident can be defined as an unusual and unexpected occurrence that interrupts the regular progress of an activity. An unexpected occurrence may or may not result in a personal injury. The concern for industrial accidents and injuries can be defended from either a cost basis or a humanitarian basis. It makes economic sense to attempt to eliminate accidents and injuries because of lost time, damaged equipment, retraining costs, insurance premiums, and other financial factors. Altruistically, an employer should feel some moral or ethical responsibility to protect his employees from unsafe working conditions.

Causes of Accidents

Accidents are caused by several factors, but such factors can usually be classified into one of two major categories: (1) unsafe chemical, physical, or mechanical conditions, and (2) unsafe personal acts. However, the causes of accidents do not represent an either-or situation; in fact, most accidents are caused by a combination of personal and mechanical factors. In the past, the concept of accident proneness was also commonly used as an explanation of why accidents and injuries occurred. Today, however, most authors discount such a theory as a reason for personnel accidents and injuries. Employee traits and environmental characteristics are usually broken down into identifiable subunits that are analyzed systematically and analytically to better understand the real causes of industrial accidents and personal injuries. Today many sophisticated techniques of analyzing accidents are available. Empirical data in the form of accident frequency rates and severity rates are perhaps the most commonly used statistical methods of analyzing accident information. Numerical ratios are also used to compare and contrast industry injury rates, direct and indirect costs associated with any accident, and other comparisons of interest to safety managers.

Although the phrases industrial safety and industrial hygiene are still quite commonly heard today, it must be realized that such terms are somewhat dated in perspective. These phrases indicate the historical evolution of health and safety in an employment setting. But all employment situations do not occur only within the industrial sector of the economy. Consequently, the modern phrases occupational health and occupational safety are today preferrable to their historical ancestors. Occupational health and safety matters will be discussed further in Chapter 10.

G. LABOR RELATIONS-COLLECTIVE BARGAINING

Labor relations and collective bargaining are other personnel subfunctions commonly associated with personnel administration. In general, these personnel subfunctions deal with contract negotiation, contract interpretation, contract administration, and grievance handling. Although many authors use labor relations and collective bargaining interchangeably, some authors make distinctions. If these phrases are not considered synonymous (i.e., when differences are noted), the usual explanation is that collective bargaining refers specifically to the area of labor-management contract negotiation, while labor relations refers generally to the day-to-day administration of labor-management activities. Collective bargaining is often a phrase used only to describe a unionized setting in which organized labor confronts and interacts with corporate management, usually within a large organization.

However, in reality, labor relations and collective interaction occur whether or not workers are organized and whether or not the organization is of a large size. Labor-management relationships, contract negotiations, and grievance handling take place in all organizations, regardless of their relative size or degree of labor organization. Labor relations and collective bargaining activities also occur whether an organization is privately owned or publicly operated. Labor relations do not take place only within an industrialized setting or environment. Any organization that employs labor is involved with labor relations. Furthermore, the collective bargaining concept is also not limited to the industrial and private sectors of the economy. Unions are more and more common within the public sector of society. Teachers, policemen, firemen, sanitary employees, and transit workers are especially current and germane examples of public employees who are often unionized today and who achieve their demands through collective bargaining. Even if workers are not formally represented by a union, employee "bargaining" is still likely to be carried on in a collective manner. Even nonunionized employees gather together to fight for common causes when bargaining for employment contracts with management representatives. Thus, to at least some extent, labor relations and collective interaction (bargaining) take place in both unionized and nonunionized settings, and within both private and public sectors of the economy.

When a union has been certified by the National Labor Relations Board, as the result of an election, as the sole and exclusive bargaining agency for a company's employees, then management, by law, must bargain with it in regard to wages, rates of pay, hours of work, and other conditions of employment. Contract negotiation, interpretation, and administration are the main concerns of the labor relations-collective bargaining function. Handling daily complaints through a progressive grievance system is also a main task and responsibility of this personnel subfunction.

The personnel-industrial relations staff plays a very significant role in labor-management relations. The personnel director (or someone with a comparable title, such as the industrial relations director) commonly serves as a (the) key member of the company contract bargaining team. In addition, while daily operating under the terms of a labor contract, first-line supervisors (foremen) often consult the personnel department about the allocation of overtime, the handling of transfers and layoffs, and the application of contract work rules. In the area of grievance handling especially, the typical personnel-industrial relations department plays a vital role. Although nearly all grievance procedures, as spelled out in the labor contract, specify that the foreman will be the first to hear about and act on an employee grievance in all but the most routine cases, the foreman typically consults the pesonnel office before giving an answer. The personnel department is usually the second or third management step in a typical grievance handling system. Often, in effect, the personnel manager is given line authority to make a binding settlement in grievance matters. Such great authority is granted in grievance handling to insure due regard for precedent and to bring about plantwide consistency of action. This is crucial; mishandling a case could cause grave consequences, since many grievances have plantwide or even companywide implications. The importance of the labor relations and collective bargaining personnel subfunctions will be discussed further in Chapter 11.

H. PERSONNEL RESEARCH

Personnel research has traditionally been identified as a subject matter area of personnel administration but, until the past fifteen years, very little has actually been accomplished in this area. Even today the majority of personnel research is being conducted by special research organizations and a limited number of professors and graduate students. Although personnel research is frequently identified by personnel managers as part of their jobs, it is usually the lowest-priority item on their list of duties and responsibilities.

In the last few decades, however, some of the largest companies have been doing at least something in the personnel research area (Cook). The field of personnel research, however, should not be confused with the product research and development function. Product research and development has always been a high priority item for aggressive and growing organizational concerns. Marketing and sales research also should not be confused with personnel research. The personnel research function only entails investigations that pertain to manpower issues. Personnel research is research related to the personnel subfunctions — such as those identified in this chapter. Research done in the areas of staffing and appraisal, training and development, compensation: wage and salary administration, compensation: benefits and services, health and safety, labor relations — collective bargaining, and manpower planning can properly be labeled personnel research. In addition, much personnel research being done today concentrates on behavioral issues, especially motivation, leadership, and communication.

Research Impact

Even today the personnel research function is a low-priority concern in most personnel departments. Its existence is directly related to the financial fortunes of an enterprise. If times are rough and retrenchment becomes necessary, personnel research activities feel the cut of the financial axe almost immediately. Unquestionably, most organizations view manpower research as a luxury, not a necessity. Such a conceptualization of the personnel research function is not only unfortunate, but it is also often unrealistic. Properly directed manpower research can do much to alleviate the type of problems that cause financial retrenchment. Personnel and human resource research will be discussed in greater detail in Chapter 12.

4. Changing Scope of Personnel Administration

The scope of personnel administration has changed over the last few decades. Although there is agreement on the fact that the personnel function has changed recently, there is no consensus about exactly what these changes are and about the pace or rate of these alterations (Cox). Some alleged and acknowledged experts see the personnel discipline in a state of turmoil in which the pace of change is so rapid that drastic adaptations must be made in order to secure the survival and continued existence of the discipline. Other observers see the field of personnel as but a slowly evolving methodical glacier that, although in motion, is relatively dead in comparison to other changes taking place within our society. Both perspectives represent extreme viewpoints, and the best interpretation lies somewhere between the two (Odiorne, 1967).

Pace of Change

Many observers would probably agree that the field and practice of personnel administration has changed relatively slowly in comparison to other academic areas of business, management, and administration. Such a viewpoint and conclusion can be reached if one compares the book and journal literatures of the various business administration disciplines over the course of the last few decades. The disciplines of finance, accounting, marketing, production management, and labor relations have all experienced tremendous changes in subject matter and operational tools and techniques of analysis when compared to the relatively static content of the personnel discipline.

Subject Matter Changes

Changes definitely are taking place in personnel administration. Some personnel subfunctions seem to be breaking away from personnel, others seem to be new subareas, while still others seem to be changing only in terms of their relative emphasis and degree of importance. Many of these changes depend on the size of the organization in which the personnel function occurs. In-coming and out-going subareas of the overall personnel function often also depend on managerial personnel philosophies, which are known to vary considerably. Recognizing that such changes at best are only drastic oversimplifications, global generalizations, and personal observations, I will still disucss the changing scope of the personnel function. These changes are not universal, but they represent movements currently taking place within some but not all organizational personnel units.

Several functions that began in personnel are now separate departments in many larger modern corporations. The most evident of these functions are labor relations, public relations, and plant security. All three of these functions have expanded in importance over the years and are now separate, unique, specialized areas and departments in all but the smaller organizations. Such subfunctions, in effect, have withdrawn often from the main personnel function, not because of their insignificance, but because of their importance (Wood, 1967B).

On the other hand, some modern personnel issues are of recent vintage, or at least they appear to be new areas because of their lack of former prominence and because of their current popularity. Examples of such incoming personnel subareas include human resource planning, organization planning, and international staffing (employment) issues. Of course, these are actually evolutionary, not revolutionary, personnel subfunctions. Such concerns were evident in the field of personnel decades ago, but today they have been given new labels (titles) and their relative degree(s) of attention and importance have increased greatly (Cook).

Change in Emphasis

Although past and present personnel topics are similar, priorities of subfunctions have changed. Employee training and especially managerial development have increased over the years. Personnel research has a much greater emphasis today. Wage and salary administration seems to have lost some of its importance over the years, partially because hour and working condition problems have at least somewhat been settled in older and larger industrial organizations where unions have long been established. Employee appraisal is another example of a personnel subarea that is declining in terms of relative importance. With the governmental push for equal employment opportunities and test validation, most companies are decreasing their concern about employee evaluations. Not all personnel subfunctions are either increasing or decreasing in emphasis and importance. Benefits and services, and health and safety are examples of employee matters that have in the past been, currently are, and in the future will remain vital personnel issues and concerns. Of course, the desired employee benefits and services have changed over the years, and the major impetus for improving health and safety working environments has also varied over time (the current pressure being due to the passage of the Occupational Safety and Health Act).

Not all these changes are taking place in all organizational personnel units. They are occurring basically in larger, well-established industrial concerns. Smaller personnel units will not display outgoing personnel subareas. Newly created personnel departments cannot neglect wage and salary administration issues. And many public institutions are just now facing issues related to managerial development and employee health and safety. Changes in emphasis and importance are hard to generalize from one personnel unit to the next but, in general, see the major movements to be as described previously. These changes within personnel practices have occurred because of several factors that are beyond the scope of this discussion. These priority shifts have come about because of changing organizational demands, employee needs, and societal concerns (Lederer).

In summary, it seems that today personnel administration has almost all of the problems (topics or subfunctions) of the past (with in many cases a shift in emphasis) as well as additional anxieties from current circumstances. There are some new issues and techniques being studied today that were missing in the past and, similarly, there are some formerly prominent topics that have currently declined in importance. However, most of the important issues of the past are still the persistent problems of the present and undoubtedly will continue to cause fatigue and frustration in the future (Miner, 1969). The evolving environment has caused constant changes throughout the entire economy. Personnel administration as an academic discipline and as a field of practice has changed significantly over the years — but not any more and in fact probably substantially less than other aspects and areas of general business administration.

Figure 2-3 summarizes the changing scope of personnel administration.

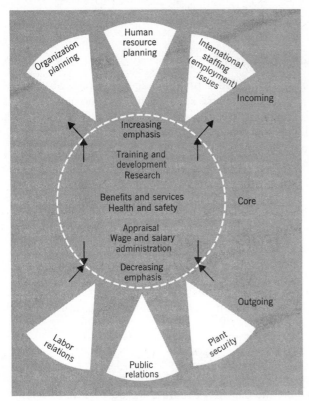

FIGURE 2-3 The changing scope of personnel administration.

Human resource planning, organization planning, and international staffing (employment) issues are shown as incoming personnel subareas. Within the personnel core, training and development and research are depicted as personnel subfunctions that are increasing in importance today, while appraisal and wage and salary administration are illustrated as personnel subareas that currently have declined in terms of their relative emphasis. Benefits and services, and health and safety are shown as personnel subfunctions of continual emphasis and importance. Finally, labor relations, public relations, and plant security are pictured as outgoing personnel subconcerns — but remember that such departings usually represent increased, decreased, organizational importance.

5. Roles of a Personnel Manager

A role can be defined as an expected behavior pattern. Personnel managers perform many roles; that is, they are expected to exhibit various behavior patterns. Some of the most commonly performed personnel roles include social conscience, counselor, mediator, company spokesman, problem solver, change agent, and miscellany — all of which will now be explained in somewhat greater detail.

A. SOCIAL CONSCIENCE

The social conscience role of the personnel manager is a behavioral role based on historical precedence. Because some of the first personnel managers had religious training, and because of the poor working conditions existing within the initial industrial factories, the social conscience role seemed to naturally be affiliated and identified with the evolution of the personnel management function (Cook). The personnel manager was seen as a concerned humanitarian who reminded management of its moral and ethical obligations to its employees. The personnel manager was seen as a "good guy" trying to prevent the "bad guys" (management) from abusing and taking advantage of the company's lowly employees. It was thought that the employed common man could have his interests and welfare made known to management through the medium of the personnel manager. The social conscience role of the personnel manager is still performed to some extent today, but such a role is at best only partially descriptive of the past and is not totally representative of the present or future activities of the typical personnel administrator.

B. COUNSELOR

Another personnel manager role is the concept of the personnel counselor. This role is both historically and currently accurate and descriptive of at least some portion of the typical personnel administrator's duties and responsibilities. In the past this role was perhaps better identified as a "chaplain" role, because the personnel officer was then thought of as someone to whom one could go to to discuss personal and religious sorts of problems. Today, the personnel manager is still the one to whom employees frequently turn to if they desire to discuss personal matters with a company representative. However, such personal matters are usually much less likely to be of a religious nature today. Marital, health, financial, mental, and career problems now comprise the bulk of the personal subject matter discussed between an employee and a personnel manager. Most personnel managers, however, know that they are not trained to be professional counselors. They usually practice a very nondirective approach in which they try to get employees to recommend their own solutions to their own problems. If severe personal problems are encountered, the wise personnel manager is one who will refer such a case to an appropriately trained and qualified professional.

C. MEDIATOR

A mediator acts as an intermediary between disputing parties in order to bring about a settlement (a peacemaker). This function relates largely to the personnel subfunction of labor relations — collective bargaining. In this capacity, the personnel manager attempts to reconcile differences existing between labor and management organizational factions. This mediator or peacemaker role can, however, refer to settling differences that occur between individuals or between groups. This is probably the most descriptive and accurate role portrayal of the job of a modern personnel manager. The typical personnel manager today attempts to act as a liaison and communicating link between individual and group, labor and management constituencies. Because this coordinating role frequently deals with entity differences, it is probably best identified as either a mediator or peacemaker function.

D. COMPANY SPOKESMAN

The personnel manager has always been a frequent spokesman for or representative of the company. Whenever someone from an organization is called on to represent that organization at some public function or occasion, the company spokesman often will be from the personnel department. This is because the personnel manager commonly has a better overall total picture of a company's operation, since he deals so intimately with so many key organizational activities and functions. This company spokesman role was performed so frequently by personnel managers that it has led to the eventual separation of public relations work from the normal scope of personnel matters in larger organizations. The personnel manager still, however, performs this public relations or company spokesman role in most small organizations.

E. PROBLEM SOLVER

The personnel manager must also serve as a problem solver with respect to the issues and dilemmas that involve human resources management. Along with being the main decision maker in regard to personnel matters, the personnel administrator also frequently helps to solve problems related to overall long-range organizational planning. Problem solving and decision making are major parts of any manager's job. The personnel officer is expected to perform these roles comprehensively in regard to specific manpower matters and supplementally with respect to general organizational issues. Some observers envision these problem-solving and decision-making functions as the core of a personnel administrator's job duties and responsibilities.

F. CHANGE AGENT

The change agent function is one of the more modern roles performed by and affiliated with the personnel administrator. The personnel manager as an agent of change is thought of as the person within an organization best suited to introduce and implement major institutional changes. The major organizational adjustments that must be made, when any physical procedural or technological changes occur, have to be made basically by the people affected by these changes. Since the personnel manager is mainly responsible for an organization's personnel, he is best suited to coordinate the manpower adjustments to change.

G. MISCELLANY

Some observers have commented that the personnel department in many organizations fulfills a miscellaneous and heterogeneous function. Any matter that needs someone's attention and that nobody else wants to do often is done by the personnel department (McLaughlin). This historically, especially, has been the case, but it is true at least to some degree today. The personnel department frequently appears to be a collection of odd jobs that other organizational departments do not want to be bothered with. The discussion in Chapter 1 about the emergence of personnel specialists seems to lend credence to this historical personnel role. Although it is generally believed that the personnel manager has to perform many miscellaneous and peripheral activities, it is also agreed that such activities are important. They are crucial to the efficient and effective operation of any organization.

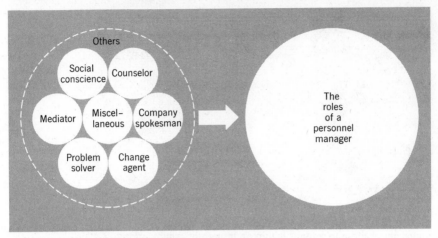

FIGURE 2-4   The roles of a personnel manager.

Although the personnel manager often performs a variety of duties, these responsibilities are essential to the proper maintenance of an enterprise.

H. OTHERS

The preceding identified personnel roles are representative, not all-inclusive. Each author will identify somewhat different roles when classifying the expected behavior patterns of personnel administrators. For example, different personnel manager roles might be identified as recruiter, record keeper, friend, social agent, recreation director, cafeteria manager, or poet laureate.

Figure 2-4 illustrates that the roles of the personnel manager are best viewed as a composite set including the specific personnel roles of social conscience, counselor, mediator, company spokesman, problem solver, change agent, miscellany, and other expected behavior patterns. Of course, these specific roles are really best envisioned as partially overlapping and interrelated phenomena instead of as totally distinct set entities.

G. PERSONNEL RATIO

This chapter has thus far presented an overview of the personnel function(s); the remainder of this chapter will discuss the relationship of the personnel function(s) to the total corporate structure.

Personnel Appearance

As an organization grows from a one-man operation into a company of larger size, numerous departmental units evolve. For example, the typical industrial

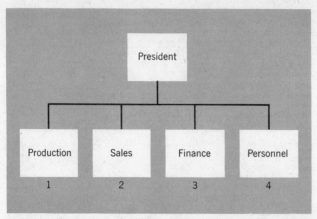

FIGURE 2-5   The personnel department is typically the fourth major department to appear within an industrial organization.

organization first grows to the point where a production department becomes necessary. Companies are formed because someone is producing a good or service that he feels can fulfill a consumer need or a societal demand. After the production department usually comes a sales or marketing department. A company must sell its product or service if it is to survive over time. Next comes the finance department, which must keep the accounting records, reports and statements of the company in proper order. Because of the scarcity of capital, its procurement and utilization must be managed competently by every organization, regardless of its size. Although many variations exist among expanding institutions, the personnel department is usually the fourth major department to evolve in the typical industrial organization. (Figure 2-5) Various manpower problems and issues eventually become important to the growing organization that a separate personnel department is formed.

Personnel Expansion

As an organization continues to grow, either other major departments will form or, more commonly, subdepartments will form under the auspices of the four original departments. If an industrial organization continues to grow and reaches the size of 3000 employees, the personnel department now will have grown to the point where it will contain personnel subfunctions in the form of separate departments in a format very similar to the personnel administration subject matter breakdown described earlier in this chapter. Figure 2-6 shows a typical industrial organization that employs 3000 workers, contains the four basic production, marketing, finance, and personnel departments, and also indicates the usual subdivision departments within the personnel area, the departments of employment (staffing and appraisal), training and development, labor relations (collective bargaining), wage and salary administration, health and safety, and benefits and services. Of course, such a model is not an exact portrayal of all industrial organizations of this size, but it is realistically representative.

The question often is asked "How large should an organization be before the personnel function becomes large enough in scope to warrant the full time services and attention of a personnel manager?" Debate continues to surround this inquiry, since the answer depends on the unique characteristics of any company. Also, "large" and "size" require additional explanation. Most people interpret size to mean the number of total employees, but it could also refer to the scope of a company's financial assets, gross or net income, plant footage, land ownership, or other measures. In reference to the number of employees criterion, an old rule of thumb used to be that a full-time personnel manager was needed as soon as a company employed 200 workers. This rule, of course, should not be interpreted to mean that if you have 199 employees, you do not need a full-time personnel manager. There is nothing especially magical about the 200 employee figure (Spencer and Singer).

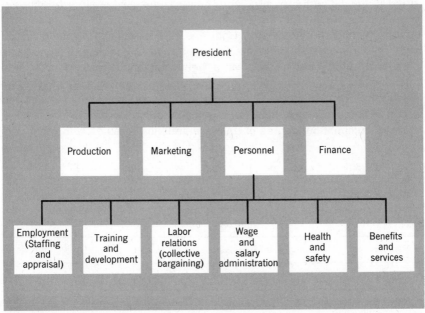

FIGURE 2-6   Typical formal structure of a medium-size industrial organization (3000 employees).

Ratio

Various survey research studies have reported data that have led to the more accurate concept of the personnel ratio (Wood, 1967A). The personnel ratio can be defined as the number of full time people working within the personnel function (exclusive of clerical manpower) per 100 company employees. Studies have shown that .60 to .90 per 100 total employees in the company are engaged in personnel work. The average thus tends to approximate .75 personnel workers per 100 company employees. This ratio works out then to recommend a full-time personnel manager approximately when an organization reaches the size of 133 total workers. In the example of the 3000 employee hypothetical company shown in Figure 2-6, we could expect to find approximately twenty-three employees engaged in some form of full time personnel work.

Ratio Determinants

The personnel ratio varies from company to company for a number of reasons. The two most important causes are managerial personnel philosophy and the size of the organization. If management believes in the importance of the personnel function, the personnel ratio will be high; if they do not so believe, the ratio will be small (Wood, 1967B). In addition, the personnel ratio tends to be closer to the .90 figure for small companies and closer to the .60 figure for large corporations because certain economies of operation can exist within the personnel department once this organizational subunit reaches a certain size. Until this size is reached, the addition of another full-time personnel manager or specialist to handle one of the basic personnel subfunctions has a more significant and direct effect on and relationship to the personnel ratio, since total company size is not yet of an extremely large magnitude. Other factors, of course, may affect the size and scope of the personnel ratio. For examples, company product or service, industry competition, degree of unionism, public pressures, and other vari-

DEFINITION	Number of full-time people working in personnel (exclusive of clerical) per 100 total company employees
RANGE	.60 — .90
AVERAGE	.75 (1 personnel person per 133 total workers)
MAIN DETERMINANTS	Managerial philosophy and organizational size

FIGURE 2-7   The "personnel ratio."

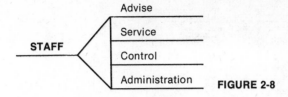

FIGURE 2-8

ables might affect the personnel ratio, although in exactly what manner and degree has not as yet been precisely determined. Figure 2-7 summarizes some of the key information related to the "personnel ratio" concept.

7. Personnel as a Staff Position

The personnel department is frequently said to be in a staff instead of a line organizational position. A staff position is advisory, service, control, or administrative in nature (Figure 2-8). A staff position theoretically does not possess any command authority over other departmental organizational entities. A staff position is said also to be outside of the direct chain of command, since it does not directly involve the production or the marketing of the company's goods or services. A staff unit is supposed to give advice, provide service, maintain control, or perform administrative tasks. Figure 2-8 shows that the staff concept is a composite of advisory, service, control and administrative role duties and responsibilities.

As an advisor, the personnel manager is called on to give advice. For example, he can screen and recommend candidates for positions, suggest performance evaluation methods to supervisors, or inform higher corporate officers about employee compensation preferences. In a service capacity, the personnel manager may supervise the company cafeteria, coordinate various recreational programs, and plan various company social functions, such as the annual Christmas party. As a control expert, the personnel administrator is expected to handle issues such as wage and salary determinations, work safety matters, and employee discipline problems. As an administrator, the personnel specialist keeps records on various manpower matters such as absenteeism, tardiness, discipline, health problems, and performance appraisal. The personnel specialist is often also the key administrator involved with the implementation of collective bargaining, training and development, benefits and services, and personnel research matters.

Line Authority

A line position is in the chain of command; that is, it has command authority or the right to tell someone what to do and to expect them to do it. Line positions directly help to produce or sell an organization's product or

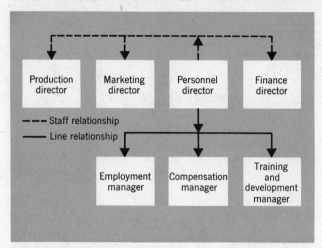

FIGURE 2-9   A personnel manager with line and staff relationships.

service. Although the personnel manager has a staff relationship to other departments, he nevertheless does possess line or command authority within his own department. Often line relationships on organization charts are indicated by solid lines, while staff relationships are shown by dotted lines. Figure 2-9 shows that the personnel director has a staff (advisory, service, control, or administrative) relationship to the production, marketing, and finance departments, but that he has a line (command) relationship to the employment manager, the compensation manager, and the training and development manager, since they are all under his direct supervision.

Line or Staff?

Today most management authors and practitioners contest the use of line and staff organizational concepts. It is difficult, if not impossible, to accurately distinguish between line and staff positions and line and staff relationships (Belasco and Alutto). For example, is finance a line or staff position? Arguments can be presented to support or refute either alternative. But even organizational positions, which appear initially to be "pure" line or staff examples, often are not upon closer examination. For example, is personnel really a staff position? It is really not in many real-world organizational settings. Frequently the personnel manager posseses line authority both within and outside of his own department. The personnel manager often does not advise or recommend alternatives; he frequently directs or even demands certain individual and organizational behaviors. He may have ultimate authority in hiring nonsupervisory personnel, he may unilaterally decide how to handle a grievance matter, he may require that certain performance appraisal procedures be followed, he may demand that certain indoctrination and training programs be required of all employees, or he may fire an employee from any department on the spot without consultation with anyone if he observes gross employee negligence or behavior. Such examples support the fact that the personnel manager, although theoretically in a staff position, can and usually does have some line authority in real-world environments, and this command authority typically extends beyond his own department into other organizational subdivisions (Coffey). Many if not most organizational positions occasionally exhibit both line and staff duties, responsibilities, and authorities. Technically, the concept of functional authority has been created to explain the situation where a staff position is given line authority outside of his own area of jurisdiction under certain circumstances. Figure 2-10 illustrates that the concept of "functional authority" is used to explain the real-world interrelationships and overlappings between the theoretical concepts of line and staff positions.

The relationship of the personnel function to an organization's total corporate structure varies from one institution to another. Organizational size can be important. Smaller organizations have personnel managers who perform more line duties than staff activities. As an organization grows, however, the need for specialization is greater, as is the likelihood that the personnel department will only perform its theoretical staff roles of advising, servicing, controlling, and administering (Sokolik). Overall top corporate managerial personnel philosophy will also affect the personnel manager's role. Some corporate officials will strongly support the personnel department and its manager by giving this function considerable latitude, while less permissive executives may prefer to stifle the overall personnel function. Of course, the unique personality, qualifications, and competency of any personnel manager will also tremendously affect the relative degrees to which he performs staff or line functions. The relative strengths and weaknesses of other

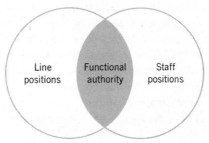

FIGURE 2-10 The idea of "functional authority" helps to explain the sometimes interrelated and overlapping nature of line and staff positions.

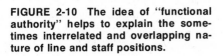

company department heads will also affect the personnel manager's scope of authority. These and other factors are meant to illustrate that a personnel administrator's relationship to the total corporate structure is not of a standard mold or format but varies markedly from one organizational setting to another.

8. Shared Responsibility

The question of final or ultimate responsibility is often asked in reference to personnel activities. Should the final decision in employment matters be made by a staff personnel officer or a line manager? This issue or question is a direct manifestation of the previously discussed but unresolved line versus staff dilemma. Whether hiring or firing, training or development, or other staffing and employment functions should be performed by either a line or staff person is a dated issue and a moot question. Today it is recognized that the responsibility for employment activities must be a "shared responsibility" (Daugherty). The personnel manager and the first-line supervisor are the two persons most involved with sharing these duties. A foreman cannot effectively perform all of his staffing activities without the assistance of the personnel manager. Of course, the reverse situation is equally true. A personnel officer cannot implement his programs without the aid of competent first-line supervisors.

Multiple Responsibility

The shared responsibility concept extends beyond merely two parties. Managers other than first-line supervisors must be concerned about employment practices. Even all nonsupervisory employees should be at least partially responsible also for their employment-related activities. Selection, safety, health, labor relations, and other personnel administration subareas are concerns and responsibilities of all company personnel — from the top corporate officer down to the newly hired employee. Personnel activities are implemented by working with many people. All organizational positions involve some degree of interpersonal relationships. Thus, ultimately, appropriate personnel practices and policies are the responsibility of an organizational group levels and individual institutional entities.

In theory, personnel employment responsibilities should be shared by all persons within an organization (Appley). In practice, usually the personnel department and the first-line supervisors share most of this operational authority. Figure 2-11 illustrates this.

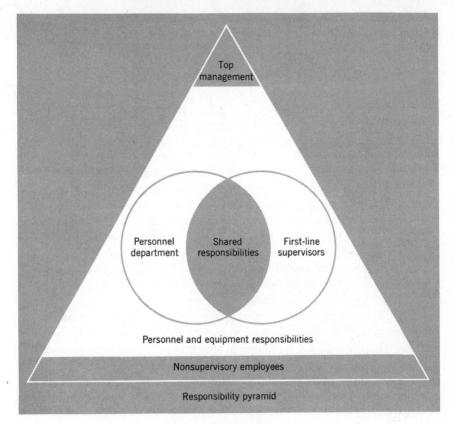

FIGURE 2-11   Multiple personnel responsibilities.

9. Summary

There are many fallacies and misconceptions associated with the overall personnel function. Some of the most common of these illusions are that personnel work involves working with people, welfare work, mainly labor relations activities, and nothing but the application of common sense.

The overall subject matter of personnel administration can be subdivided into (1) human resource planning, (2) staffing and appraisal, (3) training and development, (4) compensation: wage and salary administration, (5) compensation: benefits and services, (6) health and safety, (7) labor relations-collective bargaining, and (8) personnel research.

The scope of personnel administration has changed somewhat over the years. Human resource planning, organization planning, and international staffing (employment) issues are incoming personnel subareas. Training and development and personnel research are increasing in importance today, while appraisal and wage and salary administration currently have declined in terms of their relative emphasis. Employee benefits and services, and worker health and safety matters have continuously been important personnel concerns. Labor relations, public relations, and plant security are outgoing personnel subareas that are leaving or have left general personnel work because of their increased organizational importance.

The personnel department and the personnel manager typically perform a variety of roles. Some of the most frequently cited roles affiliated with the personnel function include the roles of social conscience, counselor, mediator, company spokesman, problem solver, change agent, and miscellany.

The personnel ratio is the number of full-time people working within the personnel function (exclusive of clerical manpower) per 100 company employees. The range of this ratio is about .60 to .90, depending on company size and organizational personnel philosophy.

Although theoretically personnel is a staff position fulfilling advisory, service, control, and administrative functions, in the real world a personnel manager frequently displays line or command authority both within and outside of his own specific institutional department. The ultimate responsibility for personnel practices and employment activities is a multiple or shared responsibility among all organizational employees — both managerial and nonmanagerial. Personnel officers and first line supervisors especially share in this employment responsibility.

DISCUSSION QUESTIONS AND ASSIGNMENTS

1. Mention and explain some of the roles commonly performed by any personnel manager.
2. What is the personnel ratio? What is the average and normal range of fluctuation for this ratio? What organizational factors affect the size of this ratio?
3. What is a staff position? Is a personnel manager in a line or a staff position? Defend your answer.
4. Compare and contrast your conceptualizations of the personnel function before and after you read this chapter.
5. What forces do you currently see within the environment that are reshaping the nature of the personnel function? Identify and explain the implications of these forces or pressures.
6. Compare and contrast the personnel functions within a small company and a large organization with which you are familiar. Visit sites and interview officials if necessary.

REFERENCES

General Book References

Beach, Dale S., *Personnel: The Management of People at Work.* New York: Macmillan, 1970, pp. 63–80.

Chruden, Herbert J., and Arthur W. Sherman, Jr., *Personnel Management.* Cincinnati: South-Western, 1972, pp. 60–117.

Flippo, Edwin B., *Principles of Personnel Management.* New York: McGraw Hill, 1971, pp. 56–72.

French, Wendell, *The Personnel Management Process: Human Resources Administration.* Boston: Houghton Mifflin, 1970, pp. 3–8, 46–72.

Jucius, Michael J., *Personnel Management.* Homewood, Ill.: Irwin, 1971, pp. 76–98.

Megginson, Leon C., *Personnel: A Behavioral Approach to Administration.* Homewood, Ill.: Irwin, 1972, pp. 45–65.

McFarland, Dalton E., *Company Officers Assess the Personnel Function,* AMA Research Study No. 79. New York: American Management Association, 1967.

McFarland, Dalton E., *Personnel Management: Theory and Practice.* New York: Macmillan, 1968, pp. 63–116.

Miner, John B., and Mary Green Miner, *Personnel and Industrial Relations: A Managerial Approach.* New York: Macmillan, 1973, pp. 3–16.

Odiorne, George S., *Personnel Administration by Objectives.* Homewood, Ill.: Irwin, 1971, pp. 90–107.

Pigors, Paul, and Charles A. Myers, *Personnel Administration.* New York: McGraw-Hill, 1969, pp. 29–51.

Ritzer, George, and Harrison Trice, *An Occupation in Conflict: A Study of the Personnel Manager.* Ithaca, N.Y.: New York State School of Industrial and Labor Relations, 1969.

Strauss, George, and Leonard R. Sayles, *Personnel: The Human Problems of Management.* Englewood Cliffs, N.J.: Prentice-Hall, 1972, pp. 348–374.

Zif, Jay J., *The Personnel Department* (Creative Studies Simulation). New York: Macmillan, 1970.

Specific Journal References

Appley, Lawrence A., "Management is Personnel Administration, *Personnel, 46* (2), 1969, pp. 1–6.

Belasco, James A., and Joseph A. Alutto, "Line-Staff Conflicts: Some Empirical Insights," *Academy of Management Journal, 12* (4), 1969, pp. 469–477.

Coffey, Thomas C., "Resolving the Conflict of Staff vs. Staff," *Personnel, 46* (4), 1969, pp. 58–65.

Cook, Arthur J. D., "Personnel Practices in a Developing Area," *Personnel Journal, 46* (5), 1967, pp. 302–306.

Cox, Arne, "Personnel Planning, Objectives and Methods: Presentation of an Integrated System," *Management International Review, 8* (4-5), 1968, pp. 104–114.

Daugherty, A. C., "A President Looks at the Personnel Function," *Personnel Journal, 47* (6), 1968, pp. 402–406.

Lederer, D. A., Jr., "Personnel Policies for the 1970's," *Personnel, 45* (5), 1968, pp. 20–29.

McLaughlin, David, "Roadblocks to Personnel Department Effectiveness," *Personnel Journal, 50* (1), 1971, pp. 46–50.

Miner, John B., "An Input-Output Model for Personnel Strategies," *Business Horizons, 12* (3), 1969, pp. 71–78.

Odiorne, George, "Yardsticks for Measuring Personnel Departments," *The Personnel Administrator, 12* (4), 1967, pp. 1–6.

Rabe, W. F., "Yardsticks for Measuring Personnel Department Effectiveness," *Personnel, 44* (1), 1967, pp. 56–57.

Rogers, Rolf E., "An Integrated Personnel System," *Personnel Administration, 33* (2), 1970, pp. 22–28.

Sokolik, Stanley L., "Reorganize the Personnel Department?" *California Management Review, 11* (3), 1969, pp. 43–52.

Spencer, Carlie, and Carmella Singer, "The Personnel Function in Medium and Small Firms," *Personnel Practice Bulletin, 26* (1), 1970, pp. 42–47.

Wood, Thomas L., "The Personnel Staff: What Is a Reasonable Size?" *Personnel Journal, 46* (3), 1967A, pp. 163–167.

Wood, Thomas L., "The Personnel Staff: What Functions Does It Perform?" *Personnel Journal, 46* (10), 1967B, pp. 640–650.

PART
TWO

Behavioral
Foundations of
Personnel
Administration

contents

learning objectives

1. To understand the importance of the behavioral topics of motivation and communication as they relate to the personnel administrator's job duties and responsibilities.

2. To become acquainted with the nature or causes of individual and group behaviors.

3. To be able to analyze and improve communication flows and systems.

4. To be able to recognize the uniqueness of each and every human being in regard to motivation and communication patterns.

Human behavior must be understood before it can be effectively managed and controlled.

3

Motivation and Communication

1. Introduction

Personnel administration involves the administration of personnel. The personnel of an organization is its manpower or human resources. It has long been recognized, especially by personnel managers, that the human inputs are the most valuable of all organizational resources. It is also generally believed that the best way to manage people is to know and learn as much as possible about global human behavior. The modern personnel manager must be well acquainted with the behavioral foundations of personnel administration. A personnel officer must be more than a specialist in general management principles and techniques. More important, he must be able to understand at least partially why people behave and act as they do. A supervisor cannot manage employees effectively without a basic understanding of individual and group behavior. Such knowledge is crucial for all managers, regardless of their departmental affiliation. This expertise is, however, especially demanded of the personnel specialist, since his bailiwick is personnel, not production, marketing, finance, or some other departmental concern.

Motivation and communication are behavioral topics that grew out of the psychology and sociology disciplines, respectively. Psychology is the study of individual behavior, and sociology is the study of group behavior. Industrial psychology and organizational sociology are basically the application of such knowledge to institutional settings and environments. Such behavioral knowledge is needed by anyone hoping to become an adept administrator of human resources.

It is impossible to thoroughly understand and comprehend employee relations without a knowledge of behavioral motivation and communication. An effective personnel or manpower manager must be able to observe, study, analyze, and understand human behavior before he can learn to cope efficiently with and handle manpower concerns and issues (Hammerton). A comprehension of communication principles, theories, and models is also a prerequisite for competent personnel administration (Happel). The two major subjects of behavioral motivation and communication constitute the subject of this chapter.

2. Motivation

The concept of motivation will be presented using the following subject matter format: (1) definition and measurement problems; (2) nature of causes; (3) role of money, and (4) roles of reward and punishment.

A. DEFINITION AND MEASUREMENT PROBLEMS

The concept of motivation is difficult to define. Laymen and acknowledged behavioral science experts do not agree on a common definition of this term. No universal meaning can be associated with the motivation concept for a number of reasons. The term motivation is used in a variety of ways. The term motivation, or its derivatives, can be used as a noun, adjective, adverb, or any other form of grammatical sentence structure. The biggest problem, however, is theoretical, not semantic. It is generally believed that behavior is motivated, but there is no consensus as to what constitutes either behavior or motivation.

Is All Human Behavior Motivated?

Some individuals have argued that all human behavior is motivated. This means that the concept of motivation should explain all forms, aspects, and variations of overt physical human movement or action. But what if an external physical force, such as an extremely strong wind, causes a person to move from position X to position Y? Was this human movement motivated? Many researchers and writers would say that the motivation concept does not explain "all" human actions, but only "internal" human behaviors. Other authors will, however, exclude certain types of even internal human behaviors, such as those taking place within a person's digestive, circulation, nervous, reproduction, and other bodily systems. An even more limited definition of motivation would include only human behavior that results because of conscious thought or cognition. If this is the preferred definition, how can habits, semiconscious, or unconscious human behaviors be explained? Because people have different ideas of what constitutes human behavior, they also have different definitions of the motivation concept. Normally, researchers define the concept of motivation in a manner related to their academic training and background and in a format conducive to their research efforts. Accordingly, engineers, physicists, biologists, psychologists, sociologists, and others all have their own preferred definitions of the motivation concept.

Motivation as a Neutral Concept

Theoretically, motivation should be considered to be a neutral concept. Unfortunately, the term motivation has a positive pragmatic connotation. For example, to say that "John is highly motivated" implies that Joe is a "good guy," and that other individuals are not motivated. Of course, all persons are motivated, some in a personally acceptable or organizationally efficient manner, and others along different lines. In this chapter I will assume both a global definition of and a neutral status for the motivation concept; that is, all human behavior ("internal" or "external," "good" or "bad," or anything else) will presumably be motivated behavior.

Measuring Motivation

Although no one really knows exactly what motivation is, this has not discouraged numerous researchers from attempting to measure it in ways that are as diverse and inconsistent as there have been definitional endeavors. Usually some form of questionnaire is given in an attempt to measure motivation, but these tests are not common. Often psychological, projective, or interest test batteries are used to evaluate human motivation. It is usually agreed that tests are able to measure what a person "can do" (ability, aptitude, intelligence, etc.), but they cannot effectively determine what an individual "will do" (motivation). Other attempts to explain and predict human behavior have been researched. Various motivation theories are based on hereditary elements, environmental components, prenatal care, the formative years, weaning habits, star constellations, head-bumps configurations, and virtually everything else imaginable. Although some of these motivation theories have more respectability than others, none of them can adequately explain all motivated human behaviors.

B. NATURE OR CAUSES

Similar to the definition and measurement of human motivation, the nature or causes of individual behavior also is (are) not know for sure. There are many different motivation theories — all of which differ at least somewhat in their underlying assumptions concerning motivated human behavior. Because of this wide variety of motivation theories, a general discussion of motivation concepts requires that such motivation models be grouped or classified into a certain limited number of categories. But even these broad categories or classifications are likely to differ in number and identification from author to author. I will group motivation theories and the nature or causes of motivation into four main subdivisions: (1) individual; (2) group; (3) environmental; and (4) systems approach. Explanations of these four motivation subgroupings will not be presented.

Individual

Individual motivation theories or the nature and causes of individual human behavior will be explained using the additional subunits of (1) needs; (2) drives; (3) tensions; (4) expectations; (5) values; and (6) combination.

NEEDS

Need theories are the most popular form or version of human motivational theories. Allegedly, needs serve as the motives or stimuli of human activities. There is no universal agreement as to what a "need" really is or how this concept can be accurately defined. For example, controversy exists concerning whether or not needs are physiological, chemical, muscular, neurological, psychological, or cultural. Nevertheless, it is commonly assumed by many psychologists and sociologists that needs cause or motivate human behavior.

Maslow. Some popular need models of motivation feature five levels or classifications of needs. For example, Abraham H. Maslow has hypothesized a "need hierarchy" similar to that shown in Figure 3-1 (Maslow, "book" reference citation). First, as this theory or model purports, an individual must fulfill physiological needs such as hunger, thirst, sleep and sex. After basic physiological needs are met, safety and security concerns become important. Satisfying safety and security needs involves building up a reserve supply of the necessities of life, such as food, water, clothing, and shelter. These two levels constitute primary needs, since they must be furnished or fulfilled before secondary or supplemental needs can serve as behavioral motivators. Social needs involve love, companionship, cooperation, and emotional considerations. If and when a person satisfies this need level, he then moves on to the self-esteem need which, in its ultimate form, is usually called self-

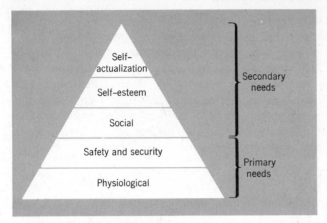

FIGURE 3-1 A need hierarchy.

actualization. Self-actualization is an overly used and abused concept that is supposed to reflect a situation where a person is utilizing his innate talents and potential to their utmost. The self-actualization concept is kin to what the younger generation today refer to as "finding your own bag," "doing your own thing," or "getting it all together." These upper levels of human needs reflect a turning inward of individual perception and attention. Self-analysis and self-insight are emphasized, and it is hoped that the application of this internalization process will lead to the general betterment of all mankind.

Criticisms of Need Theories.   Many criticisms have been levied against general and specific need theories. Within the social and behavioral sciences, there are the constantly reoccurring problems of concept definition and measurement. What is a need? How can needs be evaulated or assessed? Exactly how many needs do we have? Some models have five needs, others have six, eight, twelve, twenty or maybe just one. David McClelland is most noted for his achievement-need model of human behavior. McClelland argues that the need for achievement is the underlying force motivating many forms of human endeavor. Other need theories stress the importance of competency, sex, self-determination, or other need elements. If we have five basic needs instead of one, which five are they? Authors do not agree as to either the number or the identification of such needs. In addition, most critics today do not believe that a person cannot be concerned with or motivated by higher-order needs until lower-level needs are completely fulfilled. It is now usually contended that any individual is working to fulfill several need levels at the same time. For example, an unemployed individual may be basically concerned with survival, but he, too, has a self-image and a self-concept. On the other hand, a millionaire may spend most of his time and effort trying to satisfy self-actualization concerns, but he, too, must eat, drink, and sleep in order to survive. All human beings attempt to fulfill many needs at numerous levels at all times. Only relative rather than absolute human need vary.

Another criticism of need theories is that needs cannot directly cause or motivate behavior. Just because a person needs something does not really explain why or how he behaves in order to try to meet this need. This argument assumes that needs themselves are caused by something else, this unknown element is really the central core of motivated behavior. This rationale further assumes that a need is only a by-product or a symptom of a more fundamental and underlying human motivational concept.

DRIVES

The motivating stimuli behind human needs are often said to be human drives. Collectively, especially in psychology, there is a diversified group of theories that are best described as drive theories. Such theories see human drives as the source of human needs. In general, drive theories suffer from all of the criticisms of need theories, plus some additional maladies. Definitional, measurement, and conceptual problems are involved. The number and identification issues exist. The controversy of innate versus learned drives is introduced. And the precise relationship between needs and drives has not yet been agreed on. In addition, once the question of "what causes human needs" is answered in terms of human drives, the next logical inquiry becomes "what causes human drives." Oddly enough, some authors answer "human needs," and thus the argument or process seems to become at least cyclical, if not contradictory. Often the needs-drives dilemma and paradox turns into a chicken and the egg controversy. Other theorists, however, believe that human drives are, indeed, caused by yet another even more basic and fundamental human motivational element.

TENSIONS

A frequently espoused conceptualization is that human drives that cause human needs are caused, in turn, by human tensions. A multiplicity of theories in various academic disciplines, including both the hard and soft sciences, possess an underlying tension premise. Human tension theories emphasize the roles of mental strain, nervous anxiety, muscular contraction, physiological stretching, cultural stress, chemical changes or imbalances, social disequilibriums, and the like. Once again, definitional, measurement, conceptual, identification, and source problems and issues are encountered. What constitutes a tension? What causes human tensions? How are human needs, drives, and tensions interrelated? These and other inquiries still remain largely unanswered. Some theorists have stated that the tension concept is the same idea as needs or drives (only the label or identification has changed). Other vehemently support the abstraction that needs are caused by drives, which are caused by tensions, which are caused by something else.

EXPECTATIONS

This line of reasoning extended one step further commonly asserts that expectations cause tensions. Expectations are anticipations of or for something. Similar to other groupings of human motivational theories, there are a number of somewhat different behavioral expectation concepts. Often an expectation theory incorporates concepts such as desirability and probability. An equation such as expectation = desirability × probability is often used within expectation behavioral models. Desirability is usually expressed in terms of a valence, or a weighted numbering system. For example, if an individual desires an object or event very much, it might be rated + + +, or +10. If an object or event is very much undesired, then it would be rated − − −, or −10. A statistical and numerical figure can also be established to represent "probability." Probability estimates, that is, chances or odds, can be systematically obtained and fairly accurately measured by analyzing past experiences, former practices, and situational circumstances. Probabilities are usually expressed in decimal form; for example, .5 means a fifty-fifty risk, .9 means that this event will happen in nine out of ten possible occurrences, and so forth. In this fashion, expectations can be expressed in numerical terms. One of the more popular expectation theories that has been presented in a format similar to that just described is associated with and evidenced within the work of Victor H. Vroom (Vroom, "book" reference citation).

Although expectation theories appear to be empirical and objective, this is only an illusion. Both desirability and probability are subjective, intuitive factors, even if they are expressed in numerical terms. Multiplying intuitions and compounding subjectivities cannot produce reliable and valid concrete, objective, or empirical motivational measurements. In addition, the definition, measurement, conceptualization, identification, and source problems and issues are as much a part of expectation theories as they are part and parcel of all other forms or groups of individual motivation causes or theories.

In general, the previously discussed forms or groups of individual motivation theories progressively and respectively represent a movement from broad to narrower behavioral concepts. Figure 3-2 illustrates that in general, it can be suggested that expectations cause tensions, which cause drives,

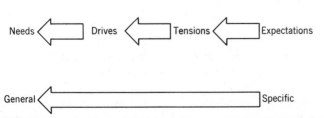

FIGURE 3-2   General and specific causes of individual human motivation.

which cause needs; this integration process sequentially and chronologically moves from very specific to more general individual motivational constructs.

VALUES

A more and more popular approach to the explanation of individual human behavior is the value or value system motivation concept. A value is a priority, preference, interest, like, or dislike for some particular object or thing. In this capacity, a value represents a social opinion, not an economic unit of measurement. A value system is a ranking of individual values along a continuum of importance; in other words, a value system is a value hierarchy.

Multidisciplinary Approach. The value approach to explaining motivated behavior today is popular for several reasons. The concept of a value is multidisciplinary. Individual, group, societal, and cultural values are studied in psychology, sociology, anthropology, political science, philosophy, religion, art, business administration, and other academic areas. Several relatively new measuring instruments, such as the Rokeach Value Survey, have recently been developed as tools for identifying human value systems. A growing body of value research data is accumulating that illustrates empirically and statistically the importance of human values as they relate to matters such as interpersonal conflict, job goals, corporate strategy, manager decision making, organizational effectiveness, supervisory competency, and career objectives (Sikula, "book" reference citations).

Emphasis on Human Cognition. One key feature of value motivation theories is that they emphasize human cognition. Values represent rational choices reached through human thought processes. Various studies performed on human beings have illustrated this cognitive component. The value approach, accordingly, is considered by many to be a better motivation theory than the needs approach, because need theories are based on studies performed on sexually deprived or hungry rats, dogs, apes, and other animals. It should not be assumed, however, that need theories have little or no relevance to the explanation of human behavior. The behavior of infants and the aged perhaps is better explained in terms of needs instead of values, since the cognitive aspects of these forms of human behavior may be relatively less existent and prevalent. For the majority of adult human behavior, however, the value or value system methodology seems to have much more to offer in terms of explanation (Sikula, "book" reference citations).

Model. The relationship of human values to both individual and collective human behavior is often queried (Ackerman). The precise relationships are exceedingly complex, and interrelated, and, in fact, are not known for sure. Nevertheless, an admittedly oversimplistic model of these relations can be pictured in terms of the formula relationships in Figure 3-3.

1. Individual Values × Situation = Individual Motivation

2. Knowledge × Skill = Individual Ability

3. Individual Motivation × Individual Ability = Individual Behavior (Performance)

4. Individual Behavior × Organizational Resources = Organizational Behavior
(Performance)

FIGURE 3-3   Value model of behavior.

Of course, the "×" and "=" notations in the Figure 3-3 equations are not literally accurate. Nevertheless, some similar types of such relationships do exist among these variables. Equation one represents the motivational aspect of human behavior. Whereas equation one concerns what an individual "will do," equation two signifies what a person "can do" (Porter and Lawler). "Can do" and "will do" components interact to produce individual behavior. Aggregated individual behaviors, assuming no intervening synergistic effects, coupled with organizational resources result in some level of organization performance.

Value Criticisms.   There are many criticisms of value motivation theories. The greatest problem concerns theoretical and conceptualization issues. There are many social science concepts similar to a value, most notably, the ideas of attitude and belief. In general, as shown in Figure 3-4*b,* values, attitudes, and beliefs are best envisioned as partially interrelated and overlapping concepts instead of being thought of as totally distinct (Figure 3-4*a*) or completely synonymous (Figure 3-4*c*) set entities. Shades of differences do exist among these concepts. Values serve as guides to behavior and,

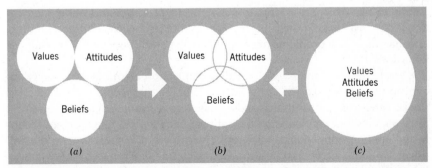

FIGURE 3-4   Values, attitudes, and beliefs as distinct, interrelated, and synonymous set entities. (*a*) Distinct. (*b*) Interrelated. (*c*) Synonymous.

although measurable, are not testable, since they represent opinions. Attitudes are not behavioral guides or standards; they are more numerous, more likely to change quickly, and less central to the motivation concept than values. Beliefs, in contrast to values, allegedly can be tested or proven to be right or wrong, and they are often seen as a result or end product of certain interrelated human values and value systems. Different authors will, however, use and define these social science concepts differently; therefore, for general purposes, the interrelatedness, not the uniqueness or the similarity of these three set entities, should be stressed and emphasized.

Simultaneously occurring with the value conceptualization issue are the problems of value definition, measurement, source, and identification. Such problems are inherent within all of the behavioral science and motivation concepts thus far presented in this chapter.

Although the value approach to explain human behavior is far from totally enlightening, many modern behavioral scientists and researchers, myself included, consider this methodology of analysis far superior to more antiquated theories of human behavior, including the need motivation models. The major feature or attraction of value theories is their inclusion of the cognitive component within their explanations of the behavior of homosapiens.

COMBINATION

The main problem with all of the individual motivation concepts discussed so far is that they each attempt to explain human behavior independently. Human behavior and motivation are much too complex and complicated to be explained in such an overly simplistic manner. The causes of individual motivation are multiple not singular (Lawler and Hall). Needs, drives, tensions, expectations, and values acting interdependently, not independently, bring about human behavior. The relative degree of importance of these various motivational concepts is subject to debate, but it is usually recognized that the most important motivational element(s) most likely varies from person to person and situation to situation. To state that individual motivation is due to a "combination" of factors recognizes the exceedingly complex dimensions of and problems existing within the study and analysis of human behavior.

A "combination" theory of individual motivation also makes it easier to explain the interrelationships between and among concepts such as needs, drives, tensions, expectations, and values. These five interrelated causes of motivation collectively constitute what I mean by the combination approach to the study of individual motivation. The interrelationships among needs, drives, tensions, expectations, and values can be illustrated by a few questions. What really is self-actualization . . . a need, expectation, value, or what? How should the sexual urge be identified . . . as a need, drive, tens. or something else? Is "achievement" really a need, an expectation, or value? Such inquiries force one to pragmatically envision the interrelatedness of these various theoretical "individual" motivation theories and elements.

Group

Many theorists and researchers believe that human behavior is not caused so much by individual factors, but by "group" elements and concepts such as roles, norms, sentiments, activities, interactions, traditions, customs, and mores. These phenomena are the result of social pressures and collective human interrelationships. A person is seen as performing behavior mandated by these various group forces. Such theories of motivation, accordingly, give much more credulity to external social instead of internal individual causes of human behavior.

ROLES AND NORMS

A closer inspection of the various group motivation concepts can help explain their underlying rationale(s). A role is an expected behavior pattern and an assumed character or function. Human beings perform many roles. An individual may be expected to behave as a boss, colleague, subordinate, friend, parent, spouse, or disciplinarian. The role "group" concept is similar to the expectations "individual" motivation concept, except now the anticipations come from others instead of from oneself. Related to the role group concept is the norm group construct. A norm is a role that serves as a rule, model, or authoritative standard. A norm is a more strictly adhered to type of role, such as a production standard. This standard is externally and socially set instead of internally and individually determined.

SENTIMENTS, ACTIVITIES, AND INTERACTIONS

Sentiments, activities, and interactions are also group motivational elements identified by some leading social researchers and academicians. Sentiments are basically feelings and emotions; activities are overt physical behavioral manifestations; and interactions are a kind of residual catchall classification that includes deviant, hybrid, or borderline paraphysical and quasiemotional social interrelationships. Of course, these three group concepts greatly overlap. Nevertheless, many behavioral scientists find such a Homans and Whyte explanation of group motivation insightful. The main Homans and Whyte thesis is that all human behavior can be identified as either one, or one of the two other, of these three sociological concepts (Homans, "book" reference citation).

TRADITIONS, CUSTOMS, AND MORES

and mores are also externally and socially produced
that direct human behavior. Traditions, customs, and
ɟ, opinions, doctrines, and practices that are transmitted
ation to generation by word of mouth, example, and written
ature. These group concepts involve the ordinary or usual manner of
doing or acting of a person or a body of persons. Other concepts such as
manners, rules, habits, folklore, and folkways are similar in conceptual
content to these three basic group constructs. Proponents of group motivation theories who stress such behavioral elements are usually sociologists
and anthropologists, while advocates of individual motivation theories are
most often psychologists.

Environmental

The environmental approach to motivation is also an external theory, but the
scope now becomes larger in dimension and therefore is best thought of as
being "cultural" instead of merely "group" in nature and perspective. Many
cultural anthropologists, urban economists, social workers, social historians,
and others believe that human behavior is basically environmentally determined. The emphasis is on a person's social, political, technological, and
economic environment, not on individual needs, drives, tensions, expectations, and values, or on group roles, norms, sentiments, activities, interactions, traditions, customs, and mores. Proponents of environmental motivation theories believe that the environment shapes and directs human
behavior. Environmental factors are pictured as determinants of, not constraints on, human activities. A person is what he is largely because of
cultural forces over which he has little or no control. Although environmental
theories are generally pessimistic or even occasionally fatalistic in perspective, they have nevertheless increased in number and popularity over the last
few years. The main criticism of environmental motivation theories is that
they underemphasize the importance of the concept of self-determination.

HERZBERG

Herzberg's "motivation-hygiene" model is an example of a research-based
concept that helps to explain the basic rationale behind environmental
motivation theories (Herzberg, "book" reference citation). Hygienic factors,
such as working conditions, company administration, salary, supervisory
relations, and benefits and services are envisioned as environmental elements that have little or no relationship to the motivation of specific job-
related behavior. The factors that can motivate a man to work harder include,
according to Herzberg, elements such as the work itself, achievement,
recognition, advancement, and responsibility. These latter factors determine

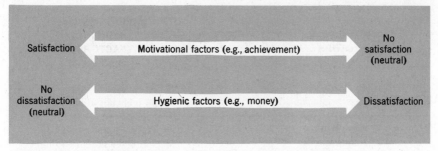

FIGURE 3-5 Satisfaction and dissatisfaction as separate continuums.

how an employee feels about his job, whereas hygiene factors only determine how a worker feels about his company or organization in general. Expressed somewhat differently, motivation factors are related to job content, whereas hygiene factors are related to job context. In addition, Herzberg has argued that an employee is either dissatisfied or not dissatisfied with hygiene factors, but that he is either satisfied or not satisfied with motivational job factors. As shown in Figure 3-5, this means that satisfaction and dissatisfaction are separate continuums and not the opposite of each other. Instead, a neutral state exists as the contrary to job satisfaction and job dissatisfaction. A worker is either satisfied or not satisfied (neutral) with motivational job factors. Similarly, an employee is either dissatisfied or not dissatisfied (neutral) with hygienic company matters.

The Herzberg rationale helps to explain why a worker may hate his job and yet remain with a company or love his job and yet quit an organization. The reason is because separate types of factors influence these two separate and distinct feelings. The elements that determine how an employee feels about his job are the motivational factors; the variables that influence how a worker feels about his company are the environmental or hygienic factors. Hygienic factors must be adequate, or employees will not be attracted to an organization. But when employed, manipulating hygienic factors cannot motivate a worker to do a better job. These key features of Herzberg's motivation-hygiene concept are summarized in Figure 3-6.

The main criticism of the motivation-hygiene concept is that initially it interpreted job and company employment factors to be totally distinct and separate set entities (House and Wigdor). Today it is recognized that these factors at times can be both "motivators" and "hygienic" in nature. Money especially seems to be a motivator in many work situations, especially those in which the employee is earning a relatively small total annual income. Motivators and hygienic factors also may vary on jobs at different organizational levels. In addition, factors that are normally environmental may become motivational (or vice versa) with certain work populations and under

	ENVIRONMENTAL
MOTIVATION	**(HYGIENIC)**
FACTORS	**FACTORS**
(Satisfiers)	(Dissatisfiers)
Job Content	Job Context
How one feels about his JOB	How one feels about his COMPANY
1. Work itself	1. Working conditions
2. Achievement	2. Company administration
3. Recognition	3. Salary
4. Advancement	4. Supervisory relations
5. Responsibility	5. Benefits and services

FIGURE 3-6 Motivation and environmental (hygienic) factors.

certain conditions. For example, "supervisory relations" for many women employees (especially secretarial and clerical types) is basically a motivational instead of a hygiene factor (Lawler and Hall).

In short, Herzberg sees motivation and hygienic factors as basically distinct set entities. Before Herzberg's theory became well known, most people assumed that hygienic factors were, indeed, also motivational ones. As shown in Figure 3-7b, the best interpretation is that motivational and hygienic factors are at least partially interrelated and overlapping in nature. To envision such entity factors as totally distinct (Figure 3-7a) or completely synonymous (Figure 3-7c) is inappropriate and not supported by the results of recent research studies (Behling, Labovitz, and Kosmo).

ENVIRONMENTAL COMPONENTS

Most environmental motivation theories are broader than the aforementioned Herzberg model (Evans). Typically, environmental motivation models

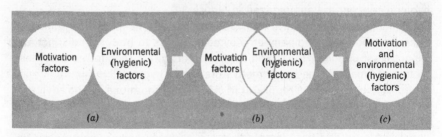

FIGURE 3-7 Three areas of motivation and environmental (hygienic) factors.
(a) Distinct. (b) Interrelated. (c) Synonymous.

are broken up into components such as social, economic, political, tech-nological, and other factors (psychological, cultural, spiritual, ethical, etc.). Human behavior is seen as a combination and manifestation of these exter-nal environmental conditions. Most objects and events within the external environment are a synthesis of these various cultural pressures and occur-rences. For example, strikes, devaluations, divorces, accidents, tax laws automation, and other external environmental acts that affect human be-havior have social, economic, political, and technological overtones and implications.

Systems Approach

The preceding discussion classifies all behavioral motivation theories into three categories, individual, group, and environmental. These three groups are so identified because of the factors that are emphasized in the theories belonging in each of these subdivisions. The systems approach to motivation should be thought as an integration of these three basic motivation-theory groupings. As shown in Figure 3-8, individual, group, and environmental

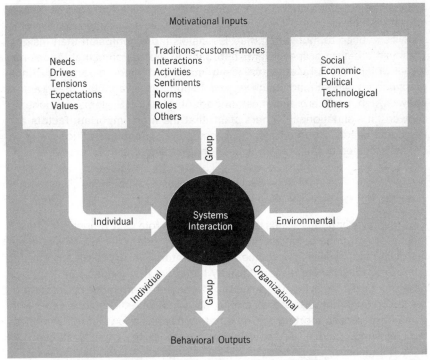

FIGURE 3-8 A systems framework to motivation and behavior.

motivation causes are seen as collective motivational inputs that interact in a systematic framework to produce individual, group, and organizational behavioral outputs. The systems interaction set framework of Figure 3-8 is the area in which individual, group, and environmental motivational causes overlap, intermingle, and become synthesized to collectively produce human behavioral outputs in the form of individual, group, and organizational outcomes.

MULTIPLE VARIABLES

In essence, the systems approach to human motivation states that an individual's (or a group's or an organization's) behavior is a result of a number of dynamic, viable, complex, and interrelated variables. A human action is a product of a multiplicity of factors manifested within a situational context (Swanson and Corbin). Although theoretically and conceptually the systems approach is the most accurate model of human motivation, pragmatically this approach offers little in the way of practical suggestions if one desires to change human behavior. What has happened now is that motivation theories have gone from one extreme to the other. Now, instead of explaining human behavior in terms of only one variable, such as the need for achievement or self-actualization, motivation is explained in terms of numerous interacting variables. Accordingly, many people have stated that systems analysis applied to motivation theories instills more confusion than insight. The main criticism of the systems approach to motivation is that it does not reveal which motivational factors are of major and minor importance. Since practitioners cannot manipulate an infinite number of variables, they want to know which ones are the most important (Frank). Systems proponents answer, "It's situational." Others claim that the most important factors are individual needs, group norms, environmental economic conditions, and so on, as indicated in the preceding sections of this chapter.

C. ROLE OF MONEY

Controversy continues to exist concerning the role that money plays as a motivator of human behavior. In general, most modern behavioral scientists are giving money less importance as a motivator, but very few if any current authors or researchers discount totally the effect that money can and does have on human behavior. The issue is not whether or not money is important, but the relative importance of money as a motivator. Opinions vary, with some observers supporting the idea that money has a low degree of motivation relevance, and others envisioning money as the primary stimulus of human endeavor.

Money Semantics

Much of this controversy is due to the semantic problems surrounding the money concept. By definition, money is anything that serves as a common medium of exchange, a standard of value, and a measure of payment of legal tender. Money conceptually is much more than dollars and cents. Gold and silver technically serve also as money. In addition, there are several forms of near-money, such as checks and credit cards. Expense accounts, paid club memberships, travel allowances, company-owned cars, homes, planes, and other items and objects also serve as paramoney and quasimotivational elements. Such factors can help motivate most employees to display more organizationally efficient behavior. Because many motivation theories interpret the concept and definition of money differently, it is not surprising that different conclusions are reached when trying to assess the motivational aspects of money.

Economic Money

Money serves basically as an economic unit of measure. Money is commonly desired because it can bring purchasing power and material happiness to its bearer. Therefore money helps to fulfill primary physiological and security needs. As an economic unit, money seems to motivate best those persons who have the least amount of it. If an individual is in desperate need of money, he often will do almost anything to get it. As an economic unit, money seems to be generally subject to the law of diminishing returns as it relates to the motivation concept. This is, as a person acquires more and more money, he commonly becomes less and less motivated by the lure of additional dollars. Although the motivational element of money may relatively decline as wealth increases, nevertheless, even as an economic unit of measurement and value, money always continues to retain some degree of motivational stimulus and attraction.

Social Money

Money also serves as a social unit of value. Individuals often judge their worth and contribution to society by the level of pay they receive for their work. In this context, money serves as a measure of prestige and status (Werniment, Toren, and Kapell). In general, the more money a person makes, the more respected he becomes. Money as a social unit of value is relatively nonexistent for persons earning only minimal incomes. But once a large degree of wealth has been accumulated, money serves much more as a social measure instead of an economic unit for those who are financially well endowed. Money can serve as a motivator of human behavior whether it basically is fulfilling a social-measure or an economic-unit role.

Money and Motivation

Essentially, money is best thought of as an environmental cause of motivation. It does possess some group and individual elements, however. Money as a social unit of value is largely a group phenomenon, and individual needs, expectations, and values are related to the economic dimension of the money-motivation relationship.

The precise relationship between money and motivation is not currently known and never can be exactly determined. This is mainly because both money and motivation are abstract concepts, and individuals cannot totally agree about how they should be defined and measured. Because no one knows for sure what motivation really is or what conditions and qualities constitute the concept of money, it should not surprise anybody that the money-motivation relationship is largely a matter of opinion and research design (definition and methodology). Because of such complications, the role of money as a motivational factor will always remain at least partially a matter of conjecture.

D. ROLES OF REWARD AND PUNISHMENT

Many theories of human behavior still stress the roles of reward and punishment. Most of these theories are the result of psychological experiments performed on animals and infants. The use of rewards to alter behavior is often referred to as positive or constructive motivation. Punitive-centered or punishment-oriented methodologies constitute a pessimistic or negative approach to the study and analysis of human motivation.

Rewards versus Punishment

Controversy has always existed concerning the question of whether or not rewards and punishments are the most effective means of changing human behavior. Over the years, the literatures of several disciplines reveal a general movement from punishment-oriented to reward-centered concepts of motivation (Sorcher and Meyer). Of course, specific individuals respond differently to various stimuli. Some individuals are reinforced by positive factors, but others react more to negative stimuli. Human beings are all unique and unalike, and what motivates one person may not influence another. Some individuals, when given complete freedom to eventually complete a task, will do nothing for an extended period of time. Others in the same situation will be challenged and will work hard to complete the job within a self-imposed time period (MacKinnon and Roche).

Not only do rewards and punishments affect human beings differently, but their individual and collective influence on any one person will also vary over time. What motivates an individual to perform at one stage in his life will not necessarily direct and influence his activities at a later time. People and times change, and thus also must appropriate motivational techniques.

Persons are not motivated solely by either rewards or punishments, but by a combination of the two. Human behaviors are altered using both positive and negative elements. Also, rewards and punishments come in a variety of forms that can influence persons differently. Rewards include more money, promotions, expense accounts, traveling allowances, company cars, and private offices. Punishments include layoffs, discharges, fines, oral reprimands, written warnings, and demotions. What is a severe punishment for one person may be less severe for someone else. A reward that motivates one employee may not stimulate a fellow worker. Rewards and punishments must be uniquely combined to influence and change the behaviors of particular individual human beings effectively.

Means, not Ends

One additional observation should be noted at this time. Sometimes the administration, application, or implementation of a reward or punishment is more important and influential than the actual event (Burke and Wilcox). If an employee is begrudgingly given a salary increase, the additional money may not serve as a motivational incentive. If an employee is sympathetically and privately reprimanded, the effects most likely will be different from what they would have been if the reprimand were public and hostile. The way and manner in which rewards are presented and punishments are imposed usually will affect human behavior more so than actual positive and negative motivational elements will.

3. The Motivation-Communication Hourglass

Both motivation and communication serve as coordinating administrative processes. As coordinating devices, motivation and communication link and integrate various organizational resources. Any organization has various inputs and numerous outputs. The motivation and communication processes bring together these institutional inputs and outputs. The motivation and communication processes join institutional inputs and organizational outputs in a similar manner to the filtering area of an hourglass; the motivation and communication processes serve as timing, linking, coordinating and filtering mechanisms that integrate institutional inputs and result in unified organizational outputs, as illustrated in Figure 3-9. Thus far the material in this chapter has dealt with behavioral motivation. The remainder of this chapter covers communication.

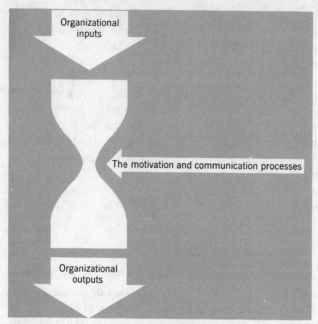

FIGURE 3-9   The motivation-communication hourglass.

4. Communication

Communication is another major concept with which the personnel or manpower function is intimately involved. Traditionally, a personnel manager was aware that individual, group, and organization communication problems existed, but he did not consider such issues to be a main functional concern inherent within his job. The modern manpower manager recognizes that communication matters are part of his central work responsibilities. No one else in a corporate setting is more strategically located than the personnel or manpower manager; thus communication phenomena can best be studied and analyzed from this organizational vantage point. Communication will be presented within this chapter under the subheadings of (1) definition and semantic problems; (2) model; (3) barriers; (4) classifications; (5) patterns or nets; (6) role of perception; and (7) role of listening.

A. DEFINITION AND SEMANTIC PROBLEMS

Communication is the process of transmitting information, meaning, and understanding from one person, place, or thing to another person, place, or thing. Although other alternative definitions of communication exist, this simple, concise definition contains the key elements that any good definition of communication must possess. There are three main ingredients to a thorough and comprehensive communication definition. First, communication must accurately be described as a process. This means that communication exists as a flow through a sequence or series of steps; it is not an isolated event or occurrence. Identifying communication as a process adds the dimension of movement to this concept. In this regard, communication should probably best be labeled or called communicating, not communication, since the sequence of steps involved are ongoing and dynamic instead of fixed and static. The specific sequence of steps involved in the communicating process will be discussed in the next major section of this chapter, which presents a communication model.

Transmitting Understanding

The second key element of an adequate definition of communication is embodied in the phrase "transmitting information, meaning, and understanding." Transmitting information alone is not communication. Communication is a two-way, not a one-way process (Howland). The information must not only be transmitted, but it must also be received and understood. If information is transmitted and received but not understood, then true communication has not occurred. When meaning and understanding are exchanged along with information, then the reception and the interpretation of the communication message can be assumed to have taken place. When information is transmitted by one party and not received by another party, or received but not accurately interpreted, then miscommunication has occurred. Miscommunication is a result of various barriers that may appear in any of the stages or steps of the overall communication process. Communication barriers will be discussed at length later in this chapter.

Human and Nonhuman Entities

The third and final main ingredient of a proper communication definition is the inclusion of both human and nonhuman entities. Many older explanations of the communication process limit this phenomenon to human interactions only, whereby a human being must be both the information transmitter and receiver. With the tremendous technological advances made recently, however, it is now possible for a machine to be one or both parties existing within a communication system. Along with human beings and machines, plants and animals can also be the entities comprising a communication channel or network. An accurate, modern definition of the communication process recognizes that information encoders and decoders may be either animate or inanimate objects.

B. MODEL

The process of communication is best explained in terms of a model featuring a sequence or series of steps. Although there is not total agreement on the exact number and precise labeling of the steps involved, a generally accepted model of the communication process is shown in Figure 3-10 (Darnell). Initially an idea or a bit of information is created; this phenomenon is usually called source or ideation within a communication system. The idea or information then must be put into some form of a coded message. This encoding may be in thought, written, oral, physical, or some other format of tentative expression. Then the message must be transmitted or sent. Transmission involves sending written messages, speaking words, acting gestures, manipulating data cards or tapes, and so on. The space, distance, mechanism, or channel a message travels through is called the communication medium. After a message has traveled through a medium, it is received by an object to which the information was directed. Upon reception, or hopefully shortly thereafter, the message is interpreted and deciphered directly or indirectly through a thought process. The human mind, a mechanical memory system, animal instincts, and other processes serve as decoding mechanisms. Action is sometimes also identified as a step within a communication system. If it is assumed that every message has an intended outcome, it can be argued that unless the objective desired is eventually obtained, the communication process has failed. If a certain behavior or action represents the purpose of a communique, and if this goal does not materialize, then perhaps the communication process was ineffective. Some communication models contain only five steps instead of seven. The first and last steps within the model shown in Figure 3-10 are often eliminated, since it can be argued that source or ideation is part of the encoding concept, and

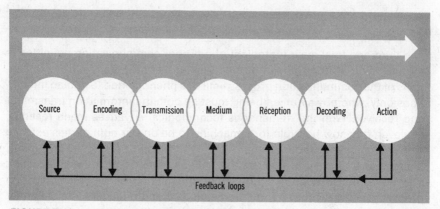

FIGURE 3-10 A model of the communication process.

action is really extraneous to and an aftermath of real communication. Note that feedback loops connect all communication steps within the Figure 3-10 model. A message can be cycled or recycled from any point in the total communication process to any other stage of the communication system (Anderson). Although it is somewhat beyond the scope of this presentation, the reader should attempt to envision concrete examples of instances and situations descriptive of specific cycling and recycling occurrences from different combinations of steps within the overall communication system.

Set Model

Figure 3-10 also illustrates the communication process by a series of interrelated set diagrams. This portrayal is accurate in as much as it is often very difficult to discern precisely where one communication stage ends and another phase begins. For example, is getting an idea part of the source stage or the encoding process? Is sending a written message or speaking orally part of the transmission or medium communication stages? When a person reads a written message or hears a spoken word, does this constitute communication reception or decoding? Because no clear lines of demarcation can be precisely established between communication process stages, the interrelated set model of a communication system seems to be an accurate representation of the actual sequential activities involved.

Presenting the communication concept in terms of a model enables one to understand better the various segmented activities involved in effective communicating. A communication model format also makes it much easier to identify and locate barriers that often exist within a total communication system or network. Communication barriers often result in either miscommunication or noncommunication.

C. BARRIERS

An interesting inquiry is "where within the communication process or model would barriers or constraints most likely appear?" This question can bring a variety of answers, because it is easy to think of communication barriers existing within and between any and all of the communication steps. Barriers within the communication process may exist in a variety of forms. For convenience and generalization, communication barriers will be grouped and classified into three main categories: (1) technical; (2) semantic; and (3) human.

Technical Barriers

In the past, technical problems seemed to dominate the prevalence and existence of communication barriers. Breakdowns in communication channels were attributed to mechanical failures, physical obstructions, technological malfunctions, concrete obstacles, and other tangible space and distance parameters evident within the transmission, medium, and reception stages of the communication process. Today, however, technical causes of miscommunication have been reduced tremendously in number and severity. The advancement and continued sophistication of inventions, such as the telephone, teletype, radio, television, automobile, airplane, train, steamship, and especially the electronic computer, have progressed to the point where these information channels are usually considered very reliable and efficient as mechanisms and mediums of communication. This is not to say that technical barriers within the communication process no longer exist. The sheer existence of space, distance, and time lags presents the possibility of totally eliminating all forms and aspects of technical communication barriers. But, in comparison to past decades, technical, physical and tangible communication constraints are much less common now than ever before.

Semantic Barriers

Semantic communication obstacles present a major complication to the effective transmission of understanding. Semantic problems are most notable between instead of within communication stages. Semantic issues revolve around the question of "what" is communicated or transferred within the communication stages. Much communication appears in the form of language. But written and spoken words mean different things to different persons when used in different situations and different contexts. Semantics, by definition, is the study of meaning. Meaning within a culture is expressed through language. But language can serve as both a communication boon and burden. Words generally assist immeasurably in the process of mutually exchanging meaning and understanding; but because words can be misinterpreted and misused, they also introduce the possibility of semantic difficulties. Semantic communication barriers are basically evident within written and oral language expressions, but semantic or meaning problems may also be inherent within the use of other forms of signs, symbols, and gestures. For example, handshakes, frowns, yawns, stretching, and other manners of expression in addition to language are especially subject to semantic problems and differences in meaning.

Human Barriers

Human barriers to communication also exist, and these constraints are considered by many to be the most serious of all communication problems. Human problems occur because of personal emotions, biases, perceptions, competencies (or incompetencies), sensual abilities (or inabilities), and the like (Breslow). Persons have different thresholds and sensitivities associated

TECHNICAL	SEMANTIC	HUMAN
Space or distance	Word interpretations	Perceptual variations
Mechanical failures	Gesture decodings	Sensitivity differences
Electrical malfunctions	Language translations	Personality variables
Time lags	Sign and symbol	Competency
Physical interferences	significancies	discrepancies
	Cue meanings	Sensual thresholds

FIGURE 3-11   Types of communication barriers.

with their mental faculties and operational senses (sight, touch, hearing, taste, and smell). These human differences can bring about major forms of communication barriers. These types of barriers or constraints exist almost exclusively in the encoding and decoding stages of the communication process. Individualized, unique, human personality factors tremendously affect how messages are encoded and decoded. Encoding and decoding are thought and mental processes, and there are extreme variations between and among human beings concerning their abilities to perform these reasoning functions. Human problems are considered to be the main forms of communication barriers today because they can never be eliminated and they are extremely difficult to reduce even slightly in frequency. Technical and even semantic barriers can be eliminated or mitigated to a large extent, but the removal of human communication problems is more difficult, because this involves the replacement of human entities with nonhuman surrogates.

Instead of being regarded as totally distinct or completely synonymous set entities, technical, semantic, and human barriers within the communication process should properly best be envisioned as partially interrelated and overlapping communication barrier classifications. To illustrate, an unwanted computerized operation is usually a combination of technical, semantic, and human errors. In addition, almost all human misunderstandings and miscommunications are caused by a combination of both human and semantic problems. Figure 3-11 summarizes the types of obstacles and elements that are frequently classifed as technical, semantic, and human communication barriers.

D. CLASSIFICATIONS

Forms and types of communications are usually grouped or classified into various categories for the purposes of study, analysis, explanation, and comparison. Numerous communication classifications exist, but in this chapter only three of the more commonly used grouping systems will be presented: (1) oral and written; (2) downward, upward, and lateral; and (3) formal and informal.

Oral and Written

Oral and written designations refer to the format of communicated messages. Many forms of communication, especially interpersonal communications, are either in spoken or written format. Because such a great percentage of human interaction occurs in these forms, various studies have been conducted to assess the merits and efficiencies of spoken and written messages. Such analyses often center around a presentation of the advantages and disadvantages of these two communicating formats. It is exceedingly risky to attempt to make generalizations about the strengths and weaknesses of spoken and written messages, because the senders of these information items differ so greatly in their abilities to accurately and clearly express themselves. However, many individuals do prefer the intimacy of spoken communications, while others recognize that precision and accuracy are usually best achieved through written communiques. Many messages appear in both forms; that is, a communication or message often will be expressed in both spoken and written forms, usually at two different times, to increase the possibility of message understanding. Many factors determine which of these two methods of communicating is most likely to be used in any given situation (Ash). Time, cost, expediency, personal preference, individual skills, available resources, and other considerations serve as decision-making criteria in reference to whether messages will occur in either a written or spoken format. For example, although numerous exceptions can easily be found, in general, oral messages are more easily and quickly transmitted and are less costly than written counterparts. Because of the prevalence and importance of these two forms of expression, high school, college, university, and extension service organizations usually offer courses in speech, business letter writing, interpersonal communication, and the like to teach community residents better communication skills and practices.

Downward, Upward and Lateral

Downward, upward, and lateral communication classifications refer to the directional flow of messages and information within a corporate structure. Again, the situation involved here is not one involving an either-or choice; instead, directional communication flows typically appear in a combination style or format (Zeyher). Downward communications include things such as face-to-face, boss-subordinate information exchanges throughout the chain of command, management bulletins, policy and procedure manuals, house organs, letters to employees, written performance appraisals, employee handbooks, and so forth. A manager has a difficult job determining what information should or should not be passed on to subordinates. Even when this decision has been made, the directional flow and mannner of presenting

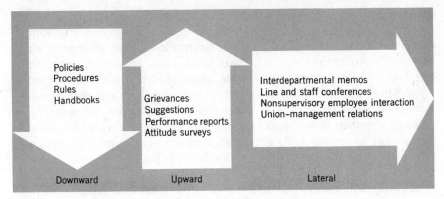

FIGURE 3-12 The directional flow of communications.

such information to nonsupervisory employees remain as crucial communicating decisions that must be made (Chase). Downward communication normally is appropriate when management wishes to communicate purely factual noncontroversial information, and where the purpose is informative, not persuasive. The upward flow of information in most companies is much less adequate than the downward flow. Certain methods, however, can be used to provide an increased upward flow or organizational information (Gelfand). In unionized shops, the formal grievance system serves as the main upward communication mechanism. Written memos, planned employee group meetings, and informal conversations with superiors are also frequently used means of upward communication. Additional techniques of upward information flows include performance reports, suggestion plans, and attitude surveys. Lateral or horizontal flows of organizational communication have been relatively ignored within the management literature. However, many business researchers currently are illustrating that horizontal instead of upward or downward information flows are really the most crucial forms and flows of internal organizational information. Virtually all direct work flow contacts involve horizontal or lateral communications. Interdepartmental and interworker exchanges of information help to link and tie an organization together and also serve as a main coordinating and unifying force within the overall corporate structure (Nathan). Of course, upward, downward, and lateral communications may be oral or written in format, and both formal or informal in style, decorum, and pattern. Figure 3-12 gives some examples of downward, upward, and lateral communication flows.

Formal and Informal

Formal and informal communication classifications refer to the styles, decorums, and patterns of organizational information flows. When messages are sent, transmitted, and received through an authoritatively determined hierarchical pattern, commonly referred to as the chain of command, then formal communication is taking place. Much information within an organization, however, is exchanged in what seems to be a less systematic and a more informal manner. Usually, an informal communication system is called a "grapevine" because of its apparent haphazard growth and development. Controlled research studies of organizational grapevines, however, have revealed a method to this illusioned madness. Cluster-chain analysis enables researchers to predict fairly accurately how informal communications will flow within and throughout an organization (Burke and Wilcox). There is disagreement as to just how important an informal communication system (grapevine) is in comparison to a formal information flow system (chain of command). This debate is not worthy of our future attention, and it can instead merely be concluded that both systems are crucial to the effective operation of an enterprise. Initially managers tried to prevent and destroy grapevine communication systems, because they thought that only gossip and rumor flowed through this pattern. Today the wise manager tries to utilize the informal communication system as a supplement to the formal chain of command (Cantor). It has been found through research, that such grapevine infromation is sometimes authoritative, although often somewhat distorted. The extremely rapid speed of operation of an informal grapevine frequently makes this alternative one that an efficient manager will want to use, not destroy (Burke and Wilcox).

E. PATTERNS OR NETS

Formal communication patterns or networks (nets) have been researched extensively. A message can be sent from one person to another by one of several plausible alternative patterns or channels of communication. Of course, some of these systems will be less efficient than others and, indeed, one such method should prove to be optimal. The study of communication patterns has been performed in an attempt to find the elusive "one best way" of communicating. There is really no one best universal way to communicate organizationally, since information and data are sent for a variety of purposes. The most effective manner of communicating messages will depend on situational factors such as speed, accuracy, cost, and time limitations. Nevertheless, an analysis of communication nets helps to determine which patterns are fastest, most accurate, most flexible, and so forth.

Communication Nets

Communication nets are usually identified according to their component configurations. Patterns such as circle, chain, wheel, all channel, star, and

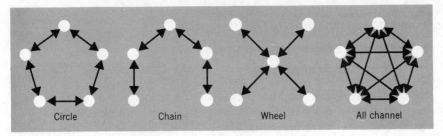

FIGURE 3-13   Communication patterns or nets.

pyramid, have been identified, labeled, and researched. For example, Figure 3-13 illustrates the design and component interrelationships of the circle, chain, wheel, and all channel communication networks. Each pattern or arrangement has certain advantages and disadvantages associated with its use. For example, the circle net is very adaptable but very slow, while the wheel pattern is fast in speed of performance but slow in flexibility to job change. Sometimes very complex organizational communication networks appear to produce results inconsistent with the conclusions reached in studies on simple five-unit laboratory communication patterns. The general conclusion commonly reached is that the best organizational results are accomplished by using various networks and media of communication instead of one alone. In this way, some of the advantages of each are secured, while inherent associated disadvantages hopefully can be counterbalanced or offset.

Communication Net Implications

There is questioned relevancy as to what, if anything, such analyses can contribute to the solution of organizational communication problems. Experiments of this type can isolate one particular variable to show its influence on communication. However, since a real organization never duplicates laboratory conditions, conclusions from such experiments cannot apply directly to operating organizations. The main value of these experiments is to show the potential influence of any variable or factor (Scanlan). In truth there is a natural tendency for groups to solve communication problems as efficiently as possible (i.e., with as little expenditure of effort as needed). This philosophy leads to the use of many adaptable and constantly changing organizational communication patterns. There is even some research evidence available to suggest that group adaptability may, in the long run, lead to substantially the same organizational productivity, regardless of network restrictions. The major shortcoming of network communication research studies is that they assume that only a formal chain-of-command information system is in existence. Of course, an informal grapevine communication network really is also operating at both the individual small group and total corporate structure organizational levels.

F. ROLE OF PERCEPTION

Within limits, people see what they want to see and hear what they want to hear. Therefore, the process of communication cannot be competently understood unless some insight is gained into the topic of human perception. Perception is the process of making sense out of occurrences and inputing meaning to experiences. Perception is a uniquely human phenomenon by which individuals interpret events around them. Persons may perceive events differently; thus perception aids but can also distort the communication process. Distorted perception is an example of a "human" communication barrier, since it serves as a constraint to mutual understanding. In terms of the communication model, perceptual distortions and barriers occur in the encoding and decoding system stages. As mentioned earlier in this chapter, semantic and human barriers (such as perception) are the most serious types of drawbacks to effective communications.

Perception and Communication

Perception is closely related to the motivation concept. The same types of factors that determine motivated behavior also determine individual perception. Individual needs, drives, tensions, expectations, and values along with group norms, roles, sentiments, activities, and interactions operating within an environmental context comprised of social, economic, political, technological, and other factors determine one's perception. These factors affect a person's self-image or self-concept, and self-perception, in turn, directly influences an individual's perception of the rest of the world. Differing and distorted individual perceptions vary because of such individual, group, and environmental experiences.

Human Senses

Differences in perception are also due to variations in the capacities and capabilities of the human senses. Perception is much more than simply a matter of visual interpretation. All human senses (sight, hearing, touch, taste, and smell) vary in sensitivity from person to person. Two persons observing an accident often picture it differently. Two potential voters hearing the same candidate's speech may interpret it in opposite fashions. Hot versus cold or pleasure versus pain may be the result of an identical condition experienced by two separate persons. Sweet versus sour or spicy versus bland are matters of perceptual opinion, as are choice in colognes, perfumes, hair sprays, and deodorants. Because of individual variations in the sensitivities, capacities, and capabilities of the human senses, perceptual problems within the communication process will always exist.

G. ROLE OF LISTENING

Listening is a human process inherent within the reception and decoding stages of the communication model. Because communication is a two-way process involving mutual understanding, listening is an essential aspect of any total communication system. A common misconception is that listening is more a part of the reception than the decoding communication stage. Hearing is with the ears, but listening is with the mind (Sigband). Effective listening is an active, not a passive process. It takes as much mental concentration to receive and decode a message as it takes to encode and send a communique.

Listening Definition

Listening involves making conscious use of the sense of hearing. In a broader context, listening involves paying attention to or heeding to the influence of any communication message — oral or written. Although the concept of listening is usually used narrowly in reference to the reception and decoding of oral messages, the basic principle can apply more universally to all forms and formats of transmitted information and data.

Listening Emphasis

Emphasis on good listening is a recent development. This new concern stems from various studies showing that approximately half of a manager's total on-the-job time is spent listening. Such studies also reveal that most individuals listen at only a 25 percent efficiency rate. However, training can increase listening comprehension by about another 25 percent (Abbatiello). In general, listening is most effective for understanding overview ideas of short-term operating problems. Listening is not effective for the receipt and long-run storage of many factual details. The human brain can process words much faster than a person can speak. Thus there is idle time involved in the listening process, and effective listeners use this time to think in terms of the speaker's objective, to weigh his evidence, to search for other clues to and examples of speaker meaning and, to review. Listening is a conscious, positive act requiring will power; it is not a simple, passive exposure to sound.

A Guide to Effective Listening

Often numerous guidelines for effective listening are presented by communication consultants. Usually most of these suggestions are nothing more than matters of behavioral courtesy. Many of these guidelines also center around a recurring theme that is, perhaps, the ultimate guideline for those trying to improve their listening skills. This theme is the idea that an effective listener is one "who keeps his mind open and his mouth shut." Effective decoding cannot be accomplished with a closed mind, and it is also impossible to be a good listener if you are always talking.

5. Summary

The modern personnel manager is expected to be well acquainted with the behavioral foundations of personnel administration. Such a foundation is built on an initial understanding of the concepts of motivation and communication.

Motivation is an abstract, complex behavioral concept whose definition, measurement, and cause are all matters of unresolved debate. In general, motivated behavior is best explained (but not predicted) in terms of a systems approach featuring a complex, dynamic interaction of multiple variables. The variables are: individual needs, drives, tensions, expectations, and values; group roles, norms, sentiments, activities, interactions, traditions, customs, and mores; and social, political, economic, technological, and other environmental factors. Motivated behavior is also strongly affected by money and by the use of other types of rewards and punishments.

Communication is the process of transferring information, meaning, and understanding from one person, place, or thing to another person, place, or thing. A model of the communication process commonly includes the steps or stages of ideation, encoding, transmission, medium, reception, decoding, and action. Many barriers can exist within and between these communication stages. Barriers can be either technical, semantic, or human. Forms and types of communication are usually grouped or classified into categories such as oral-written, upward-downward-lateral, or formal-informal. Different arrangements, configurations, or systems of transferring information, data, and messages are usually called communication patterns or nets. Both perception and listening play key roles within any communication system or pattern.

DISCUSSION QUESTIONS AND ASSIGNMENTS

1. What roles do reward and punishment play in the motivation of human behavior?
2. Define and present a model of the communication process.
3. Discuss some of the barriers or obstacles to effective communication.
4. Devise and present your own model of factors that cause human behavior.

5. Think of examples to illustrate the importance of perception and listening as elements of the communication process.
6. Explain the relative importance of money as a motivator of your own personal actions.

REFERENCES

General Book References

Bassett, Glenn A., *The New Face of Communication.* New York: American Management Association, 1968.

Breth, Robert D., *Dynamic Management Communications.* Reading, Mass.: Addison-Wesley, 1969.

Campbell, James H., and Hal W. Helper, *Dimensions in Communication.* Belmont, Calif.: Wadsworth, 1970.

Gellerman, Saul, *Management by Motivation.* New York: American Management Association, 1968.

Haney, William V., *Communication and Organizational Behavior.* Homewood, Ill.: Irwin, 1973.

Herzberg, Frederick, *Work and the Nature of Man.* Cleveland: World, 1966.

Homans, George, *The Human Group.* New York: Harcourt, 1950.

Macarov, David, *Incentives to Work.* San Francisco: Jossey-Bass, 1970.

Maslow, Abraham H., *Motivation and Personality,* second edition New York: Harper & Brothers, 1970.

McClelland, David C., *The Achieving Society.* Princeton, N.J.: D. Van Nostrand, 1961.

Sigband, Norman B., *Communication for Management.* Glenview, Ill.: Scott, Foresman and Company, 1969.

Sikula, Andrew F., *Conflict Via Values and Value Systems.* Champaign, Ill.: Stipes, 1971.

Silula, Andrew F., *Values, Motivation and Management.* Champaign, Ill.: Stipes, 1972.

Thayer, Lee, *Communication and Communication Systems.* Homewood, Ill.: Irwin, 1968.

Vroom, Victor H., *Work and Motivation.* New York: Wiley, 1964.

Specific Journal References

Abbatiello, Aurelius A., "Listening and Understanding," *Personnel Journal, 48* (8), 1964, pp. 593–596.

Ackerman, Leonard, "Let's Put Motivation Where It Belongs — Within the Individual," *Personnel Journal, 49* (7), 1970, pp. 559–562.

Anderson, John, "Giving and Receiving Feedback," *Personnel Administration, 31* (2), 1968, pp. 21–27.

Ash, Philip, "The Many Functions of Discussion," *Supervisory Management, 16* (3), 1971, pp. 21–24.

Behling, Orlando, George Labovitz, and Richard Kosmo, "The Herzberg Controversy: A Critical Reappraisal," *Academy of Management Journal, 11* (1), 1968, pp. 99–108.

Breslow, Hal S., "Employee Communication: A Personnel Man's Viewpoint," *Personnel Journal, 48* (12), 1970, pp. 995–998.

Burke, Ronald J., and Douglas S. Wilcox, "Effects of Different Patterns and Degrees of Openness in Superior-Subordinate Communication on Subordinate Job Satisfaction," *Academy of Managemet Journal, 12* (3), 1969, pp. 319–326.

Cantor, Daniel D., "Communications — The Personnel Approach," *Personnel Journal, 48* (5), 1969, pp. 337–339.

Chase, A. B., Jr., "How to Make Downward Communication Work," *Personnel Journal, 49* (6), 1970, pp. 478–483.

Darnell, Donald K., "Toward a Reconceptualization of Communication," *Journal of Communication, 21* (1), 1971, pp. 5–16.

Evans, Martin G., "Herzberg's Two-Factor Theory of Motivation: Some Problems and a Suggested Test," *Personnel Journal, 49* (1), 1970, pp. 32–35.

Frank, Edward R., "Motivation by Objectives — A Case Study," *Research Management, 12* (6), 1969, pp. 391–400.

Gelfand, Louis I., "Communicate Through Your Supervisors," *Harvard Business Review, 48* (6), 1970, pp. 101–104.

Hammerton, James C., "Management and Motivation," *California Management Review, 13* (2), 1970, pp. 51–57.

Happel, Joseph G., Jr., "To Motivate — Communicate," *Personnel Journal, 48* (12) 1969, pp. 984–987.

Herzberg, Frederick, "One More Time: How Do You Motivate Employees?" *Harvard Business Review, 46* (1), 1968, pp. 53–62.

House, Robert J., and Lawrence A. Wigdor, "Herzberg's Dual-Factor Theory of Job Satisfaction and Motivation: A Review of the Evidence and a Criticism," *Personnel Psychology, 20* (4), 1967, pp. 369–389.

Howland, John A., "Talking to or Talking with?" *Bell Telephone Magazine, 50* (2), 1971, pp. 4–9.

Lawler, Edward E., III, and D. T. Hall, "Relationship of Job Characteristics to Job Involvement, Satisfaction, and Intrinsic Motivation," *Journal of Applied Psychology, 23* (4), 1970, pp. 305–312.

MacKinnon, Neil, and William Roche, "Motivating People with Meaningful Work," *Harvard Business Review, 48* (3), 1970, pp. 97–110.

Nathan, Frederick M., "Staff Role in Communication," *Personnel Administration, 32* (4), 1969, pp. 59–62.

Porter, Lyman W., and Edward E. Lawler, III, "What Job Attitudes Tell About Motivation," *Harvard Business Reivew, 46* (1), 1968, pp. 118–126.

Scanlan, Burk K., "Improving Organizational and Personal Communication," *Supervision, 32* (6), 1970, pp. 3–6.

Sigband, Norman B., "Listen to What You Can't Hear," *Nation's Business, 57* (6), 1969, pp. 70–72.

Sorcher, Melvin, and Herbert H. Meyer, "Motivating Factory Employees," *Personnel, 45* (1), 1968, pp. 22–28.

Swanson, Lloyd A., and Carrel Corbin, "Employee Motivation Programs: A Change in Philosophy?" *Personnel Journal, 48* (11), 1969, pp. 895–898.

Werniment, P. F., P. Toren and H. Kapell, "Comparison of Sources of Personal Satisfaction and of Work Motivation," *Journal of Applied Psychology, 54* (1), 1970, pp. 95–102.

Zeyher, Lewis R., "Improving Your Three Dimensional Communications," *Personnel Journal, 49* (5), 1970, pp. 414–418.

contents

learning objectives

1. To understand what an organizational climate is and why it is important.

2. To recognize definitional and measurement problems inherent within the organizational climate and the leadership concepts.

3. To be able to compare and contrast the trait and situational approaches to the analysis of leadership.

4. To become aware of the similarities and differences between managerial philosophies and leadership styles.

Effective organizational climates and efficient leader-ship are thought induced.

4

Organizational Climate and Leadership

1. Introduction

Similar to the topics of motivation and communication, organizational climate and leadership are modern behavioral concerns of an up-to-date personnel or manpower manager. Personnel practices exist within an overall organizational setting, and this setting or climate must be analyzed and understood by a personnel manager if he expects human resource programs to be effective. Leadership styles constitute a major aspect of the total company climate, so modern personnel specialists are expected to know how to assess the existence and ramifications of various management philosophies and leadership styles. As pointed out in Chapter 2, personnel or manpower work is basically staff, not line. Accordingly, it is generally known that personnel practices are implemented and put into effect largely by first-line supervisors. The analysis of leadership discusses employer-employee relationships at all levels within an organization, including first-line supervision. Because of their importance to modern personnel management practices, this chapter will deal with organizational climate and leadership.

2. Organizational Climate

It has long been believed that the general climate existing within an organization has some bearing on the efficiency in which a company operates. This observation has led to many empirical studies that have attempted to analyze organizational climates in a more systematic and scientific manner (Strauss). What, why, and how questions related to the organizational climate phenomenon have been of concern to most personnel specialists and other management practitioners over the years. This section will attempt to answer these questions by discussing the general subject matter of organizational climate using the following subdivisions: (1) definition and semantics; (2) causes for concern; (3) relationship to productivity; (4) measurement; and (5) the most important factor.

A. DEFINITION AND SEMANTICS

What is the concept of organizational climate? This phrase is common today, yet it seldom is precisely defined. Organizational climate is a broad, nebulous, and somewhat elusive idea, and as such it is difficult to nail down semantically. In general, an organization's climate consists of its unique culture, traditions, and methods of action. An organizational climate is the sum total of the worker attitudes within a company, especially in reference to general employee health and comfort. In contrast to the common meterological usage of the term, organizational climate refers to internal instead of external company atmospheric conditions.

Morale

There are other management concepts closely related to that of organization climate. One of the most frequently referred to is the concept of morale. By definition, morale is the attitude of individuals and groups toward their work environment and toward voluntary cooperation. Morale is a state of mind with reference to confidence and zeal, especially in regard to a number of persons associated in some enterprise.

The concepts of climate and morale are closely related, but they do vary somewhat. Climate is a broader concept and refers to the entire organization. Morale is an individual or group concept. Morale is concerned basically only with attitudes, while climate also includes practices, traditions, and customs. Both climate and morale are long-run propositions, but changes in organizational climate would occur more slowly than changes in employee morale. In terms of set diagrams, Figure 4-1 shows employee morale as a subset of organizational climate.

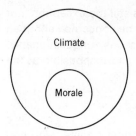

FIGURE 4-1   Morale as a subset of climate.

B. CAUSES FOR CONCERN

Not everyone is convinced that organizational climate and employee morale are matters of serious employment concern. Many managers are uncertain as to why such issues are or should be examined in reference to work environments. Unfortunately, many supervisors see climate and morale as subjective intangibles unrelated to job performance. To them, climate and morale appear to be human relations concepts related to the informal social organizational structure, but irrelevant to the effective operation of a plant. There is at least partial truth in such viewpoints, but most managers are concerned about an organization's climate for several reasons. Most causes for organizational-climate concern are either economic or humanitarian (Williams).

Economic Concern

Economic causes for climatic concern are based in terms of dollars and cents. A good organizational climate can reduce worker turnover and absenteeism, lessen the number of accidents and the degree of scrap and waste, result in more units of and less defects in production, and lead to less employee theft. This rationale of concern is based on the principle of self-interest. Happier workers sometimes are also more productive and efficient employees, and it is from this premise that economic concerns about the organizational climate originate.

Humanitarian Concern

Many managers and employees believe that executives should be concerned about an organization's climate irrespective of financial considerations. Some administrators are indeed concerned about the general well-being of their employees for truly humanitarian and altruistic reasons. Human beings deserve to be treated with respect, dignity, and kindness, whether off the job in a recreational setting or on the job in a work situation. Although many managers pay lip service to such a philosophy, the implementation of such an enlightened managerial attitude and framework is still the exception, not the rule. More and more managers, however, seem to be concerned about an organization's climate because of humanitarian reasons; unquestionably, economic motives are also at least partially at work and responsible at the same time.

C. RELATIONSHIP TO PRODUCTIVITY

Managers sometimes assume that a good organizational climate, high employee morale, and high productivity always go together. In general, there usually is some positive correlation between climate, morale, and productivity, but this correlation is not usually statistically significant. Climate reflects organizational customs, traditions, and practices, and there are a number of intervening variables between such factors and employee productivity. Even morale, which is solely an attitude measure, is not always directly or significantly related to worker productivity.

Productivity Measurement

Research studies have revealed inconsistent relationships between climate, morale, and productivity (Patrick). There are many reasons for this, but the main one is that no universal way of measuring either climate, morale, or productivity has been established. Productivity may be measured by quantity, quality, waste, number of accidents, extent of downtime and the like. Usually a composite index of productivity is established within an organization, but the factors making up this index vary from one company to another.

Organizational climate is even more difficult to measure; an intangible concept instead of a physical phenomenon is being dealt with now (Falater). The relation of climate to productivity is further complicated by conceptual confusion of climate with some of the variables that comprise it, such as morale, satisfaction, and happiness. Job satisfaction and employee happiness are also not usually positively or significantly related to productivity. Quite often unhappy workers ruled by an autocratic manager are the most productive and efficient employees (Miljus). Furthermore, there is no common agreement as to what factors or variables make up job satisfaction, employee happiness, worker morale, and organizational climate. Given such a diversity of ideas, concepts, and measurements, it should not surprise the reader to learn that no definite conclusions about the relationship between climate and productivity can be made. Such a relationship is too complex and involves the interrelationships of too many other variables to be stated in anything but situational terms.

D. MEASUREMENT

How to measure an organization's climate is an inquiry of common concern. This measurement problem exists also for the related concepts of morale, job

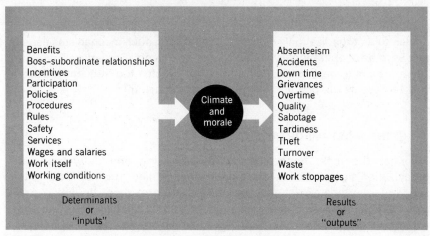

Benefits	Absenteeism
Boss–subordinate relationships	Accidents
Incentives	Down time
Participation	Grievances
Policies	Overtime
Procedures	Quality
Rules	Sabotage
Safety	Tardiness
Services	Theft
Wages and salaries	Turnover
Work itself	Waste
Working conditions	Work stoppages

Determinants or "inputs"

Climate and morale

Results or "outputs"

FIGURE 4-2 Climate and morale: "inputs" and "outputs."

satisfaction, and happiness. Usually some sort of composite index of many factors is used to try to assess an organization's climate. The type of factors that might make up such an index include labor turnover, productivity, waste and scrap, quality records, absenteeism and tardiness, reports of counseling, insurance, grievances, exit interviews, accident reports, medical reports, suggestions, and training records. Some of these items are direct measures of organizational climate, while others are indirect. Such factors are often used to evaluate an organization's climate because such information in most cases is readily available, these data are objective, and records of this nature are a good measure of trends over a period of time. Together these reports form a valuable regular supplement to periodic company surveys and continuous face-to-face interpretations of an organization's climate. Figure 4-2 summarizes some of the most frequently used measures of organizational climate and employee morale. Figure 4-2 also indicates that these measures are often thought of as results of or outputs from climate and morale conditions that are caused by yet a different set or type of determinants or inputs.

Surveys

Often employee surveys are used to evaluate a company's climate. Such surveys are sometimes called attitude or morale surveys. Employee surveys help to identify climatic problems and to improve organizational planning, organizing, controlling, motivating, communicating, decision making, staffing, and leadership efforts. Morale surveys may be objective, descriptive, or projective in format, depending on their design and structure. These surveys are usually conducted by the personnel department or by outside consultants. Although employee surveys represent a considerable investment of company time, money, manpower, and other resources, the information related to an organization's climate gathered from such mechanisms usually proves to be of operational value to corporate officers (Carnarius). Employee surveys seem to be most beneficial if not conducted too frequently. Once a year represents the practice of most organizational units.

E. THE MOST IMPORTANT FACTOR

Thus far the most important variable affecting and determining an organization's general climate has not been identified. This key factor is the superior-subordinate relationships that prevail throughout the entire company. Climatic traditions, customs, practices, and attitudes are all to a large extent basically dependent on established employer-employee relationships. The formal and informal relations a manager has with his subordinates will significantly affect how these workers envision the organization's total climate.

Multiple Climates

Actually, many organizational climates may exist within the same institution (Shepherd). Superior-subordinate relationships vary from job to job, department to department, and plant to plant. In addition, boss-subordinate relationships exist at various institutional levels, ranging from a first-line supervisor overseeing the work of nonsupervisory personnel to the chairman of the board observing the company president's behavior. In general, the higher up in the corporate hierarchy an executive is, the greater will be his total impact on the overall condition of an organization's climate. Nevertheless, the general corporate climate is at least to some degree comprised of the summation of all manager-subordinate relationships at all echelon levels throughout the entire enterprise structure.

Measuring Superior-Subordinate Relationships

It is difficult to assess in quantitative terms the precise relationship between a supervisor and his subordinates. Attitude surveys and measures such as those identified in the previous section are again often used to make this evaluation. Although there is no general agreement about how this relationship can be measured, it is still commonly accepted that superior-subordinate relationships are the main variables affecting an organization's total climate. Superior-subordinate relationships are usually analyzed in terms of managerial philosophies and leadership styles; these matters remain to be covered in this chapter.

3. Leadership

Leadership directly affects an organization's climate. Leadership will be presented in this chapter using the following format: (1) definition; (2) importance and semantics; (3) two approaches to the analysis of leadership; (4) modern leadership axioms; and (5) managerial philosophies and leadership styles.

A. DEFINITION

Leadership is an administrative process that involves directing the affairs and actions of others. Leadership is a behavioral process performed by "leaders" who are human beings who steer and guide the efforts of other human beings. Scores of other definitions of the concept of leadership exist but will not be presented so as to preserve definitional simplicity. Suffice it to say that often many authors have put together very complicated definitions of the leadership concept. This is because although the concept itself is simple, the explanation(s) of the concept are often extremely perplexing. Unfortunately, some authors, when defining the concept of leadership, like to incorporate theories of motivation into their definitions. In short, theories of leadership and motivation differ and, consequently, so do many definitions of leadership.

Key Leadership Ideas

Certain key words are contained within the above explanation of leadership. First, it is a process, which means that it is a movement through a series of events. Second, leadership involves directing. Other terms used to describe this directing might be guiding, steering, inspiring, or actuating. Third, leadership involves directing the affairs, actions, and efforts of others. These affairs, actions, and efforts may be either physical or mental. An effective leader directs not only actual motion, but he also inspires and guides mental activities such as planning, organizing, and controlling. Finally, leadership is performed by leaders who are human beings who steer and guide the efforts of other human beings. In general this statement may be correct, but a very broad definition of leadership would not restrict itself to only human beings. The above human definition of leadership is somewhat fallacious in two respects. First, it assumes that all leaders are human beings. Strictly speaking this may be erroneous. Second, and even more erroneous, is the limited viewpoint that leaders only direct the efforts of human beings. Leaders also may direct the efforts of machines and other mechanical and technological devices, such as a computer. In this chapter we will discuss the concept of leadership only from the human perspective, although a broader, more accurate, and more all-inclusive conceptualization of leadership should also include mechanical as well as human aspects and components of leadership.

B. IMPORTANCE AND SEMANTICS

Some individuals grossly underemphasize the importance of the concept of leadership. Leadership, which is the quality or capacity of a leader to lead and direct, is vital to the survival of any business or organization. An organization may have adequate planning, controlling, and organizing procedures and yet still not survive because of the lack of proper leadership. Conversely, many organizations utilizing inefficient planning, organizing, and controlling techniques have managed to survive because of dynamic leadership. The tremendous importance of leadership as the key determinant of corporate survival cannot be overemphasized.

Leadership as an Invaluable Asset

Numerous empirical research data have been gathered that illustrate the impact of organizational leadership. For example, reasons for corporate failures and bankruptcies are almost always due to the combined inseparable problems of lack of capital and managerial incompetency (Joyce). The competency of leadership within any organization is an invaluable asset in that competent leadership is priceless, but also invaluable because such leadership quality cannot be noticeably discovered by looking at the profit and loss statement or the balance sheet of any enterprise. An executive who possesses leadership qualities is an asset to his organization that cannot simply be estimated in terms of this executive's annual salary. Leadership ability is a rare and demanding quality that directly leads to organizational growth or decay. Some people today are advocating a system of human assets or human resource accounting as an attempt to recognize more properly in financial terms the vital importance of such leadership qualities (Likert, "book" reference citations).

Neutrality

One semantic problem associated with the concept of leadership is the connotation of "good," which most people attach to and associate with the concept of a leader. A leader is assumed to be a "good" leader. Someone who is identified as one who possesses leadership quality is often assumed to possess "good" or "competent" leadership qualitites. Theoretically, leading, leader, and leadership are all neutral concepts. Leaders may be "good" or "bad," "effective" or "ineffective," "competent" or "incompetent." However, the root word "lead" does possess a positive connotation and consequently so do derivative terms such as leading, leader, and leadership.

Although theoretically I recognize the intrinsic neutrality of the leading and leadership concepts, I do not normally use the terms indifferently, but accept and use positive interpretations of such concepts. The readers should, however, be made aware of such semantic problems and be advised to interpret such concepts in terms of their total verbal contexts.

C. TWO APPROACHES TO THE ANALYSIS OF LEADERSHIP

Leadership has been studied through the use of two major approaches, the trait approach and the situational approach. Chronologically, early management theorists emphasized traits, whereas modern theories of leadership stress the situational approach.

Trait Approach

Trait theory suggests that leaders can be identified by certain characteristics that they inherently possess. Such theories were popular until the mid-1940s, when the rationale of this approach was seriously questioned. The earliest trait theories believed that such characteristics were inherited, that is, carried in the genes and passed along from one generation to the next. This belief was eventually modified and expanded to include the idea that traits could be acquired also through the learning process and experience. Trait theory originated as an intuitive explanation of leadership behavior. Many leaders were assumed to possess similar personalities, physical traits, and psychological characteristics. However, when empirical research was performed in an attempt to study these traits more systematically, no traits or very few traits seemed to be common to all leaders.

TRAIT CRITICISMS

Many critics of trait approaches appeared. It soon became apparent through research that universally accepted traits as characteristics of leadership ability did not exist. It became known that no two individuals trying to explain leadership through traits came up with identical or sometimes even similar listings of leadership traits. The number of such traits was also an unresolved issue. The relative degrees of possession and importance of such traits also could not be precisely determined. The identification by name and the nonmutually exclusive nature of traits were other problems of this approach. Leadership traits used to identify future potential and current ability of leaders also seemed to be somewhat incongruent. These and other considerations led many individuals, and especially behavioral researchers, to conclude that the trait approach to leadership could at best be only a partial explanation of the total leadership phenomenon. Apparently, other situational factors in addition to character traits had some bearing on the explanation of leadership behavior. Before abandoning the traits approach in favor of the situational approach, the two basic classifications of trait theories, physical and personality, should be discussed.

PHYSICAL TRAITS

The earliest and crudest forms of trait theories were of the physical trait variety. Potential and current leaders were often described in physical terms. Physical characteristics of one's anatomy and physique were emphasized. Characteristics of a human being's framework, structure, and constitution were considered important. Height, weight, strength, posture, and muscle tone factors were believed to be associated with leadership potential and ability. Such thinking is reminiscent of our pioneering heritage and even perhaps our distantly former barbaric existence. During such past periods of existence, physical attributes undoubtedly were important for leadership and perhaps even for survival. Many people believe that our society really has not changed all that much, and that physical survival of the fittest is still the case, especially in the less highly developed nations of the world. Undoubtedly, such physical characteristics may still be required as leadership prerequisites in some situations, but most people believe today that when society matures, when rationality replaces emotions as the ultimate decision-making criterion, and when peace, not war, is the general state of affairs, physical traits as prerequisites to leadership ability will not be nearly so important. Most research studies performed in an attempt to evaluate empirically physical trait theories usually conclude that no universal physical traits can be identified. There are always, however, some studies that do show a significant correlation between a physical trait, such as height, and leadership ability. But for every such study showing a direct positive relationship, usually several studies indicating a negative relationship can also be found. The general consensus today is that leaders cannot be identified by whether or not they are tall or short, fat or skinny, blonde or brunette, black or white. Although many individuals who are physically big and strong seem also to have an awesome mystique associated with their person, such characteristics should not properly be envisioned as prerequisites of leadership ability.

PERSONALITY TRAITS

After empirical researchers consistently and statistically revealed the fallaciousness of the physical trait doctrine of leadership, trait theorists did not abandon their basic premises; they simply redefined their central focus of attention. Instead of identifying physical characteristics, newer trait theories began to stress personality and psychological traits. Factors such as honesty, loyalty, ambition, initiative, and intelligence were now emphasized. People possessing a high degree of such factors were considered to be better leaders than those who possessed less of these desirable psychological traits. This type of thinking or reasoning also was challenged by empirical researchers, who again, through a series of studies, revealed the erroneousness of such a rationale. Again, conflicting research conclusions were sometimes evident, but repeatedly the general conclusion was that no universal personality leadership traits exist. A person does not have to be exceptionally honest, loyal, ambitious, or intelligent in order to be a good leader. Usually a leader has at least an "average" relative amount of such factors, but an extremely high absolute or relative degree of such traits does not necessarily identify or associate with leadership ability. This does not mean that personality trait theories are useless. It merely means that personality traits, like physical traits, are only at best a partial explanation of leadership ability.

METHODOLOGICAL PROBLEMS

Other types of methodological problems are also partially responsible for the inconsistent empirical research conclusions arrived at through many behavioral leadership studies. One operational problem is how to measure leadership. Do you measure it in terms of a person's title, salary, status, number of subordinates, hierarchical position, or what? An even more perplexing and inconsistent variable is the procedure used to measure the degree of human possession of certain personality traits, such as loyalty, honesty, ambition, initiative, and intelligence. Such factors can be measured in several ways, not all of which will reveal consistent results. Operational problems such as these have also contributed to the demise of those who advocate personality trait theories.

PHYSICAL VERSUS PSYCHOLOGICAL TRAITS

Still another problem is trying to distinguish between physical and personality (psychological) traits. Many traits such as stamina, drive, aggressiveness, gregariousness, and forcefulness are both quasiphysical and quasipsychological. Such traits cannot solely be identified as either only physical or psychological in nature because they simply are not totally distinct conceptual entities. Figure 4-3 illustrates that stamina, drive, aggressiveness, gre-

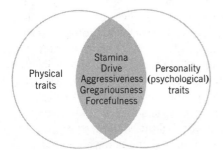

FIGURE 4-3 The interrelatedness of physical and personality (psychological) traits.

gariousness, and forcefulness are traits that are both paraphysical and parapsychological.

Situational Approach

The conclusion usually reached from trait theories is that trait characteristics are important in some circumstances but not in others. Personality and sometimes even physical traits often identify leadership ability in some environments, but such characteristics are not universal to all situations. Factors other than the mere identification of the traits of the leader are crucial within a leadership arrangement. In the late 1940s, various theories were introduced that attempted to identify these factors. Although such theories often varied in terminology, it soon became common and fashionable for leadership theories to consist of a central core of variables (Hill). I will identify these variables as (1) traits of the leader, (2) characteristics of the followers, (3) characteristics of the task, (4) characteristics of the organization, and (5) characteristics of the external environment. Leadership was considered as an output of all of these five input variables. It was seen as a system comprised of many interrelated, dynamic, overlapping, and constantly changing variables that individually could not explain leadership ability, but when pictured collectively could account for the many factors comprising the leadership phenomenon. The situational approach to leadership purports that leadership is situational; that is, it depends on unique factors, variables, and circumstances within the total environmental context. Because such factors and circumstances change frequently and often rapidly, leadership cannot be studied by a static theory or a complacent concept, but can best be approached by a systems methodology that incorporates many intervening variables existing within an environmental milieu. The five key sets of variables within this situational approach to leadership are discussed below.

TRAITS OF THE LEADER

This component is identical with the previous discussion of the traits approach. The traits approach is not totally discarded as an attempt to explain leadership behavior; it is simply now envisioned as only one of many important variables. It is true that some situational theories give very little credulity to the trait theories, especially some of the earliest situational theories. However, most modern situational theories give at least some credence to this earlier approach (Hersey and Blanchard). In some situations, individual traits, either personality or physical in nature, are important as identifying characteristics of leaders. For example, if one were to attempt to identify leadership ability on the football field, physical traits may be major variables determining leadership potential; a player's height, weight, strength, and speed are crucial to leadership ability. In other situations psychological and personality traits may be determinants of leadership ability. Many research studies support the conclusion that successful salesmen are aggressive, ambitious, friendly, initiatory, persistent, and gregarious. Such characteristics are often important for certain types of salesmen, but for other types of leaders, or salesmen selling a different product, or even salesmen selling the same product to a different clientele (e.g., retail versus wholesale), such traits may not be indicative of leadership ability. Individual traits are important in any situation, but each setting is different, and thus the required traits of a successful leader in one environment are different from the characteristics of an effective leader in another circumstance (Maier and Sashkin).

CHARACTERISTICS OF THE FOLLOWERS

Situational theories stress that the characteristics or traits of the followers in any leadership relationship are at least as important as the traits of just the leader alone. The appropriate leader is accordingly the one who is best suited and matched to those who comprise the group to be led. This, however, does not mean that the leader of the group has to have traits similar to those characteristic of the group. It just means that a certain type of leader may not be harmonious with a certain group of followers. Thus, in choosing or electing the leader for a group, the prime consideration should be the composition of characterisitcs within the group and not the traits of the leader. Perhaps an extreme example can illustrate this point. Generally, a young, white, middle-class male with several years of work experience and with both undergraduate and master's degrees would be considered a prime candidate for a leadership position. However, if the potential followers are all minority group members who have all dropped out of high school and who are currently classified as hard-core unemployables, it probably would be unwise for this white male to be put in a leadership role directing such a group. This same individual may not perform well as a supervisor of an all-female work group either or perhaps even as the director of an all-male group of employees who are considerably older than this young man. Additionally, if the young man is Polish, Catholic, or Republican, he may or may not be properly matched or fitted to the predominant characteristics of the followers in a group to be led. Educational, racial, age, sex, religious, political, ethnic, economic, social, cultural, and other characteristics of the followers are important factors within any leadership situation. The leader assigned to work with a group may not need to possess all of the group's characteristics, but his traits should be at least somewhat compatible with and not in severe contrast to the identification features of the group.

CHARACTERISTICS OF THE TASK

In some situations the job itself decides who would best fulfill a leadership role in regard to such a task or job. In all leadership settings the task should be at least an influential variable if perhaps not the crucial determinant of the appropriate leader in this situation. The traits of the leader and the characteristics of the followers are usually recognized as important leadership variables, but the significance of the job itself is often a neglected leadership element, even within some modern situational approaches to leadership. The actual duties and responsibilities associated with a task frequently and uniquely qualify or disqualify potential leaders of that task. A job or position may involve and require certain activities and behavior that many people cannot provide. Tasks vary in terms of physical requirements, mental prerequisites, managerial ability, and other such factors. Each job or position has specialized assignments and procedures associated with it, and because a person has proven himself to be a leader in performing some other function does not necessarily mean that he will be a good leader of a different task. For example, the captain of the high school football team may not be a good student council president; he may not even be the best candidate for captain of the basketball team; and probably he would not be a good head cheerleader. Similarly, all industrial organizations have numerous examples of men and women who were good workers but bad supervisors. Educational institutions also frequently find that extremely competent professors often become inept administrators. This is often not due to leader or follower traits or lack thereof; but, instead, it is due to the varying nature of different tasks. The characteristics of the task determine not only who the appropriate leader should be, but they also dictate to a large degree how the task is to be accomplished or performed. The leadership situation on an assembly line or in a managerial position operates within the limitations and constraints placed on this situation as specified by the job itself.

CHARACTERISITCS OF THE ORGANIZATION

Many modern situational theorists combine into one factor the variables of "characteristics of the task" and "characterisitcs of the organization." They are similar, but their scope and dimension vary, so I will discuss them separately. Both the characteristics of the task and of the organization are grossly underestimated as determining variables within a leadership setting. The nature of an organization often determines what type of person is best suited for a leadership role within such an organization (Shetty). Very often the nature of an organization is due to the managerial philosophy or leadership style prevalent within the institution. The institution may display a very authoritarian style of management, or it may practice a very democratic approach to supervision. Obviously, most organizations are best characterized in terms of a management philosophy or style somewhere between these two extreme positions. A certain type of leader can best operate in an organization of a certain managerial style or philosophy. Normally, there should be an appropriate match between an individual's managerial style and an organization's philosophy. It must be realized, however, that organizational styles and philosophies exist at various levels — institutional, divisional, regional, departmental, and so on. The managerial philosophy or style of a leader is most effective when it is similar to and reinforced by the prevailing philosophy inherent within his immediate subunit. A person practicing a participative-group management philosophy within a benevolent authoritarian environment represents a somewhat misplaced leader in an incongruent and potentially disruptive setting. Leadership styles and philosophies will be discussed in greater detail later.

Organizational Mission. Other factors besides managerial style and philosophy such as basic purpose, habits, customs, traditions, and structure, also determine an organization's characteristics. Readers should attempt to illustrate for themsleves hypothetical or practical examples where these and other organizational factors may affect a leadership situation. Only one other type of frequently encountered institutional variance will be noted here. The basic purpose of various organizations differs. Organizations and institutions may be large or small, private or public, profit making or nonprofit making, product oriented or service oriented, task centered or socially centered, and so forth. The ideal leader in such situations again varies according to the match between the manager and the organization. The amount of congruence again need not be perfect, but large discrepancies are and should be the exception and not the rule. A leader in a military situation may or may not be an effective politician. A successful industrialist may or may not be able to transfer his skills in order to become an efficient administrator of an eleemosynary institution. An acknowledged hospital administrator may or may not be able to transmit and convey his abilities successfully to fulfill the requirements of the presidency of an educational institution. These organizational characteristics, however, affect much more than just the leader in a leadership situation. The followers, the tasks, and the environment are also tremendously changed and influenced by organization characteristics. Obviously the task and personnel within a public, nonprofit-making institution will be markedly different from the job and manpower existing within a private, profit-oriented establishment. Organizations vary in their characteristics, and thus the leadership situations and requirements within these organizations also differ.

CHARACTERISTICS OF THE EXTERNAL ENVIRONMENT

Characteristics of the external environment (political, economic, social, and technological factors) may also influence a leadership situation. A change in political parties may alter tax bases, inflationary pressures, peace prospects, the allocation of government contracts, and virtually all other aspects of the external environment, and thus such a change can directly and indirectly affect any and all organizations. Certainly economic factors such as depression, inflation, and devaluation also affect institutional procedures. More specifically, if an institution is in a financial bind, relatively authoritarian and strict leadership styles and situations often prevail. External social factors such as discrimination and nepotism can easily influence a leader-followers situation. Additionally, technological advances within society in general, within a firm's industry, or within the firm itself obviously and drastically affect the leader-followers-task state of affairs. Time constraints and limitations also may alter work relationships. Managerial philosophies and styles are especially prone to change from more to less democratic if time pressures are encountered. Passages of time may also account for the instances in which an individual may at one time possess leadership ability but then lose it, or he may initially not possess this skill but eventually later acquire it over the course of many years. These and other external environmental factors change organizational settings both directly and indirectly and, conse-

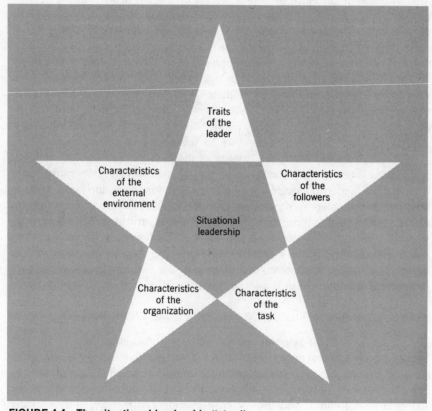

FIGURE 4-4   The situational leadership "star."

quently, leadership situations within such organizational settings are also altered.

Figure 4-4 summarizes the situational approach to the study of leadership. The situational leadership "star" indicates that five factors or sets or variables must be taken into account when analyzing the leadership phenomenon. As identified and explained earler, these five contingencies include: (1) traits of the leader; (2) characteristics of the followers; (3) characteristics of the task; (4) characteristics of the organization; and (5) characteristics of the external environment.

D. MODERN LEADERSHIP AXIOMS

Many principles and maxims are associated with modern situational approaches to leadership. Such statements represent in adage format many of the key ideas contained within situational theories of leadership. These axioms do not represent precise truisms or strict rules but, instead, they reflect the general rationale contained within modern versions of situational leadership theories. Many of these propositions are similar and interrelated in nature. I will briefly discuss four of these sayings: (1) leaders are made, not born; (2) leadership can be learned; (3) everyone has leadership potential; and (4) leadership is a relationship.

Leaders are Made, Not Born

Early versions of trait theories stated that leaders were born, not made. A philosophy sometimes identified as the "great man theory" initially prevailed, and its underlying rationale stressed the idea that leadership traits were hereditary in nature and passed from one generation to the next by biological genes and chromosomes. Such a belief initiated from ancient feudal governing systems that contained kings, queens, princes, and princesses. Caste systems also were, to some degree, a part of every culture, and certain classes of people in many societies were virtually excluded from various types of leadership positions. Although in some cultures leaders are still born, not made, most civilized and advanced societies recognize that leaders generally acquire or should acquire their positions through knowledge, power, ability, expertise, and experience, not through inheritance. A rational society recognizes that the ability to perform is a much better basis for leadership than one's lineage. This shift in thinking has been apparent and is now becoming accepted only within the last few decades, and only within the more culturally advanced societies.

Leadership can be Learned

Modern situational theories also stress that leadership can be learned. Just because an individual does not display early signs of leadership potential does not necessarily mean that he cannot eventually learn to be an effective leader through indoctrination, training, and development. Leadership does not come naturally; it is a skill and an ability usually acquired through education and experience. Leadership skills can be taught by a variety of classroom methods, such as lecture, discussion, films, role playing, case studies, and programmed instruction. Instructors can teach leadership principles, and pupils can learn and practice leadership skills. Leadership ability is not a permanent either-or condition where an individual either has leadership ability or he doesn't. The ability to lead is a long-run educational process that can be learned and acquired through deliberate study and prolonged practice. Some individuals do not learn leadership skills until later in their lives.

Everyone has Leadership Potential

Even after it was recognized that "leaders are made, not born" and that "leadership can be learned," it was still some time before it was generally believed that "everyone has leadership potential." It was once assumed that there were relatively few individuals who could learn leadership skills and thus become leaders. Today situational theories explicitly or implicitly state that everyone has some leadership potential. Perhaps this potential is not always actualized or developed, but this potential is inherent in all human beings. In the proper situation (i.e., given the proper unique combination and configuration of followers, tasks, organizations, and external environmental factors), there is an ideal situation for every individual. Anyone can be a leader if he finds the situations that are especially well suited for him. Such undeveloped existing human potentials are of infinite value both economically and socially.

Leadership is a Relationship

"Leadership is a relationship" summarizes the philosophy of situational approaches to leadership. A leadership situation is a relationship or a system of relationships among factors and variables, such as the traits of the leader, the characteristics of the followers, the characteristics of the task, the characteristics of the organization, and the components of the external environment. This relationship is dynamic and viable, not static and complacent. Although this relationship is among people, objects, things, and events, the most important aspects are the interpersonal relationships in the leadership situation. First, leadership is a relationship among persons. A leader and his followers form ties and bonds that identify this leadership relationship. Using formal organization terminology, such relationships can be identified as authority, power, responsibility, and accountability relationships. Informal organizational relationships between a leader and his followers can be described by concepts such as values, status, roles, norms, sentiments, morale, activities, and interactions.

E. MANAGERIAL PHILOSOPHIES AND LEADERSHIP STYLES

Managerial philosophies and leadership styles are also approaches to the analysis of leadership, but they were not included in the earlier section of this chapter so entitled because their basic purposes are different from those of trait and situational leadership theories. Trait and situational leadership theories were devised to explain how to best choose leaders for leadership positions. Explanations of managerial philosophies and leadership styles do not emphasize this notion of proper leadership choice. Instead, managerial philosophies and leadership styles explain established leadership relations. Philosophies and styles concentrate on descriptions of the real present world instead of on projections of the ideal future world. The choice of optimal leaders is not the intent; managerial philosophies and leadership styles focus on attempts to explain concrete relationships that exist between managers and their subordinates.

Managerial philosophy and leadership style have different meanings. Managerial philosophy describes an executive's internal system of interpreting knowledge, facts, and events according to his inherently based assumptions about and conceptualizations of reality, validity, and value. Leadership style refers to a manager's specific mode, fashion, and distinctive manner of administrative performance and conduct. Managerial philosophy is broader in scope than leadership style. A better distinction is that managerial philosophy refers to an administrator's theories and leadership style refers to an administrator's practices. A person's managerial philosophy is his mental model, and his leadership style is the operational procedures and techniques a person uses to implement and actuate this model. Using the set-systems approach, the best interpretation of managerial philosophy and leadership style is to see these two concepts as partially overlapping and interrelated phenomena, as shown in Figure 4-5b. These constructs are not totally distinct (Figure 4-5a) or completely synonymous (Figure 4-5c). In the real world it is usually very difficult or impossible to always make clear distinctions between these two concepts, although theoretically managerial philosophies consist of thoughts, and leadership styles consist of actions.

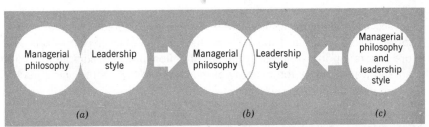

FIGURE 4-5 Managerial philosophy and leadership style as distinct, interrelated, and synonymous set entities. (a) Distinct. (b) Interrelated. (c) Synonymous.

There have been many recent attempts to research and understand managerial philosophies and leadership styles better. We will look, in chronological order of appearance, at four methodologies: (1) Theory X and Theory Y; (2) managerial grid; (3) exploitive authoritative-benevolent authoritative-consultative-participative group; and (4) autocratic-custodial-supportive-collegial. The first two are attempts to analyze managerial philosophies, while the last two are attempts to study leadership styles.

Theory X and Theory Y

The late Douglas McGregor, in his well-known and frequently cited book, *The Human Side of Enterprise,* developed the concepts of Theory X and Theory Y (McGregor, "book" reference citations). Theory X describes a management philsophy that is often labeled as authoritarian or autocratic. Theory X is a managerial philosophy based on a certain set of assumptions about people and work. These assumptions are that people are inherently lazy and avoid work; if work is to be accomplished people must be coerced, manipulated, controlled, directed, and disciplined by management, because most human beings basically lack initiative, creativity, imagination, ingenuity, self-direction, self-control, and self-motivation, and therefore shirk responsibility. Theory Y is the opposite managerial philosophy, based on a contrasting set of assumptions, attitudes, values, and beliefs. These opposing assumptions are that people enjoy working and that the expenditure of physical and mental effort in work is as natural as play and rest. Furthermore, the majority of human beings have the capacity and ability for self-direction, self-control, self-motivation, and self-actualization. The average person also seeks instead of avoiding responsibility, since such situations provide opportunities to display imagination, ingenuity, and creativity.

Theory X and Theory Y are managerial motivational inputs that directly affect a manager's leadership style and thus also influence the behavior of his subordinates. The usual conclusion reached when discussing Theories X and Y is that Theory Y is generally the more optimisitc, realistic, humane, practical, and even the more economical alternative. Many authors have interpreted McGregor's concepts somewhat differently, but the implications of such ideas are especially subject to debate. Writers are already modifying and extending Theory X and Theory Y to meet their own interpretations and analyses of managerial philosophies (Morse and Lorsch). For example, another theory, such as Theory Z, can be and has been hypothesized as a more accurate portrayal of a certain set of philosophical assumptions about man and work held by the majority of managers today (Morse and Lorsch).

THEORY X OR THEORY Y?

Modern interpretations are that Theory X and Theory Y do not represent an either-or choice situation. All managers are both relatively positive and

THEORY X	THEORY Y
Employees are lazy	People are industrious
Employees avoid work	Work is as natural as play and rest
Employees need to be controlled and directed	People are self-motivated
External discipline is required	People are self-disciplined
Employees avoid responsibility	People seek responsibility
Employees lack initiative and ingenuity	People are creative and competent

FIGURE 4-6   Theory X and Theory Y "assumptions" about human beings.

negative in perspective at different times and in different situations through-out the course of any normal workday. Of course, some managers are relatively much more optimistic (pessimistic) than other supervisors. Managers display both Theory X and Theory Y assumptions at different times and in different work situations. The basic assumptions underlying Theories X and Y are summarized in Figure 4-6.

Managerial Grid

The managerial grid concept was developed by Robert Blake and Jane Mouton to analyze managerial philosophies (Blake and Mouton, "book" reference citation). The grid is a two-dimensional diagram with a horizontal axis labeled "concern for production" and a vertical axis labeled "concern for people." Blake and Mouton annually conduct numerous grid seminars for businessmen to help managers analyze their administrative philosophies more correctly. By answering a number of questions, respondents can "plot" themselves on the grid. Certain plots or positions are represented by certain abscissa numbers. Figure 4-7 depicts the managerial grid concept. Positions on the grid represent differing combinations of concern for production and concern for people. According to mathematical custom, the fist abscissa number represents a location on the horizontal dimension, and the second abscissa point represents the appropriate position on the vertical axis. For example, position 1-1 shows small concerns for both production and people; position 9-1 reveals a high concern for production but a low concern for people; position 1-9 depicts a large concern for people but a small concern for production; and position 5-5 is a middle-of-the-road position. Blake and Mouton argue that most people fall along a south-west to north-east diagonal when plotted; that is, they fall into positions such as 3-3, 5-5, and 7-7, as shown by the shaded diagonal area in Figure 4-7. They also argue that the best position to be in is 9-9, since this represents the maximum concern for both production and people.

THIRD DIMENSION

The management grid concept is useful for analyzing managerial philos-ophies. It, like Theories X and Y, is being modified and extended by

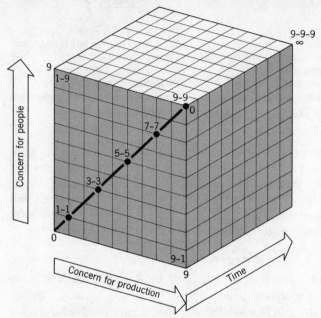

FIGURE 4-7   A three-dimensional managerial grid.

numerous management authors and practitioners. Already some theoreticians have suggested the extension of the grid to include another dimension (Reddin). The third dimension, which might be called thickness, depth, or consistency, usually represents the time dimension. The best manager is now the one who is 9-9-9 individual, because he has the maximum concern for both production and people and because this optimal dual concern is consistent or lasts indefinitely through time instead of being temporary, sporadic, and transitory. The third hypothetical dimension of the managerial grid is also shown in Figure 4-7. Many people consider Blake and Mouton's managerial grid idea to be a better concept than McGregor's Theories X and Y (Gordon). This is because Theory X is usually associated, perhaps mistakenly, with only a concern for production, and Theory Y is often interpreted to mean only a concern for people, but the management grid concept vividly points out that this is not an either-or situation. Concerns for production and people may be high, medium, or low, individually or jointly.

Exploitive Authoritative-Benevolent Authoritative-Consultative-Participative Group

The previous two techniques are modern attempts to analyze managerial philosophies. Leadership styles are also more and more under research scrutiny. One of the most popular and most publicized methods of studying leadership styles was developed by Rensis Likert, formerly Director of the

Institute for Social Research at the University of Michigan (Likert, "book" reference citations). Likert has devised a fourfold, classification system of leadership styles either individually referred to as system 1, system 2, system 3, and system 4 or, alternatively, exploitive authoritative, benevolent authoritative, consultative, and participative group. Similar to the management grid technique, managers can "plot" themselves into one of these systems by responding to specific questions about key administrative areas and activities such as leadership, motivation, communication, decisions, goals, and control. A sample question from the decisions area might be "Where are decisions made?" with optional answers ranging from "top management" to "upper and middle management" to "upper, middle, and lower management" to "all managerial and employee levels." These optional answers chronologically would correspond with Likert's systems 1, 2, 3, and 4. A series of twelve to twenty such questions are asked in each of the six areas. By checking the appropriate response, an individual can determine his leadership style. Likert usually has respondents answer such questions twice, once as a description of actual and existing conditions, and second as a model of how an ideal organization should operate. When this is done, composite leadership profiles usually fall between systems 2 and 3 in the real world, but the ideal profile normally as a composite falls between systems 3 and 4. Using such a technique, Likert concludes that system 4, the participative group leadership style, is the best approach to leadership. Likert states that the participative approach is best socially and economically, if the long-run and human factors are considered. The long run, Likert points out, may vary from company to company and may be anywhere from one to five to ten years or perhaps even more. Human factors can be taken into account economically by a theoretical but as yet somewhat impractical method that Likert has labeled "human asset accounting." In human asset accounting an estimated dollar value is attached to the worth of a human asset. An executive accordingly could hypothetically be shown on a balance sheet as an asset of a certain stated amount. Although most management authors and practitioners are not so certain and convinced as to the conclusions and implications arrived at by Likert by this system, most people nevertheless conclude that this is one of the best ways of currently analyzing such managerial styles. Figure 4-8 shows the four Likert systems of leadership styles and the six general areas of managerial concern. Approximate positions of actual and ideal composite managerial profiles are also indicated by the shaded areas. Recall that such profiles are determined by aggregating replies from respondents who answer a series of questions in each of the six areas using a checking procedure.

Autocratic-Custodial-Supportive-Collegial

Keith Davis, a widely read management author from Arizona State University, has also attempted to synthesize and integrate much of the current manage-

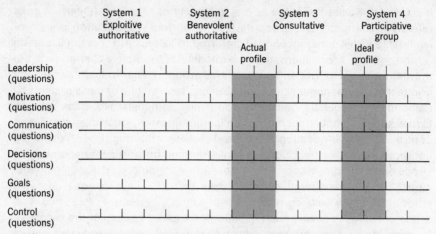

FIGURE 4-8 Likert's fourfold leadership style classification system.

ment literature pertaining to leadership styles into a fourfold classification system (Davis, "book" reference citation). The Davis synthesis consists of a matrix of terms and phrases that respectively correspond to one of his four terms descriptive of the four leadership styles (autocratic, custodial, supportive, and collegial) and that also correspond to a certain framework variable. Framework variables include managerial orientation, employee orientation, employee psychological result, employee needs met, performance result, and morale measure (Davis). Figure 4-9 illustrates this method.

LEADERSHIP STYLES

		Autocratic	Custodial	Supportive	Collegial
FRAMEWORK VARIABLES	Depends on:	Power	Economic resources	Leadership	Mutual contribution
	Managerial orientation:	Authority	Material rewards	Support	Teamwork (integration)
	Employee orientation:	Obedience	Security	Performance	Responsibility
	Employee psychological result:	Personal dependency	Organizational dependency	Participation	Self-discipline
	Employee needs met:	Subsistence	Maintenance	Higher-order	Self-realization
	Performance result:	Minimum	Passive cooperation	Awakened drives	Some enthusiasm
	Morale measure:	Compliance	Satisfaction	Motivation	Commitment to task and team

FIGURE 4-9 Davis' fourfold leadership style classification system. Adapted from: Keith Davis, *Human Behavior at Work: Human Relations and Organizational Behavior.* (New York: McGraw-Hill Book Company, 1972), p. 498.

The major contribution of the Davis analysis is the matrix of terms that constitute the heart of Figure 4-9. Such terms allow leadership styles to be compared, contrasted, and analyzed in a readily understandable manner. This matrix also incorporates some of the more popular and current behavioral management concepts, such as teamwork, self-realization, participation, and maintenance, and fits them into a well-defined conceptual framework. The labels of the leadership styles described are well-chosen, and the framework variables identified represent behavioral concepts that are now at the forefront of managerial concern and analysis. The Davis matrix can integrate and synthesize modern behavioral management concepts, such as Maslow's hierarchy of needs, McGregor's Theory X and Theory Y, Blake and Mouton's managerial grid, Herzberg's motivation-hygiene theory, and McClelland's achievement motivation concept.

LIKERT AND DAVIS COMBINED

The Davis and Likert systems possess many similarities and a few differences. The similarities and differences are all but a matter of relative degree of emphasis on certain factors and variables. The four leadership styles in each classification system do not correspond exactly. Their interrelatedness, however, can be shown by envisioning a leadership style continuum now not broken up into two extremes, such as a Theory X or Theory Y breakdown, nor broken up into a fourfold categorization system, such as Likert and Davis individually purport but, instead are broken up into a eightfold segmented continuum. Figure 4-10 illustrates this classification system, which is a combination of the previous Likert and Davis fourfold classification systems with individual managerial styles positioned on the leadership continuum according to their respective degrees of authoritarianism.

Other Classifications

Many other classification systems exist. Many of them are somewhat dated, others are new, but not as comprehensive or as popular as the preceding classification systems. The previous examples represent current, in vague management thinking (Mathis). Other classification systems use somewhat different terminology, such as bureaucratic laissez-faire, rigid-flexible, inorganic-organic, dictatorial-democratic, hierarchical-free form, closed-open, or permanent-temporary, to portray a continuum similar to that presented in Figure 4-10. Different writers and researchers also may have a different number of subunit classifications along their continuums. A key point to remember is that such a methodology is, indeed, best seen as a *continuum*. By definition, a continuum is a union of uninterrupted continuous parts or segments. Clear distinctions among parts or segments, whether they be two, four, eight, or some other amount in number, cannot be precisely determined. Gray areas instead of black and white areas normally

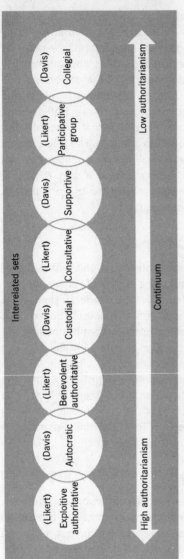

FIGURE 4-10 An eightfold leadership style classification continuum.

exist. Overlapping interelationships instead of definite demarcation lines represent the general state of affairs. Whatever the number of leadership styles identified, set-systems analysis can and should be used properly to explain and understand the interrelatedness of dichotomies, continuums, or any classification system in between. Accordingly, Figure 4-10 also illustrates the leadership style classification continuum by means of eight partially interrelated and overlapping set entities.

Variability in Philosophies and Styles

Variations in managerial philosophies and leadership styles exist theoretically and operationally. The immediately preceding sections dealt mainly with theoretical variations in terms of the labeling and the number of subunits contained within various classification systems of managerial philosophies and leadership styles. Operational variance also exists within these phenomena.

FLEXIBILITY?

There is debate today among management academicians and practitioners about whether or not an actual practicing manager should possess a fixed managerial philosophy or leadership style (Sadler). Should a manager always strive to be Theory Y or 9-9-9 oriented? Is participative management always the best style? Although there are no universally accepted answers to such questions, people are answering such inquiries more and more by stating that managerial philosophies and leadership styles should be situational. A manager should adapt his leadership style and probably even his managerial philosophy if the situation dictates such a change (Miljus). Previously in this chapter I stated that the situational approach to leadership views the directing function as an output of many interrelated variables. Depending on the characteristics of the leader, the followers, the task, the organization, and the external environment, one type of managerial philosophy and style may be appropriate for one situation but not for another. For example, can participative management be applied practically in a penal institution or an insane asylum? Some limited examples of successful participative approaches used within such institutions can be found; however, it is generally believed that a more autocratic leadership style is better suited for such environments. Some people have contested that leadership styles might be flexible, but managerial philosophies should be firmly rooted and stable. Again, this argument centers around relative issues. If managerial philosophies and styles must both not be static, as most people admit, then they must, by definition, also be relatively flexible to some degree. There is probably wisdom and insight in the assertion that styles should be relatively more flexible than philosophies, but both managerial philosophies and leadership styles must adapt and change if the situation merits such alterations. It is bewildering to note that virtually all management authors and practitioners believe and accept the idea that managerial philosophies can and should change from being less to being more democratic, but that few individuals ever advocate changes in the reverse direction, from being less to being more autocratic. If flexibility and adaptibility are sincerely advocated, it must be recognized that change is multi- instead of singly dimensional and directional.

SAME TIME FRAME

There is a final dimension to this variability phenomenon. If one accepts the idea that managerial philosophies and leadership styles can and should change, it is often assumed that the time period has also changed. This may or may not be true. Changing philosophies and styles may also occur during the same moment in time, consciously or unconsciously. For example, many and probably most managers knowingly or unknowingly exhibit one form of managerial philosophy and style when dealing with their superiors and yet display a different and often quite radically changed managerial philosophy and style when working with their subordinates (Wernimont). A manager is usually more Theory Y oriented when interacting with his boss. Theory X oriented when dealing with his workers.

4. Summary

This chapter has dealt with organizational climate and leadership. An organizational climate is the total of the culture, traditions, methods of action, and worker attitudes within a company, especially in reference to general employee health and comfort. Causes for organizational-climate concern are both economic and humanitarian. However, in general, research studies have revealed inconsistent relationships between climate, morale, and productivity. One reason is because there is no universal measurement of organizational climate or employee morale. Usually some sort of composite index is used. Such an index might include factors such as labor turnover, productivity, waste and scrap, quality records, absenteeism and tardiness, reports of counseling, insurance premiums, grievances, exit interviews, accident reports, medical reports, suggestions, training records, and morale surveys. Nevertheless, the most important variable affecting and determining an organization's general climate is the superior-subordinate relationships that prevail throughout an entire company.

Leadership styles directly affect an organization's climate. Leadership is a behavioral process performed by leaders who are human beings who steer and guide the efforts of other human beings. Executive leadership is the key determinant of corporate survival and growth. Leadership has been studied basically by the use of two major approaches, the trait approach and the situational approach. Human leadership traits can be classified as physical or personality (psychological), although these two groupings are not totally distinct. The situational approach is the generally accepted belief today, because it incorporates and then expands on trait theory ideas. Situational approaches to leadership explain the directing function in terms of: (1) traits of the leader; (2) characteristics of the followers; (3) characteristics of the task; (4) characteristics of the organization; and (5) characteristics of the external environment. Often the conclusions reached from situational leadership analysis are expressed in terms of axioms.

The concepts of managerial philosophy and leadership style are closely related. However, one distinction is that managerial philosophy refers to an administrator's theories or thoughts, while leadership style refers to a manager's practices or actions. There are many somewhat different (similar) author interpretations, explanations, and analyses of both managerial philosophies and leadership styles. Four of the currently most popular attempts to study these phenomena include: (1) McGregor's Theory X and Theory Y; (2) Blake and Mouton's managerial grid; (3) Likert's exploitive authoritative-benevolent authoritative-consultative participative group systems: and (4) Davis' autocratic-custodial-supportive-collegial methodology. The first two are attempts to analyze managerial philosophies, and the last two categorizations are attempts to study leadership styles. Many other classification systems exist, but they are either more dated, not as comprehensive, or less popular than the preceding four groups. Variations in managerial philosophies and leadership styles exist both theoretically and operationally. A more and more popular practical suggestion today is that a manager should adapt and alter his leadership style and probably even his managerial philosophy if the situation dictates such a change.

DISCUSSION QUESTIONS AND ASSIGNMENTS

1. Define and explain what is meant by an organizational climate.
2. What factors can be measured in an attempt to assess an organization's climate? Which factors seem to be the most important and influential?
3. Explain what is meant by the situational approach to the study of leadership.
4. Interview a few first-line supervisors in a nearby industrial organization and ask them what relationship, if any, they see between organizational climate and human productivity.
5. Try to invent some leadership axioms that reveal your own personal philosophy of leadership and style of management.
6. Evaluate the merits of the McGregor and Blake-Mouton explanations of managerial philosophies and the Likert and Davis approaches to the study of leadership styles.

REFERENCES

General Book References

Blake, Robert R., and Jane S. Mouton, *The Managerial Grid*. Houston, Texas: Gulf, 1964.

Blum, Milton L., and James C. Naylor, *Industrial Psychology*. New York: Harper & Row, 1968.

Davis, Keith, *Human Behavior at Work: Human Relations and Organizational Behavior.* New York: McGraw-Hill, 1972.

Dubin, Robert, George C. Homans, R. D. Mann, and Delbert C. Miller, *Leadership and Productivity.* San Francisco: Chandler, 1965.

Fiedler, Fred E., *A Theory of Leadership Effectiveness.* New York: McGraw-Hill, 1967.

Leavitt, Harold J., *Managerial Philosophy.* Chicago: University of Chicago Press, 1964.

Likert, Rensis, *New Patterns of Management.* New York: McGraw-Hill, 1961.

Likert, Rensis, *The Human Organization: Its Management and Value.* New York: McGraw-Hill, 1967.

Lippitt, Gordon L., *Organizational Renewal.* New York: Appleton-Century-Crofts, 1969.

McGregor, Douglas, *The Human Side of Enterprise.* New York: McGraw-Hill, 1960.

McGregor, Douglas, *The Professional Manager.* New York: McGraw-Hill, 1967.

Rosen, Ned A., *Leadership Change and Work-Group Dynamics.* Ithaca, N.Y.: Cornell University Press, 1969.

Sikula, Andrew F., *Management and Administration.* Columbus, Ohio: Merrill, 1973.

Sutermeister, Robert A., *People and Productivity.* New York: McGraw-Hill, 1969.

Specific Journal References

Carnarius, Stanley E., "After the Attitude Survey," *Personnel, 45* (5), 1968, pp. 65–68.

Davis, Keith, "Evolving Models of Organizational Behavior," *Academy of Management Journal, 11* (1), 1968, pp. 27–38.

Falater, Frederick L., "The Study of Organizational Environment," *Personnel Journal, 49* (3), 1970, pp. 200–205.

Gordon, Michael, "Grid on the Grill," *Management Today,* September 1970, pp. 41–48.

Hersey, Paul, and Kenneth H. Blanchard, "Life Cycle Theory of Leadership," *Training and Development Journal, 23* (5), 1969, pp. 26–34.

Hill, Walter, "A Situational Approach to Leadership Effectiveness," *Journal of Applied Psychology, 53* (6), 1969, pp. 513–517.

Joyce, J. R., "The Search for Leaders," *Personnel Journal, 49* (4), 1970, pp. 308–311.

Maier, Norman R., and Marshall Sashkin, "Specific Leadership Behaviors that Promote Problem Solving," *Personnel Psychology, 24* (1), 1971, pp. 35–44.

Mathis, Robert L., "Organizational Development," *The Personnel Administrator, 15* (5), 1970, pp. 25–28.

Miljus, Robert C., "Effective Leadership and the Motivation of Human Resources," *Personnel Journal, 49* (1), 1970 pp. 36–40.

Morse, John J., and Jay W. Lorsch, "Beyond Theory Y," *Harvard Business Review, 48* (3), 1970, pp. 61–68.

Patrick, John F., "Organization Climate and the Creative Individual," *Public Personnel Review, 31* (1), 1970, pp. 31–35.

Reddin, W. J. "The 3-D Management Style Theory: A Typology Based on Task and Relationships Orientations," *Training and Development Journal, 21* (4), 1967, pp. 21–30.

Sadler, Phillip, "Leadership Style, Confidence in Management, and Job Satisfaction," *Journal of Applied Behavioral Science, 6* (1), 1970, pp. 3–20.

Shepherd, Jim, "Functional Specialization and Work Attitudes," *Industrial Relations, 8* (2), 1969, pp. 185–194.

Shetty, Y. K., "Leadership and Organization Character," *Personnel Administration, 33* (3), 1970, pp. 14–20.

Strauss, George, "Human Relations — 1968 Style," *Industrial Relations, 7* (3), 1968, pp. 262–276.

Wernimont, Paul F., "What Supervisors and Subordinates Expect from Each Other," *Personnel Journal, 50* (3), 1971, pp. 204–208.

Williams, Edgar G., "Changing Systems and Behavior," *Business Horizons, 12* (4), 1969, pp. 53–58.

PART THREE

Personnel Administration Subsets

contents

learning objectives

1. To comprehend the definition and importance of human resource planning.

2. To be able to understand individually and collectively the components of the human resource planning process.

3. To know the similarities and differences between and among the concepts of human resource planning, manpower planning, manpower programming, organization planning, organizational development, human resource auditing, and human resource forecasting.

4. To learn human resource planning objectives and to become acquainted with human resource planning action programs.

If you don't know where you're going, any road will get you there.

5

Human Resource Planning

1. Definition and Semantics

Definition

Human resource or manpower planning has been defined as "the process of determining manpower requirements and the means for meeting those requirements in order to carry out the integrated plans of the organization" (Coleman). A "man-plan" involves determining the required types of skills or capabilities and the number of people needed. The location and timing of manpower needs is also important. Human resource planning involves having the right number and the right kinds of people at the right places, at the right times, doing the right kind of things, which results in long-run maximum individual and organizational benefits.

Future Orientation

Human resource planning involves projecting and forecasting present personnel functions into the future. Setting up a "man-plan" involves anticipating the future patterns of an organization and of the business environment and then relating manpower requirements to these conditions. Both internal and external factors must be considered during human resource planning endeavors.

Systems Orientation

The application and implementation of a man-plan requires a systems approach, since several interrelated and interacting stages of activities are involved (Morrissey). Such an integrated view of the personnel systems of an organization allows individual managers to make improved day-to-day decisions that can be consistent with total organizational long-run needs. This systems perspective and the more complete explanation of the actual steps involved in the total man-plan process will be discussed later in this chapter.

Semantics

Human resource planning takes different forms and labels, depending on the length of the time span involved. In general, man-plans for the coming year or the near future are called proposed personnel budgets, and man-plans for the distant future are usually termed manpower forecasts.

Human Resource Planning versus Manpower Planning

Human resource planning and manpower planning are synonymous. In the past the phrase manpower planning was used most, but today there is a movement toward replacing this sexually limited phrase with the human resource distinction. Women especially do not appreciate personnel planning being identified with a male dominating label. Accordingly, although these two phrases are interchangeable, I have emphasized the use of the broader based human resource planning terminology.

Manpower Planning versus Manpower Programming

Another semantic problem is trying to distinguish between manpower planning and manpower programming. These two terms are not used consistently within the management literature. Sometimes the phrases are used as interchangeable concepts but, more commonly, the former term refers to the man-plan per se, whereas the latter term refers to the implementation of the man-plan (Maki). Thus the distinction (when it is made) is basically between thoughts and actions. Instead of being thought of as totally distinct (Figure 5-1a) or completely synonymous (Figure 5-1c) manpower activities, Figure 5-1b indicates that manpower planning and manpower programming should properly best be envisioned as partially interrelated and overlapping personnel concepts.

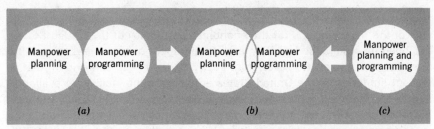

FIGURE 5-1 "Manpower planning" and "manpower programming" as distinct, interrelated, and synonymous set entities. (*a*) Distinct. (*b*) Interrelated. (*c*) Synonymous.

2. Importance

Human resource planning is important for the same reasons that planning is important. Maximum utilization of resources, manpower or otherwise, does not just happen. Optimal efficiency can only result after careful planning and after goals, steps, and actions have been implemented. The most productive use of any organizational input can only be achieved through conscious and prolonged attention to planning details. This importance of planning has far-reaching dimensions, but the basic benefits accrue at three main levels; individual, organizational, and national.

Individual Importance

Human resource planning is important to each individual because it can assist him in improving his skills and using his capabilities and potential to the utmost. Personal satisfaction can be achieved more easily through proper career planning. Less frustration, stress, and anxiety also usually accompany the person who has definite job goals, work objectives, and career plans.

Organizational Importance

Corporations use human resource planning to improve their long-run efficiency and productivity. Companies must recruit and hire enough qualified individuals to provide themselves with the basic productive resource (manpower) of which all organizations are composed. Because most organizations follow the policy of promoting from within, initial or beginning human manpower is the source for present and future management talent in all organizations. Only when there are capable employees in the lower levels are there potential managers to promote (Batholomew).

National Importance

One of the main reasons for the economic supremacy of the United States has been its systematic selection and development of employees to staff its business enterprises. However, in the early 1970s it has been evident that a current limitation of the United States economy is the lack of an available supply of adequately trained and developed personnel for the rapidly expanding activities associated with technological advancement. If the United States is to remain preeminent in the economic realm, it must plan to perpetuate the supply of managerial, technical, and skilled employees to meet the growing and changing needs for increased productivity and enhanced social responsibility (Wright).

3. Human Resource Planning Components

Human resource planning is best thought of as a systematic procedure featuring a planned sequence of events or a series of chronological steps. These steps or events are the components of the human resource planning process; they incorporate (1) objectives; (2) organization planning; (3) human resource auditing; (4) human resource forecasting; and (5) action programs including affirmative action and EEOC. Each of these components will now be explained in more detail.

A. OBJECTIVES

Human resource planning activities fulfill many objectives. Individual, organizational, and national needs, such as those mentioned in the previous section of this chapter, are met by such personnel planning procedures. Although many related goals and derived objectives may be associated with human resource planning activities, the ultimate mission or purpose of human resource planning is *to relate future human resources to future enterprise needs so as to maximize the future return on investment in human resources.* In effect, this main mission is one of matching or fitting employee abilities to enterprise requirements with an emphasis on future instead of present arrangements (Cox).

Objectives and Time Spans

Although the major purpose of human resource planning remains unchanged through time, more specific goals and objectives of man-plans depend on the scope or width of the time period under consideration. For example, a short-term goal (an objective to be reached in one year or less) might be to hire ten black trainees. A long-run purpose (an end to be achieved in five to ten years) might be to have minority group members

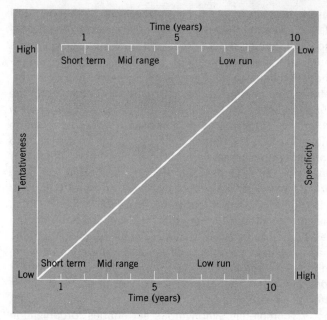

FIGURE 5-2 Objectives and time spans.

eventually in positions of middle and upper management. As shown in Figure 5-2, objectives with a short-term perspective are high in specificity and low in tentativeness, while long-run goals are low in specificity and high in tentativeness. The longer (shorter) the time span, the higher (lower) the tentativeness and the lower (higher) the specificity.

Interrelatedness of Objectives

All human resource planning objectives, regardless of their time dimension and degrees of specificty and tentativeness, are intimately interrelated. Because the long run is composed of numerous short runs, and because an overall purpose can be achieved only by fulfilling several initial subgoals or minor end-states, human resource planning objectives are imminently and inevitably linked together in a highly integrative fashion. The final purpose can only be achieved by the construction and achievement over time of numerous sibling subparts.

B. ORGANIZATION PLANNING

Organization Planning versus Organization Development

Setting manpower objectives is the first step in the human resource planning process. The next step is to assess the future adaptations and changes an organization will have to make in its internal structure and design because of alterations in its internal and external environments. This adaptation process is currently identified and labeled differently by different authors. Common phrases include organizational development, planned change, organizational renewal, and applied behavioral sciences. I will use the term organization planning to refer to this change process. Organization planning is the conscious activity undertaken by an enterprise to effect a positive change in its well-being and growth capacity as a purposeful work organization (Steiner). Organization planning is an organic, process-oriented approach to organizational change and management effectiveness. It effects change and improvement by involving all members of the organization in problem analysis and planning. When organization planning stresses individual human adaptation and development, it is referred to as OD (organizational development). OD is an educational strategy that involves the strengthening of the human processes in organizations that improve the functioning of the organic system so as to achieve its objectives. Another difference between organization planning and organization development is that the former concentrates on adapting to external environmental occurrences while the latter focuses on internal adjustments and changes. Instead of being thought of as totally distinct or completely synonymous set entities, organization planning and organization development should be thought of as partially interrelated and overlapping change concepts.

Organization Planning versus Human Resource Planning

The concepts of organization planning and human resource planning are highly interrelated. Because manpower is the most crucial institutional input, organization planning must, in effect, be manpower planning (Burckhardt). Of these two concepts, organization planning is usually given a broader viewpoint and interpretation and, in this capacity, all resources (land, capital, equipment, raw materials, buildings, etc., in addition to manpower) are viewed from a planning and allocative perspective. It is best to view human resource planning and organization planning as partially interrelated and overlapping activities. To envision these planning concepts as totally distinct or as completely synonymous activities is inaccurate.

Many environmental factors, which are basically external but also occasionally internal in nature, affect organization planning activities. Some of the most important variables affecting organization planning include (1) business forecasts, (2) expansion and growth, (3) design and structural changes, (4) management philosophy, (5) role of government, (6) role of union, (7) product and human-skills mix, and (8) international competition. These factors or variables and their impact on organization planning will now be explained in greater detail.

Business Forecasts

Business forecasts predicting the general economic swing in national manufacturing activities have a drastic effect on the organization planning process. Predictions about inflation, wages, prices, costs, and raw material supplies have a direct bearing on the future plans of all institutions. The eventualities and contingencies of general economic business cycles always have had, and always will have, an influence on the short-range and long-run plans of all organizations (Swerdloff).

Expansion and Growth

Organization planning efforts must also anticipate future enterprise expansion and growth movements. Most organizations hope to grow in size and scope over the years, and such expansion cannot take place smoothly without advance preparation. Often such enlargements involve additional plants and relocated facilities. Growth is more and more often also attained by the acquisition of or merger with other enterprises. Expansions of this magnitude especially may present many enormous problems unless prolonged advance planning has occurred.

Design and Structural Changes

Most organizations must also plan to make structural adjustments over the years. Changes in personalities, philosophies, product mix, and mechanical technology often make structures designed for the past inadequate for the present and especially for the future. The rising proportions of white collar jobs and women employees also point out the need for organizational restructuring. Revised management philosophies and leadership styles are more participative and democratic today, and this enlightened thinking usually must also lead to and result in structural and design changes within institutional entities.

Management Philosophy

Many people think that changing managerial philosophies are the key force behind both environmental changes and institutional responses involving organization planning. The general educational level of managers is rising, and democratic-participative leadership styles are being taught, learned, and implemented more and more. Managerial philosophies are becoming more flexible and permissive, and organization planning activities have been expanded so as to try to come up with newer ideas as to how to best put such new thinking into new practices.

Role of Government

Another factor affecting the increasing use of organization planning is the changing role of government. Especially at the federal level, governmental intervention into business activities has increased in recent years. State and local governments are also more involved with corporate activities. Government contracts and new federal employment laws contain provisions that require organization planning. The always changing corporate tax laws and government product subsidies are constant contingencies that demand enterprise adaptation and adjustment. The role of government at all levels changes over time; thus, institutional plans for the future must also change. The total impact of governmental changes usually affects larger international corporations the most, although the relative effect may also be of a do-or-die magnitude for smaller enterprises.

Role of Union

Firms must also make plans to either accommodate or combat unionization activities. Unions seem to be gaining a new foothold today in formerly nonunionized work settings. More and more white-collar workers and professional employees are being attracted to unionization attempts, especially in the public sector of the economy. The unions that have been established for a long time are increasing their demands for additional wages and benefits. The wise and prudent manager plans his responses to predicted union reactions. Management strategies and tactics are prepared in advance for collective bargaining and contract negotiation sessions. The greater the amount of planning done before the negotiating session, the less drastic the required management adjustments after the collective bargaining process ends will be.

Product and Human-Skills Mix

Very often organization planning is a result of changes in the amount or kind of product or service produced. Plans must be made when increased amounts of the current product are to be produced in the future, but plans especially need to be made when new products are to be added to or are to replace a company's current offerings. New products demand new production skills, and thus human manpower adjustments must also accompany changes in technology (Crowley). Organization planning takes place so that product and human-skills transformations may occur with a minimum of disturbance to the total organizational entity.

International Competition

During the early 1970s one of the newest and most forceful causes of increased organization planning was stepped up international competition.

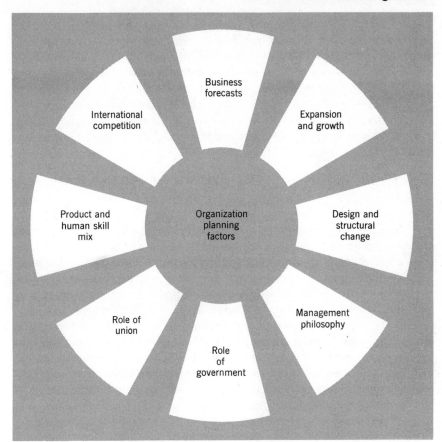

FIGURE 5-3   Organization planning factors.

International trade agreements, increased industrialized capacity abroad, changing prestige of the dollar, and other factors made foreign goods more competitive with domestic products. Beef, oil, steel, grain, and other commodities are now traded more freely among nations of the world. The result has sometimes been declining profit margins for American industries. Declining profit margins have led to increased organization planning in an effort to find new or better ways of managing current facilities.

The previously discussed organization planning factors are summarized in Figure 5-3, which indicates that these eight factors and variables include business forecasts, expansion and growth, design and structural changes, management philosophy, role of government, role of union, product and human-skills mix, and international competition.

C. HUMAN RESOURCE AUDITING

The next major component of human resource planning is human resource auditing. Auditing is an intensive, investigative, analytical, comparative process. Audits are systematic searches that gather, compile, and analyze data in depth for an extended period of time — usually a year. Most audits are designed to compare information about an individual firm or agency with norms, standards, and composite reports from other similar organizations. Internal comparisons among departments and divisions are also part of the auditing process (Heiser).

General Management Audits versus Human Resource Audits

The coverage or scope of audits varies from those that involve a comprehensive overview of the entire management process to others that consider only one department or a single area of management responsibility. The most common audits are financial, because the opportunities for malpractice are most obvious in this area. However, audits are more and more being applied to nonfinancial areas and matters. For example, formal audits of employment relationships have achieved wide and growing acceptance. Formal appraisals of employment relations are often called human resource or manpower audits. The coverage or scope of manpower audits also varies widely. Such audits may involve formal checks on the effectiveness of some or all current personnel programs, including program areas such as job analysis, recruiting, testing, interviewing, training, management development, promotion and transfer, personnel appraisals, labor relations, employee benefits and services, employee attitudes and moral, employee communications, employee counseling, wage and salary administration, and personnel research. Many human resource audits today attempt to follow a "whole man" approach. The modern audit of human resources management reviews the entire systemwide range of personnel programs in which management secures, develops, allocates, and supervises human resources in the organization.

In this chapter we are not concerned with general management audits, nor are we concerned with the entire scope of activities, which might fall under the comprehensive heading of a human resource or manpower audit. Instead, we will concentrate our attention on aspects of human resource auditing that relate specifically to the human resource planning concept. Accordingly, the features of human resource auditing to be discussed further in this chapter involve the issues of manpower quality, inventory, expected losses, and internal moves.

Quality of Work Force

The human resource auditing of an enterprise's personnel should involve examining the present quality of the work force. The aim, of course, is to improve the quality of the work force over time. Improved quality can be achieved by employing high-quality manpower to replace low-quality personnel, or quality can be enhanced through the experience, training, and development of present employees. In general, the development of present personnel is the technique used most within organizations of relatively constant size. Rapidly expanding enterprises must concentrate on external labor supplies to improve work force quality. All firms, however, will at times implement both internal and external work force quality improvement measures.

Determining Quality

Job analysis can be used to determine the qualitative aspects of a company's work force. Job analysis is used to determine the duties, responsibilities, working conditions, and interrelationships between a particular job as it exists and other jobs with which it is associated. It can be defined as the process of gathering pertinent information and determining the component elements of a job by observation and study. Job analysis records details concerning training, skills, required efforts, qualifications, abilities, experiences, responsibilities, and so forth, which are needed for a job. This process of job analysis evaluates all the qualitative demands of a job, and thus this procedure is used when a job is being analyzed for any purpose, whether it be for the recruitment, placement, or evaluation of future employees, or for the establishment of salary scales, performance standards, work simplification methods, and the like for present workers. Job analysis, or some variation of it is the main process used to assess the quality of a work force during a human resource auditing procedure.

Skills Inventory

Computerized personnel systems today make use of human resource skills inventories. A skills inventory contains data about each employee's skills, abilities, work preferences, and other items of information that indicate an employee's overall value to the company. A skills inventory is very helpful for various reasons, but it is especially useful when a firm has an opening that it wants to fill with one of its present employees. Very sophisticated computerized skills inventories are commonly referred to as MIS or "manpower information system(s)" (Walker, 1971). Regardless of the degree of complexity, however, human resource information system is incapable of providing or creating anything more than a compilation or analysis of the data committed to the system. The kinds of data and information used as inputs for such a system are indicated in Figure 5-4. Such a record is kept on every employee as part of a well-managed manpower human resource information system.

1. PERSONAL FACTORS

Age	Dependents	Name
Sex	Handicaps	Social Security number
Citizenship	Security clearance	Permanent address
Military Status	Birthplace	Telephone number
Marital Status	Occupation of parents	Medical status

2. EDUCATION AND TRAINING

Schools attended	Highest level of education
Class rank	School locations
Years in attendance	Means of financial support
Degree areas	Other educational programs

3. EXPERIENCE AND SKILLS

Job areas	Certification — Licenses
Job titles	Reasons for leaving
Job dates	Supervisory responsibilities

4. ADDITIONAL INFORMATION

Salary data	Travel preference
Appraisal data	Location preference
Absenteeism record	Testing results
Disciplinary record	Performance ratings
Benefit preference	Vacation preference
Career plans	Location of relatives

FIGURE 5-4   Data and information used in skills inventories and manpower information systems.

"Skill" Definition

An accurate description of employee skill can substantially increase the usefulness of information derived from any human resource data system. But the concept of a skill is being constantly redefined as jobs move from requiring less and less physical skills to demanding more and more mental abilities. Persons do not possess a skill, they possess skills. Different types and degrees of skills must be differentiated within human resource information systems. For example, types of skills may be problem-solving ability, manual dexterity, emotional stability, response time, the abilities to plan, organize, control, and coordinate. As jobs become more specialized, it becomes more important to identify the needed and critical skill elements on which successful performance depnds.

Expected Losses

Human resource auditing procedures must include provisions for estimating labor turnover. Because vacancies are created when employees leave the company, human resource planning techniques must estimate statistically how many are likely to leave. This can be accomplished by using labor turnover calculations. Such calculations make it possible to learn about the expected number of job vacancies, even though who specifically is to leave cannot be ascertained. Such estimates can be made in terms of past turnover rates. By examining past personnel records, future human resource needs can be projected with adjustments made for anticipated growth or non-growth trends.

Replacement Tables

Expected human resource losses can also be predicted and planned for by the use of personnel replacement tables. As shown in Figure 5-5, quits, retirements, deaths, and promotions can be estimated. Replacement tables are most commonly used to estimate managerial turnover, and the projection period or time span is commonly five years. More complicated replacement tables may include dismissals, layoffs, and other separations using projections for longer than five years.

Internal Moves

Along with external departures, human resource audits must also be aware of internal organizational moves. Internal moves involve promotions, demotions, and transfers. Although such personnel are not lost to the total organization, nevertheless, such movements can be just as upsetting as new hires or permanent dismissals within organizational subunits or departments. The total effect within an organization may also be significant, since

FIVE-YEAR EXECUTIVE REPLACEMENT PLAN[a]

Position	No. of Positions	Quits	Normal Retirement	Death and Early Retirement	Total	Cumulative Promotions
President	1	—	1	—	1	1
Executive staff	13	—	4	—	4	5
General staff	39	—	11	5	16	21
Fourth level	115	6	40	14	60	81
Fifth level	162	2	36	19	57	138
	330	8	92	38	138	246

[a]Briefly, we must be prepared (1) to produce at least one new top executive, (2) to produce four department managers per year, (3) to upgrade 15 people per year at the middle management level, and (4) to hire and retain annually 14 young people with good management potential.

FIGURE 5-5 Five-year executive replacement plan.

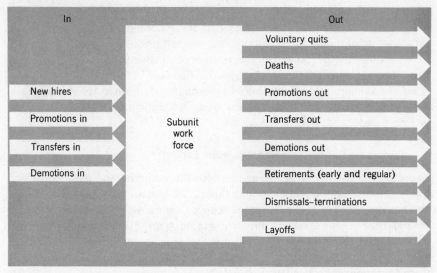

FIGURE 5-6   The changing composition of an organizational subunit work force.

every internal move is, in effect, two moves (i.e., a movement out of one job and a movement into another position).

The work force for any subunit of an organization is constantly changing in terms of past, present, and future size. As shown in Figure 5-6, additional manpower is gained through new hires, promotions in, transfers in, and demotions in, but personnel is lost through voluntary quits, dismissals-terminations, layoffs, deaths, retirements (early and regular), promotions out, transfers out, and demotions out.

The human resource auditing section of this chapter is summarized in Figure 5-7. Although comprehensive human resource audits may involve

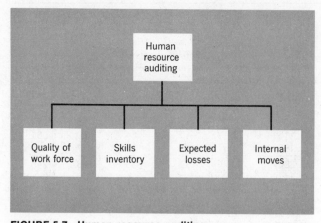

FIGURE 5-7   Human resource auditing.

other matters, four main components of any human resource auditing process are assessing and determining for any organization its quality of work force, skills inventory, expected losses, and internal moves (Heiser).

D. HUMAN RESOURCE FORECASTING

Auditing versus Forecasting

Human resource forecasting is the fourth major human resource planning component. Human resource forecasting is very similar to human resource auditing except that forecasting emphasizes the future, while auditing is more concerned with the present (Rowland, 1968). Another distinction is that human resource auditing concentrates on internal organizational adjustments, while human resource forecasting focuses on institutional adaptations resulting from external pressures and changes (Peterson). Instead of being thought of as totally distinct (Figure 5-8a) or completely synonymous (Figure 5-8c) set entities, Figure 5-8b illustrates the interrelatedness of the human resource auditing and human resource forecasting concepts.

Human resource forecasting must take place because of various external pressures and future contingenices. Examples of the types of factors and variables that affect human resource forecasts are amount of production, technological changes, supply and demand conditions, and career planning. The impact of each of these factors on human resource forecasting endeavors is discussed next.

Amount of Production

Human resource forecasts are influenced drastically by production levels. These production levels may be internal or external in origin and effect. The degree of production of a firm's suppliers and competitors can severely curtail the operations of any manufacturer. If raw materials cannot be obtained, manufacturing processes have eventually to be reduced. The production capacity of competitors can also have ramifications on any organization's

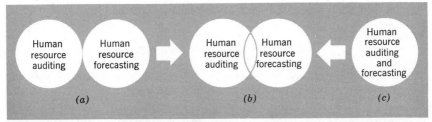

FIGURE 5-8 "Human resource auditing" and "human resource forecasting" as distinct, interrelated, and synonymous set entities. (a) Distinct. (b) Interrelated. (c) Synonymous.

operations. Markets can only be saturated to a certain level or extent and, if competitors capture a good portion of this amount, less total industry market is left available.

Production capacity can also fluctuate for other reasons. Seasonal adjustments, enhanced automation, depleted inventories, new international and domestic markets, rising income levels, improved product quality, enhanced consumer demand, less industry competition, and other factors may be reasons why a company directly instead of indirectly increases its means of production. When production levels rise, for most companies, especially those that are labor-intensive, human resource utilization must also be increased. If production levels fall, less personnel are needed. In short, the amount of production varies because of direct-internal factors and because of indirect-external variables, and these changes necessitate human resource forecasting activities in order to lessen change adjustments (Walker, 1969).

Technological Changes

Human resource forecasting must also take place to account for changes in technology. Again the change may be internal or external. A common type of human resource forecasting that takes place is the personnel planning that accompanies the introduction of a new piece of highly automated machinery. If workers are displaced, either these workers must be permanently dismissed, temporarily laid off, retrained, or relocated. In addition to former employee and current worker adjustments, new employees may also have to be hired to operate the new piece of machinery. New skills, abilities, and expertise may be needed. In the past, the introduction of new technology has led to the introduction of more white-collar, professional, or quasi-professional positions and the elimination of numerous blue-collar, unskilled jobs (Bassett).

Although the installation of a new piece of machinery does not take very long, the proper introduction and human preparation of the newer technology often takes months and sometimes years to implement. Human resource forecasts aiming for the utilization of new technology often involve years of preparation and planning. The major adjustments to be considered are human, but other types of changes must also be planned for.

Supply and Demand Conditions

In forecasting future human resource needs, many employers study the national labor market as well as the one in which they operate (Rowland and Sovereign). A labor market is an ill-defined geographical area in which the supply of people looking for work interacts with the demand of employers for workers in such a way that wages are affected and determined. In actuality, both local and national labor markets perform the function of determining the number of employees in various skills that are available and the price that must be paid for their services.

Supply and demand conditions within labor markets have changed over time. In general, three major modifications have taken place within the labor force during the last several decades. First, the kinds of industry in which workers are employed have changed from the agricultural and extractive industries to manufacturing and service activities. Second, the site or location at which workers perform their activities has shifted from the rural, agricultural areas and the small towns to large, suburban, metropolitan areas. In this regard, the work environment has changed from an agrarian culture to an industrial milieu. Finally, the kinds of work being performed have been modified. Manual labor and unskilled jobs have been replaced by activities that require skill, scientific knowledge, technological acumen, and professional training (Travis). Such modifications necessitate a different kind of work force, and they require human resource forecasting to bring such a labor force into existence. Several changes in the labor force are now occurring to meet these new demands. Some of these changes include increasing the number of employed persons; increasing the number of employed young people; increasing the number of part-time and full-time women employees; increasing the number of nonwhite employees; increasing the number of service-related industries and jobs; and increasing the variety and composition of occupational and career patterns. Declining hours of work, rising employee productivity, more and more white-collar employees, increasing educational levels of the work force, and other additional pressures also affect labor supply and demand conditions. All such conditions should be anticipated by human resource forecasting procedures if a company expects to adapt optimally to local, regional, national, and international environmental employment pressures and changes.

Career Planning

Human resource forecasting must also recognize the occurrence and importance of career planning. Career planning, or career management, as it is sometimes called, refers to the forward-looking organizational employment policies and programs that apply usually to only high-talent or critical manpower categories. The basic purpose of career planning is to unite organizational human resource planning with individual needs, capabilities, and aspirations. The study of past promotional paths and career movements of professional and managerial personnel has led to the current organizational formulation of career policies and strategies in many companies. Such policies and strategies recognize that occupational movements frequently go

beyond any one particular organization. Career planning as a human resource forecasting technique must be done both on an individual basis and
on a collective basis. Each managerial career movement within a company
must be planned, and the resulting impact on other career paths must be
analyzed if human resource forecasting procedures are to be organizationally useful.

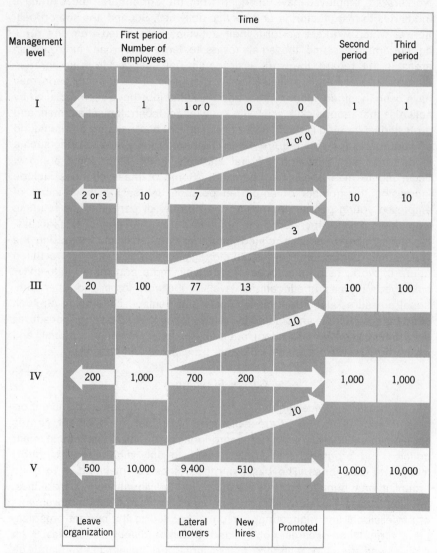

FIGURE 5-9 **A model of human resource career movements over time (Haire).**

Haire's Model

Several models are available that illustrate the flow of people into, through, and out of an organization (Berry). The examination of such flows enables an organization to predict its short-run human resource needs. One such model developed by Mason Haire is shown in Figure 5-9 (Haire). Given past experience with managers leaving the organization (e.g., twenty, on the average, quit, retire, are discharged, or become ill in management level III) and managers being promoted (e.g., ten, on the average, will be promoted from level IV to level III), the model predicts how many new managers must be hired at each level to maintain a stable system. The model can also be used to predict the consequences of other contingencies, such as promotion-from-within policy or the impact of increased or decreased recruitment and turnover. Such models aid in the analysis of career planning and human resource forecasting.

This human resource planning chapter section is summarized in Figure 5-10. Four human resource forecasting factors or variables are shown: amount of production; technological changes; supply and demand conditions; and career planning. Although other factors and variables are involved,

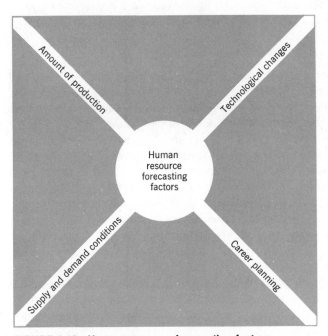

FIGURE 5-10 Human resource forecasting factors.

these four suffice to serve as representative human resource forecasting contingencies. Human resource forecasts are the result of such eventualities and conditions.

E. ACTION PROGRAMS INCLUDING AFFIRMATIVE ACTION AND EEOC

The final human resource planning component is action programs. After human resource objectives are set, organization planning takes place, and human resource auditing and forecasting has occurred, then the application and implementation of human resource planning concepts necessitate the utilization of action programs. The action programs are designed and structured with reference to the data and information obtained and analyzed in previous components of the human resource planning process. Action programs are intended to move human resource planning activities from the conceptual-intangible realm to the operational-tangible world. Previous human resource planning efforts may occur for naught unless direct concrete programs are brought into existence. Human resource action programs may be implemented in a number of general personnel areas, but the examples that follow are among the most frequently found general operational program arenas. These general action-program areas are recruitment-selection, employee training, management development, labor relations-collective bargaining, and benefits and compensation.

Recruitment-Selection

Special recruitment and selection programs are often the end result of human resource auditing and forecasting activities. Such employment efforts are designed to hire the types of employees whose skills will be in the greatest demand and the shortest supply in the future. The search for engineering talent and managerial potential has, in the past, been the focus of such action endeavors. The use of special manpower recruitment and selection procedures is often an indication that the required organizational human resource needs for the future cannot be met simply by a promotion-from-within policy. Such a condition is most commonly found in rapidly growing enterprises. The exact and precise actions and activities occurring within the special human resource recruitment and selection program, of course, vary from program to program and from company to company. Actions that could be involved are recruiting trips to university campuses, mass media advertising of available positions, simplified selection procedures featuring the elimination of certain testing procedures, unusual compensation and benefit packages, and special seniority-priority classification (Rosenbaum).

Employee Training

Often special employee training programs are the result of human resource planning efforts. This alternative form of action recognizes that future organizational human resource needs can be met at least partially by training current employees to perform jobs that will be prevalent in the future (Clague). Often this process is best described as a retraining instead of a training effort, since new skills and abilities are to be taught to current workers who possess dated capabilities and expertise in areas that will not be in demand in the future. A common example of retraining is teaching workers to be computer technicians and programmers after previously being semi-skilled employees operating assembly-line machinery. Retraining often involves making professional white-collar wor'ers of formerly nonprofessional blue-collar employees. The purpose of employee training and retraining programs is to obtain necessary future manpower skills from current members of an organization's work force.

Management Development

When employee training occurs at the supervisory or administrative level of an organization, it is usually referred to as management development. Managerial positions are just as likely to change in scope, assigned duties, and required responsibilities as nonsupervisory jobs do. Administrative talent is difficult to develop unless planned steps are taken to this end. More and more managerial expertise is being required in almost all organizations as machine technology gradually replaces the need for human physical efforts. Mental instead of physical abilities are more frequently in demand. An enhanced number of middle management positions especially seem to be needed in the future of many organizations. A variety of techniques, such as job rotation, job enlargement, job enrichment, planned progression, and multiple management, are often used in the management development process. All such efforts are designed to enhance the administrative acumen of managers to prepare them better for future, more demanding leadership positions. Action programs in the area of management development are found in all organizations that attempt human resource planning, auditing, and forecasting procedures systematically and on a continual basis.

Labor Relations-Collective Bargaining

Human resource planning programs must often also involve labor relations and collective bargaining issues. If antiquated jobs are to be phased out, union security provisions often require worker relocation and retraining efforts. New worker skills and employee abilities to be demanded at a later date may be areas of current or future labor discontent. Often contract negotiation strategies and tactics may be part of the human resource planning process. Whether workers are moving from a unionized job to a nonunionized position or vice versa, human resource planning activities should focus future labor-management relationships. This necessitates the formulation of tentative policies, procedures, and rules that will apply to future work environments.

Benefits and Compensation

Other human resource action programs require special employee benefits and worker compensation arrangements. White-collar and blue-collar workers differ in their economic and noneconomic job expectations. Professional and nonprofessional employees vary in their demands for direct and indirect compensation sources. Managerial and nonmanagerial members of an organization are motivated by different means. Thus, when the composition and mix of an employment setting change, so should the methods of financial and nonfinancial recompense. Unique special remuneration pack-

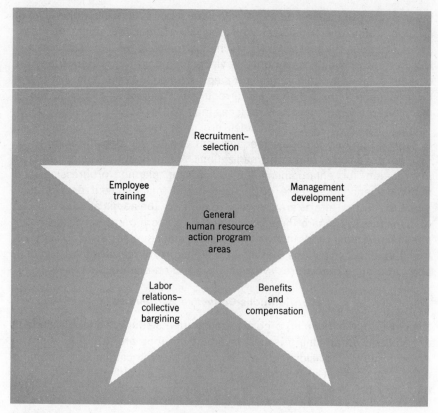

FIGURE 5-11   General human resource action program areas.

ages may be needed to attract future talent in high demand and short supply (Cheek). In any event, because "money talks," many manpower action programs directly involve rearranged financial compensation systems, and all personnel action endeavors have at least an indirect remuneration base and rationale.

Although human resource action programs may occur in other personnel areas, the five general types of action activities just mentioned, recruitment-selection, employee training, management development, labor relations-collective bargaining, and benefits and compensation, are the most common, and are identified and brought together in Figure 5-11.

Specific Legislatively Induced Action Programs

Some specific human resource planning action programs today are a direct result of legislative statutes at the state and federal levels. Nondiscrimination and even reverse-discrimination are often mandatory behaviors required of employing organizations by legislative enactments. The most important laws today leading to specific human resource planning action programs usually are collectively labeled fair employment legislation.

Fair Employment Legislation

Within the last thirty years, over half of the states in this country have passed fair employment practice laws. Nevertheless, the greatest impact on equal opportunity in employment came in 1964 at the federal level with the passage of the Civil Rights Act. A key feature of the Civil Rights Act of 1964 is Title VII, which is a provision that prohibits discrimination in employment based on race, color, religion, national origin, or sex. This provision applies not only to employers but also to labor unions and employment agencies. Most of the discrimination complaints brought under Title VII concern race and sex. These complaints have increased dramatically over the years. Figure 5-12 shows the number of race, sex, and total charges brought under Title VII from 1966 to 1971. The projection for 1974 is that EEOC will investigate some 33,000 complaints.

EEOC

Title VII is enforced by the Equal Employment Opportunity Commission (EEOC). Under the 1964 Civil Rights Act, EEOC tried to effect compliance by persuasion, conciliation, and mediation confrontations with the parties involved. If this procedure failed, EEOC had the power to request that the Attorney General bring a civil suit against the employer. But, over the years, it was found that these powers were too slow and too weak, and in 1972 amendments were passed so that EEOC can now directly bring enforcement actions to and through the federal courts. EEOC jurisdiction applies to all employers with the exception of the very smallest, who do not engage in interstate commerce.

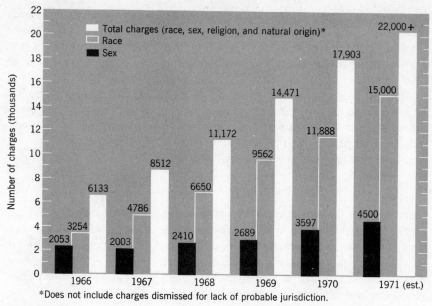

FIGURE 5-12   **Race and sex as the basis of discrimination in employment.**

OFCC

Another program that the federal government uses to enforce antidiscrimination practices is provided for under executive orders that apply to all government contractors. The most significant of these is Order No. 11,246, which was issued in 1970 and applies to some 90,000 organizations that employ about one third of the entire American labor force. Like EEOC, this order prohibits employment discrimination, but it also requires employers to take affirmative action to make sure that discriminatory practices of the past will not be continued into the future. This order is enforced by the Office of Federal Contract Compliance (OFCC) within the U.S. Department of Labor. OFCC has the authority to terminate present contracts and to prevent companies from bidding on future government contracts if they do not follow through on affirmative action programs. Because of such powers, the potential impact of OFCC is greater than that of EEOC but, to date, OFCC has suffered from lack of personnel, inefficiency, and administrative conflicts with the EEOC. OFCC regulations apply only to nonconstruction industries, and they focus on employers with contracts of $50,000 or more and fifty or more employees.

Affirmative Action

Today the phrase affirmative action is used to describe both a general philosophy and a specific activity. As a general philosophy, affirmative action is closely related to the idea of social responsibility, except that affirmative action is directed at minority groups, not at a total population, and also the emphasis is on nondiscrimination in employemnt practices instead of charity, protecting the ecological environment, and the like. Affirmative action as a general philosophy is a commitment to improve the plight of certain minority groups in our society. In this capacity, affirmative action means doing the most to improve the general well-being of all minority group members.

Specific Activity

As a specific activity, affirmative action means complying with EEOC or OFCC orders to develop nondiscriminatory employment practices. Instead of a maximum general philosophy, this is often a minimum specific employment practice plan. Affirmative action programs for EEOC or OFCC purposes include the analysis of the distribution of jobs within a company by sex, race, color, and so forth. If inequities are found, affirmative action as a specific activity requires exact steps and timetables to correct injustices. Specific affirmative action programs examined by EEOC or OFCC are especially designed to correct the underutilization of females and racial minorities. The criteria used to test fair representation are what percentage each group has of the total population and the availability of skills in each group at the present time or potentially after training. Specific affirmative action goals for improvement are significant, measurable, attainable, and scheduled on the basis of time. One of the forms that EEOC requires employers to fill out is indicated in Figure 5-13, which shows Section D of the form EEO-1; its intent is to examine the distribution of minorities at various employment levels.

Affirmative action both as a general philosophy and a specific activity developed out of a concern for certain groups in our society. Discrimination in employment practices especially stimulated the development of the affirmative action movement. The most serious forms or types of employment discrimination have been based on race, sex, and age.

Racial Discrimination

Many minority ethnic groups have found it harder than usual to find and retain jobs. Much of this was and is due to discriminatory employment practices. The affirmative action movement currently is helping to correct this situation. Corrections are taking place within all facets of the employment spectrum including recruitment, selection, hiring, placement, indoctrination, appraisal, training, and development. Today over 20,000 companies have developed minority employment programs (Janger and Schaeffer, book reference citation). One of the keys to success of such programs is to have a program director or plant manager in daily contact with the disadvantaged. Other conditions needed for successful programs include supportive coun-

Employment at this establishment—Report all permanent, temporary, or part-time employees including apprentices and on-the-job trainees unless specifically excluded as set forth in the instructions. Enter the appropriate figures on all lines and in all columns. Blank spaces will be considered as zeros. In columns 1, 2, and 3 include ALL employees in the establishment, including those in minority groups.

Job categories (See Appendix 4 for definitions)	Total employees in establishment			Minority group employees (See appendix 5 for definitions)							
				Male				Female			
	Total employees including minorities (1)	Total male including minorities (2)	Total female including minorities (3)	Negro (4)	Oriental (5)	American Indian[a] (6)	Spanish surnamed American (7)	Negro (8)	Oriental (9)	American Indian[a] (10)	Spanish surnamed American (11)
Officials & managers											
Professionals											
Technicians											
Sales workers											
Office & clerical											
Craftsmen (Skilled)											
Operatives (Semiskilled)											
Laborers (Unskilled)											
Service workers											
TOTAL →											
Total employment reported in previous EEO-1 report											

(The trainees below should also be included in the figures for the appropriate occupational categories above)

	(1)	(2)	(3)	(4)	(5)	(6)	(7)	(8)	(9)	(10)	(11)
Formal On-the-job trainees White collar											
Production											

[a]In Alaska include Eskimos and Aleuts with American Indians

1. NOTE: On consolidated report, skip questions 2-5 and Section E.
2. How was information as to race or ethnic group in Section D obtained?
   1 Visual Survey   2 Employment Record   3 Other—Specify
3. Dates of payroll period used

4. Pay period of last report submitted for this establishment
5. Does this establishment employ apprentices?
   This year?   1 Yes   2 No
   Last year?   1 Yes   2 No

FIGURE 5-13 EEOC Employer Information Report, Section D, EEO-1 Employment Data.

seling and supervision, remedial basic reading and oral skills training, and effective orientation programs. Helping minority group members handle personal problems that interfere with work attendance is also sometimes helpful. Also crucial to the success of such programs is the adequate training of the supervisors involved. Providing better employee orientation, training, and development programs so as to make such workers ultimately promotable is also crucial to the long-run effectiveness of these programs. Such conditions, when developed appropriately, usually require years and years of implementation time.

Sex Discrimination

Problems relating to sex discrimination have emerged during the 1970s as a major concern for personnel managers. As shown in Figure 5-12, the EEOC has faced an increasing number of sex discrimination complaints over the years. One problem involved with sex discrimination cases is that some sex discrimination is permissible where sex is a "bona fide occupational qualification" (BFOQ) necessary to an employer's normal operation. What constitutes a BFOQ is subject to different interpretations in various courts, although this provision is becoming narrower in scope. Courts have held that waitresses, barmaids, and stewardesses need not necessarily be female, nor that truck drivers, trash collectors, or construction workers need always be male. General assumptions of characteristics and stereotypes of men and women often no longer stand up in court. For example, women cannot be denied jobs as sales people because they are considered less aggressive than men. A few jobs may, however, still be reserved only for men or women on the basis of community standards of morality or propriety, as in the case of restroom attendants.

The historic issue of not hiring women for jobs that require certain physical strengths has generally not been upheld in court. The Occupational Safety and Health Act of 1970 limits the amount of weight to be handled during certain jobs, and these limitations typically do not eliminate women from doing the normal job routine. Also, some cases have proven that many women are stronger than their male counterparts who are performing the same type of job requirements. In general, courts have upheld the EEOC position that weight-lifting requirements do not constitute a bona fide occupational qualification.

Women are underrepresented in the better paying and higher-status jobs in the United States (Verway). The Census Bureau found in 1970 that women earn about half the pay men do for the same jobs. There are, of course, industries and jobs in which women have done reasonably well, but many of these are sex-typed jobs such as nursing, social work, elementary education, fashion design, retailing, advertising, public relations, and banking. Departmentally and functionally, more women are found in personnel and marketing than in operations and accounting (Buckley).

Age Discrimination

Public policy and federal legislation with respect to the employment of older workers has changed considerably over the years. For example, the Social Security Act of 1935 was designed to encourage older people to retire from the labor market by the age of sixty-five. Most employers have instituted private pension funds to augment federal social security benefits. By the mid-1960s, there were signs that the public policy of encouraging older workers to leave the labor force was having some negative effects. The percentage of older people in the population was increasing steadily, but the job opportunities for men and women declined markedly when they reached the age of forty-five. One reason for this was the high cost of funding adequate retirement benefits for older workers. Eventually Congress enacted the Age Discrimination Act of 1967, which provides many of the same prohibitions against discrimination in employment for persons aged forty to sixty-five that Title VII of the Civil Rights Act of 1964 provided with respect to race, sex, religion, and national origin. There are, of course, certain exceptions for BFOC's based on age, such as the federal regulations that limit the age of airline pilots. The Age Discrimination Act of 1967 is not enforced by the EEOC, but is, instead, administered by the U. S. Department of Labor with little provision for effecting remedies for older workers suffering discrimination. Thus the impact so far of the Age Discrimination Act on personnel practices has been much less than the influence generated by the Civil Rights Act.

The typical way in which pensions are funded makes it more expensive to employ older workers. But much research is available to show that older workers (i.e., those over age forty), often do more accurate work, plan ahead better, and even learn as well as younger employees do. Also, just because pension costs are higher for older workers does not mean that total expenses are higher for employers who hire and retain older employees. This is so because workmen's compensation, sickness, accident, absenteeism, training, and other costs are either higher with younger workers or do not vary appreciably between younger and older workers (Fjerstad).

State Discrimination Statutes

A number of states and even some cities have passed fair employment practice laws outlawing discrimination on the basis of race, color, religion, and national origin. These laws vary considerably in enforcement provisions and applicable penalties, and they have been known to change in coverage over the years. In addition, some states even have passed laws prohibiting age and sex discrimination in employment. Figure 5-14 shows which states have statutes constraining employment decisions in these ways.

State	Type of Illegal Discrimination		
	Racial, religious	Sex	Age
Alabama	–	–	–
Alaska	×	×	×
Arizona	×	×	–
Arkansas	–	–	–
California	×	×	×
Colorado	×	×	×
Connecticut	×	×	×
Delaware	×	×	×
District of Columbia	×	×	–
Florida	–	–	–
Georgia	–	–	×
Hawaii	×	×	×
Idaho	×	×	×
Illinois	×	×	×
Indiana	×	×	×
Iowa	×	×	×
Kansas	×	×	–
Kentucky	×	×	×
Louisiana	–	–	×
Maine	×	–	×
Maryland	×	×	×
Massachusetts	×	×	×
Michigan	×	×	×
Minnesota	×	×	–
Mississippi	–	–	–
Missouri	×	×	–
Montana	×	×	×
Nebraska	×	×	×
Nevada	×	×	–
New Hampshire	×	×	×
New Jersey	×	×	×
New Mexico	×	×	×
New York	×	×	×
North Carolina	–	–	–
North Dakota	–	–	×
Ohio	×	–	×
Oklahoma	×	×	–
Oregon	×	×	×
Pennsylvania	×	×	×
Puerto Rico	×	–	×
Rhode Island	×	×	×
South Carolina	–	–	–
South Dakota	–	×	–
Tennessee	–	–	–
Texas	–	–	–
Utah	×	×	–
Vermont	×	×	–
Virginia	–	–	–
Washington	×	×	×
West Virginia	×	×	×
Wisconsin	×	×	×
Wyoming	×	×	–

Source. Compiled from Bureau of National Affairs, Inc., *Fair Employment Practices* (Washington, D.C., 1972), pp. 25-28, 451.

FIGURE 5-14   State fair employment practice laws.

Very often state fair employment practice laws are more powerful than the federal law because state agencies usually have the power to take direct action against violators. When both state and federal laws cover a discrimination situation, first the complaint is brought to the state agency where, if it is not settled, it must wait sixty days before going to the federal EEOC. When conflicts appear, federal requirements take precedence over state statutes.

4. Total Systems Model

The components of human resource planning have been discussed in previous sections of this chapter. These components are objectives, organization planning, human resource auditing, human resource forecasting, and action programs including affirmative action and EEOC. These components, when pictured properly, should be thought of as interrelated sequential steps, as shown in Figure 5-15. Often it is difficult to tell where one step ends and the next step begins. In addition to being cyclical, the human resource planning process is also recyclical, as shown by the feedback loop in Figure 5-15. Human resource planning activities are formulated and reformulated on a continual basis. All components and facets of the human resource planning process are intimately interrelated in a dynamic ongoing fashion (Walker, 1970). Manpower objectives are part of the organization planning process. Human resource auditing and forecasting activities are closely related, and only their time perspectives vary. Action programs implement the conclusions reached during planning, auditing, and forecasting stages. Action programs result in new manpower objectives, and the entire human resource planning sequence begins anew.

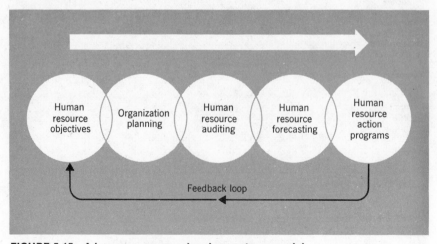

FIGURE 5-15   A human resource planning systems model.

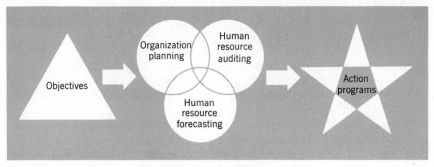

FIGURE 5-16   The human resource planning process.

An alternative diagrammatic portrayal of the human resource planning process is shown in Figure 5-16. Again the sequence of human resource components is illustrated, but now the especially highly interrelated nature of the middle component steps is emphasized. Organization planning, human resource auditing, and human resource forecasting are shown as partially overlapping set entities. These aspects of human resource planning in reality are often performed simultaneously instead of separately (Miller and Haire). They are not totally distinct activities either in time nor in scope of operation. Collectively they lead to and result in human resource action programs. These relationships and interrelationships among human resource planning components are so indicated in Figure 5-16.

5. Summary

Human resource planning is the process of determining personnel requirements and the means for meeting those requirements in order to carry out the integrated plans of an organization. Human resource planning activities are important in individual, organizational, and national arenas in order to bring about the optimal utilization of human resources. Human resource planning is best thought of as a systematic procedure featuring a planned sequence of events or a series of chronological steps. These steps or events are the components of the human resource planning process. Human resource planning components include: (1) objectives; (2) organization planning; (3) human resource auditing; (4) human resource forecasting; and (5) action programs, including affirmative action and EEOC. All components and facets of the human resource planning process are intimately interrelated in a systematic, dynamic, ongoing fashion. The middle steps within the process, organization planning, human resource auditing, and human resource forecasting, are especially highly interrelated in nature, time, and scope.

DISCUSSION QUESTIONS AND ASSIGNMENTS

1. Define the human resource planning concept.
2. Discuss the importance of human resource planning activities.
3. Explain the similarities and differences between human resource auditing and human resource forecasting procedures.
4. Describe in your own words the relationship between human resource planning and organization planning.
5. Develop your own total systems model of the components of the human resource planning process.
6. Formulate a detailed five-year plan for yourself relating to your career goals and objectives. Include all relevant projected job experiences, educational opportunities, changes in the family unit, and other anticipated events and activities that will affect your personal development during the next five years.

REFERENCES

General Book References

Beaumont, R. A., *Manpower and Planning.* New York: Industrial Relations Counselors, 1970.

Burack, Elmer H., *Strategies for Manpower Planning and Programming.* Morristown, N.J.: General Learning, 1972.

Burack, Elmer H., and James H. Walker, *Manpower Planning and Programming for Change.* Boston: Allyn and Bacon, 1973.

Ginzberg, E., *Manpower Agenda for America.* New York: McGraw-Hill, 1968.

Glueck, William F., *Organization Planning and Development.* New York: American Management Association, 1971.

Greenlaw, Paul S., and Robert D. Smith, *Personnel Management: A Management Science Approach.* Scranton, Pa.: International Textbook, 1970.

Heneman, H. G., and G. Seltzer, *Employer Manpower Planning and Forecasting.* Washington, D.C.: U.S. Department of Labor, Manpower Research Monograph No. 19, Government Printing Office, 1970.

Janger, Allen, and Ruth Schaeffer, *Managing Programs to Employ the Disadvantaged.* New York: Studies in Personnel Policy No. 219, National Industrial Conference Board, 1970.

Lecht, L. A., *Manpower Needs for National Goals in the 1970s.* New York: Praeger, 1969.

Manpower Report of the President. Washington, D.C.: U.S. Government Printing Office, 1971.

Morrison, E. J., *Developing Computer-Based Employee Information Systems.* New York: American Management Association, 1969.

Towers, Perrin, Forster, and Crosby, *Corporate Manpower Planning.* Philadelphia: TPF/C, 1971.

Wasmuth, William C., et al., *Human Resources Administration: Problems of Growth and Change.* Boston: Houghton-Mifflin, 1970.

Weber, Arnold, Frank Cassell, and Woodrow Ginsburg (eds.), *Public-Private Manpower Policies.* Madison, Wisc.: Industrial Relations Research Association, University of Wisconsin Press, 1969.

Wikstrom, W. S., *Manpower Planning: Evolving Systems.* New York: Conference Board, 1971.

Specific Journal References

Bartholomew, D. J., "Decision-Making in Manpower Planning," *Operational Research Quarterly, 19* (2), 1968, pp. 129–132.

Bassett, Glenn A., "Manpower Forecasting and Planning, Problems and Solutions," *Personnel, 47* (5), 1970, pp. 8–16.

Berry, William F., "What a Personnel EDP System Should Do," *Personnel, 46* (1), 1969, pp. 18–21.

Buckley, John, "Pay Differences Between Men and Women in the Same Job," *Monthly Labor Review, 94* (11), 1971, pp. 36–39.

Burckhardt, Wenzel, "Planning for Manpower Utilization," *Personnel Administrator, 15* (3), 1970, pp. 36–40.

Cheek, L. M., "Personnel Computer Systems," *Business Horizons, 14* (4), 1971, pp. 69–76.

Clague, Ewan, "Government Employment and Manpower Planning in the 1970's," *Public Personnel Review, 31* (4), 1970, pp. 279–282.

Coleman, Bruce P., "An Integrated System for Manpower Planning," *Business Horizons, 13* (5), 1970, pp. 89–95.

Cox, Arne, "Personnel Planning, Objectives and Methods: Presentation of an Integrated System," *Management International Review, 8* (4-5), 1968, pp. 104–114.

Crowley, M. F., "Projected Requirements for Technicians in 1980," *Monthly Labor Review, 93* (5), 1970, pp. 13–17.

Fjerstad, Robert, "Is it Economical to Hire the Over Forty-Five Worker?," *Personnel Administration, 28* (2), 1965, pp. 24–30.

Haire, Mason, "Approach to an Integrated Personnel Policy," *Industrial Relations, 9* (2), 1968, pp. 107–117.

Heiser, R. T., "Auditing the Personnel Function in a Decentralized, Multi-Unit Organization," *Personnel Journal, 47* (3), 1968, pp. 180–183.

Maki, Dennis, "A Programming Approach to Manpower Planning," *Industrial and Labor Relations Review, 23* (3), 1970, pp. 397–405.

Miller, James R., III, and Mason Haire, "Manplan: A Micro-Simulator of Manpower Planning," *Behavioral Science, 15* (6), 1970, pp. 524–531.

Morrissey, Charles A., "Long-Range Planning in Personnel: Impact of the Computer," *Personnel Administration, 31* (2), 1968, pp. 35–38.

Peterson, Richard B., "The Growing Role of Manpower Forecasting in Organizations," *Business Topics, 10* (4), 1969, pp. 7–14.

Rosenbaum, B. L., "The Manpower Inventory — A Powerful Tool," *Personnel Journal, 46* (2), 1967, pp. 85–88.

Rowland, Kendrith M., "Forecasting Current Practices," *Personnel Administrator, 13* (1), 1968, pp. 23–27.

Rowland, Kendrith M., and Michael G. Sovereign, "Markov-chain Analysis of Internal Manpower Supply," *Industrial Relations, 9* (1), 1969, pp. 86–90.

Steiner, George, "Rise of the Corporate Planner," *Harvard Business Review, 48* (5), 1970, pp. 133–139.

Swerdloff, S., "How Good Were Manpower Projections for the 1960's?" *Monthly Labor Review, 92* (11), 1969, pp. 17–22.

Travis, Sophia C., "The U.S. Labor Force: Projections to 1985," *Monthly Labor Review, 93* (5), 1970, pp. 4–5.

Verway, David, "Advance to the Rear for Women," *MSU Business Topics, 20* (2), 1972, pp. 53–62.

Walker, Alfred J., "Evaluating Existing Computerized Personnel Data Systems," *Personnel Journal, 49* (9), 1970, pp. 742–745.

Walker, James W., "Forecasting Manpower Needs," *Harvard Business Review, 47* (2), 1969, pp. 152–164.

Walker, James W., "Models in Manpower Planning," *Business Horizons, 14* (2), 1971, pp. 87–95.

Wright, Robert, "Managing Man as a Capital Asset," *Personnel Journal, 49* (4), 1970, pp. 290–298.

contents

learning objectives

1. To envision and understand the overall importance of the staffing or employment function.

2. To be able to identify and explain the techniques used within the staffing subsets of recruitment, selection, placement, indoctrination, and appraisal.

3. To recognize the integrative and omnipresent nature of the human resource appraisal process.

4. To become aware of and acquainted with both traditional and modern appraisal methods.

Human resources are the most important and valuable resources of any organization.

6

Staffing and Appraisal

1. Staffing and Appraisal Semantics

Employment and staffing are interchangeable personnel concepts. Staffing involves the employment function as it relates to all organizational personnel, not to only those in staff instead of line positions. I prefer the term staffing to employment because staffing is more of a dynamic concept and thus more descriptive of actual organizational employment activities. The "ing" ending of staffing helps to emphasize that all aspects of the employment function are ongoing and viable. The term employment has a static and dormant connotation that instills one with a heavy feeling of inertia rather than a lively sense of change (Martin).

Staffing and Human Resource Planning

The concept of human resource planning is often similar to the staffing (employment) concept. These terms overlap considerably, but there is a major difference between them. Staffing concerns itself largely with present or current employment activities, while human resource planning focuses on future manpower needs and requirements. Staffing deals with real facts and figures, while much of planning is concerned with forecasted and projected data.

Staffing Subprocesses

Many subprocesses or subfunctions are associated with the overall staffing or employment concept. The exact number and precise labeling of these subareas are unknown. In this chapter, I will discuss recruitment, selection, placement, indoctrination, and appraisal. These activities are considered the main components of the overall staffing or employment function by most personnel practitioners and authors.

Appraisal versus Assessment

The appraisal portion of the overall staffing function is similar in many respects to what a modern manpower manager means by assessment. This appraisal or assessment in the past often emphasized current job performance, but now the stress is usually on future organizational potential. Appraisal is concerned with current job performance and "here and now" situations, while assessment concentrates on future company potential under hypothetical "there and then" conditions.

Assessment Emphasis

The term assessment is preferred by many modern manpower managers to older personnel concepts such as testing, appraisal, evaluating, and merit rating for a number of reasons. The term assessment is more neutral in connotation than emotionally laden terms such as those just mentioned. Individuals prefer to be assessed instead of tested, appraised, or evaluated (Greer). Also, the term assessment implies a much more scientific, objective, and comprehensive analysis than that provided by an evaluation, appraisal, or test. Assessment procedures are usually many and varied in scope and dimension. Subjective and qualitative judgments, although not completely eliminated, are minimized. Current job performance is only one of many employee behaviors assessed. Social, educational, human relations, and other skills often are also judged with an eye toward the future. Additionally, the term assessment is in vogue today, and it is somewhat of a fad and status symbol for a company to possess an assessment employee procedure. Assessment concepts are being used by many of the leading and progressive companies in various industries. Any company can gain a measure of this avant garde feeling if and when it introduces a new comprehensive (or renames its old antiquated) employee appraisal system. But, in reality, the assessment concept is more than a flippant fad; it is a serious movement away from biased, negatively oriented, pressure-filled, unscientifically based, superficial, job-related work appraisals to more objective, positively oriented, comprehensive, global organizationally related employee assessments. The assessment concept will be discussed in greater depth in a later appraisal topic subdivision in this chapter.

2. Recruitment

Recruitment is the act or process of an organization attempting to obtain additional manpower for operational purposes. Recruiting involves acquiring further human resources to serve as institutional inputs. When new supplies of men for service have been gathered, recruitment has taken place. The goal of recruitment is to create a large pool of persons who are available and willing to work for a particular company. The recruitment function is positive in that it persuades people to apply for work at a particular company or institution.

Internal-External

Institutionally, recruitment may be done internally or externally. When a person is needed to fulfill a vacant organizational position, this individual may eventually come from inside or outside the company. Some companies prefer to recruit from within, since this aids employee morale, loyalty, and motivation. Other corporations prefer to recruit externally to prevent inbreeding and to encourage new ways of thinking. Although recruitment policies vary considerably from one organization to another, the general rule is to promote from within whenever anyone in the company has the necessary and required qualifications needed for the vacant position (Mayfield).

Internal Sources

Additional manpower resources may be acquired by an organization in different ways. Internally, job applicants are frequently found by reviewing performance records and by a job posting or bidding system (Travaglio). Often additional employees are obtained by nepotism, that is, by asking current employees to inform their friends and relatives that the company is going to hire some additional workers. Often managerial positions, especially lower-level ones, can be staffed by checking the company personnel records, including performance evaluation reports, determining which current employees deserve a promotion, and then offering the unoccupied post to a worthy current employee. Some companies expand this basic idea into a formal job bidding or posting system. This involves the practice of announcing all job vacancies on company bulletin boards and inviting employee bids or applications. The bulletin board notice specifies the job title, rate of pay, and qualifications that the employee must possess. The principal virtue of the job post and bid system is that it grants every qualified employee a fair opportunity to obtain a better job. In addition, it reduces the likelihood of special deals and favoritism from entering into recruitment and selection processes.

External Sources

External sources of manpower include public employment agencies, private employment agencies, labor unions, walk-ons, advertising, college recruiting, and professional association contacts. Public employment offices concentrate their efforts heavily on certain occupational groups, such as domestic service, farm and construction labor, unskilled and skilled factory work, and retail store sales clerks. Many private employment agencies concentrate on white-collar office and retail sales personnel, because demand is generally high, and turnover is great. It is primarily in those occupations in which the employees are represented by craft unions that much of the hiring process is carried on through union hiring halls (e.g., construction, longshoring, maritime, clothing, and popular dance bands). For jobs requiring only routine abilities and skill, many employers are able to fill their labor needs largely by means of direct hiring of "walk-on" job applicants. Many organizations advertise for manpower in newspapers, trade magazines, and professional society journals. College and university recruiting is done for engineering and scientific personnel primarily by larger companies. Often also some companies seek additional professional personnel by contacting professional societies and associations and asking them for their assistance in finding properly qualified persons for their current executive job openings.

Recruitment Criteria

Many factors and criteria affect organizational recruiting practices and choices. Of course, applicant qualifications are important. The issue of inside versus outside priority must be decided. The obligation of social responsibility to disadvantaged groups is an alternative consideration. Mandatory federal legislation, executive orders, and suggested state guidelines dictate certain company recruiting policies. The exact role of nepotism and friendship within the recruitment function must also be made perfectly clear through appropriate policy statements. All of these criteria and factors make employee recruitment a much more complicated employment function than it first appears. Because organizations weigh such considerations differently, recruitment practices and policies deviate tremendously within and among various organizations. Figure 6-1 summarizes the above discussion of recruitment sources and recruitment criteria.

RECRUITMENT

SOURCES	CRITERIA
1. College placement offices	1. Agency guidelines
2. General public	2. Applicant qualifications
3. Job bidding or posting	3. Executive orders
4. Labor unions	4. Federal legislation
5. Private employment agencies	5. Nepotism
6. Professional associations	6. Social responsibility
7. Public employment agencies	7. State laws

FIGURE 6-1   Recruitment "sources" and "criteria."

3. Selection

Selecting is choosing. Any selection is a collection of things chosen. The selection process involves picking out by preference some objects or things from among others. In reference to staffing and employment, selection refers specifically to the decision to hire a limited number of workers from a group of potential employees. The objective of employment selection is the sorting out or elimination of those judged unqualified to meet job and organizational requirements (Bahn).

Negative Process

Recruitment was explained as a positive process; selection is somewhat negative, because it rejects a large portion of those who apply. Recruitment involves selling the organization to the potential employee, while selection requires the employee to sell himself to the organization (Owens and Jewell).
It is very difficult to define where recruitment ends and selection begins. It is intuitively obvious and commonly assumed that selection occurs after recruitment takes place. But the line of demarcation between the employment recruitment and the selection processes is ambiguous and unclearly defined.) *Cumulins*

Hiring

Some authors refer to the employment selection process as the hiring process. Hiring and selection are similar and interchangeable employment concepts when the term hiring is interpreted broadly. If the term hiring is interpreted literally and more specifically, however, it constitutes only a minor aspect of the total employee selection process. An employee is either hired or not hired at the tail end of the selection process. Potential employees go through a battery of tests and interviews, an employment decision is made, and then actual hiring or not hiring takes place. Because the hiring process is interpreted by both a broad and a narrow perspective, in general the term selection is preferable to the term hiring.

Unfortunately, often company recruitment and selection policies are not in perfect alignment. Some organizations spend exorbitant amounts for recruiting purposes trying to attract numerous potential employees to the corporation when, in fact, they can financially and structurally afford to select only a few of these many applicants. Such discrepancies often exist, especially in larger companies, because these two functions are not always carried out or even supervised by the same person. Much more must be done to coordinate employee recruiting and staff selection policies and practices within many institutions.

Selection Techniques

Managers use various techniques to assist them in employee selection. The most common devices are the application blank, tests, interviews, a background investigation (including reference checks), and a medical examination (Rabourn, Schilz, and Holland). These techniques chronologically are usually used within the overall employee selection process in the sequence in which they were presented above. These individual selection techniques and devices will now be discussed in greater detail.

A. APPLICATION BLANK

An application blank is usually the initial source of information an employer has about a particular employee. Virtually all organizations use some form of an application report or questionnaire. Such data enable a prospective employer to get a quick look at a job seeker's general background and qualifications (Meyer). Although almost everyone agrees that application blanks are needed, there is no general consensus about what type of information should be requested or filled in on this application form (Hershey). Federal and state laws often now prevent the inclusion of certain types of data on application questionnaires. Even the most rudimentary types of information today are being contested by some concerned group or challenged within the judicial court system by some organization that feels discriminated against. Women often do not want a sexual distinction to be noted on application forms. Young and old employees are trying to prevent the inclusion of age information. Racial and religious information has now been banned from most application questionnaires, although such data are still commonly recorded on other forms for governmental reporting purposes. The validity of data relating to an individual's personal background, such as his marital status, number of dependents, length of residency, and even his former employers, has also been questioned. The use of a person's name has even been said to be a discriminating factor, especially if the application blank asks one to identify whether or not he or she is a "Mr.," "Miss," or "Mrs." The relevance of every item of information on an application blank is being challenged today (Goldstein). As a consequence, many employers really do not know what is the best information to ask for via the application form. Although this dilemma continues to exist, nevertheless, all employers use some form or type of application blank, because nothing has yet been suggested or invented that gathers such needed general employee information in a more efficient or effective manner (Novack).

B. TESTING

In our society tests are used for a variety of purposes. In an employment setting, tests are primarily used for the selection of new employees (Inskeep). However, tests are also used to place or assign persons to jobs, to choose employees for promotion and transfer within the organization, to determine candidates for assignment to a company training program, and to act as an aid for diagnosis when counseling individual problem employees.

Test Definition

The concept of a test has been defined in many ways. In essence, a test is a systematic procedure for sampling human behavior. Tests are used in order to compare the behavior of two or more persons. Tests are designed to sample various aspects of an individual's behavior or performance and attitude.

Declining Emphasis

Until recently, testing programs have generally achieved increasing significance in company selection matters. However, a higher percentage of large companies use tests than small ones do. Within the last few years, many large and small companies are beginning to stress testing less because of governmental pressures to validate testing procedures (Mosher). When faced with the mandatory alternatives of validating one's tests or not using tests at all, many companies have abandoned their testing programs almost completely. It takes considerable time, effort, and money to validate a test battery. Instead of going through these expenses and complications, many organizations have simply dispensed with testing activities, and they have no immediate plans to acquire and establish properly validated tests.

Testing Rationale

Valid tests may aid company selection procedures in a number of ways. One result is the hiring of better qualified employees. This, in turn, can lead to less turnover, lower training costs, higher output, and better quality of work. Better job adjusting and fewer placement errors can also result from valid testing techniques. Valid tests can add significantly to the accuracy of predicting job success.

Even valid tests should, however, only be used as supplemental selection techniques. No test should ever be used as the sole criterion for applicant selection. Test results must be used with discretion and must never be substituted for thoughtful judgment. When valid tests are regarded as only a part of the total selection process, they are performing the role for which they were intended and are best suited.

Types of Tests

Tests can be classified according to the type of human behavior measured. Tests commonly are classified as (1) aptitude, (2) achievement, (3) vocational interest, (4) personality, and (5) projective.

APTITUDE ⋏

Aptitude tests measure the latent or potential ability to do something. Some aptitude tests measure general mental ability or intelligence, while other aptitude tests gauge special aptitudes, such as mechanical aptitude dexterity, clerical ability, sales knowhow, vision, and perception. Psychological testing began with mental ability or intelligence testing around 1900. More work has been done in creating, developing, experimenting, and refining general intelligence tests than with any other type of test. Some of the most commonly used general aptitude tests include the Otis Employment Tests, the Adaptability Test, the Wesman Personnel Classification Tests, and the Wonderlic Personnel Test. Most of these tests contain several alternative versions, some designed for people of different educational attainments, and others equivalent in difficulty level to minimize the change of a person obtaining a higher score than he normally would simply because he had recently taken the exact same test elsewhere (Bennis).

A great number and variety of special aptitude tests currently are available (Bemisse). For example, mechanical aptitude tests measure the capacities of spatial visualization, perceptual speed, and knowledge of mechanical matter. Abilities such as manual dexterity, motor ability, and eye-hand coordination are measured by psychomotor types of special aptitude tests. Clerical aptitude tests, measuring ability items such as spelling, computation, comparisons, copying, and work meaning have also been created to measure specific capacities involved in office work.

ACHIEVEMENT ✗

Achievement tests, which are also often called proficiency tests, measure an achieved skill or an acquired knowledge. Usually this acquired skill or knowledge is obtained as the result of a training program or because of on-the-job experience. Achievement tests ordinarily are classified into two categories. One measures job knowledge and may be either written or oral. The other category is labeled work sample, since it involves administering a typical portion of an actual job as a test.

VOCATIONAL INTEREST ✗

Vocational interest tests are inventories of the likes and dislikes of people in relation to occupations, hobbies, and recreational activities. The basic idea and assumption behind these tests is that a definite pattern of interests exists for those who are successful in any occupation. If a person seeking a career has similar interests to those who have proven to be successful at a particular vocation, such a person should then consider this occupation as his calling, because he, too, is likely to be successful in this field. In general, interest tests are more useful for vocational guidance than they are for employee selection because it is possible to fake or slant respondent replies in a manner believed to be preferred by an employer. Currently, the Strong Vocational Interest Blank and the Kuder Preference Record are the most popular and commonly used interest tests.

PERSONALITY √

Personality tests seek to evaluate characteristics such as emotional maturity, sociability, responsibility, conformity, objectivity, ascendancy, and nervous symptoms (Cannedy). Most personality tests are of the objective type (i.e., they are paper and pencil tests or personality inventories). Personality inventories, like interest inventories, can be faked by sophisticated candidates and thus also are best used for counseling instead of for selection purposes (Sparks). Among the most commonly used personality tests are the Bernreuter Personality Inventory, the Humm-Wadsworth Temperament Scale, the Guilford-Martin Personnel Inventory, and the Minnesota Multiphasic Personality Inventory.

PROJECTIVE

Projective tests are special types of personality tests. In a projective test, the subject is asked to project his own interpretation into certain standard stimuli situations. The meanings that a person ascribes to these stimuli depend on his own values, motives, and personality. Two of the most widely used projective tests are the Rorschach ink blot test and the Thematic Apperception Test. Projective tests also can be faked and thus are better for counseling than for selection purposes. Projective tests have been especially criticized recently because they are unscientific and often are more revealing of the personality of the test designer, administrator, or evaluator than they are of the test subject (Cannedy).

Guides to Testing

There are many rules and principles that should be followed and observed whenever the testing alternative is considered. The following conditions are frequently suggested as testing guidelines.

1. Tests as supplements. No test should ever be used as the sole criterion for anything, whether it be selection, placement, promotion, transfer, or whatever. Even valid tests represent only a small sample of a person's total pattern of behavior.

2. Tests are better at predicting failure than success. Much empirical evidence is available to support the contention that testing procedures often determine what subjects will not or cannot perform a job satisfactorily, but they are not adept at determining who can or will perform such duties in a very effective and efficient (successful) manner (Korman).

3. Tests as a screening device. Tests are useful when it is necessary to pick a small, select group from many applicants. When hundreds of candidates are applying for a few job openings, testing can properly serve as a preliminary selection technique.

4. Test scores are not precise measures. Because tests are samples of behavior, they cannot be totally accurate predictors of anything. A test score of 90 does not precisely reveal a 90 percent grasp of the testing subject matter. Test subjects with the highest test scores are not always better choices for a job than are those scoring lower.

5. Tests must be validated. Every test should be validated within the particular organization in which it is being used. The validity of a test is the degree to which it measures what it is intended to measure. It is always necessary to test the test itself before any degree of confidence can be placed in its ability to predict successful performance on the job. The only way to validate a test is to conduct a research investigation within the environment in which the test is being used. This practice, which is now often required by federal law, frequently is not done because of ignorance and the expense involved. Besides being valid, tests must also be reliable. The reliability of a test is the consistency with which it yields the same score throughout a series of measurements. This means that a person should receive the same score whenever (in time) he takes a test, unless some significant educational process has taken place between testing dates.

C. INTERVIEWING

Interviewing is the most common selection method. All organizations use interviews to help assess candidates for employment; most employers use multiple interviews during the employment process. An interview may be thought of as a conversation or verbal interaction, normally between two people, for a particular purpose. Selection interviews have numerous objectives. An interviewer is interested in determining whether or not a candidate is suitable for employment in the organization he represents. The interviewee's qualifications for a particular job are analyzed and discussed. Most interviews are designed so that a candidate is given sufficient information about the organization, the job, and the company manpower situation so that he is able to make an intelligent decision on acceptance or rejection of the job if it should be offered to him. Another objective of the selection interview is to create a feeling of good will between the applicant and the company and its management.

Types of Interviews

Many types of interviews take place within organizations. Some are intended for selection purposes, while others concentrate on appraisal, counseling, or data gathering. Types of interviews can also be classified according to their techniques or structure. The planned interview, which has also been referred to as the depth interview or the action interview, is semistructured in nature and utilizes questions in key areas that have been outlined or stated in advance by the interviewer. Typical subjects discussed include the candidate's home life, education, previous work experience, attitudes, and recreational interests. On the other hand, the interviewer provides institutional information about the organization, nature of work, pay, opportunities for advancement, and demands made on the employee. This type of interview is a compromise between the completely directive and the completely nondirective philosophies of interviewing. Very strict directive interviews are often called patterned or standardized interviews. Such interviews use a comprehensive questionnaire format and are highly structured. The subjects covered in this form of interviewing are similar to that of the planned interview except now such considerations are covered in greater detail. Interviews are also said to be unstructured when they are highly nondirective and relatively nonplanned as to format.

A final common interview is the stress interview. During a stress interview, the interviewer assumes a role of hostility toward the subject. The interviewer plays the role of an interrogator as he attempts to put a candidate on the defensive by deliberately seeking to annoy, embarrass, or frustrate him. In general, stress interviews are inappropriate as selection techniques except when interviewing candidates for work where action under stress is an essential ingredient of the job (e.g., in police work).

Structures of Interviews

The general format of interview situations varies considerably. The respective roles of an interviewer and an interviewee often differ immensely from one selection setting to another. It is usually assumed that the interviewer must initially take the lead in establishing rapport and a relaxed atmosphere. However, it is generally agreed that the total time allocation should be approximately equally divided in terms of who should do the most talking. Questions and information should mutually be exchanged between the employer representative and the potential employee. Also, in general, broad, leading, open-ended questions should be used by both parties when interviewing each other instead of specific inquiries that can be answered by either a simple "yes" or "no".

Hazards of Interviewing

There are many hazards that must be avoided if at all possible during the interviewing process. Interviewers must beware of biases, prejudices, and subjective emotions (Pickens). Such factors cannot be totally eliminated, but they can be discounted if an interviewer is fully aware of his attitudes and emotions. Interviewers must also guard against the condition called the "halo effect." The halo effect occurs when a single prominent characteristic of a candidate dominates an interviewer's judgment of all his other traits. This impression may be either positive or negative. For example, if a person is neat and clean-cut, an interviewer might also assume that he is intelligent, alert, ambitious, or dependable. On the other hand, if a candidate is sloppy and slovenly, the employer representative might conclude that he is also ignorant and lacking in essential skills and job knowledge. A final pitfall is the failure to listen. Often interviewing parties have a tendency to talk too much and listen too little. In addition, when they do appear to be listening, they too often are hearing but not comprehending the conversation (Asher).

Interview Research Findings

During the last decade, the selection interview has been subjected to a great deal of criticism (Carlson). Most of this criticism has stressed a general lack of evidence concerning the interview's reliability and validity. Much research about interviewing techniques has taken place, but often such studies present conclusions that are not always in agreement. Although skepticism about the relevance of the selection interview continues, no employment technique or device has yet been found that is better suited than the interview as a pragmatic employee appraisal and assessment methodology. In spite of the fact that there has been little coordinated research to date, there are enough consistent results to make a few fairly definite statements about what is and what is not true about the selection interview (Wright).

1. Intra-rater reliability of the interview appears to be satisfactory. This in essence means that an interviewer reinterviewing the same interviewee arrives at approximately the same rating he did originally.

2. Inter-rater reliability is extremely low if the interview is unstructured. In other words, when the interviewer-interviewee format is loose and nondirected, two different interviewers will not have consistent ratings of the same employee candidate.

3. Inter-rater reliability is satisfactory if the interview is structured. When two different interviewers are forced into evaluating the exact same candidate information, they usually agree on their assessment and evaluation of the employee data.

4. Even if an interview is proven to be reliable, it still may not be valid. Just because an interview gathers consistent data and judgments is no real indication that the interview measures what it is supposed to measure (which allegedly is potential, productive employee performance).

5. High interview assessments are not directly related to later performance. High interview appraisals given by individual interviewers are not related to eventual employee success on the job.

6. Team interviewing increases the <u>validity possibility</u>. When interviewers work together as a board or when interviewers converse separately with an applicant and later pool their judgments, candidate appraisals seem to be better related to later job success and performance.

7. Attitudes and biases of an interviewer affect interviewee appraisals. Such factors can be guarded against and discounted, but they can never be totally eliminated.

8. Interviewers are influenced more by unfavorable than favorable information. An interview is primarily a search for negative data.

9. Interviewers make employment decisions early during an unstructured interview. Preliminary application blank information and first visual impressions of an applicant's personal appearance are the bases on which many interviewers make their candidate-employment decision. This decision is often formed within the first few minutes of an unstructured interview.

10. During unstructured interviews, the interviewer generally talks more than the interviewee. This finding violates the frequently stated rule that the interviewee should do slightly more than half of the talking during an employment interview.

D. BACKGROUND INVESTIGATION AND REFERENCE CHECKS

Background investigations rely on the general principle that the best guide to what a person will do in the future is what he has done in the past. Sources of such information include school and college officials, previous employers, character references, and other persons familiar with the life or work of the candidate. If the employment manager himself is doing the checking, such information is best gathered by telephone or by personal visit instead of by reference letters, which tend to be of a standard format and are generally less frank and specific. When background checks are used, it is important to get more than one or two viewpoints (Nash and Carroll). It is vitally important also for such references to indicate how long and in what capacity they had contact with an applicant. There is wide variation in industry today pertaining to the degree to which employing organizations use background investigations and reference checks as part of their overall selection program (Gunn). Some employment managers feel that such investigations are useless because it is a rare person who will list on his application persons who would supply anything but a most favorable recommendation. Other employers consider reference checking to be an integral part of the total overall selection and assessment program (Gannon). This selection background component is used frequently, since it requires only a little time and money and a minimum amount of effort (Browning).

E. MEDICAL EXAMINATION

A preemployment physical is standard procedure in most organizational selection processes. It serves four major purposes. First, it determines whether an applicant's physical qualifications are sufficient to meet the requirements of the work he is being considered for. Second, it identifies an applicant's physical condition at the time of hiring in the event of a workmen's compensation claim for an injury that occurs later. Third, it prevents the employment of candidates with contagious diseases. Fourth, it assists in the employee placement process by determining personal physical abilities and shortcomings of employee candidates. Many large companies employ a full-time staff physician. Most smaller organizations use the services of a private medical practitioner on either an individual fee or an annual retainer basis. In some organizations, the physical examination selection procedure is a farce and merely a rubber stamping aftermath often approved within a few minutes and without a candidate ever having really been examined by a qualified physician. In other employment situations, especially whenever a top-executive-post candidate is being seriously considered, the medical examination may be a two- or three-day hospital affair that ultimately determines whether or not a candidate is offered a job.

F. TWO GENERAL SELECTION PHILOSOPHIES — SUCCESSIVE HURDLES VERSUS THE COMPENSATORY APPROACH

There are two general selection and assessment philosophies in existence today (Bray and Moses). The majority of employee selection programs are

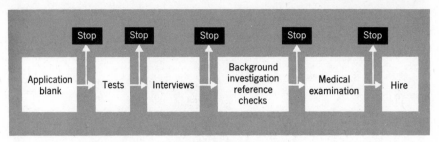

FIGURE 6-2 The "succesive hurdles" selection approach.

based on the successive hurdles concept. This means that to be hired, applicants must successfully pass every screening device (the application blank, tests, interviews, background check, and medical examination). For a candidate to pass all hurdles successfully, he must meet or exceed the requirements for each hurdle. The compensatory selection approach, which is less commonly used, is based on the assumption that a deficiency in one factor can be counterbalanced by an excess amount of another factor. In essence, a low evaluation on one selection criterion may be offset by a high assessment on a different employment criterion. A candidate is routed through all selection stops before a final employment decision is made. Often such a procedure involves compiling a composite assessment score index on which a final hiring decision is based.

Controversy exists as to which of these two selection approaches should be most frequently utilized (Walker, Luthan, and Hodgetts). Both methods are advantageous under differing circumstances. If an applicant is grossly un-qualified to pass even the preliminary interview because he lacks essential abilities and experience, there is no point in sending him through the remaining hurdles. If, however, a candidate looks promising on the early hurdles but is slightly below par on some other minor employment factor, there is logic in giving such an applicant the full treatment before making a final employment decision (Didato). Figures 6-2 and 6-3 attempt to convey the underlying philosophies and rationales of the successive hurdle and com-pensatory selection approaches.

4. Placement

The concept of employee placement is often interpreted in one of two ways. The layman uses the term placement as a general term referring to finding employment for a worker. This interpretation has come about because of the placement activities of public and private employment agencies and the job searching responsibilities of college and university placement services. The

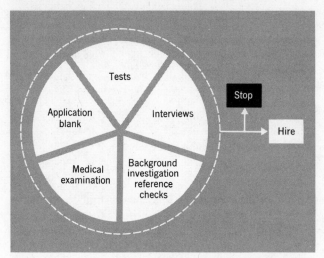

FIGURE 6-3 The "compensatory" selection approach.

idea of employee placement, when envisioned in this broad context, means simply finding a job for candidates and applicants.

A second interpretation of the placement concept is more specific and more related to a unique aspect of overall employment practices as performed by any personnel department within an organization. In this capacity, placement means matching or fitting a person's qualifications and a job's requirements (Thompson). Matching or fitting attempts to determine unique human capacities and abilities and to pair these with unique position duties and responsibilities. This interpretation of placement means more than just finding employment for a person; it means that after selection and hiring have already been determined, the proper place, job, or position within the organization must also then be determined. It is in this second interpretation and format that the concept of employee placement will be used in the remainder of this text.

Candidate selection and placement are best thought of as partially interrelated and overlapping employment activities instead of as totally distinct or completely synonymous employment entities. A person is not normally selected by a company before any consideration is given as to what exact post he will occupy within the organization. On occasion, very large corporations will hire extremely promising potential employees without much if any consideration as to exactly what type of job such an applicant will be assigned to; however, such examples are the exception, not the rule. On the other hand, when a very strict job description or job specification system exists, when an organizational vacancy occurs, and when recruitment efforts concentrate on finding a unique personality to fit a particular job description and specification exactly, at this time employee selection and employee placement approximate the idea and condition of being synonymous or interchangeable concepts. Usually, however, neither of these two extreme positions are seen in actual practice during the employment of most company personnel. "Selection and placement as distinct concepts" is descriptive of the hiring philosophy for lower-level employees by some large companies, and selection and placement as synonymous concepts may be true of the recruitment approach for the top executive posts in many organizations regardless of size; but, in general, the employee selection and placement processes are best envisioned as highly interrelated concepts, although currently unresolved debate about the extent or degree of this interrelationship exists.

Continuous Placement

Employee placement is best seen as a continuous process instead of as an isolated event. Employees cannot be placed on a job and then forgotten. People change and jobs change and thus what might initially start out to be a proper fit or match may not later remain so. Most workers want greater and greater job duties and responsibilities in the form of promotions as time goes by. Increased automation and technology make the pace of job change extremely fast in many mechanical work situations. Such factors make a continuous placement philosophy mandatory in any efficiently run employment setting today.

Continuous placement does not necessarily mean continuous promotion. Placements can be in the form of promotions, transfers, demotions, layoffs, retirements, and firings. Technically, a promotion (demotion) is a movement within an organization from one position to another that involves either an increase (decrease) in pay or an increase (decrease) in status. Transfers do not involve pay or status alterations. Employee separations may be in the form of temporary layoffs, permanent firings, voluntary early retirements, mandatory-age retirements, formal employee resignations, and informal work quittings. Promotions are usually based on employee ability, while demotions and firings are caused by worker inability. Transfers and layoffs, which are mainly based on employee seniority or juniority, are usually caused by structural and technological changes within an organization or economic and financial factors within the external environment. Resignations and quittings are usually due to better job opportunities elsewhere, while retirements are an aftermath of the human aging process.

Placement Underemphasis

The employee placement process is grossly underemphasized in most organizations. Sometimes thousands of dollars are spent for naught by organizations in recruiting and selection activities because of inappropriate placement procedures or the lack of mutual coordination of all employment subfunctions. This is true especially in larger organizations where recruitment, selection, and placement activities may all be carried on by and ultimately may be the responsibility of different persons. Unfortunately, it is all too common to find instances when thousands of dollars were spent to recruit and select hundreds of candidates when, in fact, the organization structurally and financially could only properly place a few dozen of these candidates. The sports world is probably the best (worst) example of where recruiting and placing activities are often way out of alignment. On occasion, athletic franchises pay a multimillion dollar compensation package to a player whom they then will eventually place on the bench for several years perhaps later trade away. To prevent such atrocities, placement must not only be considered as a continuous process, but it must also be given equal importance to employee recruitment and selection activities.

A. JOB EVALUATION, JOB ANALYSIS, JOB DESCRIPTION, AND JOB SPECIFICATION

Employee placement and job fitting or matching are often done on a systematic basis in most larger organizations. The usual employment procedures and concepts involved include job evaluation, job analysis, job description, and job specification. Some authors see job evaluation and job analysis as interchangeable concepts, while other writers use the phrase job evaluation as the broader concept that includes the subset of job analysis. Also, some personnel authors reserve the idea of job evaluation to describe the analysis of jobs in reference to wage and salary considerations while, to them, job analysis pertains to analyzing jobs in reference to only employee selection and placement activities. Job evaluation is really all activities involved in the evaluation of a job, and job analysis is all activities involved in the analysis of a job. The employment concepts of job evaluation and job analysis are best thought of as partially interrelated and overlapping staffing subfunctions instead of as totally distinct or completely synonymous job staffing entities. Since the concept of job analysis is usually used in reference to staffing activities, I will use the job analysis concept in preference to the job evaluation concept in the remainder of this chapter.

Job Analysis

Job analysis is the process of obtaining all pertinent job facts. Uusally this involves the creation of two separate written statements. One is the job description, which is a statement describing the job in terms such as its title, location, duties, working conditions, and hazards. The second is the job

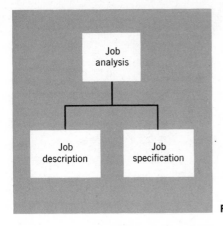

FIGURE 6-4 Components of job analysis.

specification, which is a statement of the human qualifications necessary to do the job. The job specification usually contains items such as required levels or degrees of education, experience, training, judgment, initiative, physical effort, skills, and responsibilities needed in order to perform a certain job properly. The relationship among the job analysis, job description, and job specification concepts as seen from this perspective is shown in Figure 6-4.

Job Description–Job Specification

Some personnel authors and practitioners, however, make no distinction between a job description and a job specification. In practice, an organization often will combine both of these written statements into one form. Many organizations, especially larger ones, will use separate job description and job specification statements, but many organizations do not follow this convention. When only one form is used, it may be called either a job description or a job specification.

Position Description

Some authors also use the concept of a position description in reference to job analysis matters. A position description is a job description for a managerial position. Normally position descriptions are broad in scope and more general in format than job descriptions are. Not all personnel specialists make a distinction between a job description and a position description. Figure 6-5b illustrates that the concepts of job description, job specification, position description are best envisioned as partially overlapping and interre-

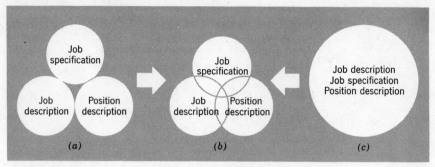

FIGURE 6-5 Three views of job analysis subsets. (*a*) Distinct. (*b*) Interrelated. (c) Synonymous.

lated constructs instead of being thought of as totally distinct (Figure 6-5*a*) or completely synonymous (Figure 6-5*c*) set entities.

Application of Job Analysis, Job Description and Job Specification Techniques

Many controversial issues surround the question of whether or not organizations should set up and follow a rigid job description–job specification system. The above materials may have left the reader with the notion that such techniques are commonly and unquestionably accepted by all organizations today. This is not the case. Many items of concern surround the organizational usage of job analysis techniques.

UTILITY

First is the question of usefulness or utility. Of what benefits are such techniques? Job analysis was first undertaken to set up systematic and fair wage and salary procedures. Job analysis information can also aid proper employee recruiting, selecting, and placing activities. Training and development needs of a company can be determined by job analysis, as can certain health and safety institutional matters. Manpower planning, job design, performance appraisal, and other employee concerns can also be aided by gathering better job information. Unfortunately, in the past, separate job analysis studies were undertaken for every one of these organizational purposes. A job analysis study was done to determine a proper compensation system, then a job analysis study was performed to determine training needs, then another job evaluation project was designed to analyze safety conditions, and so forth. Today, companies that use job analysis systems try to coordinate their efforts so that one or two job studies will gather all of this information for them simultaneously.

Some organizations, both large and small, believe that job analysis efforts are a waste of time. The basic idea is that jobs should be shaped around people instead of having people conform to job molds. In addition, jobs and people change so rapidly that attempts to classify either are useless according to this viewpoint. Furthermore, a few companies have learned, through bitter experience, that as soon as you put down on paper what a person is expected to do in a job, he will not do anything except what is specifically called for and indicated in the job description. Last, job analysis techniques are costly. Often a full-time person or even an entire staff may be needed to formulate and constantly revise an organization's job descriptions and job specifications. Because of these and other problems and issues, some companies prefer not to use any formalized job analysis sytem.

COST

The cost criteria is important enough to be considered as a separate issue. A full-time worker or staff in this type of work may cost an organization tens of thousands of dollars annually. Many companies believe in the philosophy of job analysis but are dismayed because of the costs involved. As an attempt to alleviate or mitigate the expense factor, many companies utilize standard references and sources of job information. For example, by referring to *The Dictionary of Occupational Titles,* a personnel specialist can find job information that can be used to formulate crude job descriptions for positions within his organization. Information within the *Dictionary* is expressed in terms of *duties, tasks, positions, jobs, occupations,* and *careers.* In general, as shown in Figure 6-6, these terms move from specific to general job information. Although the precise definitions of these terms are not crucial for our introductory purposes, it is nevertheless important to note that distinctions can be and have been made among these terms in order to promote the cause of more economical job analysis techniques and procedures. In general, organizational reference to such standard sources is recommended as a starting point only. A company cannot and should not expect to obtain a valid job analysis system of its own merely by referring to a standard resource publication dealing with such matters.

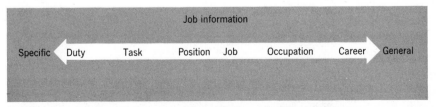

FIGURE 6-6 Specific-general job information terminology continuum.

SPECIFIC VERSUS GENERAL

The issue of whether or not job descriptions should be general or specific has also been raised. Specific descriptions tell precisely what is to be done, whereas general descriptions are much more vague and ambiguous. Specific statements have the advantage of telling a working person, in definite terms, what the job duties are, while general statements allow considerably more flexibility. Unions prefer specific descriptions, but management prefers general statements. This is not really an either-or situation, however. The most frequent solution is a specific description that includes a final general statement item such as "and all house keeping and other chores indirectly related to the performance of this job." Such a statement helps to prevent the situation where workers refuse to do any work not specifically called for or identified on their job descriptions. As noted earlier in the chapter, the specific versus general format issue is involved not only when job descriptions for nonsupervisory employees are being considered, but also when position descriptions for managers are being formulated.

NORMATIVE VERSUS DESCRIPTIVE

Another concern is whether or not job descriptions should be descriptive or normative. Should job descriptions describe what is done or what should be done? Should a norm or standard be set realistically or ideally? In practice, almost all job descriptions in use are descriptive rather than normative. Often the only real difference among job descriptions in terms of this dimension is not whether or not standards or norms are set (they always are), but the variations exist only grammatically in that descriptive statements use directing verbs such as "is" and "are," whereas "normative" descriptions utilize a lot of "could's" and "should's." In addition, all job descriptions, regardless of their grammatical format, tend to be more normative than descriptive because new hirees are not as yet totally familiar with the work situation.

UNION ROLE

Another issue centers around the proper role of a union in formulating an organization's job descriptions and specifications. Traditionally, job analysis is and has been considered a management prerogative. Often management will formulate the job description and submit it to the union for final approval. In essence, the union commonly has a veto power. A union representative may actually help in the analysis of a job or in the final writing of the job description.

WHO PERFORMS THE ANALYSIS

Another issue is who should actually perform the job analysis and have ultimate responsibility for drawing up the final job statements. Usually either the personnel department or an engineering department performs the actual job analysis. If an organization is nonindustrial this job invariably becomes the duty of the personnel department or some outside consulting agency. Engineering departments are commonly involved because much of the job analysis procedure involves time and motion studies. Usually the first step in formulating a job description is to have a worker write up his own description of his job. The worker's immediate supervisor then reviews, corrects, and adds to this initial statement. Often it is absolutely amazing to see the tremendous discrepancies that exist between how an employee sees his job and what his boss expects him to do. The personnel department usually has the final responsibility for writing up job descriptions and specifications. The personnel manager is aided in the total job analysis process, however, by workers, supervisors, engineers and, occasionally, maybe even also by external consultants or labor union representatives.

5. Indoctrination

Indoctrination, as a staffing subfunction, refers to the guided adjustment of a new employee to the organization and its work environment. Employee indoctrination involves the process of recognizing one's position in relationship to other persons, positions, departments, and factors within the external environment. Other terms, such as induction or orientation are also used to describe this staffing subfunction. Although most people feel that indoctrination, induction, and orientation are synonymous, personnel practitioners and authors occasionally may differentiate among these three concepts.

Placement versus Indoctrination

It is difficult to determine where placement ends and indoctrination begins. Many of the activities involved in arranging and determining the proper position for a newly hired candidate are both placement and orientation in nature and purpose. Employee placement and indoctrination are best thought of as partially interrelated and overlapping staffing subfunctions instead of as totally distinct or completely synonymous employment activities.

Indoctrination versus Training

Although it is commonly believed that employee training occurs *after* employee indoctrination, it is impossible to determine precisely where indoctrination ends and training begins. In general, indoctrination involves a general orientation to the whole work environment, while training pertains to specific work skills and duties relating to a particular job setting. However, indoctrination and training should be considered partially overlapping and interrelated staffing subfunctions instead of totally distinct or completely synonymous employment activities.

Indoctrination Purposes

Indoctrination has many purposes. It seeks to establish favorable employee attitudes toward the company, its policies, and its personnel. Orientation procedures help to instill a feeling of belonging and acceptance which, in turn, help to generate enthusiasm and high morale. By-products of a well-run indoctrination program may be fewer rules violations, discharges, quits, grievances, and misunderstandings. However, dysfunction aspects of indoctrination may also exist in the form of conformity, group thinking, and emphasis on peer loyalty instead of work achievement.

Indoctrination Information

There is no standard format for organizational indoctrination procedures, but Figure 6-7 lists the actions and items of information that are commonly included in many company orientation programs.

Indoctrination Underemphasis

The employee indoctrination program is often severely neglected. It is assumed that the new employee can orient himself automatically by being on the job for a certain period of time. Research indicates the financial wisdom

INDOCTRINATION INFORMATION

Collective bargaining agreement
Company history, policies, and practices
Company plants and facilities
Company products or services
Company responsibilities to the employees
Company service programs
Departmental and plant tours
Employee appraisal and performance systems
Employee responsibilities to the company
Health and benefit plans
Introductions to fellow employees
Organization structure
Pay policies and procedures
Promotion policies
Rules of conduct
Safety program
Training and development opportunities
Work assignment and schedule

FIGURE 6-7 Employee indoctrination information.

of a good company indoctrination program. Such programs frequently lead to reduced job-learning time, higher output, better attendance, less waste, and improved product quality (Inskeep). This occurs because of lowered employee anxiety and stress, which have resulted directly from the well-planned company orientation program. These programs are usually supervised by the personnel department, but the immediate supervisor of a new employee typically also plays a key role in the overall indoctrination process.

The amount of time, effort, and money devoted to employee indoctrination programs perhaps should not be equal to that spent on the employee recruiting, selecting, and placing staffing subprocesses but, some concerted attempt should be made by all organizations to orient all of their new employees. Per dollar return on investment, such a program is a wise financial decision. The best-run organizations usually devote considerable attention to the indoctrination and orientation of newly hired employees (Korman).

6. Appraisal

Definition

Employee appraising is the systematic evaluation of a worker's job performance and potential for development. Appraising is the process of estimating or judging the value, excellence, qualities, or status of some object, person, or thing. The appraisal of individuals in an employment setting has been labeled and described over the years by personnel authors and practitioners in a number of different ways. Some common descriptions include performance appraisal, merit rating, behavioral assessment, employee evaluation, personnel review, progress report, service rating, and fitness report (Oberg). Some personnel specialists use such concepts interchangeably, while others attach special interpretations to some of these appraisal phrases.

Employee appraisal is part of all the other staffing subprocesses. It is hard to conceptualize mentally and to illustrate diagrammatically the relationship of the employee appraisal process to the other staffing subprocesses. Figure 6-8, which shows that employee appraisal is individually and collectively part of the recruitment, selection, placement, and indoctrination staffing subfunctions, is the most accurate portrayal. All of these employee activities involve the evaluation and assessment of company candidates or workers to some degree. Other activities are also part of the recruitment, selection, placement, and indoctrination staffing concepts, so employee appraisal is shown in Figure 6-8 as a composite of only smaller segments of all of these staffing activities and subprocesses.

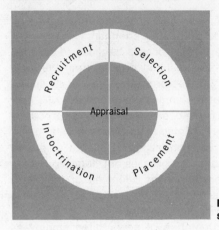

FIGURE 6-8 The role of appraisal as a staffing subset.

The employee appraisal process is probably more accurately labeled as the employee appraising process because the term appraising is more accurately reflective of the real meaning of the process. *Appraising is a dynamic concept, while appraisal is static. Employees are always being evaluated either formally or informally and the "ing" ending on the identification of this process connotes this continuance and helps to illustrate that employee appraising is an evolutionary process, not an annual or semiannual event.

"Who"

The matter of employee appraisal can easily and logically be covered in a simple "who," "what," "why," "when," "where," and "how" format. The "who" question actually involves two inquiries: "who should be appraised" and "who should do the appraising." All organizational employees should be evaluated. Janitors, the president, and all jobs and positions in between should be analyzed in terms of their performance. The second inquiry is much more difficult to answer. Most commonly employees are evaluated by their immediate supervisor. However, peer evaluation, self-evaluation, and subordinate evaluation methods are sometimes used (Bassett and Meyer). A panel made up of several supervisors or superiors is also common (Miner). The composition of such a panel could also consist of colleagues or other employees at various organizational levels. Often someone from the personnel department is used as an employee evaluator. In addition, appraisals for managerial employees are often performed by outside consultants who are experts in the field of employee appraisal. Usually an employee's immediate boss is the main employee appraiser, but other appraisal sources are frequently also used both on a formal and an informal basis.

"What"

"What" should be appraised is best answered in terms of two employee dimensions: current performance and future potential (Kavanaugh). There is debate as to which of these two factors is the most important. Often non-supervisory employees are judged by their current performance, whereas managers are often evaluated in terms of their future potential. Appraising in reference to the staffing or employment function and in reference to the "what" appraisal inquiry concerns only the appraisal of human beings, not the evaluation and assessment of other organizational resources.

Traits or Results

The "what" question also involves the issue of what human criteria or factors to evaluate. Should personal traits such as intelligence, aggressiveness, decisiveness, and maturity be appraised, or should accomplished goals or performance results be measured? In the past appraisal methods concentrated on personal traits, but today the emphasis is on achieved objectives. The management-by-objectives concept and movement that will be discussed later in this chapter are largely responsible for this trend. Employee appraisal systems exist today that combine traditional trait analyses and modern MBO assessments.

"Why"

There are a number of reasons "why" employee appraising takes place. Appraisals help to create and maintain a satisfactory level of performance from employees on their present jobs (Brumback and Vincent). Worker evaluations help to highlight employee needs and opportunities for personal growth and development. Employee appraising aids decision making for promotions, transfers, layoffs, and discharges (Korman). Many organizations relate the size and frequency of pay increases to the rating assigned to the employee during the performance appraising process. In addition, the accuracy and validity of predictions made in the employee staffing subprocesses (recruitment, selection, placement, and indoctrination) are often determined by comparing or correlating performance ratings with test scores, interviewers' evaluations, and so on. If carried out properly, the entire appraisal process can facilitate mutual understanding between the supervisor and his subordinates.

"When"

"When" employee appraising takes place depends on whether the reference is to the formal or informal appraisal process. Formal employee appraisals usually occur annually or semiannually, but informal evaluations take place continually. In actuality, it is often hard to identify an informal evaluation from a formal appraisal, since the latter sometimes is determined by the former.

"Where"

The location "where" employee appraisals take place also varies. Formal appraisals often take place in the office of an employee's immediate boss. Formal appraisals also occur at the subordinate's job site or work location. If consultants are used, the appraisal process may take place away from company premises. Informal appraisals take place anywhere and everywhere, both on the job in work situations and off the job in social and recreational settings.

"How"

The most difficult and complicated inquiry to answer is the "how" appraisal question. Various appraisal methods are used within organizations today. These methods and techniques will be discussed in the next section, after which a discussion of general appraisal problems will be presented.

A. APPRAISAL METHODS

Employee appraisal methods utilized within organizations are many and varied; traditional methods include: (1) rating scales; (2) employee comparisons; (3) checklists; (4) free form essays; (5) interviews; and (6) critical incidents.

Rating Scales

Rating scales are the oldest and most widely used employee appraisal procedure. A rater is given a printed form that contains a number of employee qualities and characteristics to be judged, such as quantity of work, quality of work, job knowledge, cooperativeness, dependability, industry, attitude, initiative, leadership, creative ability, decisiveness, analytical ability, and emotional stability. These traits are then evaluated on a continuous (a continuum) or discontinuous (consisting of appropriate boxes or squares to check) scale, and the scale may be represented by and be broken down into three, five, seven, ten, or more parts or points. The rating scale appraisal method is easy to construct, easy to use, and easy to understand. However, rating scales have some serious drawbacks. There is an illusion of precision when definite numbers are assigned to an appraiser's opinions that, in fact, are only subjective judgments. In addition, ratings cluster on the high side when this appraisal system is used. Figure 6-9 illustrates an example of a hypothetical rating scale.

Attitude

No interest	Indifferent	Interested	Enthusiastic	Very enthusiastic

Job knowledge

Serious gaps	Some minor deficiencies	Satisfactory	Well informed	Exceptional expertise

Contacts with others

Very little	Departmental only	Several departments	Multidimensional internally	Multidimensional internally and externally

FIGURE 6-9   An employee appraisal rating scale.

Employee Comparisons

Employee comparisons are of two common types, rankorder and forced distribution. The ranking method asks the appraiser to rank employees on an overall basis according to their job performance and value to the organization. One person only can occupy any ranking or position, whether it be high, low or in the middle. The forced-distribution procedure requires an assessor to distribute his evaluations in a pattern to conform to a normal frequency distribution (e.g., 10-20-40-20-10 percent categories). Other variations of employee comparisons are common. For example, an appraiser may simply be asked to place his rates into groups such as the lowest third, the middle third, and the upper third; or he may be instructed to use a paired-comparison technique, which involves contrasting each ratee with all other ratees in the group, one at a time. There are several disadvantages to the ranking method of employee comparisons. It does not reveal the difference between persons in adjacent ranks. Rankings can tell how a person stands relative to others in the group, but they do not indicate how much better or worse one person is than another. Also, this method does not consider specific aspects of behavior, since ratees are ranked on a "whole man," total contribution basis only. The main fault with the forced-distribution method, which involves interval instead of ordinal numbers, is that it is highly unlikely that the performance of employees in any small group will conform to a normal curve.

Checklists

Checklist appraisal methods are weighted or forced choice. The weighted checklist consists of many statements that describe various behaviors for any particular job (or job family). Each statement has a weight or scale value

MOST	LEAST	
A	A	Seldom makes mistakes
B	B	Respected by subordinates
C	C	Fails to follow through assignments completely
D	D	Feels his job is more important than other jobs
E	E	Does not express his own views with confidence

FIGURE 6-10 Forced-choice checklist statement format.

assigned to it in accordance with the way judges evaluated the degree of importance of this statement. When appraising an employee, the assessor checks all the statements that closely describe the individual's behavior. The checklist is then scored by averaging the weights of all the descriptive statements marked by the rater. The main drawback is that it is costly in terms of staff development time because a separate checklist must be established for each different job or job family. The forced-choice checklist is a variation of the weighted checklist. It consists of sets of tetrads, or groups of four or five statements each. For each tetrad the appraiser must check the most and least descriptive statements as they pertain to a particular employee. The statements are grouped and designed so that two statements appear favorable and two appear unfavorable. However, the real or actual values or weights of the statements are not known by the ratee or the rater. The assessor, when evaluating a person, does not know which statements will count for or against the rated individual. The main limitations of this appraisal method are the installation expense and the fact that it is difficult for an appraiser to discuss ratings afterwards with a ratee because he himself does not know how the items are (were) scored. Figure 6-10 illustrates the forced-choice checklist statement format.

Free Form Essays

Free form essays do not involve rating scales, checklists or any other standard format devices. Free form essays merely require an appraiser to write down his impressions of the ratee on a blank sheet of paper. Problems also exist with this appraisal technique: considerable time and effort are required if it is to be done properly; appraisals depend more on the appraiser's literary skills than on an employee's abilities and performance; and it is hard to evaluate and to compare employees.

Interviews

Interviews are also frequently used (Burke and Wilcox). The various types and structures of interviews were discussed previously in this chapter. In general, structured interviews are preferred to unstructured interviews as appraisal techniques. Interviews also require a lot of time and effort. Another limitation is that they usually also have to be supplemented with written records and reports.

Critical Incidents

Critical incidents are noteworthy events or happenings related to the behaviors and performances of organizational employees. Whenever an employee does an exceptionally good or poor work-related activity, his supervisor is told to make a written record, which will be referred to when formal performance evaluations are to occur. Usually this method of appraisal encourages frequent recordings and involves categorizing employee behaviors and notations. Facts are observed and recorded; therefore subjective judgments are deemphasized. The drawbacks of this system are that it requires a lot of time and effort; appraisal must be done only by an employee's immediate supervisor; and it can lead to overly close supervision and poor worker morale if employees feel that everything they do is being observed and recorded.

Other Appraisal Methods

Other employee evaluation techniques exist; two popular current assessment methodologies are the assessment center concept and management by objectives (MBO). Human asset accounting, although not as popular, is also a new, widely discussed technique sometimes used today as a performance appraisal method. The newer appraisal techniques of the assessment center concept, management by objectives, and human asset accounting will be discussed, respectively, after the next section.

B. GENERAL APPRAISAL PROBLEMS

Specific shortcomings of the traditional appraisal methods have already been mentioned. However, certain general types of rating problems are common to many, if not all, of these methods. These common problems include: (1) the halo effect; (2) leniency or strictness; (3) central tendency; (4) personal bias; and (5) appraisal purposes.

Halo Effect

As noted earlier in this chapter, the halo effect occurs when an appraiser evaluates an entire set of employee characteristics in the same way that he evaluates one specific employee trait for which he feels he has an accurate assessment basis. This global assessment may be positive or negative in nature and direction. Even if an appraiser can reliably evaluate an individual's aggressiveness, this is no assurance that he can validly also assess this individual's intelligence, emotional stability, dependability, creativity, and leadership potential. When an appraiser gives the same rating to unknown characteristics that he has given to known traits, the halo effect has occurred.

Leniency or Strictness

Many raters are too lenient in their ratings (Sharon and Bartlett). High scores may be assigned to all employees, irrespective of merit. A less frequent problem is the reverse situation where all individuals are rated too severely. Such problems arise because of varying performance standards among appraisers and because of different interpretations of observed employee performances and behaviors.

Central Tendency

Central tendency is when a rater assigns mostly middle-range scores or values to all individuals being appraised. Extremely high or low evaluations are avoided. Usually central tendency is caused by a lack of information. If a rater is unfamiliar with a ratee, if forced to evaluate, he will play it safe by neither condemning nor praising.

Personal Bias

The way an appraiser personally feels about a ratee will drastically affect the appraiser's objectivity. Many research studies have been performed to support this contention. The appraiser and others must learn and know about such biases, and then discount and perhaps reevaluate certain ratings if this problem warrants such considerations under certain circumstances.

Appraisal Purposes

Often ratings depend on the way such information is to be used. The classic example is the boss who tends to rate his subordinates highly when pay increases are being determined, but who often stresses employee weaknesses and deficiencies when attempting to assess promotable employees. Occasionally, the best subordinates are not promoted because they are so crucial to a superior's success, while poor performers may be promoted to get rid of unproductive personnel. One universal assessment, instead of separate employee appraisals for different staffing purposes, is a possible solution to this problem.

Figure 6-11 summarizes the last sections dealing with the employee appraisal process. It brings together the answers to all of the "who," "what," "why," "when," "where," and "how" inquiries.

APPRAISAL QUESTIONS

<u>WHO</u>

Appraised: All employees   Appraisers: Immediate supervisor   Subordinates

                                        Other supervisors   Personnel manager

                                        Peers or colleagues   External consultant

                                        Self   Group combination

<u>WHAT</u>

Object: Human   Time Frame: Current performance   Specifics: Personal traits

        beings   Future potential   Achieved results

<u>WHY</u>

Maintain work force   Basis for promotions, transfers,

Improve performance   layoffs, discharges, etc.

Determine organizational   Basis for pay increases

   training needs   Aid in recruitment, selection, placement and

Determine personal   indoctrination processes

   development opportunities   Feedback and communication

                                   mechanism

<u>WHEN</u>

Formal: Annually   Informal: Weekly

        Semiannualy   Daily

        Quarterly   Continuously

<u>WHERE</u>

On the job: Boss's office   Off the job: Consultant's office

             Subordinate's work location   Social or recreational setting

             Everywhere   Everywhere

<u>HOW</u>

Methods: Rating scales   Problems: Halo effect

                Employee comparisons   Leniency or strictness

Traditional   Checklists   Central tendency

                Free form essays   Personal bias

                Interviews   Appraisal purposes

                Critical incidents

              Assessment centers

Modern   Management by objectives

              Human asset accounting

FIGURE 6-11 Appraisal questions.

C. ASSESSMENT CENTER CONCEPT

Definition

The simplest definition of an assessment center is that it is a place where assessments are made. Assessments, in this context, are the pooled judgments of several specially trained managers who use a variety of criteria to evaluate an employee's performance as he goes through several different test situations. Multiple judgments by many evaluators, upon observations of employee performance in several situations, is the crux of the assessment center concept.

AT&T

Historically, the assessment center concept began in 1965 as part of a new American Telephone and Telegraph Company (AT&T) training and development program. Today, well over fifty assessment centers are operating in various parts of the Bell System. Many other larger corporations in other industries also now use some modified form of the original assessment center concept.

Purpose

Assessment centers are used mostly to help select men and women for the first-level (lowest) supervisory positions. Assessments are aimed at determining employee potential. Actual promotions are still made by line officials responsible for the operations into which an employee will be promoted.

Assessment Activities

An employee assessment is generally a half-week process, with a dozen or so management aspirants going through at a time. Assessments may involve paper and pencil tests, interviews, and situational exercises. Bell uses three paper and pencil tests: one a test of general mental ability; a test of ability to reason; and a test of knowledge of current affairs (Wikstrom). The interview is of the depth variety, but it is conducted by a line manager, not a psychologist. It is a much more searching interview than the average manager is apt to conduct when selecting applicants for promotion to a foreman's position.

The most distinctive aspect of the assessment center concept is the use of situational exercises. Bell uses four situational tests: an in-basket exercise, a business game, a role-playing incident, and a leaderless group discussion exercise involving a labor dispute. Other assessment centers have used different combinations of individual and group activities and exercises.

Assessors

Six Bell staff members and the training-assessment director spend several days evaluating the results of assessment tests. The staff members are drawn from experienced managers of proven ability from levels above that for which promotions are being considered. A staff member assignment to an assessment center is temporary, usually for six months. A three-week training period prepares new staff members for the work they will be doing. After six months, staff assessors are transferred and replaced so as to keep fresh vision within the appraisal process.

Staff members individually and collectively rate all employees, and each candidate eventually is assigned to one of four categories: more than acceptable, acceptable, less than acceptable, and unacceptable. The director prepares a summary report supporting an employee's final classification. Feedback on a face-to-face basis is given to all candidates who request it (usually about 85 percent). Modifications of these Bell procedures have taken place within other companies who have taken this basic idea and adapted it to meet specific institutional needs.

Longitudinal research studies have shown that the assessment center concept is a better method of identifying managerial potential than any other personnel method currently available (Wollowick and McNamara). Those persons judged promotable within the center usually do advance within the corporate structure, while those labeled unacceptable do not go on into managerial positions. This is more than a self-fulfilling prophecy, however, since promotion decisions are still ultimately determined by responsible line managers, not by assessment center results.

The main drawbacks of an assessment center are that an organization usually has to be fairly large to reap the potential gains, and also that the average cost per candidate assessment during the early 1970s was around $450 (Byham). This includes the costs of operating the center, the salary, travel and living expenses at the center of the persons being assessed, and other related expenses. The key features of the assessment center concept as developed by AT&T are summarized in Figure 6-12.

FEATURES OF THE ASSESSMENT CENTER CONCEPT

1. Advisory final report	8. In depth interviews
2. Bell development	9. Multiple criteria
3. Emphasis on managerial potential	10. Pooled judgments
4. Face-to-face feedback	11. Situational exercises
5. Groups of from 10-15	12. Temporary company assessors
6. Approximately a half-week process	13. Test batteries
7. High success prediction	14. Approximately $450 per candidate

FIGURE 6-12   Key features of the "assessment center" concept.

D. MANAGEMENT BY OBJECTIVES

Management by objectives is both a philosophical concept and a set of operational procedures (Frank). Management by objectives, which is usually referred to today as MBO, represents a way of managing people in work organizations. MBO activities in specific reference to employee appraising procedures often is identified as appraisal by results. There are several steps involved within the MBO concept. First, an employee gets together with his immediate supervisor and they mutually define, establish, and set certain goals or objectives that the employee should attempt to achieve within the next few months. Ways of measuring employee progress are also a matter of supervisor-subordinate discussion. Goals that become set are supposed to be work related and career oriented. Then, periodically, the employee meets with his superior to evaluate or reevaluate the employee's goal progress. Goals and appraisal criteria may then be revised if necessary. Frequent feedback and supervisor-subordinate interaction are the key features of the MBO concept. The supervisor tries to play supportive, counseling, and coaching roles. Feedback and interaction continue, as old objectives are reached and new goals become established.

Ends Not Means

The MBO process focuses on results accomplished and not on personal traits or operational methodologies. A person is not judged in terms of initiative, cooperativeness, attitude, emotional stability, or any other human characteristics. The only question of relevance is, "Did the employee reach his goals?" If he did, he is appraised positively; if he did not, he gets a poor performance rating. Results are what count. The methodology, or how one manages to achieve or obtain these objectives, is of no or only minor importance (so long as everything is done legally, ethically, and courteously). A final feature of the MBO appraisal system, which contrasts with traditional appraisal methods, is its emphasis on the present and the future instead of on the past.

Variations

Many variations of the basic MBO concept exist, and each variation often possesses its own unique descriptive title. However, almost all MBO programs in operation today have been applied only to technical, professional, supervisory, or executive personnel. MBO is less applicable for hourly workers because their jobs are usually too restricted.

Evaluation

Most MBO programs are superior to traditional appraisal systems (Tosi and Carroll). Basic requirements for success with this method are that subordi-

MBO FEATURES

Supervisor-subordinate interaction
Supervisor-subordinate mutually set goals
Supervisor-subordinate mutually set performance criteria
Emphasis on present and future
Emphasis on results (not means)
Frequent feedback
Goal reassessment
Performance criteria reassessment
Work-related and career-oriented goals

FIGURE 6-13 Key features of the "management by objectives" appraisal concept.

nates must be ambitious, creative, and interested in their work and in the organization. When such employees are found, the MBO approach has been successful. Participation and self-determination are the underlying forces that motivate employees involved with a MBO appraisal program. Often both employee attitudes and actions change favorably when MBO appraisal techniques are implemented within an organization. The main drawbacks of an MBO appraisal system are the amount of supervisory time needed and the often less than total employee interest in and commitment to both the organization in general and the MBO assessment system in particular. In general, the MBO approach has a lot to offer, but it is not a solution to all management and staffing problems.

The modern human resource manager often has replaced or at least supplemented traditional appraisal methodologies with MBO. This assessment concept emphasizes whether or not workers achieve goals mutually set by subordinates and their supervisors. If worker goals are achieved, the individual is assessed positively but, if performance objectives are not met, then the employee appraisal is much less complimentary. MBO is replacing other forms of individual human resource appraisal because it stresses concrete results instead of employee personality traits or methodological assessment gimmicks. The key features of the MBO assessment concept are summarized in Figure 6-13.

E. HUMAN ASSET ACCOUNTING

One of the newest methods of individual appraisal is human asset accounting. This concept is based on the rationale that human beings are assets that should be treated similarly to physical plant and equipment. This means that human assets should be shown on a corporation's balance sheet and income statement and, in general, should be valued and devalued (depreciated) similarly to other capital assets. Human beings represent investments above and beyond simply their worth as indicated currently only by wage or salary expense designations. Human beings represent long-term capital investments for an organization and should be treated accordingly.

Human asset accounting refers to activity devoted to attaching dollar estimates to the value of a firm's internal human organization and its external customer goodwill. If able, well-trained personnel leave the firm, the human organization is worth less; if they join it, the firm's human assets are increased. If distrust and conflict prevail, the human enterprise is devalued; if teamwork and high morale prevail, the human organization is a more valuable asset.

It is now possible to develop procedures to appraise the current value of a firm's human organization (Pyle). This requires extensive use of the measurement resources developed by the social sciences. Various alternative approaches may be used to develop such a human assessment procedure. The basic step in developing procedures for applying human asset accounting to a firm's human organization is to undertake periodic measurements of key causal and intervening enterprise variables (Likert, "book" reference citation). Causal variables are independent variables that determine the course of developments within an organization and the results achieved by the organization. These causal variables include only the independent variables that can be altered or changed by the organization and its management. Such variables include the structure of the organization and management's policies, decisions, business, and leadership strategies, skills, and behavior. Intervening variables reflect the internal state and health of the organization. These measures include the loyalties, attitudes, motivations, performance, goals, and perceptions of all members and their collective capacity for effective interaction, communication, and decision making. Causal and intervening variable measurements must be made over several years time to provide the data necessary for human asset accounting computations.

A handful of firms today are using human asset accounting methods. Such procedures are still not part of generally accepted accounting practices and principles. Firms using such a system usually prepare two sets of financial statements, one incorporating human asset accounting techniques for internal purposes and one without such procedures for external audit purposes. Figure 6-14 illustrates a hypothetical corporation balance sheet indicating and including human asset accounting data.

7. Affirmative Action and EEOC Staffing Implications

The concept and practice of affirmative action and the requirements of EEOC were mentioned in detail in the previous chapter, so they will not be dealt

BALANCE SHEET

ASSETS

Accounts Receivable	$ 10,000.00
Buildings	100,000.00
Cash	10,000.00
Equipment	50,000.00
Inventory	10,000.00
Land	50,000.00
Raw Materials	10,000.00
Internal Human Relationships	20,000.00
External Customer Goodwill	20,000.00
Managerial Expertise	20,000.00
TOTAL ASSETS	$300,000.00

Human Asset Accounting Data {Internal Human Relationships, External Customer Goodwill, Managerial Expertise}

LIABILITIES

Accounts Payable	$ 20,000.00
Accrued Expenses	10,000.00
Dividends Payable	20,000.00
Federal Taxes Withheld	80,000.00
Notes Payable	30,000.00
Mortgage	30,000.00
State Taxes Withheld	10,000.00
Common Stock	40,000.00
Preferred Stock	20,000.00
Retained Earnings	40,000.00
TOTAL LIABILITIES	$300,000.00

FIGURE 6-14 A balance sheet with human asset accounting data.

with at length here. The main point to note is that the areas of personnel decision making that may be affected by fair employment practice regulations are not limited to the hiring process. Complaints to the EEOC have involved promotion opportunities and seniority systems, and there is increasing concern with the lack of minorities and women in higher-paying occupations and managerial positions. However, the major thrust has been against hiring practices that result in discrimination, whether deliberate or inadvertent. Rulings by the EEOC that have been upheld in federal courts, for example, include one that prohibits an employer from using arrest (but not conviction) records as a basis for hiring decisions, even though the policy is applied objectively and fairly between applicants of various races. This results from a discrimination policy against black candidates because blacks are arrested more frequently than whites.

Although the total staffing process is subject to scrutiny under fair employment practice regulations, the employment practice that has received the greatest criticism is psychological testing. Of the total number of complaints filed with the EEOC (about 40,000 from 1967 to 1970), about 20 percent concern the use of tests. As a result, both EEOC and OFCC have issued detailed guidelines related to the use of tests and testing procedures. This concern with the use of tests was anticipated by various members of Congress when the Civil Rights Act of 1964 was passed. Title VII of this Act includes a provision indicating that testing for selection purposes is legal only so long as the test is not specifically designed, intended, or used to discriminate. Despite this provision, the crucial issue in testing and hiring practices, according to the U.S. Supreme Court, is not the employer's "intent," but the "result." If the practice results in discrimination against a minority group and cannot be shown to be related to job performance, then the practice is prohibited. The significance of this ruling for employers is that they must be able to show that tests and other hiring and staffing procedures are proven measures of job performance.

8. Summary

Employee staffing includes the employment subprocesses of recruitment, selection, placement, indoctrination, and appraisal. Employee recruitment is the act or process of an organization attempting to obtain additional human resources for operational purposes. Employee selection involves taking or picking out by preference a limited number of workers from a group of potential employees. The most commonly used selection devices include the application blank, tests, interviews, a background investigation including reference checks, and a medical examination. Employee placement means matching or fitting a person's qualifications and a job's requirements. This matching or fitting process is aided by procedures such as job evaluation, job analysis, job description, and job specification. Employee indoctrination refers to the guided adjustment of a new employee to the organization and its work environment. Employee appraisal is part of all staffing subprocesses. Employee appraisal is the systematic evaluation of a worker with respect to his current performance on the job and his potential for future development.

Figure 6-15 shows the chronological and sequential relationships between and among the recruitment, selection, placement, indoctrination, and appraisal processes. Appraisal is the linking component for these staffing subfunctions, as indicated by the arrows in Figure 6-15. Figure 6-15 also shows that recruitment precedes selection, which precedes placement

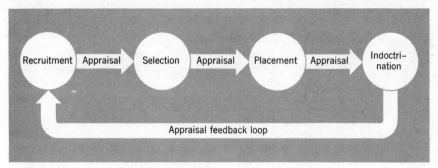

FIGURE 6-15 Interrelationships between staffing and appraisal subsets.

which, in turn, precedes indoctrination. Note also in Figure 6-15 that appraisal serves as a feedback loop connecting the staffing subprocesses in a circular or cyclical fashion. This accurately portrays employee recruitment, selection, placement, indoctrination, and appraisal as continuous processes. When employee recruitment, selection, placement, indoctrination, and appraisal are thought of as continuous processes, it is easier to understand the partially interrelated and overlapping nature of these employment subprocesses. Currently, EEOC and OFCC decisions, along with affirmative action programs, are having an effect on all the subprocesses within the overall staffing concept.

DISCUSSION QUESTIONS AND ASSIGNMENTS

1. Identify the subprocesses within the overall staffing process.
2. How are employees normally selected? Which selection techniques do you personally feel are the most valid and reliable?
3. Identify and briefly explain the most commonly used performance appraisal methods.
4. Present your personal viewpoints concerning the advantages and disadvantages of testing and interviewing.
5. Which do you feel is more important, proper selection or proper placement? Defend your answer.
6. Draw a figure representing the relationships between recruitment, selection, placement, indoctrination, and appraisal.

REFERENCES

General Book References

Anastasi, Anne, *Psychological Testing.* New York: Macmillan, 1968.

Barnette, W. L. (ed.), *Readings in Psychological Tests and Measurements.* Homewood, Ill.: Irwin-Dorsey, 1968.

Barrett, R. S., *Performance Rating.* Chicago: Science Research Associates, 1966.

Blum, M. L., and J. C. Naylor, *Industrial Psychology: Its Theoretical and Social Foundations.* New York: Harper & Row, 1968.

Burns, T. J., *The Behavioral Aspects of Accounting Data for Performance Evaluation.* Columbus, Ohio: College of Administrative Science, Ohio State University Press, 1970.

Campbell, J. P., M. D. Dunnette, E. E. Lawler, and K. E. Weick, *Managerial Behavior, Performance, and Effectiveness.* New York: McGraw-Hill, 1970.

Coss, F., *Recruitment Advertising.* New York: American Management Association, 1968.

Dunnette, Marvin, *Personnel Selection and Placement.* Belmont, Calif.: Wadsworth, 1966.

Finkle, R. B., and W. S. Jones, *Assessing Corporate Talent.* New York: Wiley, 1970.

Ghorpade, J., *Assessment of Organizational Effectiveness.* Pacific Palisades, Calif.: Goodyear, 1971.

Guion, R. M., *Personnel Testing.* New York: McGraw-Hill, 1965.

Hagglund, G., and D. Thompson, *Psychological Testing and Industrial Relations.* Iowa City: University of Iowa Press, 1969.

Jaquish, Michael P., *Recruiting.* New York: Wiley, 1968.

Korman, A. K., *Industrial and Organizational Psychology.* Englewood Cliffs, N. J.: Prentice-Hall, 1971.

Likert, Rensis, *The Human Organization: Its Management and Value.* New York: McGraw-Hill, 1967.

Rosen, D. B., *Employment Testing and Minority Groups.* Ithaca, N. Y.: New York State School of Industrial and Labor Relations, Cornell University Press, 1970.

Wikstrom, W. S., *Management By- and With-Objectives.* New York: National Industrial Conference Board, 1968.

Specific Journal References

Asher, J. J., "Reliability of a Novel Format for the Selection Interview," *Psychological Reports, 26* (4), 1970, pp. 451–456.

Bahn, Charles, "Economy of Scientific Selection," *Personnel Journal, 49* (8), 1970, pp. 651–654.

Bassett, G. A., and H. H. Meyer, "Performance Appraisal Based on Self-Review," *Personnel Psychology, 21* (4), 1968, pp. 421–430.

Bennis, S. E., "Occupational Validity of the General Aptitude Test Battery," *Journal of Applied Psychology 52* (3), 1968, pp. 240–244.

Bray, D. W., and J. L. Moses, "Personnel Selection," *Annual Review of Psychology, 23* (1), 1972, pp. 545–576.

Browning, R. C., "Validity of Reference Ratings from Previous Employers," *Personnel Psychology, 21* (4), 1968, pp. 389–393.

Brumback, G. B., and J. W. Vincent, "Jobs and Appraisal of Performance," *Personnel Administration, 33* (4), 1970, pp. 26–30.

Burke, R. J., and D. S. Wilcox, "Characteristics of Effective Performance Review and Development Interviews," *Personnel Psychology, 22* (3), 1969, pp. 291–305.

Byham, William C., "Assessment Centers for Spotting Future Managers," *Harvard Business Review, 48* (4), 1970, pp. 150–160.

Cannedy, Rodney C., "The Development and Validation of Psychological Tests to Predict Employee Tenure," *Dissertation Abstracts International, 30* (3), 1969, p. 1391.

Carlson, R. E., et al., "Improvements in the Selection Interview," *Personnel Journal, 50* (4), 1971, pp. 268–275.

Didato, Salvatore V., "Some Reminders about Selecting Good Managers," *Personnel Journal, 49* (6), 1970, pp. 489–491.

Frank, Edward R., "Motivation by Objectives—A Case Study," *Research Management, 12* (6), 1969, pp. 391–400.

Gannon, M. J., "Sources of Referral and Employee Turnover," *Journal of Applied Psychology, 55* (3), 1971, pp. 226–228.

Goldstein, I. L., "The Application Blank: How Honest Are the Responses?" *Journal of Applied Psychology, 55* (4), 1971, pp. 491–493.

Greer, Thomas V., "Some Behavioral Aspects of Training," *S.A.M. Advanced Management Journal, 35* (3), 1970, pp. 55–63.

Gunn, Bruce, "The Polygraph and Personnel," *Personnel Administration, 33* (2), 1970, pp. 32–37.

Hershey, Robert, "The Application Form," *Personnel, 48* (1), 1971, pp. 36–39.

Inskeep, Gordon C., "Statistically Guided Employee Selection: An Approach to the Labor Turnover Problem," *Personnel Journal, 49* (8), 1970, pp. 15–24.

Kavanaugh, M. J., "The Content Issue in Performance Appraisal: A Review," *Personnel Psychology, 24* (4), 1971, pp. 653–668.

Korman, A. K., "The Prediction of Managerial Performance: A Review," *Personnel Psychology, 21* (4), 1968, pp. 295–332.

Martin, Robert A., "Our Primitive Employment Process," *Personnel Journal, 49* (2), 1970, pp. 117–122.

Mayfield, Eugene C., "Management Selection: Buddy Nominations Revisited," *Personnel Psychology, 23* (3), 1970, pp. 377–391.

Meyer, Pearl, "How to Read a Resume," *Dunn's Business Review, 96* (4), 1970, pp. 48–52.

Miner, J. B., "Management Appraisal: A Capsule Review and Current References," *Business Horizons, 11* (5), 1968, pp. 83–96.

Mosher, Lawrence, "Court Rules Against Job Tests Screening Out Blacks," *National Observer,* March 15, 1971, p. 6.

Nash, A. N., and S. J. Carroll, "A Hard Look at the Reference Check," *Business Horizons, 13* (5), 1970, pp. 45–49.

Novack, Stanley R., "Developing an Effective Application Blank," *Personnel Journal, 49* (5), 1970, pp. 419–423.

Oberg, Winston, "Making Performance Appraisal Relevant," *Harvard Business Review, 50* (1), 1972, pp. 61–67.

Owens, W. A., and D. O. Jewell, "Personnel Selection," *Annual Review of Psychology, 20* (4), 1969, pp. 419–446.

Pickens, William, "The Interview—The Black's Viewpoint," *Business Horizons, 13* (5), 1970, pp. 13–22.

Pyle, William C., "Human Resource Accounting," *Financial Analysts Journal, 26* (5), 1970, pp. 69–78.

Rabourn, Owen N., James H. Schilz, and Charles W. Holland, "A Successful Selection Technique," *Personnel Journal 46* (4), 1967, pp. 211–213.

Sharon, A. T., and C. J. Bartlett, "Effect of Instructional Conditions in Producing Leniency on Two Types of Rating Scales," *Personnel Psychology, 22* (3), 1969, pp. 251–263.

Sparks, Charles P., "Validity of Psychological Tests," *Personnel Psychology, 23* (1), 1970, pp. 39–46.

Thompson, David W., "Selective Trait Matching Sequence: An Alternative Approach to Management Selection and Promotion," *Personnel Journal, 49* (1), 1970, pp. 45–49.

Tosi, Henry L., and Stephen J. Carroll, "Managerial Reaction to Management by Objectives," *Academy of Management Journal, 11* (4), 1968, pp. 420–425.

Travaglio, Ray F., "Response Differences Among Employment Applicants," *Personnel Journal, 49* (7), 1970, pp. 593–597.

Walker, James W., Fred Luthan, and Richard M. Hodgetts, "Who Really Are the Promotables?" *Personnel Journal, 49* (2), 1970, pp. 123–137.

Wikstrom, Walter S., "Assessing Managerial Talent," *Conference Board Record, 4* (3), 1967, pp. 39–44.

Wollowick, H. B., and W. J. McNamara, "Relationship of the Assessment Center to Management Success," *Journal of Applied Psychology 53* (2), 1969, pp. 348–352.

Wright, O. R., "Summary of Research on the Selection Interview Since 1964," *Personnel Psychology 22* (3), 1969, pp. 391–413.

contents

learning objectives

1. To understand the similarities and differences between the concepts of training, development, education, and learning.

2. To become knowledgeable about training and development methods.

3. To be aware of the purposes of, responsibilities for, and methodologies of evaluating training and development programs.

4. To comprehend the extension of training and development concepts to the "group" and "organizational" entity levels.

The vast majority of human potential remains un-realized.

7

Training and Development

1. Definitions and Semantics

Training is a short-term educational process utilizing a systematic and organized procedure by which nonmanagerial personnel learn technical knowledge and skills for a definite purpose. Development, in reference to staffing and personnel matters, is a long-term educational process utilizing a systematic and organized procedure by which managerial personnel learn conceptual and theoretical knowledge for general purposes (Steinmetz). Thus training and development differ in four ways: "what" is learned, "who" is learning, "why such learning takes place and "when" the learning occurs. More and more today training refers only to the instruction of technical and mechanical operations, while development refers to more philosophical and theoretical educational concepts. Training is designed for nonmanagers, while development is aimed at managerial personnel. Training courses are typically designed for a short-term, stated set purpose, such as the operation of some piece(s) of machinery, while development involves a broader education for long-run general purposes (Campbell). These training and development distinctions are summarized in Figure 7-1.

LEARNING DIMENSION	TRAINING	DEVELOPMENT
Who	Nonmanagers	Managers
What	Technical-mechanical operations	Theoretical-conceptual ideas
Why	Specific job-related purpose	General knowledge
When	Short term	Long run

FIGURE 7-1 Training and development distinctions.

Training versus Development

Often an explanation such as that shown in Figure 7-2 is used to describe the differences existing between the training and development concepts. This portrayal is usually credited to Robert L. Katz, who first presented these ideas in 1955. Nonmanagerial instructional needs are largely technical and human relations, but they are not conceptual in nature. Managerial educational needs are basically conceptual and human relations, but they are not technical in nature. Nonmanagerial training and management development both stress human relations skills. It is generally believed that effective personnel must be able to learn basic human relations skills, such as communication, motivation, and leadership, at all organizational levels (Mosvick). Lower-echelon employees must also be taught technical skills, such as how to operate mechanical equipment, while higher level managers must learn theoretical concepts, such as planning, organizing, and controlling (Moulds). When technical instead of conceptual skills are stressed, this instructional process is usually called training. Conversely, development is the label given to educational procedures designed to teach conceptual instead of technical skills. In reality, the training and development concepts overlap because there are no clear-cut distinctions or lines of demarcation between and/or among technical, human relations, and conceptual skills.

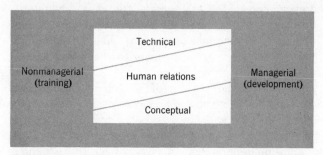

FIGURE 7-2 Nonmanagerial and managerial needs for different skills.

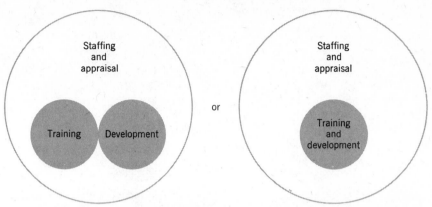

FIGURE 7-3   Training and development as subset(s) of staffing and appraisal.

Relationship to Staffing and Appraisal

Sometimes training and development are considered part of the overall staffing or appraisal concept. Figure 7-3 illustrates that training and development, individually or collectively, can be considered subsets within the overall staffing and appraisal set concept. I will discuss training and development in a separate chapter because of the tremendous importance currently given to these employment subfunctions.

Relationship to Indoctrination

A final semantic difficulty concerns the training function and its relationship to the indoctrination concept. Training and indoctrination (induction or orientation) should be regarded as partially interrelated and overlapping concepts instead of as totally distinct or completely synonymous set entities. However, many personnel authors and practitioners think that indoctrination is a subset of the overall training concept, as shown in Figure 7-4. This interpretation sees indoctrination as an intitial type of training that is broad and generally company related. Through this perspective, only later forms of employee training become specifically job related.

2. Relationships to and Role of Education

The relationship of education in general to the more narrow concepts of development, training and learning is shown in Figure 7-5. Education is the broadest instructional concept, and learning is the most specific of these instructional processes, with development and training falling between these two extremes.

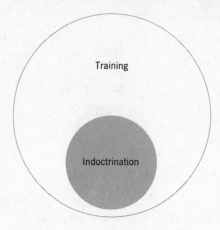

FIGURE 7-4 Indoctrination as a subset of training.

Education as Capital

Instruction within organizations is moving from the idea of training to development and eventually on to education. This movement progresses from specific job skills to wider organizational concepts and even, at best, includes general personal enlightenment. Although most organizations have not reached the stage where educating employees is done only for purely worker self-actualization, there now is at least a beginning of a movement to this end (Wright). Immediately after World War II, managers began to think of the immense training task that had been accomplished during the war. From this experience arose a new sense of the importance of manpower and its potential if people are properly trained or educated. For the first time, the idea developed that education and training should be thought of as invest-

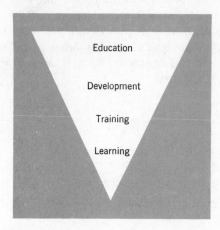

FIGURE 7-5 The education, development, training, and learning relationship.

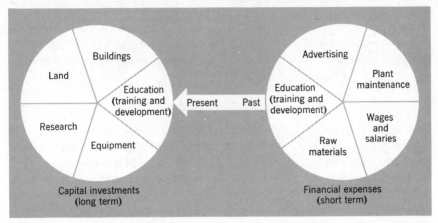

FIGURE 7-6   Education as a long-term capital "investment."

ments in human resources, or even as a capital investment. The next step was to measure the rate of return on this investment. This measurement task, however, was and still is quite complex (Kelley). Such measurement attempts are called human asset accounting. Human asset accounting shows the value of an organization's human resources on the actual company balance sheet. However, it is usually agreed among progressive manpower managers that education does not have to be justified on purely economic grounds. There are many advantages in having an educated population that cannot be measured by monetary means.

Figure 7-6 illustrates the central idea that the education of organizational personnel should be considered a capital investment, not a financial expense. Land, buildings, equipment, and research are often considered capital investments, since they appreciate in value in the long run. Financial expenses such as plant maintenance, wages and salaries, raw materials, and advertising are often seen as short-run expenditures. In reality, the differences between a short-run financial expense and a long-run capital investment are often impossible to discern. Nevertheless, in the past, manpower education (training and development) was usually thought of as a short-run financial expense, but it is presently more properly envisioned as a long-term capital investment.

Human Potential

In general, human potential is an unlimited and underutilized organizational resource. People are capable of much more than they are normally called on to do, and they can learn much more than was formerly thought possible. Employees possess an untapped intellectual reservoir that can serve as an organizational creativity pool and resource if properly managed (Drucker). Almost all workers are anxious to extend and explore these cognitive capacities and capabilities if given a chance to do so. Such observations and findings make the "education as capital" idea a reality instead of only an adroit adage or a verbal platitude.

Long-Run Process

Throughout the American economy and society, a changed attitude toward education is taking place. Instead of educating an elite group, learning and instruction are meant for the entire populace. Instead of thinking about going to school for a fixed number of years and feeling that this a terminal education, the idea of continuing education is being considered. Instead of trying to cram everything a person needs to know for the rest of his life into a limited number of years while he is young, the notion of returning to school from time to time throughout one's life is now evident (Odiorne).

Lifelong Processes

Learning and education are lifelong processes. The high school dropout must complete school if he intends to advance personally and organizationally. Junior colleges have been established to fulfill many local community needs, one of which is to teach trade-related subjects to high school graduates. Small, private, four-year colleges are geared to teach the liberal arts to their enrolled students. Large public undergraduate and graduate universities have been created to prepare enrolees for the professions. Master and doctoral programs have been enacted to train and develop specialists in many fields. Even postdoctorate instruction is now offered in the areas of expertise that tend to change rapidly because of frequent technological and theoretical breakthroughs and discoveries (Moulds).

Within any work organization, employee education is also a continuing process. Assembly line workers must be trained and retrained as new automated equipment is introduced. Technicians must attend seminars and conferences to keep abreast of the latest technical developments in their fields. Managers must attend workshops and extension courses to learn the latest planning, organizing, and controlling techniques, and so on.

The idea of lifelong education is frightening to many people, but it is now an economic and social fact of life. Those who do not accept this concept usually find it difficult to adjust to and cope with our fast moving, constantly changing, achievement-oriented American style of life. The modern manpower manager accepts the concept of continuous educational assessment, and a good portion of his time and effort involves establishing procedures and methods for dealing with and implementing this idea within the organization that employs him.

Federal Legislation

For the first century of this nation's history, education for work, except at the professional level, was regarded as largely inappropriate in the public educational system. Slow change away from this early policy can be noted. Private vocational schools emerged to meet the demands for manpower with specialized vocational training. Public funds provided collegiate training in medicine, law, and education. Teacher colleges were created to meet the rapidly growing demands in public education. In the early twentieth century, federal support became available for high school courses in agriculture, the trades, and home economics (Smith-Hughes Act, 1917). These programs were granted additional federal support by the George-Barden Act on 1946. Meanwhile, both federal and state support sought to encourage apprenticeship training for the skilled crafts.

Postwar Policy

World War II marked a sharp turn in public policy in the United States and around the world. Wartime shortages of skilled craftsmen threatened the success of military operations. Special training programs in this nation, such as the Training Within Industry program or T.W.I., tried to overcome the handicap imposed by shortages of skills. Following the war, the National Defense Education Act of 1958 provided federal support for educating skilled workers essential to defense industries. Even more spectacular, however, was the worldwide interest in education as the key to industrialization and economic development. Education and training became the recognized magic words for speeding industrialization and the race toward prosperity. In the United States this movement led to federal legislation initiating a whole new national manpower development program.

Symbolic of this new public policy are the stated intentions of the Manpower Development and Training Act (MDTA) of 1962 and the Vocational Education Act of 1963. The former made it the obligation of the Secretary of Labor to search for and identify skill and capability needs in our economy and to initiate and financially support the special educational programs thus prescribed. The latter initiated the updating of vocational education throughout the nation to attune such programs to present and prospective demands for specialized competence. Today's MDTA programs have been modified and amended by other federal programs, such as the War on Poverty (1964), Neighborhood Youth Corps (1964), Job Corps (1964), and especially by the Job Opportunities in the Business Section program (JOBS) of 1967. Many of the original provisions contained within MDTA are now provided for by the Comprehensive Employment and Training Act of 1973, which has superseded MDTA.

Although consensus about the future is not totally clear, many observers believe that public policy can be expected to support a much wider range of educational programs and to provide more financial support in the years ahead. Reasons for this include the growing economic significance of educational attainment and the speeding pace of technological change. The shape of things to come and suggestions as to the future of public policy may be seen in the proposed Human Investment Act. This measure, first introduced in 1965, proposed to grant a tax adjustment for training costs, other than for manager and professional training, thus encouraging apprenticeship, job training, and MDTA programs.

3. Relationships to and Role of Learning

As previously shown in Figure 7-5, the beginning of education, development, and training is rooted within the learning process. Today there is an emphasis on the learning process itself. Models of human learning are being studied to try to find out why some individuals seem to learn at a faster rate than others. Environmental conditions and resources for learning are also being evaluated and stressed. Some external environmental conditions seem to foster learning, while others hinder it. Human and physical variables are being analyzed in an effort to arrive at general learning principles.

"How," Not "What"

Learning theories concentrate on "how" an individual learns instead of "what" he learns. From such studies, learning cycle models similar to life cycle models have resulted. Human learning, like human growth, seems to advance rapidly at some points, to level off at others, and to decline eventually in still other periods. The reasons and conditions for such periods are the focal point of learning analysis. Such research is important because knowing how a person learns can assist individuals, groups, and organizations in specific skill training and general educational development.

Learning concepts and theories are relatively new concerns for organizations, but these concepts are based on firmly rooted and well-grounded educational and psychological principles (This and Lippitt). We cannot deal with all of the details and developments of teaching-learning theory here, but some of the most significant aspects of current learning theory are listed to serve as a behavioral foundation for the study of current personnel administration practices related to the manpower training and development function.

Learning Principles

1. All human beings can learn. Individuals of all ages and of various intellectual capacities have the ability to learn new behaviors.

2. An individual must be motivated to learn. This motivation may exist in a variety of forms, such as self-actualization, promotional possibilities, or financial incentives. However, most learning motivation is self-motivation.

3. Learning is active, not passive. Effective education requires action and involvement from all participants.

4. Learners may acquire knowledge more rapidly with guidance. Feedback is necessary because trial and error are too time consuming and inefficient.

5. Appropriate materials should be provided. Educators should possess a reasonable repertoire of training tools and materials, such as cases, problems, discussion questions, and readings.

6. Time must be provided to practice the learning. Part of the learning process requires a great deal of time for student internalization, assimilation, testing, acceptance, and confidence.

7. Learning methods should be varied. Variety should be introduced to offset fatigue and boredom.

8. The learner must secure satisfaction from the learning. Education must fulfill human needs, desires, and expectations.

9. Learners need reinforcement of correct behavior. Positive and immediate rewards reinforce and cement desired behaviors.

10. Standards of performance should be set for the learner. Goals or bench marks should be established so that individuals can judge their educational achievements and progress.

11. Different levels of learning exist. Learning may involve awareness, changed attitudes, or changed behavior. Some learning involves mental processes, while other instructional activities concentrate on physical maneuvers. Different time and method requirements are needed to bring about different levels of learning.

12. Learning is an adjustment on the part of an individual. Actual learning represents a change in the student, and all changes require adjustments.

13. Individual differences play a large part in the effectiveness of the learning process. What can be learned easily by some individuals may be very difficult for others because of differences in basic abilities or cultural backgrounds.

14. Learning is a cumulative process. An individual's reaction in any lesson is conditioned and modified by what has been learned in earlier lessons and experience.

15. Ego involvement is widely regarded as a major factor in learning. Each participant learns most when he sees the training opportunity as related to the attainment of his personal goals.

16. The rate of learning decreases when complex skills are involved. Simple skills can be learned easier and quicker than complex activities.

17. Learning is closely related to attention and concentration. The learning process is more effective if distractions are avoided.

18. Learning involves long-term retention and immediate acquisition of knowledge. Such retention is encouraged by understanding, emphasizing, and repeating.

19. There are upward spurts of understanding followed by plateaus in the curve of learning. New knowledge is always gathered in a sporadic fashion.

20. Accuracy generally deserves more emphasis than speed during the learning process. Speed can be improved, but accuracy is more difficult to control.

21. The law of effect states that a particular response becomes more certain the more often it occurs. In other words, repetition tends to fix the response or adjustment.

22. Sleep affects learning. Sleeping immediately following (but not during) a learning experience often improves retention.

23. Learning should be reality based. Education should be highly related to the learner's life experiences.

24. Learning should be goal oriented. Specific purposes and rewards affiliated with the learning effort generally enhance educational attainment endeavors.

From such educational principles and research findings, many management training and development guidelines and adages have emerged. For example, manpower development is inevitably self-development. No firm or manager can develop people; managers can only provide opportunities and incentives for people to develop themselves. Another managerial guideline is that education is not effective in solving all organizational problems. An important question for managers concerns the relationship between problems to be solved and the likely usefulness of instruction for that purpose.

4. Purposes of Training and Development

There are many reasons why companies install employee training and management development programs. In general, the reasons for beginning an employee training program are similar to or identical with the purposes of initiating a management development procedure. These purposes concern: (1) productivity; (2) quality; (3) human resource planning; (4) morale; (5) indirect compensation; (6) health and safety; (7) obsolescence prevention; and (8) personal growth. Collectively these eight purposes directly relate to and comprise the ultimate purpose of organizational training and development programs, and that purpose is to enhance overall organizational effectiveness. Each of these purposes will now be discussed briefly except for obsolescence prevention, which will be covered in greater detail because of its increasing importance.

Productivity

Training and development apply not only to new employees but to experienced people as well. Instruction can help employees increase their level of performance on their present job assignments. Increased human performance often directly leads to increased operational productivity and increased company profits (Scott). Increased performance and productivity, because of training and development programs, are most evident with new employees who are not yet fully aware of the most efficient and effective ways of performing their jobs (Baum, Sorensen, and Place).

Quality

Proper training and development not only improve the quantity of output, but they usually also improve the quality of output as well. Better informed workers are less likely to make operational mistakes. In addition, more highly educated and enlightened managers attempt to utilize more participative styles of employee interaction. Thus quality increases may be in a relationship to the company product or service, or in reference to the intangible organizational employment atmosphere (Boocock).

Human Resource Planning

Proper employee training and development can help a company to fulfill its future personnel needs and requirements. Organizations that have a good internal educational program will have less drastic manpower changes and adjustments to make in the event of sudden personnel alterations. When the need arises, organizational vacancies can more easily be staffed from internal sources if a company initiates and maintains adequate instructional programs for both its nonsupervisory and managerial employees (Fine).

Morale

The general organizational climate and atmosphere are usually improved when proper educational programs exist within a company. There are many reasons for this. An endless chain of positive reactions can result from well-planned company instructional programs. For example, productivity and product quality may rise, financial incentives may then be increased, internal promotions become stressed, less supervisory pressures ensue, and base-pay rate increases result. Increased morale may be due to many factors, but one of the most important of these is the current state of an organization's educational endeavors. (Greer).

Indirect Compensation

Many workers, especially managers, consider educational opportunities part of their total employee-employer remuneration package. They expect the company to pay the bill for programs leading to their increased general knowledge and skill expertise. Many organizations accordingly offer special training and development programs as recruitment techniques to attract highly qualified potential employees (Jones and Moxham).

Health and Safety

An employee's mental health and physical safety are often directly related to an organization's training and development efforts. Proper training can help prevent industrial accidents and a safer work environment can lead to more stable employee mental attitudes. Managerial mental states can also be improved if supervisors know that they can better themselves through company-designed development programs (Florsheim).

Obsolescence Prevention

Continuous employee training and development efforts are needed so as to keep workers abreast of the current improvements in their respective fields of work, whether they are mechanical or managerial. Old skills and antiquated ideas will bankrupt an organization. Training and development programs foster employee initiative and creativity and thus help to prevent manpower obsolescence (Aronoff and Litwin). There is no way to prevent machinery obsolescence, but the more serious problem of antiquated manpower can be at least partially alleviated through a continuous program of educational assessment.

Employee obsolescence is the discrepancy that exists between an employee's expertise and the demands of his job. Many employees lack the training and experience necessary for them to fulfill their work roles efficiently and effectively (Drucker). Supervisors may be matched to their positions compatibly at one point in time but, as additional time passes, jobs change, and so do human personalities, and these movements are not always in the same direction. There are many causes of employee obsolescence, such as lack of training, insufficient human intellectual capacity, time constraints, environmental pressures, and cultural and societal alterations. However, the primary casual factor of employee obsolescence is technological change.

Technological changes can involve technique, tool, or process alterations. New statistical decision tools and the expanded use of the computer are two technological changes that affect production, marketing, finance, personnel, research, and other organizational capacities and capabilities. The accelerating pace of scientific and technological innovation is a continuing threat to an employee's knowledge and expertise. Every major technological advance threatens the relevance of human knowledge and experience. Managerial employees and nonsupervisory workers are subject to obsolescence possibilities. It is now apparent that both employee skills and managerial knowledge display the same vulnerability to obsolescence, as do physical plant and equipment materials.

Managerial obsolescence is often analyzed by the concept of "half-life." The "half-life" idea describes the situation that exists when half of the relevant knowledge in a particular area or expertise has eroded away or become obsolete because of newer scientific innovations and discoveries. Managerial half-lives are lessening in all fields, but at differing rates (Boocock).

Various organizational policies and programs can be initiated in an attempt to control employee obsolescence. Corporate officers must deal with the need for managerial upgrading as well as the recruitment of new skills. Greater attention must be paid to individual development and training (Sims). Such changes will, of course, also require new executive financial manpower commitments. Management, especially top management, has a key role in initiating and responding to technical changes. Recognizing this interrelationship between corporate policy and technological change is an essential first step in controlling and combating manpower obsolescence. Top managers must be able to anticipate future external technological changes and then plan for the necessary internal human and nonhuman resource adjustments. This process inevitably leads to restructuring the work place and realigning manpower experience and educational needs.

Other aspects of the organizational environment besides those directly involved in the formal planning processes also play important roles in determining individual and corporate adaptability to change. A supportive climate is one such dimension. New technological innovations are most smoothly introduced when all organizational levels interact and participate in the installation of a new procedure or technique. Along with participation, a gradual change introduction is usually preferable to a rapid operational alteration.

Individual adaptability also affects employee obsolescence. Motivation, temperament, and age are basic factors involved in individual obsolescence (Wohlking). Self-actualization, self-development, and self-determination are also crucial variables influencing a person's ability and willingness to adapt. New career paths are always available to the worker who is constantly ready to learn new skills in order to advance himself. Promotional inducements have always served to enhance individual coping efforts. Manpower audits reported job vacancies and new positions, and announced upcoming educational and trainining opportunities are other organizational inducements (Labovitz).

Employee obsolescence can be controlled through continuing and sophisticated attention to the forecasting of manpower needs, monitoring technological changes in terms of their employment impact, and altering indi-

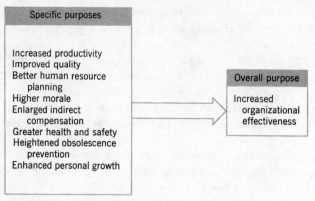

FIGURE 7-7   Purposes of training and development.

viduals to opportunities as well as to the hazards of technical change. The challenges presented by technological change can only be met through personal supportive relationships. structured organizational training development, and other programs that bring the full resources of an enterprise to bear on the problems of employee obsolescence.

Personal Growth

Not all of the benefits of company training and development programs accrue only to corporate entities. Employees on a personal basis also gain individually from their exposure to educational experiences (Bowley and Schriver). Management development programs especially seem to give participants a wider scope of knowledge, an increased feeling of competence, an aroused sense of awareness, an enlarged skill repertoire, an enlightened altruistic philosophy, and other considerations indicative of enhanced personal growth (Wiener and Attwood). The aforementioned purposes of training and development efforts are summarized in Figure 7-7.

5. Responsibilities for Training and Development

The question is often asked "Who has ultimate responsibility for an organization's training and development programs?" In terms of final authority, a company's top executive usually has the ultimate say. Many personnel and training directors have had to learn the hard way that unless top management is convinced of the vital importance of the training and development function, all personnel educational programs inevitably will fail in the long run. Top line commitment to organizational educational plans is needed as a prerequisite to all company training and development efforts. Although top line executives often possess the ultimate or latent responsibility for training and development company activities, other corporate constituencies share the manifest or operational educational responsibilities. Company officers basically determine training and development policy issues only. They determine the overall company philosophy or attitude in regard to manpower education programs in general. After instructional policy issues have been decided, other employee levels are charged with the responsibilities of putting these policies into actual operation.

Personnel Responsibility

The personnel manager or one of his subordinates, who might be identified as a training director, is the staff person usually most involved with company educational matters. This individual must take top management training policies and convert them into definitive planned educational programs. The training and development director is the one who is usually ultimately concerned with establishing and later evaluating a company's instructional programs. In smaller organizations, the personnel manager may have to assume these duties as part of his total job. The proper planning, establishment, and evaluation of training and development programs may take several years. Various forecasting techniques are used during the efforts to set up instructional manpower programs. Management inventories, career paths, obsolescence tables, replacement charts, maturity curves, and various other projective devices aid the training director in his attempt to establish the most appropriate training and development programs possible for his organization.

Supervisory Responsibility

After policy and planning matters have been decided, the training and development responsibility burden now shifts largely to all supervisors, individually and collectively. Once the educational program has been established, usually the implementation or application of the program depends on the efforts of the managers who are either training or developing their subordinates. No instructional program can succeed without the supportive backing of an organization's managers. They are the ones who serve as the direct training link to the employees. Putting an educational plan, or any other program for that matter, into effect depends ultimately on the cooperative efforts of an organization's supervisors and managers.

Employee Responsibility

Some training and development responsibility also rests with the employees or trainees themselves. It often has been said that ultimately all learning and all education is self instruction. Without the proper worker attitude or frame of reference, even well planned and effectively implemented training and development efforts may still fail. Employee motivation, trust, loyalty, and other factors also indirectly will influence employee proneness to be trained. Virtually all employees have the capacity or ability to be trained, but not all of them possess the desire or willingness to be so developed. Thus, some of the educational responsibility for training and development also is vested within the employees or trainees themselves. This responsibility when assumed is usually expressed in the forms of feedback and proposed training and development program revisions.

Multiple Responsibilities

Although other responsibilities and constituencies are involved, the training and development duties and obligations are the responsibilities of four main groups: top line management, the personnel department, supervisors, and employees. Top management sets training policy; the personnel department plans, establishes and evaluates the instructional program; supervisors implement and apply development procedures; and employees provide feedback and revision suggestions for corporate educational endeavors. In short, many individuals within an organization must share the company's training and development responsibilities. Some positions are ultimately responsible for some aspects of the total educational program, while other company personnel have the final obligation in other facets of the total training and development effort. However, responsibilities may overlap considerably in real life. Figure 7-8 shows the four basic organizational constituencies with their ultimate respective training and development responsibilities.

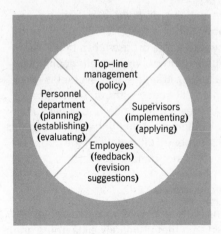

FIGURE 7-8 Responsibilities for training and development.

6. Training Methods

Earlier it was stated that training is a short-term educational process utilizing a systematic and organized procedure by which nonsupervisory personnel learn technical knowledge and skills for a definite purpose. This chapter section deals with the methods used to bring training about and the next major chapter section deals with "development methods." There are a number of commonly used training methods. The ones that we will now discuss in greater detail include: (1) on-the-job; (2) vestibule; (3) demonstration and example; (4) simulation; (5) apprenticeship; (6) classroom methods (lecture, conference, case study, role playing and programmed instruction); and (7) other training methods. The particular training method used depends on considerations of time, cost, effort, availability, instructor preferences, number of persons to be trained, depth of knowledge required, background of the trainees, and many other factors.

A. ON THE JOB

Most training is of the on-the-job variety. Some estimates are that at least 90 percent of all job knowledge is acquired through on-the-job training methods (Scoville). It is hard to pinpoint exactly what procedures and techniques constitute on-the-job training. Some of these procedures are informal and haphazard while others are formal and systematic. Simple observation and practice, which are informal techniques, are two of the greatest sources of on-the-job training knowledge. A person learns his job simply by watching others doing it and then eventually duplicating or copying these observed behaviors. Other aspects of on-the-job training may be much more formal in format. A senior employee may be assigned to a new employee to help "break him in" on the proper way to run a certain machine. Some on-the-job training may include the use of procedure charts, pictures, manuals, sample problems, demonstrations, and other training aids (Mollenkopf).

The primary responsibility for on-the-job training rests with an employee's immediate supervisor. Often, however, the supervisor delegates at least part of this obligation to a senior nonsupervisory employee. Unfortunately, on-the-job training is too often envisioned as a burden instead of a necessity. The on-the-job training function is a role that all supervisors must be taught to perform competently and sympathetically. It is the job of the personnel department to see to it that supervisors are adequately trained so that they can in turn be responsible for the on-the-job training of their subordinates.

On-the-job training is most appropriate for teaching knowledge and skills that can be learned within a few days or a few weeks. Only a few trainees should be going through on-the-job training at the same time for the same job. The most common types of jobs in which on-the-job training is used are unskilled or semiskilled in nature, such as clerical jobs or sales work. The main advantage of on-the-job training is that the trainee learns on the actual equipment and in the real environment of his job. The main drawback of this training method is that it is often highly disorganized and not properly supervised.

B. VESTIBULE

A vestibule is an isolated chamber or separate area set apart from but contained within, the walls of some housing entity. As a training method, the vestibule technique is comprised of a school or workshop usually organized in an industrial plant to introduce new workers into the work setting by means of a few weeks of practice for a specific job. Vestibule training is often done in a classroom setting for the purpose of teaching semiskilled production and clerical routines. This method is most appropriate when many new employees are being trained for the same kind of work at the same time. Although an attempt is made to duplicate the actual material, equipment, and conditions that will later be found in the real work situation, during the vestibule training period, emphasis is placed on learning instead of production. This training often deals, at least somewhat, with theory as well as practice. The type of skills being learned usually take from a few days to a few months to acquire. Vestibule schools tend to be well supervised by competent and concerned instructors. Examples of the types of jobs that are often learned through a vestibule school training method include typists, testers, clerks, bank tellers, machine operators, and inspectors.

C. DEMONSTRATION AND EXAMPLE

A demonstration is a showing and explanation of how something works or how something is done. A demonstration involves describing and displaying something through the use of experiments or examples. Often the easiest and most direct way for a manager to teach an employee how to do something is for the supervisor to actually perform the activity himself and to go through a step by step explanation of "why" and "how" he is doing what he is doing. Demonstrations are a very effective training method for a number of reasons. One reason is because of all the senses, sight is one of the best for learning. It is often much easier to simply show a person how to do a task instead of to tell him or have him read a description of the steps involved. Most demonstrations, however, are usually combined with other learning aids including lectures, pictures, text materials, discussions, et al. Demonstration seems especially appropriate as a "training" technique, but it may also be used for managerial "development" purposes. Management by example is an instance in which demonstration can be used as a managerial development device.

An example is a representative specimen deserving of imitation. Examples serve as models or cases identical with or similar to something under consideration. The example training method can be used for either teaching mechanical operations or interpersonal relationships. Training examples used for mechanical operations are actually the same instructional method as demonstration that was discussed previously. The example method, however, is also appropriate to teach interpersonal relationships, job duties and responsibilities, informal group standards, supervisory expectations, and the like. If a boss works hard, is cordial, punctual, and efficient, more than likely his subordinates will be likewise. It is virtually impossible to get desired and productive employee behavior if supervisor examples are to the contrary. Management by personal example is a tremendously powerful training technique, but one which has been grossly underestimated in importance over the years. Most employees make deliberate and conscious efforts to duplicate and copy the actions of their superiors for they assume that such behaviors are what is organizationally required in order to advance upward through the corporate hierarchy. Training by example and management by example are two major instructional concepts whose relevancies are just now becoming appreciated.

D. SIMULATION

A simulation is a situation or event that takes on the appearance or form of reality but is, in fact, an imitation of reality. In reference to training, a simulation is any kind of equipment or technique that duplicates as nearly as possible the actual conditions encountered on the job. The vestibule training method described earlier is a kind of simulation. The numerous varieties of the now popular business gaming technique are also, in essence, business simulations. The most widespread use of simulation techniques has taken place within the aerospace industry. First, pilots were taught to fly new types of airplanes in realistic working models of the actual ships. Later astronauts were trained for moon flights in lifelike space capsules and eventually even the moon atmosphere and its environment were replicated for training purposes.

Simulation Semantics

The term simulation is subject to much semantic confusion. Some people refer to any model or theory of reality as a kind of simulation. This is a rather loose and liberal interpretation of the simulation concept. Models and theories are attempts to represent reality and real world situations, although many such conceptualizations are very abstract and ambiguous. More frequently, the term simulation is reserved to identify a model that is very, very close to reality itself. Often it is extremely difficult to tell a "good" simulation from the actual experience of reality. The same cannot be said about most other types of models or theories of reality. The idea of simulation also involves a physical as well as a mental replication of actual conditions. Life size models of objects are commonly included. In contrast, many models and theories are conceptual and abstract only and do not involve or incorporate any physical matter or objects.

Simulation is usually a very expensive training technique, but it is useful or even necessary where actual on-the-job practice could result in a serious injury, a costly error, or the destruction of valuable company materials or resources. Typically, training interest and employee motivation are both high in simulation exercises because the trainee actions taken closely duplicate real world conditions.

E. APPRENTICESHIP

The apprenticeship training method is a way of developing skilled craftsmen that historically evolved as a descendant of the craft guild system of the Middle Ages. An apprentice is any learner or beginner who is usually bound by a legal agreement to serve in a certain position or capacity for a fixed period of time in order to learn a trade or business. During the era of the Industrial Revolution, apprentices were indentured and received no wages other than room, board, and clothing. Training was basically on-the-job in nature and lasted usually for seven years (Hammond).

In 1937 the Fitzgerald Act was passed in Congress and new apprenticeship standards were formalized. All apprentices must now be at least sixteen years of age. Work experience must now be supplemented with at least 144 hours of trade related classroom instruction per year. Apprentices are now paid on a program that features a progressively increasing schedule of wages. Proper supervision and periodic evaluation are also required within any modern apprenticeship system.

Apprenticeship Definition

Apprecticeable trades today are those requiring at least 4000 hours (two years) of training experience through employment. Over 300 skilled occupations today have apprenticeship training programs. Although the time period of apprenticeships vary from two to seven years, most programs take four or five years to complete.

Apprenticeship Variability

The apprenticeship systems in this country do not conform to a standard format. Within general guidelines, employers can operate apprenticeship programs according to their own organizational needs and desires since there are no strict requirements to conform to state or federal trade standards. Thus, journeymen of different caliber are commonly found within the apprenticeable trades. The apprenticeship system permits a continuous supply of highly skilled manpower to be continuously introduced into the overall industrial system. Today trainees receive decent wages while learning and later acquire a specialized skill that often commands a wage rate greater than that earned by beginning professional employees. Although the apprenticeship training periods are extended in length, the eventual financial rewards are great enough to attract an abundance of beginners into nearly all of the apprenticeable trades.

F. CLASSROOM METHODS

Much organizational training that takes place today utilizes conventional classroom methods of instruction. In many instances, these classroom methods are indeed used in actual training classrooms, but very often also, the setting might be the shop floor or actual work area. Although there is much controversy about the effectiveness of traditional classroom methods of instruction, the current lack of more effective pedagogical techniques often inevitably leads to the use and reuse of conventional teaching methodologies. Certain aspects of all jobs are more easily learned in the classroom than on the job. This is especially true if philosophy, concepts, attitudes, theories, and problem solving abilities must be learned. Technical, professional, and managerial personnel are examples of positions where trainees are expected to acquire considerable depth of knowledge during the training period. Several specific techniques are commonly used for training purposes in classroom settings. The classroom methods most frequently identified are: (1) lecture; (2) conference; (3) case study; (4) role playing, and (5) programmed instruction.

Lecture

A lecture is a discourse delivered aloud for instructional purposes. Lectures are formal organized talks on specific subject matters or areas. Lecturing has always been the traditional, most commonly used instructional method found in college and university classrooms. Lecturing permits a topic to be presented in a systematic, organized, and rigorous fashion. The main advantage of the lecture method, however, is that it can be used for very large groups and thus the cost per trainee is low. Nevertheless, the lecture method is increasingly criticized today as an instructional technique for a number of reasons. Trainees or learners are passive instead of active; only one-way communication is involved; no feedback from the audience takes place; lecturing violates the concept of learning by doing; presentations must be geared to a common level of knowledge; lecturing tends to stress the accumulation and memorization of facts and figures; and lectures do not stress the application of knowledge. Because of these disadvantages, it is usually recommended that the lecture technique be combined with other instructional methods so as to at least partially alleviate the aforementioned shortcomings.

Conference

A conference is a formal meeting in which a discussion or consultation on some important matter takes place. Conferences emphasize small group discussions, organized subject matter, and active participant involvement. Learning is facilitated basically through oral participation and member interactions. Trainees are encouraged to contribute ideas of their own that are then discussed, evaluated and perhaps modified by the ideas and opinions of others. Conferences, although they may have a leader, are intended to be mutual exchanges of information. In essence, participants learn from each other instead of from only one individual instructor. Conferences may, however, vary considerably in format. Some conferences may be "directed" or semistructured. Other types of conferences feature consultative or group problem solving methodologies. Most conferences are limited in number to fifteen to twenty persons because larger groups often prohibit active participation on the part of all conferees. Because mutual discussion is emphasized, conference participants are expected to have at least some knowledge of the subject matter to be discussed before coming to the conference. The conference training method is useful primarily for the development of conceptual knowledge and for the creation and modification of attitudes. Its principal drawbacks are that it is limited to small groups and progress is often slow because all those desiring to speak on a point are generally allowed to do so.

Case Study

A case study is a written or oral miniature description and summary of a real or hypothetical business situation and problem. When given a case to analyze, students are usually asked to identify the problem(s) and to recommend tentative solutions to the problem(s). This method provides for learning by doing and is intended to promote analytical thinking and problem-solving ability. The case method also encourages openmindedness and serves as a means for integrating knowledge obtained from a number of foundation disciplines. Although students quickly learn that there is no single answer or solution to a case problem, they are, nevertheless, expected to derive useful generalizations and principles from the cases. Case studies are extensively used in graduate professional schools of law and business administration and in supervisory and executive training programs in industry. Law, human relations, personnel management, labor relations, marketing, production management, and business policy are topics and disciplines that frequently make wide use of the case study method of instruction.

Role Playing

Role playing occurs whenever an actor assumes a part, character, or function. By definition, a role is an expected behavior pattern. When a person acts out or pretends to be fulfilling a behavioral role, then role playing exists. During role playing, two or more trainees are assigned parts to play before the rest of the group. These parts or characterizations, however, do not involve memorized lines or set behavioral actions. Role participants are simply informed of a situation and the respective roles they are to play within this hypothetical context. After some time for preliminary planning, the situation is then acted out by the role participants. Often role playing problems involve man-boss relationships such as the hiring, firing, or disciplining of a subordinate. Role playing is primarily used to give trainees an opportunity to learn human relations skills through practice and to develop insight into their own behavior and its effect on others. The advantages of the role playing method of instruction are: (1) learning by doing is emphasized; (2) human sensitivity and interactions are stressed; (3) knowledge of results is immediate; and (4) trainee interest and involvement tend to be high.

Programmed Instruction

Programmed instruction involves a sequence of steps set up, often through the control panels of an electronic computer, as guides in the performance of a desired operation or group of operations. Programmed instruction incorporates prearranged, proposed, or desired plans or courses of proceedings related and pertaining to the learning or acquisition of some specific skill or general knowledge. Programmed instruction can be carried out through a book, manual, or teaching machine. Programmed instruction involves breaking information down into meaningful subunits and then arranging these segments in a proper way so as to form a logical and sequential learning program or package (Feldman and Szabo). The major advantages of programmed instruction are: (1) students learn at their own pace; (2) material to be learned is broken down into small units; (3) immediate feedback is available; (4) active learner participation takes place; (5) individual differences can be taken into account; and (6) training can be done at odd times and in odd places. The main disadvantages of programmed learning include: (1) the impersonality of the instructional setting; (2) the fact that advanced study cannot occur until preliminary information is learned; (3) only factual subject matters can be programmed; (4) philosophical and attitudinal concepts along with motor skills cannot be taught through this methodology;

and (5) the cost of creating any such program is very great (Nash, Muczyk, and Vettori).

G. OTHER TRAINING METHODS

It is virtually impossible to comprehensively, in an all-inclusive fashion, identify and classify all the various techniques and methods used to train employees. Various types of classes, seminars, lectures, conferences, short courses, and the like are often used as employee training methods. These training methods are continuous offerings instead of once-in-a-lifetime affairs. Courses and seminars may be given on an academic degree or nondegree basis. In either case, the instruction may occur at a college, a university, a high school, a resort, the company itself, or some other location. The program may take place during the day, night, or weekend. The variety and variance of these training methods are multifaceted in scope and dimension (Carroll, Paine, and Ivancevich).

Associations

Memberships in professional or trade associations also are considered to be a type of training method. Tradesmen and other specialists continuously learn new techniques and ideas within their vocations because of these memberships. Many organizations encourage such memberships to the extent that they will pay a person's membership dues and perhaps even his expenses to various membership annual conventions. Both informal social contacts and formal association publications help to maintain and support an employee's area of expertise thus minimizing the possibility of skill obsolescence.

Audio-Visual Aids

Many companies use records, tapes, films, and video tape training methods (Bienvenu). The audio and visual aids are often a welcomed relief from traditional instructional methods. These media resources are pedagogically best used, however, in conjunction with other more conventional teaching methods.

Planned and supervised reading programs are another commonly used training technique. Specified books and journal articles are often maintained in a company library for reference and use by organizational trainees (Henry).

Overview

Figure 7-9 can serve to summarize the preceding discussion of employee training methods and shows a training methods subdivision labeled class-room methods consisting of lecture, conference, case study, role playing,

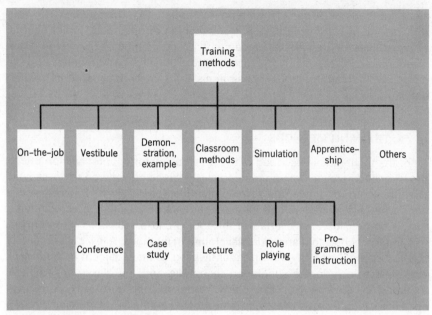

FIGURE 7-9 Training methods.

and programmed instruction elements. It also illustrates a higher order or level of training methods consisting of on-the-job, vestibule, demonstration-example, simulation, apprenticeship, classroom methods, and other elements. It must be recognized by the reader that these training methods are not all distinct instructional devices. For example, a man learning how to run a drill press may be utilizing aspects of on-the-job, vestibule, demonstration-example, simulation, apprenticeship, and other various forms of training all at the same time. Even the specific classroom methods of instruction are not easily identifiable and separable into totally complete and distinct entities. The various forms and types of employee training methods are highly interrelated, and it is consequently difficult if not impossible to tell by observing an employee who is being trained which training method or combination of methods is actually being used.

7. Development Methods

Development is the instructional process that utilizes a systematic and organized procedure by which managerial personnel learn abstract concepts and theoretical knowledge for long-run general educational purposes (Rhea and Bruskotter). Some of the most commonly used management development methods include: (1) training methods; (2) understudies, (3) job rotation and planned progression; (4) coaching-counseling; (5) junior boards of executives or multiple management; (6) committee assignments, staff meetings, and projects; (7) business games; (8) sensitivity training; and (9) other development methods. These items will now be discussed in greater detail.

A. TRAINING METHODS

All of the techniques described in the previous major chapter section under the label of employee training methods also can be considered to be, at least to some degree, managerial "development methods" as well. Because some employees are managers and all managers are employees, there obviously has to be considerable overlap in the topics and discussions of employee training methods and managerial development methods. A few of the training methods described earlier are frequently used as management instructional aids. These include the simulation technique and the classroom training methods of conference, case study, and role playing. Many personnel specialists would argue that these instructional methods are more accurately described as development devices instead of as training aids since the trainees involved are more likely to be in managerial organizational capacities rather than being from nonmanagerial jobs.

B. UNDERSTUDIES

An understudy is a person prepared to perform the work or fill the position of another. He is a trainee who at a future time will assume the duties and responsibilities of the position currently held by his immediate supervisor. The understudy concept is a manpower planning technique that insures a company that a fully qualified person will be available to take over a manager's job whenever this manager leaves his position due to promotion, transfer, retirement and so forth. The understudy managerial development technique is similar to the on-the-job training instructional method. Learning by doing is emphasized although usually an understudy does not have to perform the full range of duties and responsibilities that would be expected of him if he did in actuality occupy the position for which he is training. The understudy basically plays the role of an administrative assistant. The assistant handles only those administrative matters that his supervisor chooses to delegate to him. In addition, the manager may discuss the handling of his daily operating problems with his understudy so as to give the trainee some background and experience in such matters. Frequently, assistants are asked to investigate and make written recommendations about problems and projects related to their unit work duties. An understudy also frequently supervises a small task force in order to experiment with and to establish a certain leadership style and philosophy. Understudies are also commonly called on to attend executive meetings either with or in the place of their supervisors.

Trainee interest and motivation are usually high when the understudy development technique is used. Its greatest strength, however, is the fact that the understudy concept permits long-range manpower planning to take place on a systematic and coordinated basis. The main drawbacks of the understudy development technique exist in the forms of inbreeding and favoritism. Understudies tend to perpetuate existing practices and thus new ideas and creativity can be stifled under this training method. Also, jealousy and friction within a department may result because of an understudy program. The motivation of all other employees in the unit may decrease since the incentive to get ahead is partially destroyed when one particular subordinate is identified in advance as the one who will be the next occupant of a higher level managerial position (Dhir).

C. JOB ROTATION AND PLANNED PROGRESSION

Job rotation involves the transferring of trainees from job to job and sometimes from plant to plant on a coordinated planned basis for educational-learning purposes. Planned progression is about the same idea except that movements do not involve equal status and pay positions, but instead, each relocation involves the assumption of more and more duties and responsibilities. Often job rotation is designed for beginning level managers while planned progression is more likely to occur at higher managerial levels (Bedrosian).

Job assignments under a rotation or progression system typically last from three months to two years. Positions involved are not of the understudy nature or stature. A trainee is given the full duties and responsibilities that are part and parcel of these rotated positions. Activities are monitored and supervised in the same manner in which all normal organizational positions are evaluated and assessed.

Advantages

Job rotation and progression are intended to give a trainee a broad perspective of total corporate activities. Diversified instead of specialized skills and knowledge are emphasized. All top executive positions require generalists who have had a variety of job experiences. Departmental provincialism can be prevented and interunit cooperation can be enhanced under job rotation and planned progression managerial development methods. When a number of managers have served in each other's units, they can more readily understand the reasons why a certain function has to be done in a particular way.

Disadvantages

Position rotations promote new organizational thinking and allow for corporate manpower development. However, these movements are hard on the management trainees because so many relocations are involved. Many of the last rotated positions in such a program involve movements to different geographical locations. Because rising young executives must continually be on the move, the home or family life of those involved often suffers immeasurably. Job rotation programs also may undermine organizational morale and efficiency. Subordinates must continually adjust and readjust their behaviors to conform to new leaders. Also, occasionally rotating executives are envisioned by other company employees as an elite corps and this may lead to jealousy, friction, and other noncooperative and dysfunctional forms of human behavior.

D. COACHING-COUNSELING

In reference to managerial development, coaching is a procedure by which a superior teaches job knowledge and skills to a subordinate. The supervisor indicates what tasks he wants done and he suggests methodologies of attaining these ends. Periodic feedback and evaluation are also a part of the coaching activity. The role of a job coach is to guide a subordinate in the performance of immediate job assignments.

Counseling, on the other hand, involves a discussion between an employee and an organizational superior in matters pertaining to a worker's personal hopes, fears, emotions, and aspirations. Managers typically perform a counseling function much less than they perform a coaching role (Wohlking).

Coaching versus Counseling

Figure 7-10 illustrates the differences between the coaching and counseling managerial functions or roles. Coaching is usually done by an immediate supervisor and concerns operational, job-related issues. Counseling often is

COACHING	COUNSELING
Immediate supervisor	Personnel specialist
Job related	Personal
Long run	Short run
Frequent	Infrequent
Line relationship	Staff relationship
All employees	Few employees
Aggressive supervisory role	Passive supervisory role
Coach approaches employee	Employee approaches counselor

FIGURE 7-10 Coaching versus counseling

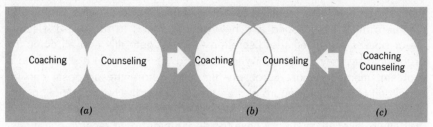

FIGURE 7-11 Three views of the relationships between coaching and counseling. (a) Distinct. (b) Interrelated. (c) Synonymous.

performed by a personnel specialist and involves human, personal problems. Coaching is intended to be a long-run process performed frequently while counseling is supposed to be infrequent in occurrence and short-run in duration. Coaching is basically a line relationship a superior should maintain with all of his subordinates, but counseling is a staff relationship a specialist has with but a few employees. Usually a coach goes to the work area to direct and instruct employee behavior, but a counselor often stays in his office, is approached by an employee, and then performs passive, nondirective, and listening roles. These differences are summarized in Figure 7-10.

Of course the managerial development concepts of coaching and counseling are similar in many respects. When a supervisor is interacting with a subordinate, it is often difficult if not impossible to clearly define whether he is performing a coaching or counseling role or function. Theoretically these concepts may differ, but pragmatically it is not possible to totally separate these two management development techniques. Figure 7-11b illustrates that the coaching and counseling management concepts are best envisioned as partially interrelated and overlapping training and development methods, instead of totally distinct (Figure 7-11a) or completely synonymous (Figure 7-11c) set entities.

E. JUNIOR BOARDS OF EXECUTIVES OR MULTIPLE MANAGEMENT

The concept of multiple management, or the junior board of executives system, as it is sometimes called, was begun in 1932 by Charles P. McCormick in his firm McCormick & Company in Baltimore. This managerial development system features permanent advisory committees of managers who study problems of the company and then make recommendations to higher management. A junior board is different in structure from the ordinary committee found in most business settings. Junior boards are formally organized under a set of bylaws. Often junior board members are paid extra compensation for their services. Members evaluate each other and have specific terms of office, and only effective members are allowed to remain on the junior board. For each succeeding term of office, some of the old members must be dropped and new people added to the board. Usually junior boards are given the discretion to investigate any and all company problems that they so desire. When a board has arrived at a solution to a problem, members must agree unanimously before the proposal can be submitted to the senior board of directors (which is the regular stockholder-elected board). Junior boards serve in a staff and advisory capacity only, and thus senior executives do not have to adopt junior board recommendations. However, in the vast majority of cases, senior directors do adopt junior board proposals.

Advantages

As a management development method, multiple management or the junior board of executives system has the following advantages: (1) it is relatively inexpensive (indirect opportunity costs are, however, involved); (2) a considerable number of managers can participate within a reasonable period of time; (3) members gain practical experience in group decision making and teamwork; (4) it helps identify good executive talent; (5) sound business recommendations arrived at through multiple judgments are obtained for company use; (6) board members broaden their administrative horizons since they are forced to be generalists instead of specialists; and (7) general improvements in organizational efficiency, productivity, and morale are often found as byproducts under this managerial development system (Core). The main difficulty with this method is that alleged "prima donnas" are identified and this identification can lead to lower motivation for those not belonging to the "in" group.

F. COMMITTEE ASSIGNMENTS, STAFF MEETINGS, AND PROJECTS

Committee Assignments

A committee is a body of persons appointed or elected to consider, investigate, take action on, and usually to report concerning some matter of business. Committees come in all forms, shapes, and sizes. A committee may be two people or it may be twenty or more. Committee members may be appointed or elected. In addition, committees may be formal or informal and temporary or permanent. Some committees serve in staff capacities while others perform line functions, some are comprised of nonmanagerial personnel while others are made up of top level executives. The committee structure is used to obtain the more detailed analysis of problems by a few key committee members. Subcommittees are formed to investigate and research certain issues and then recommendations are usually made to the committee as a whole for approval and modification if necessary. Committees promote the mutual sharing and discussion of points of interest by many individuals so as to arrive at consensus opinons. Assignments to committees have always been and will in the future continue to be a widely used technique of developing managers into general administrators.

Staff Meetings

Staff meetings exist when top level executives get together formally to discuss organizational problems and issues. Executives from both line and staff departments usually participate in staff meetings. Management trainees are frequently asked to informally observe staff meetings and occasionally they may even make formal reports and presentations before such a group. Actually, meetings of an organization's staff (and thus staff meetings) can occur at any company level; but as a managerial development technique, the staff meeting concept is usually reserved to refer only to top level executive staff meetings.

Projects

A project is a planned undertaking, a proposed scheme, a definitely formulated piece of research, or a mental projection. Projects are tasks or problems that involve the learning of some phase of company operations and that call for constructive thought and action. Management trainees are given or assigned projects on an individual or group basis and the results of these projects are evaluated by executive managers. A complicated project utilizing a large group of personnel is often called a task-force. Projects and task-forces, like committees, come in a variety of forms because of size, duration, composition, formality, and other functional, structural, and organizational differences.

G. BUSINESS GAMES

Business games are classroom simulation exercises in which teams of individuals compete against each other or against an environment to achieve given objectives. Business games, or management games as they are sometimes called, are designed to be representative of real life conditions. Most business games are expressed in the form of a mathematical model controlled and manipulated through the aid of an electronic computer. Usually management games consist of several teams that represent competing companies. Teams make decisions concerning prices, production volume, research expenditures, and advertising effort in an attempt to maximize hypothetical profits in this simulated environment. Team actions and decisions are fed into a computer that has been programmed according to a particular model of the market. Although a computer can handle much complex mathematical data in a very brief period of time, not all business games feature computer assistance. "Manual" business games, in which calculations are made by hand or with a desk calculator, also are found and used often today as managerial development techniques.

Business games are intended to teach trainees how to make management decisions in an integrated manner. Some business games concern management in general, while others focus more specifically on a particular functional field of general management such as production control, sales, financial management, or labor relations. Business game participants learn by analyzing problems and by making trial and error decisions. A main feature of business games is the consolidation of the time dimension. Business decisions and their repercussions can be determined in the space of a few hours instead of a few years. Management games illustrate the organizational existence of various group processes including communication, conflict resolution, leadership emergence, and the development of friendship ties. Business games are fun and they do stress the concept of integration, but their true educational validity is not yet really known. Games may be accurate simulations, but they never can be totally realistic. There is no concrete evidence to support the fact that those successful in a business game situation also will be successful in a real job environment. It is usually recommended that business games be used in conjunction with other more conventional training and development methods.

H. SENSITIVITY TRAINING

Sensitivity training is currently one of the more widely discussed management development techniques in existence. The topic of sensitivity training will be presented using the following topic format: (1) definition and semantics; (2) history and evolution; (3) components; (4) goals; (5) variance; and (6) evaluation. This longer than usual presentation of a development method will take place because of the tremendous impact sensitivity training has had on both the academic and business worlds.

Definition and Semantics

Sensitivity training is subject to definitional difficulties. There is no common agreement as to what sensitivity training is or is not. Many terms are often used synonymously with sensitivity training. Such terms might be: laboratory training, group dynamics, T-grouping, confrontation groups, awareness experiences, human capacity movements, sensitivity retreats, marathons, and encounter sessions (Buchanan). Accordingly, sensitivity training means different things to different people. On a very general basis, sensitivity training can be a phrase descriptive of any training or development technique that attempts to increase or improve human sensitivity and awareness. As a specific concept of management development, however, the idea of sensitivity training usually has a much more narrow interpretation, and accordingly it usually refers to a set of more rigidly defined procedures. Because the phrase "sensitivity training" is used in so many ways, I will not attempt to define the concept but will instead attempt to describe its procedures and to fit it into its proper evolutionary perspective and context.

One major semantic difficulty is the misconception of equating sensitivity training to (with) T-grouping. As the terms are normally used, T-grouping is but one aspect or component of sensitivity training, albeit, usually one of the most important and dramatic parts.

History and Evolution

Sensitivity training began in Bethel, Maine, in 1947 by an association later to be called the National Training Laboratory (NTL). After a rather slow start, sensitivity training began to gain greater momentum by 1960. It initially became part of management training programs in business and industry, but later gained favor in many religious and educational enterprises. Although sensitivity training is only some twenty-five years old, its availability and quasiacceptance now can be seen and found throughout most parts of the world.

Today some business schools conduct sensitivity training programs for managers from industry as well as for their own students. Even large corporations sometimes conduct internal sensitivity programs for their own executives and other employees. In this way, sensitivity training has spread throughout the country and is today commonly used within management development programs. However, the bulk and vast majority of educational programs in existence currently, which are identified as sensitivity training endeavors, are performed within churches and educational institutions. It is hard to find any church, college, or university of any size today that does not in some way make use of sensitivity training techniques. These programs are designed to improve personal self insight and they also stress vocational guidance and emotional adjustment, and they usually are not supervised by NTL associates. In short, what began as an NTL management development technique has now become introduced within many types of organizations as a device for increasing interpersonal awareness and sensitivity.

Components

Sensitivity training is basically composed of three types of activities: (1) T-grouping; (2) exercises; and (3) theory sessions.

T-GROUP

The most talked about and controversial aspect of sensitivity training is the "T-group." The T stands for training, but some people prefer to label these groups as "D" or "L" groups to reflect their "development" or "learning" emphasis. The T-group is a largely unstructured group typically consisting of from eight to twelve persons. Usually the T-group has no leader, no agenda, and no stated goals. The group is expected to develop interaction and on-going experiences in whatever fashion group members so desire. These interactions and experiences serve as the real substance of the learning process. Participants are encouraged to give feedback to each other on their personal feelings and reactions to what is happening in the group and on their reactions to one another's behavior. The emphasis is on the "here and now" and on "face-to-face" interactions and confrontations. T-groups meet together with a trainer to learn about themselves, others, and how groups develop and function, and they represent a significant departure from many other learning approaches for group members are asked to generate their own data for scrutiny and consideration (House). This approach is sometimes referred to as experientially based learning. Sensitivity training also is referred to as "learning how to learn." As part of this learning approach, it has been found helpful in T-groups to encourage participants to deal with "here and now" instead of "there and then" issues. In early T-group sessions, group members are faced with unstructured, purposively ambiguous situations. Most individuals feel very uneasy in these nonagenda situations and the sharing of these feelings is frequently the first data the group has to consider. As the group progresses, other information is generated, considered, and made available for everyone. In the struggle to grow as a group, to become a viable, mature, miniature society, it becomes possible for the group members to reveal to and learn from each other about their individual strengths and weaknesses, to learn how to listen to one another, and how to give and receive help. During this process there is an emphasis on face-to-face interaction featuring the use of immediate and frequent feedback.

EXERCISES

Sensitivity training exercises are similar to the techniques used in assessment center "situational" tests. In-basket exercises, panel discussions, role-playing, intergroup competitive exercises, leaderless groups, business games, tape recorded activities, cases, incidents, self-insight questionnaires, group decision problems, micro or mini labs, and the like are part and parcel of sensitivity training exercises. Sensitivity training "exercises" are designed to have participants learn by actually experiencing and experimenting with different forms of behavior. Direct experience is often the best teacher. Exercises are intended to physically illustrate concepts discussed and presented during the theory sessions.

THEORY SESSIONS

Sensitivity training theory sessions are usually some kind of information giving and sharing meeting, with an additional effort often made to involve

SENSITIVITY TRAINING COMPONENTS

T-group	Exercises	Theory Sessions
Confrontation	Business games	Blake and Mouton's managerial grid
Emphasis on "here and now"	Cases—incidents	Herzberg's motivation-hygiene theory
Face-to-face interaction	In basket	Likert's four leadership systems
Feedback	Leaderless groups	Maslow's hierarchy of needs
No agenda	Micro or mini labs	McClelland's achievement motive
Unstructured	Panel discussions	McGregor's Theory X and Theory Y
Eight to twelve persons	Role playing	Odiorne's management by objectives

FIGURE 7-12 Sensitivity training "components."

the audience more directly in the educational process. Theory sessions attempt to explain theoretically or conceptually what is happening during the T-grouping and exercise activities. Theory sessions are often simply lecture sessions in which much group participation takes place. Often wide use is also made of visual aids and mechanical resources, such as records, films, tape recorders, cameras, video tapes, and the like. Theory sessions are formal or semiformal structured attempts to inform participants about the concepts, principles, and theories underlying human and organizational behavior. Theory sessions include discussions of Maslow's hierarchy of needs, McClelland's achievement motivation, Herzberg's motivation-hygiene concept, McGregor's Theory X and Theory Y, Blake and Mouton's managerial grid, Odiorne's management by objectives, Likert's fourfold classification of leadership systems, and other theoretical concepts. Figure 7-12 summarizes the three major components of sensitivity training and gives some features and examples of these three components.

Goals

The objectives of sensitivity training are to help people understand themselves better, to create better understanding of others, to gain insight into the group process, and to develop specific behavioral skills. Laboratory training also seeks to improve communication skills. In addition, participants are expected to learn how to work more effectively as group or team members and how to perform leadership roles.

The goals of sensitivity training vary tremendously depending on what organization the program is designed for, what the major focus of intent is considered to be, and what degree of insight is expectd to be gained. For

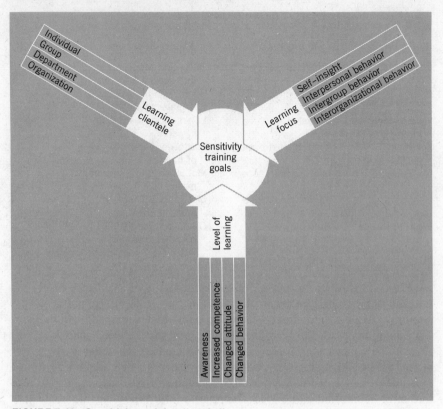

FIGURE 7-13 Sensitivity training "goals."

example, the "ultimate client" may be the individual or an organization. The learning "degree" may be awareness, increased competence, changed attitudes, or changed behavior. The "focus" of the learning or "what the learning is about" may be individual behavior, interpersonal behavior, intrapersonal retrospection, group behavior, intergroup behavior, organizational behavior, interorganizational behavior, individual versus group relations, group versus organizational behavior, or individual versus organizational behavior. In short, the goals of sensitivity training vary tremendously because of different learning levels, topics, and clientele.

On an individual, personal basis, the goal of sensitivity training is simply greater self insight. Participants are encouraged to find out more about themselves through personal meditation and retrospection, and by encouraging group feedback and analysis of individual and group behaviors. A climate of trust, openness, and love is encouraged so that participants can honestly and mutually discuss personal feelings, sentiments, attitudes, values, beliefs, and emotions.

Figure 7-13 denotes the complexity and variety of sensitivity training goals. These goals depend on three mainstream factors: learning focus, level of learning, and learning clientele. The possible alternatives within these three mainstream variables are also shown in Figure 7-13.

VARIANCE

Sensitivity training programs vary tremendously in content and caliber. One reason for this as indicated above is because of the different goals of different sensitivity groups. The relative amounts and proportions of time spent on theory sessions, exercises, and T-grouping also instills uniqueness into every laboratory experience. Group compositions always vary. Some groups are homogeneous, but others are composed of people with wide fluctuations in age, race, income, ethnic, educational, religious, political and work backgrounds, and experiences. In addition, sensitivity training sessions also range in length from a few hours to a few weeks. Some sessions are put on at resort communities, some on company, school or church premises, while others periodically change their location(s). Usually training sessions are continuous but they may involve returning to one's home or work environment and then periodically coming back for more sensitivity training encounters. Also the qualifications and methodologies of sensitivity trainers vary greatly. Some trainers are high school dropouts; others are medical physicians or psychiatrists. Some trainers play hostile, confrontation roles, while other leaders are passive within or physically absent from the group. In short, sensitivity training groups vary in design, homogeneity, length, degree of isolation, goals, and trainer activities. There is a limitless number of combinations of these factors. In essence, all individuals are unique; sensitivity groups are composed of individuals and thus each laboratory experience must also be characterized as unique instead of a standard format. Figure 7-14 summarizes the sensitivity training "variance" factors.

EVALUATION

It is difficult to make a global overview assessment of sensitivity training because of the marked variation in programs that use the "sensitivity training" identification label. Some laboratory training is of superior quality, some is worthless, but most of it is of average training caliber. Many extreme critics

---

SENSITIVITY TRAINING—VARIATIONS IN:

1. Goals	**5.** Location
2. Group homogeneity	**6.** Number of sessions
3. Learning components	**7.** Trainer qualifications
4. Length per session	**8.** Trainer role

FIGURE 7-14 Sensitivity training "variance" factors.

and proponents of sensitivity training programs are easily found. Some people see laboratory training as the best development and educational technique under the sun, while others vehemently attest to its faddishness. Most people agree that NTL sensitivity training programs are relatively worthwhile, but some other development techniques, such as "marathons," which claim to be "sensitivity training" experiences are run by fast-buck operators. In fact, recently some nudist colonies and wife-swapping organizations also have claimed to be conducting research through "sensitivity training" methods and programs.

A number of controlled research experiments have been conducted recently seeking to determine the outcomes and results of sensitivity training programs. However, not all of these studies support the concept of laboratory training (Fulmer). Most individuals enjoy and say that they learn something from sensitivity programs, but when asked to identify exactly and precisely what they learned, they are often unable to mention specifics. Research studies have, however, often noted the following changes in participants who have gone through a sensitivity training program: increased skill in interpersonal relations and greater capacity for collaboration; increased openness, receptivity, and tolerance of differences; and improved understanding and diagnostic awareness of self and others (Buchanan). The main criticism of sensitivity training is that the openness, trust, and equalitarianism that are emphasized in the lab sessions clash with the reality of the business world that is harsh, aggressive, autocratic, secretive, and extremely competitive. It also has been argued that a brief exposure to a sensitivity lab is unlikely to achieve really lasting improvements or changes in a person's life style and general philosophical beliefs, since personality components are relatively stable and ingrained after early childhood.

Layman and expert opinions evaluating sensitivity training programs range from totally positive to completely negative evaluations with most feedback falling somewhere on the continuum between these two extremes (Powell and Stinson). Generally, sensitivity training is best used as a technique for self insight instead of organizational development. Contrary to the opinions of some, it must be recognized that sensitivity training is not a panacea for all personal, organizational, and societal ills and malfunctions. The best run sensitivity training groups have clearly defined objectives and well-trained leaders. In addition, sensitivity training programs that have generally proved to be useful to organizations also have a great deal of "structure," that is, they emphasize exercises and theory sessions instead of T-groupings.

I. OTHER DEVELOPMENT METHODS

Other instructional methods, in addition to those development devices mentioned, are used for management educational purposes. Blake and Mouton's managerial grid and McGregor's Theories X and Y are examples of additional commonly used managerial development procedures. Although it is impossible to single out all of the many management development methods in existence today, those previously identified and discussed in this chapter are among the most frequently used.

Overview

In review, the development methods identified in this chapter section include: training methods; understudies; job rotation-planned progression; coaching-counseling; junior board of executives-multiple management; committee assignments, staff meetings, and projects; business games; sensitivity training; and, other development methods. It again must be recognized by the reader that these development methods are not all totally distinct instructional devices. For example, an executive giving an assignment to a subordinate manager may be utilizing aspects of understudy, planned progression, coaching, multiple management, project, and other forms of development all at the same time. Similar to the employee training methods described earlier in the chapter, the management development methods are not easily identifiable and separable into totally complete and distinct entities.

8. Evaluation of Training and Development Programs

If an organization invests in employee training and management development programs, it expects to derive some tangible benefits from these programs. Training and development directors in companies have to be able to defend the use and necessity of these programs before corporate officers will invest in them. It is not easy to statistically measure the effectiveness and justify the existence of company training and development programs. Generally, the usefulness of training and development methods is inversely proportional to the ease with which the evaluation can be done (Blumenfeld and Holland).

Participant Reaction

The easiest and least statistically valid way to evaluate a training or development program is to simply ask the participants if they learned anything. This information is usually gathered in the form of an opinion survey or questionnaire. This assessment procedure is almost totally useless, however, for often educational programs are rated by participants in terms of their entertainment value, ease, grade outcome, or personality characteristics of the instructor, instead of for their informative content (Carroll and Nash).

Before and After Test Scores

A more effective appraisal methodology involves before and after test scores. A participant is given a test before the training and development course and then regiven the same test after the completion of the instructional program. Allegedly, a significantly increased test score would indicate the informative value of the course. Several problems arise with this evaluation method. Participants do not especially like to be given a test even before the course officially begins. Tests in general are being criticized because of their general cultural biases and lack of validity. Also, increases in the test scores may not be due to the instructional program per se. And, finally, increased test scores do not usually or necessarily mean increased organizational performance or improved job competency (Cote).

Before and After Performance Measures

A third and better assessment alternative is to use before and after job performance measures. Some index of actual job performance is determined, program participants are evaluated before the training and development course is given, the educational program ensues, and at the end of the instruction participants are reevaluated using the same job performance index. Increased scores should reflect increased job competence and performance. Although this assessment technique solves some appraisal problems, many still remain. Increased scores could be due to factors other than the educational program. Additional on-the-job training and practice over time may by themselves be the real reasons for the increased job performance (Schein). To investigate these possibilities a more sophisticated research methodology is needed.

Experimental and Control Groups

The best evaluation programs feature before and after job performance measures and both experimental and control groups (Schmidt). Figure 7-15 illustrates the design of this evaluation methodology. Comparable groups A and B are matched in terms of intelligence, learning ability, and other educational considerations. Group A becomes the experimental group and Group B is designated as the control group. Both groups are evaluated through some index of general job performance. The experimental group (Group A) then goes through the designed training or development course while the control group members (Group B) simply remain on the job possibly gathering job knowledge and skill merely by performing their work over an extended period of time. The control group is not subjected to the formal training or development course. At the conclusion of the training or development course, various comparisons of job performance measures are made. Group A[1] is the experimental group after the completion of the training

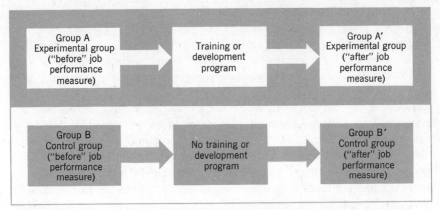

FIGURE 7-15 Experimental design for evaluating training and development programs.

or development program; group B^1 is the control group after the passage of time during which the educational program was given to Group A (but not to Group B). The effectiveness of the instructional program is evident only if A^1 scores are significantly greater than both A scores *and* B^1 scores. If A^1 indices are significantly greater than A measures, some learning has taken place. But if A^1 scores and B^1 scores are not significantly different, then the learning is due to job practice or some other educational factors instead of being a result of the training or development course effort (Thorley).

In general few research studies of the sophistication described have taken place in an effort to evaluate organizational training and development programs (Warr). The reasons for this are usually expressed in terms of time, manpower, and economic constraints. It takes considerable amounts of time, effort, and money to perform these investigations and most companies are not willing to make such investments. For example, one very time consuming and expensive problem is establishing a valid job performance measure or index. This index is extremely hard to determine and usually different indices are needed for different jobs (White). Of those organizations that have made these evaluation studies, the vast majority of them have not statistically supported the usefulness or effectiveness of employee training and managerial development programs. This, of course, is very disappointing to corporate executives, personnel managers, and training and development directors. Usually, it is discovered that A^1 job measures are significantly greater than A or B scores, but that no statistically significant differences can be noted between A^1 and B^1 job index measures. The conclusion usually reached is that on-the-job training and development accounts for the vast majority, often 90 percent or more, of all job education that occurs in most work situations and environments (Glasner).

9. Training and Development Model

Employee training and management development must be approached organizationally today in a systematic fashion and an integrated manner (Prieve and Wentorf). Training and development goals, methods, programs, and evaluations must all proceed logically and sequentially if educational endeavors are to exist efficiently within large scale institutions. In like fashion, these training and development choices must be the result of decisions based on various recognized alternatives and contingencies. For examples, training and development goals should result from individual needs and organizational objectives; training and development methods should be based on learning theories and learning methods; training and development programs have to be an outgrowth of top management support and corpo-

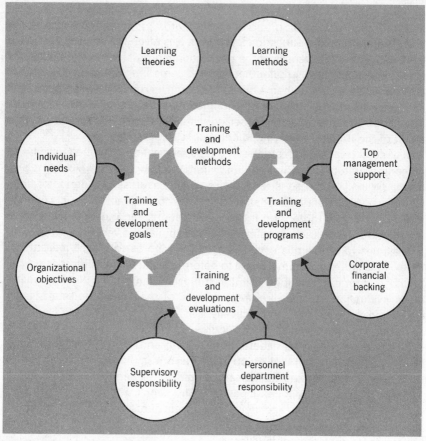

FIGURE 7-16 Training and development model.

rate financial backing; and the responsibility for training and development program evaluations must be shared by the personnel department and all organizational supervisors. Such factors considered collectively constitute a systematic training and development model featuring continuous and cyclical relationships in the manner as illustrated in Figure 7-16. Training and development goals, methods, programs, and evaluations are highly interrelated and are determined by other individual and organizational factors in a cause-and-effect systematic and sequential manner.

10. Group Development and Group Dynamics

The training and development subject matter discussed in this chapter has focused on the education of *individuals*. The next two major sections will extend the training and development horizon to incorporate the education of *groups* and *organizations*. Accordingly, the topics of group dynamics and organizational development constitute the bulk of the remaining subject material within this chapter.

Group Dynamics

Individuals exist within and achieve results through groups. Therefore, the first logical extension of the preceding chapter discussion that dealt with the training and development of individuals is the presentation of subject matter dealing with the training and development of groups. The instructional analysis of groups often exists and takes place under the label or heading of group dynamics. The concept of group dynamics will be presented using three main subdivisions entitled: (1) definition; (2) within organization meetings; and (3) teamwork.

1. *Definition.* Group dynamics is the social process by which people interact in small groups. Group dynamics is both an area of research and an area of practice, and it is closely related to sensitivity training. However, sensitivity training usually focuses on the individual, while group dynamics stresses group behavior. The concepts of laboratory training, encounter sessions, T-grouping, confrontation experiences, et al. are also kin to the group dynamics and sensitivity training concepts.

Synergism

Both research and experience make it clear that groups have properties of their own that are different from the characteristics of the individuals who make up the group. Groups display the phenomenon of "synergism." Synergism means that one plus one plus one equals more than three. One individual plus one individual plus another individual results in much more than three persons. One and one and one does not equal three when human beings are the additive units, because the "and" factor represents complex interactions and interrelationships between the human units involved. In a group there is no such thing as two or three persons only, for the "dynamics" of group and interpersonal relationships always produces a sum that is greater than the total of its additive discrete human parts.

A Group has a Purpose

A final distinction needs to be made between a group and a mere aggregation of persons. A group refers to two or more persons who are interacting with regard to a common, explicit purpose. A collection of people on a busy city street corner do not constitute a group because although they are physically gathered together, they mentally are not jointly pursuing a common or shared objective.

2. *Within organization meetings.* From an organizational perspective or point of view, group dynamics refers to the activities that take place "within organization meetings." Organization meetings usually appear in the form of committees that are institutional subgroups, which meet face to face to discuss work-related problems. By definition, a committee is a specific type of meeting in which group members have been delegated the responsibility, and sometimes even the authority, to analyze a particular problem in depth. Typically, each committee member possesses the power or influence of one vote. Meetings and committees are commonly convened for many purposes, such as information, advice, decision making, negotiation, coordination, and creative thinking.

Size Factor

Behavioral research reveals that the size of a meeting or committee affects the manner in which it works. When membership rises above seven, interpersonal communications tend to become centralized because members do not have adequate opportunity to communicate directly with one another. Often five persons are recommended to be the optimum number of meeting participants. Smaller meetings have difficulty functioning because of power conflicts. For example, when three man groups meet, there is a tendency for two persons to form a combination against the third. Four man committees are not encouraged because frequently a fifth lot is needed to break vote ties.

Level Composition

The hierarchical membership composition of a meeting is also important. Role conflicts often result when subordinates are given equal voice (and vote) on committees that also include various managerial levels. Higher corporate officials often informally control these meetings even though subconsciously they are not deliberately trying to do so. Most subordinates will not confront their superiors even when given a chance to do so because of the fear of reprisal.

Task and Social Leaders

Social research also has shown that most groups usually require two leadership roles: a task leader and a social leader. It is very infrequent that the same person fulfills both of these roles. The task leader attempts to formally get the work done while the social leader informally tries to keep everyone happy and satisfied. Although production and pleasure are not always in direct conflict, there often tends to be some degree of incompatibility between the simultaneous achievement of both of these goals.

Interaction Factor

Research in group dynamics has discovered that the more frequently persons interact, the stronger their feelings are about one another. These feelings may be in either a positive or a negative direction depending on the progress a group is making toward the achievement of an acceptable group goal. Group members tend to like one another if they are moving toward a common goal, but dislike intensifies when the objectives of group members are not shared.

Advantages

Group meetings and committees display certain organizational advantages. Three such advantages commonly observed are: improved performance, supported decisions, and increased creative thinking. Group meetings allow for membership participation that, in turn, often results in higher quality decisions — providing a problem-solving atmosphere exists. Probably the most important outcome of a meeting is that people who participate in making a decision feel more strongly motivated to carry it out. An individual who has helped make a decision is obviously more interested in seeing it implemented. Groups often may aid creative thinking by providing an environment of enthusiasm, excitement, and enjoyment. Brainstorming meetings, for example, encourage creative thinking by allowing all ideas to be presented before they are analyzed, evaluated, or criticized. "Deferred judgments" or delayed evaluations, when used within group meetings, often result in increased membership creative thinking capacity.

Disadvantages

Group meetings and committees often possess certain disadvantages, such as: slow results, divided responsibility, and inferior decisions (leveling). Time is money and because meetings consume time (sometimes exorbitant amounts of it), they are expensive and often inefficient (in addition to sometimes being ineffective). Mathematical formulae are available to illustrate how much longer it takes a group to make a decision in comparison to one person. Because groups decide issues collectively, it is hard to pinpoint who is ultimately responsible for a committee decision. Shared responsibility makes specific accountability difficult if not impossible. In addition, group discussions place a premium on conformity and compromise. This results in "leveling," which is the tendency of a group to bring individual thinking in line with the average (lower) quality of the group's thinking. In essence, leveling leads to agreement for agreement's sake. One final criticism of groups is that they can lead to a "groupthink philosophy" and the destruction of individualism and personal initiative. Some persons become addicted to groups so much so that group membership becomes an end in itself instead of a means toward an end.

3. *Teamwork.* Meetings and committees feature group members *talking* together, but teamwork emphasizes group members *working* together. Teamwork can be defined as "coordinated action by a cooperative small group in regular contact wherein members contribute responsibly and enthusiastically toward task achievement." Coordination and cooperation are essential aspects of teamwork. Cooperation is a voluntary human attitude, but coordination is an involuntary overt activity. Human beings may desire to cooperate, but this in and of itself will not automatically result in coordinated effort, unless a common goal and synchronized procedures designed to bring about the goal accompany the cooperative attitudes. A group is able to function together as a team only after each person knows the work roles of all the others with whom he will be interacting. In addition, teamwork assumes that each person possesses the necessary abilities to perform his function. Being complex and dynamic, teamwork is sensitive to all aspects of the organizational environment. Before teamwork can be developed, it is especially important that management first establish a supportive environment for it.

11. Organizational Development

After individual training and group education comes the topic of organizational development. Just as there is a synergistic effect from individuals to groups, so also is there a synergistic effect when moving from the study of groups to the analysis of organizations. Organizational behavior is much more than simply the summation and aggregation of group behaviors. Today the analysis and assessment of organizational performance and behavior often occurs under the title of organizational development.

Organizational development, usually referred to as O.D., is a new integrated type of analysis that originated in the 1960s (Mathis). In essence, O.D. is both an educational strategy and implemented courses of action that focus on the whole culture of an organization in order to bring about planned change. O.D. attempts to alter human attitudes and values as well as organizational designs and structures so that work institutions can better adapt to technology and live with the fast pace of change (Goodacre). Many observers feel that organizational development already has or in the near future will have more of an impact on society than has sensitivity training. However, because the focus of this chapter is on individual employee training and development instead of total institutional change, only the basic premises of O.D. will be presented at this time.

Characteristics

Numerous authors have attempted to identify O.D. characteristics (Kegan). Characteristics such as the following are usually mentioned.

1. O.D. is an *educational strategy* that attempts to bring about planned change.
2. O.D. relates to *real organizational problems* instead of hypothetical classroom cases.
3. O.D. uses *sensitivity training methods* and emphasizes *experientially based learning.*
4. O.D. *change agents should be external consultants* outside of the organization being changed.
5. O.D. external change agents and internal organization executives must establish a *collaborative relationship* involving mutual trust, jointly determined goals and means, and mutual influence.
6. O.D. external change agents are *humanists* seeking to establish a social and altruistic philosophy within organizations.

Words and ideas that are frequently mentioned in O.D. sessions, include team building, consensus, openness, feedback, trust, confrontation, intergroup conflict, and strategy. Sensitivity training is the educational technique most used in O.D. Because individual values and managerial philosophies are also stressed, the McGregor, Blake and Mouton, Likert, Davis, et al. approaches to the study of leadership styles and managerial philosophies (as explained in Chapter 4 of this text) are often part and parcel of O.D. training and educational sessions (Huse and Beer). In essence, O.D. to a large extent is simply the application of individual and group educational concepts to the analysis of organizations.

12. Summary

Training is a short-term educational process utilizing a systematic and organized procedure by which nonmanagerial personnel learn technical knowledge and skills for a definite purpose. Development is a long-run educational process utilizing a systematic and organized procedure by which managerial personnel learn conceptual and theoretical knowledge for general purposes.

Instead of being thought of as totally distinct (Figure 7-17a) or completely synonymous (Figure 7-17c) set entities, Figure 7-17b illustrates that the administrative and personnel concepts of employee training and management development are best envisioned as partially interrelated and overlapping instructional constructs. Also closely related to the training and development concepts are the sibling concepts of education and learning.

The purposes of or reasons for having employee training and management development programs concern issues of increased productivity, quality, human resource planning, morale, indirect compensation, health and safety, obsolescence prevention, and personal growth. Obsolescence prevention is especially a matter of enhanced importance today. However, the ultimate purpose of organizational training and development programs is to enhance overall organizational effectiveness.

Although actually other responsibilities and constituencies are involved, the training and development duties and obligations are the responsibilities of four main groups: top line management, the personnel department, supervisors, and employees.

The most commonly used employee training methds include: (1) on the job; (2) vestibule; (3) demonstration and example; (4) simulation; (5) apprenticeship; and (6) classroom methods (lecture, conference, case study, role playing and programmed instruction).

The most frequently utilized management development methods include: (1) training methods; (2) understudies; (3) job rotation and planned progression; (4) coaching-counseling; (5) junior boards of executives or multiple

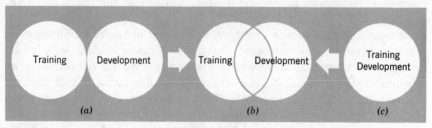

FIGURE 7-17 Training and development as distinct, interrelated, and synonymous set entities. (a) Distinct. (b) Interrelated. (c) Synonymous.

management; (6) committee assignments, staff meetings and projects; (7) business games; and (8) sensitivity training.

Training and development programs are usually evaluated by analyzing participant reactions, before and after test scores, before and after performance measures, and experimental and control groups.

Systematic training and development models reveal the relationships between training and development goals, methods, programs, evaluations, and other individual and organizational factors.

The extension of individual training and development educational concepts to the group dimension and the organization level concerns and involves the concepts of group dynamics and organizational development.

DISCUSSION QUESTIONS AND ASSIGNMENTS

1. Define and explain the similarities and differences between the training and development concepts.
2. Identify and briefly explain some of the most commonly used training and development methods.
3. Differentiate between sensitivity training, group dynamics, and organizational development.
4. From your own personal perspective, which classroom methods of instruction seem best suited to your individual learning needs? Explain the rationale behind your preferences.
5. Design an analytical methodology for evaluating an actual training or development program with which you are familiar.
6. Which of the learning principles cited within this chapter make the most and least sense to you? Be prepared to defend your choices.

REFERENCES

General Book References

Andrews, Kenneth R., *The Effectiveness of University Management Development Programs.* Boston: Graduate School of Business Administration, Harvard University, 1966.

Argyris, Chris, *Intervention Theory and Method: A Behavioral Science View.* Reading, Mass.: Addison-Wesley, 1970.

Beckhard, R., *Organizational Development: Strategies and Models.* Reading, Mass.: Addison-Wesley, 1969.

Belasco, James A., and Harrison M. Trice, *The Assessment of Change in Training and Therapy.* New York: McGraw-Hill, 1969.

Bennis, Warren G., *Organization Development: Its Nature, Origin, and Prospects.* Reading, Mass.: Addison-Wesley, 1969.

Bienvenu, Bernard J., *New Priorities in Training.* New York: American Management Association, 1969.

Blake, Robert R., and Jane S. Mouton, *Corporate Excellence Through Grid Organization Development.* Houston: Gulf, 1968.

Bradford, L.P., J. R. Gibb, and K. D. Benne (eds.), *T-Group Theory and Laboratory Method.* New York: Wiley, 1964.

Broadwell, Martin M., *The Supervisor and On-the-Job Training.* Reading, Mass.: Addison-Wesley, 1969.

Glueck, William F., *Organization Planning and Development.* New York: American Management Association, Research Study No. 106, 1971.

Howard, Janet, *Please Touch: A Guided Tour of the Human Potential Movement.* New York: McGraw-Hill, 1970.

Jakubauskas, Edward B., and C. Philip Baumel (eds.), *Human Resources Development.* Ames, Iowa: Iowa State University Press, 1967.

Maier, Norman R. F., *Problem Solving and Creativity: In Individuals and Groups.* Belmont, Calif.: Brooks/Cole, 1970.

Myers, C. A., *The Role of the Private Sector in Manpower Development.* Baltimore: Johns Hopkins Press, 1971.

Odiorne, George S., *Training by Objectives.* New York: Macmillan, 1970.

Shaw, Marvin E., *Group Dynamics: The Psychology of Small Group Behavior.* New York: McGraw-Hill, 1971.

Stroh, Thomas F., *The Uses of Video Tape in Training and Development.* New York: American Management Association, Research Study 93, 1969.

Tracey, William R., *Evaluating Training and Development Systems.* New York: American Management Association, 1968.

United States Department of Labor, *Apprentice Training.* Washington, D.C.: Government Printing Office, 1968.

West, J. P. and D. R. Sheriff, *Executive Development Programs in Universities.* New York: National Industrial Conference Board, 1969.

Specific Journal References

Aronoff, J., and G. H. Litwin, "Achievement Motivation Training and Executive Advancement," *Journal of Applied Behavioral Science, 7* (1), 1971, pp. 215–229.

Baum, Bernard H., Peter F. Sorensen, and W. S. Place, "The Effect of Managerial Training on Organizational Control: An Experimental Study," *Organizational Behavior and Human Performance, 5* (1), 1970, pp. 170–182.

Bedrosian, Hrach, "Selecting Supervisors for Training — What Motivates the Boss?" *Personnel, 48* (1), 1971, pp. 44–47.

Bienvenu, Bernard J., "Changing Concepts in Training," *Personnel, 46* (1), 1969, pp. 55–63.

Blumenfeld, W. S., and M. G. Holland, "A Model for the Empirical Evaluation of Training Effectiveness," *Personnel Journal, 50* (4), 1971, pp. 637–640.

Boocock, Sarane S., "Technology and Educational Structure," *Educational Technology, 9* (1), 1969, pp. 19–21.

Bowley, Roger L., and William R. Schriver, "Nonwage Benefits of Vocational Training: Employability and Mobility," *Industrial and Labor Relations Review, 23* (4), 1970, pp. 500–509.

Buchanan, Paul C., "Laboratory Training and Organization Development," *Administrative Science Quarterly, 14* (3), 1969, pp. 466–480.

Butkus, Alvin A., "Should Executives Go Back to School?" *Dunn's Review, 96* (9), 1970, pp. 38–40.

Campbell, J. P., "Personnel Training and Development," *Annual Review of Psychology, 22* (1), 1971, pp. 565–602.

Carroll, S. J., and A. N. Nash, "Some Personal and Situational Correlates of Reactions to Management Development Training," *Academy of Management Journal, 13* (1), 1970, pp. 187–196.

Carroll, S. J., F. T. Paine, and J. J. Ivancevich, "The Relative Effectiveness of Training Methods — Expert Opinion and Research," *Personnel Psychology, 25* (1), 1972, pp. 12–25.

Core, G. J., "The Management Internship," *Academy of Management Journal, 11* (2), 1968, pp. 163–176.

Cote, D. Phillias, "Measuring Results of Supervisory Training," *Training and Development Journal, 23* (11), 1969, pp. 38–46.

Dhir, Krishna S., "The Problem of Motivation in Management Development," *Personnel Journal, 49* (10), 1970, pp. 837–842.

Drucker, Peter F., "The Relevance of Management Education," *Perspectives in Defense Management,* December, 1969, pp. 11–15.

Feldman, John F., and Michael Szabo, "A Review of Developments in Computer Assisted Instruction," *Educational Technology, 9* (4), 1969, pp. 32–39.

Fine, Sidney A., "The Use of the *Dictionary of Occupational Titles* as a Source of Estimates of Educational and Training Requirements," *Journal of Human Resources,* Vol. 3, No. 3, 1968, pp. 363–372.

Florsheim, Henry, "Employee Training Vital for Reduction of Costs: Problems to Get Worse," *Supervision, 32* (7), 1970, pp. 5–8.

Fulmer, Robert, "Making Sense of Sensitivity Training," *Association Management, 22* (6), 1970, pp. 48–52.

Glasner, Daniel M., "Why Management Development Goes Wrong: Five Reasons," *Personnel Journal, 47* (9), 1968, pp. 655–658.

Goodacre, Daniel M., "Organization Development: The Name or the Game?" *Training and Development Journal, 23* (5), 1969, pp. 22–25.

Greer, Thomas V., "Some Behavioral Aspects of Training," *S. A. M. Advanced Management Journal, 35* (3), 1970, pp. 55–63.

Hammond, Reese, "Effective Preparation for Apprenticeship," *Monthly Labor Review, 93* (4), 1970, pp. 43–46.

Henry, Pamela, "Methods of Training Semi-Skilled Workers in 26 Manufacturing Firms," *Personnel Practices Bulletin, 26* (3), 1970, pp. 175–186.

House, Robert J., "T-Group Training: Good or Bad?" *Business Horizons, 12* (6), 1969, pp. 69–77.

Huse, E. F., and M. Beer, "Eclectic Approach to Organizational Development," *Harvard Business Review, 49* (5), 1971, pp. 103–112.

Jones, Alan, and John Moxham, "Costing the Benefits of Training," *Personnel Management, 1* (4), 1969, pp. 22–28.

Kegan, D. L., "Organizational Development: Description, Issues, and Some Research Results," *Academy of Management Journal, 14* (2), 1971, pp. 453–464.

Kelley, Roger T., "Accounting in Personnel Administration," *Industrial Relations, 7* (2), 1968, pp. 24–28.

Labovitz, G. H., "Organizing for Adaptation," *Business Horizons, 14* (3), 1971, pp. 19–26.

Mathis, Robert L., "Organizational Development," *The Personnel Administrator, 15* (5), 1970, pp. 25–28.

Mollenkopf, W. G., "Some Results of Three Basic Skills Training Programs in an Industrial Setting," *Journal of Applied Psychology, 53* (4), 1969, pp. 343–347.

Mosvick, R. K., "Human Relations Training for Scientists, Technicians, and Engineers: A Review of Relevant Experimental Evaluations of Human Relations Training," *Personnel Psychology, 24* (2), 1971, pp. 275–292.

Moulds, Warren, "Corporate Colleges: The Boom in Executive Finishing Schools," *Generation, 2* (2), 1969, pp. 26–31.

Nash, A. N., J. P. Muczyk, and F. L. Vettori, "The Relative Practical Effectiveness of Programmed Instruction," *Personnel Psychology, 24* (4), 1971, pp. 397–418.

Odiorne, George S., "Adult Education in the Multiversity," *Michigan Business Review, 21* (1), 1969, pp. 17–20.

Powell, R. M., and J. E. Stinson, "The Worth of Laboratory Training," *Business Horizons, 14* (4), 1971, pp. 87–95.

Prieve, E. Arthur, and Dorothy A. Wentorf, "Training Objectives — Philosophy or Practice?" *Personnel Journal, 49* (3), 1970, pp. 235–240.

Rhea, Richard E., and James R. Bruskotter, "Management Development: Uniform Opportunities in Diversified Operations," *Personnel, 46* (3), 1969, pp. 48–55.

Schein, V. E., "An Evaluation of a Long-term Management Training Program," *Training and Development Journal, 25* (12), 1971, pp. 28–34.

Schmidt, Warren A., "How to Evaluate a Company's Training Efforts," *California Management Review, 12* (3), 1970, pp. 49–56.

Scott, L. C., "The Economic Effectiveness of On-the-Job Training," *Industrial and Labor Relations Review, 23* (2), 1970, pp. 220–236.

Scoville, James G., "A Theory of Jobs and Training," *Industrial Relations, 9* (1), 1969, pp. 36–53.

Sims, James K., "They Go Back to School . . . Without Leaving Plant," *The Personnel Administrator, 13* (6), 1968, pp. 9–12.

Steinmetz, Lawrence J., "Age: Unrecognized Enigma of Executive Development," *Management of Personnel Quarterly, 8* (3), 1969, pp. 3–10.

This, Leslie E., and Gordon L. Lippitt, "Learning Theories and Training," *Training and Development Journal, 20* (4), 1966, pp. 2–12, and *20* (5), 1966, pp. 10–19.

Thorley, S., "Evaluating an In-Company Training Program," *Training and Development Journal, 35* (3), 1970, pp. 55–63.

Warr, Peter, "Evaluating Management Training," *Personnel, 2* (2), 1969, pp. 27–29.

White, Tom, "How to Evaluate Your Management Development Program," *Industrial Management, 12* (12), 1970, pp. 8–11.

Wiener, E. L., and D. A. Attwood, "Training for Vigilance: Combined Cueing and Knowledge of Results," *Journal of Applied Psychology, 52* (8), 1968, pp. 474–479.

Wohlking, Wallace, "Attitude Change, Behavior Change: The Role of the Training Department," *California Management Review, 12* (2), 1970, pp. 45–50.

Wright, Robert, "Managing Man as a Capital Asset," *Personnel Journal, 49* (4), 1970, pp. 290–298.

contents

1. Introduction and Semantics
2. Principal Wage and Salary Issues and Problems

   A. Pay Level

   B. Pay Structure

   C. Individual Pay Determination

   D. Payment Method

   E. Incentives

   F. Indirect Compensation

   G. Pay Control

   H. Special Problems

3. Wage and Salary Criteria

   A. Prevailing Pay

   B. Ability to Pay

   C. Union Bargaining Power

   D. Cost of Living

   E. Living Wage

   F. Productivity

   G. Job Requirements

   H. Supply and Demand Market Factors

4. Job Evaluation Systems

   A. Ranking

   B. Grade Description

   C. Point

   D. Factor

   E. Time Span of Discretion

5. Summary

learning objectives

1. To understand the semantic and definitional problems associated with the compensation concept.
2. To become acquainted with the principal issues and problems associated with wage and salary administration.
3. To become knowledgeable about wage and salary criteria.
4. To learn the philosophies behind and the mechanics of job evaluation systems.

Money is a relevant but relative manpower motivator.

8

Compensation: Wage and Salary Administration

1. Introduction and Semantics

In order to attract and maintain a work force, an organization must adequately pay its personnel. Personnel pay considerations involve the concept of "compensation" and the practice of "wage and salary administration." These considerations are the subject matter of this chapter.

Semantics

The process of wage or salary administration (or, "compensation" as it is sometimes called) involves the weighing or balancing of accounts. A compensation is anything that constitutes or is regarded as an equivalent or recompense. In the employment world, financial rewards are the compensation resources provided to employees for the return of their services. The terms "remuneration," "wage," and "salary" also are used to describe this financial arrangement between employers and employees. A remuneration is a reward, payment, or reimbursement for services rendered. Most forms of remuneration are financial, although these reimbursements on occasion also may be nonfinancial in nature. Remunerations are usually in the form of

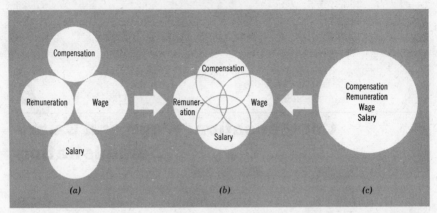

FIGURE 8-1 Compensation, remuneration, wage, and salary as distinct, interrelated, and synonymous set entities. (a) Distinct. (b) Interrelated. (c) Synonymous.

wages or salaries. In general, a wage is anything given as a recompense or requital; however, more specifically, wages are money paid for the use of something. The concept of wages usually is associated with the process of paying hourly workers. A salary is a recompense or consideration paid, or stipulated to be paid, to a person at regular intervals for performed services. Salaries are fixed compensations paid, to holders of official, executive, or clerical positions, on a regular basis such as by the year, quarter, month, or week. The above discussion indicates that the pay concepts of compensation, remuneration, wage, and salary have both similarities and differences between one another. Area b of Figure 8-1 illustrates that the pay concepts of compensation, remuneration, wage, and salary are best envisioned as partially interrelated and overlapping phenomena instead of being thought of as totally distinct (Figure 8-1a) or completely synonymous (Figure 8-1c) set entities. Figure 8-2 shows that compensation and remuneration are more

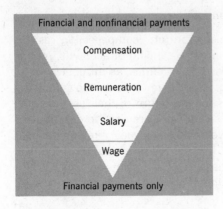

FIGURE 8-2 The comprehensiveness of pay concepts.

comprehensive pay concepts than are the ideas of salary and wage that normally include a financial but not a nonfinancial dimension.

Compensation

In general the term compensation is preferred today as the term most descriptive of organizational pay practices, because the concept of compensation is broader in scope than are the other pay concepts. Wage, salary, and remuneration pay concepts stress only direct financial reimbursements, but the compensation pay construct includes both direct financial payments and indirect nonfinancial rewards. In short the term compensation usually is selected to describe the total employer-employee payment arrangements because it is broader in perspective than are the pay concepts of remuneration, wage, and salary.

Systems

Often the term "systems" is used in connection with wage, salary, or compensation administration. The systems term within the phrase compensation systems indicates the rational, objective, and systematic approach taken by most organizations today in an effort to solve their payment problems. Exact and precise wage and salary principles, methods, and guidelines are usually used when setting up an organization's payment or compensation system or systems. This systems identification also reveals the ongoing and organizationally interrelated nature of any modern company payment and reimbursement methodology.

In this chapter and in the next, wage and salary administration and employee benefits and services will be discussed. Wage and salary administration concerns itself with direct financial payment issues while benefits and services involve indirect financial and nonfinancial employee considerations, as indicated in Figure 8-3. Collectively the areas of wage and salary administration and employee benefits and services make up the total compensation concept.

The remainder of this chapter deals with the subject matter of wage and salary administration. Although there are slight differences between the wage and salary payment concepts, as explained previously, these two remuneration methods have similar problems and issues associated with their use. Accordingly, wage and salary administration is best envisioned as a common body instead of as separate administrative entities. Wage administration and salary administration is wage and salary administration, which involves the administration of wages and salaries. The administration of wages and salaries will be explained in this chapter by exploring and presenting three general remuneration subtopics or subareas: principal wage and salary issues and problems; wage and salary criteria; and job evaluation systems.

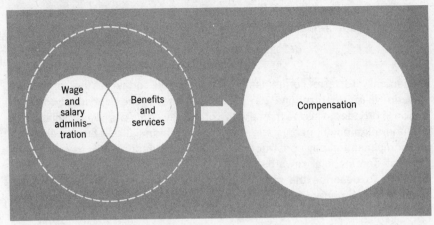

FIGURE 8-3 Compensation components.

2. Principal Wage and Salary Issues and Problems

The main compensation problem of all organizations can be reduced to seeing that every employee is fairly paid for his efforts. This objective is usually readily accepted, but there is much less agreement about the manner of accomplishing this goal. For purposes of analysis, it is useful to subdivide the main compensation problem facing all organizations into the following categories: (1) pay level; (2) pay structure; (3) individual pay determination; (4) payment method; (5) incentives; (6) indirect compensation; (7) pay control; and (8) special problems.

A. PAY LEVEL

The problem of pay levels is concerned with whether the entire structure is high, average, or low in comparison to the general labor market (Sawhney and Herrnstadt). If the pay level is too low, companies will be unable to attract and maintain top-notch employees. Conflicts with regulatory bodies, minimum wage laws, and public contract agreements also may result. In addition, low pay levels may cause union pressure or union organization activities. High pay levels can usually solve low pay level problems, but normally other types of complications occur when high pay levels exist. High pay levels mean high organizational costs, and excessive expenses cause financial control problems and often a deteriorated competitive firm position in the product market. High labor costs lead to high product prices that can cause organizational and competitive loss of sales (Schweitzer).

Many factors influence organizational pay levels. Some of the major considerations are: competitive rates in the labor market, industry pay levels, financial strength of the company, management pay policies, public pay policies, and union pay contracts (Bailey and Schwenk). State laws and federal legislation often set lower and upper pay limits and, within these limits, the greatest influence on pay levels is the amount of pay paid in the area or industry for comparable work. Wage surveys are used to collect this information. Once this information has been gathered, various other considerations will then be assessed in an effort to arrive at a general company pay level. These considerations are often in the form of "pay criteria," which will be discussed later in this chapter. These considerations vary in importance over time, and the main determinants of a pay level in one situation and at one point in time may be quite different from the main pay level determinant(s) under changed circumstances in a different environment (Masters).

The pay level problem is intuitively and pragmatically the first major compensation issue faced by an organization. Some solution to the pay level problem is usually called for before other pay problems can be confronted.

B. PAY STRUCTURE

The issue of pay structure concerns the hierarchy of pay rates, pay grades, and job classifications existing within an organization. After an organization solves the problem of pay levels, which relates company wages and salaries to external labor market and industry conditions, then the internal pay structure issue must be handled. The relationship of internal jobs must be determined in terms of pay and salary rates. All jobs within a company are not of equal caliber or difficulty; some jobs require professional managers, others call for skilled craftsmen, while others can be performed by unskilled workers. The pay structure question concerns the matter of determining exactly what the relationships are among these internal organizational positions. Normally job evaluation is the method used for determining these internal relationships. Jobs are compared in terms of their required degrees of intelligence, expertise, effort, safety, stamina, and other human qualities needed to successfully perform the involved job duties and responsibilities. Job evaluation, however, is not the only method developed to compare jobs. Other informal and formal techniques such as management judgments or collective bargaining arrangements have been used to determine pay structures.

Although pay structures can be determined in a variety of ways, the logic used is essentially the same. First, a study of the jobs in the organization must be undertaken. After this job information is obtained, the next step is to decide what factor or factors place a job at a higher point in the job hierarchy and, therefore, command a higher rate of pay. Then a system is developed that permits the evaluation of jobs according to these key factors. This system is used to establish and set up a logical job hierarchy and, lastly, specific wage or salary rates are assigned to the jobs within the hierarchy (Gerwin).

The internal pay structure problem within an organization is just as important as the external pay level issue, in fact, often the internal pay structure is even more important to employees. Although qualified employees may be attracted to a company by a proper pay level, they may leave if they observe pay inequities within the organization. Preventing such pay inequities from arising and correcting them when they do occur involves the problem of constructing a sound internal pay structure.

C. INDIVIDUAL PAY DETERMINATION

Pay levels concern the relationship of all organizational jobs to external labor and industry markets. Pay structures involve the internal interrelationships of all jobs and positions within the company itself. The issue of individual pay determination centers around the question of how much should a specific individual receive in wages or salary for the performance of his required job. Should two people performing the exact same job get equal pay? What if one person does a much better job at his work than someone else doing a similar task? What personal qualities or factors determine precisely how much an individual should earn in pay? These are the types of questions that the individual pay determination problem attempts to answer (Boynton).

Individual pay assignment begins by classifying people into job titles and pay grades, then a range of pay for each grade must be determined, and finally, how much money each person is entitled to within the range must be decided. Where an individual employee will be placed within a pay range is at least partially determined through a performance appraisal process. Highly rated employees receive the top rates within a range whereas poor performers are assigned the lowest range rates (Schuster and Clark).

A controversial issue is whether all individuals on the same job should necessarily receive the same pay (Bass). Where a variation in payment to different individuals on the same job is permitted, such variation may be accomplished in one of two ways. One is an incentive method of pay whereby the base rate is set for the job and the employee's pay is determined largely by his own efforts. The other method involves the use of pay ranges featuring minimum, standard, and maximum rates. Once such ranges are established, some procedure must be devised for moving individuals through the range. The most commonly used possibilities include: automatic increases based on seniority; increases based on performance appraisal; and a combination seniority-performance measure (Giles and Barrett). Figure 8-4 illustrates a pay structure featuring increasing rate ranges.

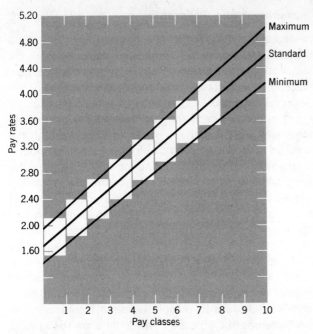

FIGURE 8-4 Pay structure with increasing rate ranges.

D. PAYMENT METHOD

In general, there are two main payment methods — payment on the basis of time (that is, by the hour, day, week, or month), and payment on the basis of output (that is, by the piece produced, or dollar's worth of goods made or sold, or the amount of time or money saved). Most organizations use a combination of these methods depending on work arrangements, organizational needs, and worker preferences. The problem of choosing the method of measuring employee contribution appears simple, but actually it is not. One reason for this illusion is because time spent on the job often measures elapsed time instead of employee contribution. In addition, job results attained may be difficult to appraise directly because the assessment of these variables involves the evaluation of worker effort, fatigue, and other factors.

Time versus Output or Wage versus Incentive

The question of time versus output is often explained in terms of wage versus incentive payments. A person is either paid a flat wage per unit of time, or he is paid some rate or incentive per unit of output. Thus, these two payment philosophies can be described either as time-wage or wage-incentive pay methods.

Advantages and Disadvantages

There are certain advantages and disadvantages associated with both time and output pay methods. Time wages are simple to calculate and are convenient for payroll accounting purposes. Often unions and employees prefer time wages because of the certainty provided by employment of the time unit. The complexity of incentive wages and the uncertain relationship between money and motivation also may be reasons for using time payments. Often management lacks the ability or desire to go through the steps necessary to establish a proper incentive output payment methodology. The main disadvantage of time payments is the fact that time rates are unrelated to productivity. With time pay, there is no direct relationship between what an employee does and what he gets paid. Because time pay arrangements provide no recognition of individual differences among employees, time wages penalize outstanding employees. In addition, from a management perspective, time rates make it difficult for an employer to plan unit labor costs in advance. Much wider fluctuations in labor cost occur under time pay than under systems of output pay. Output or incentive pay possesses the advantage of basing compensation on results obtained from work. This in turn permits employers to reliably estimate their labor unit costs. Also, individual differences in employee performance are recognized and compensated. The biggest disadvantage of output pay methods is the opportunities they provide for upsetting employer-employee relationships. Worker competition may result, large pay differences within similar job classifications can occur, employee grievances often become more frequent, and various union charges and complaints commonly increase. Management also is faced with increased accounting and administration costs. In addition, management must develop consistent work standards and provide uniform and dependable work conditions if it uses an incentive pay system.

Approximately two-thirds of the employees in this country are paid on a time basis. There is, however, a great deal of variation by industry and area. There is a considerable amount of evidence to suggest that output pay, in many but not all instances, has resulted in greater output per man-hour, lower unit costs, and higher wages. Some critics, nevertheless, argue that these gains are really mostly attributable to improved management practices that accompany the installation of an incentive pay system (Kinyon).

Time versus Output Considerations

The decision as to whether to pay for time or output involves many considerations. In general it appears that time (output) payment is more applicable when: (1) units of output are difficult (easy) to distinguish and measure; (2) workers are unable (able) to control product quantity; (3) there is not (definitely) a clear relationship between effort and output; (4) delays in the work are frequent (infrequent) and not (are) employee controllable; (5)

quality considerations are important (unimportant); (6) good and fair supervision exist (are lacking); and (7) precise advance knowledge of unit labor costs is unnecessary (necessary). Community attitudes, employee preferences, labor relations climate, and technological considerations also are important factors affecting the time or output payment decision.

Of course, in reality, the time or output decision is not an either-or situation. There are various combinations of these basic pay methods. In fact, it is quite common to find employees who are paid on the basis of a mixture of these two concepts. For example, most salesmen get paid a regular salary plus an extra commission based on a percentage of their sales. In addition to set monthly salaries, most executives also receive financial supplements in the form of expense accounts, profit sharing, bonuses, stock options, and other financial contingencies and incentives.

E. INCENTIVES

If it has been decided to adopt an incentive pay system, there are several types of systems from which to choose. All incentive systems have different characteristics, purposes, and methods of installation and operation. Today, most incentive plans possess a guaranteed base rate that is paid to all workers, even those who fail to reach standard production. Thus, in essence, most incentive pay plans contain at least some elements of both the time-based or output-based compensation methods.

Variations

An unusually large number of incentive plans have been devised. Incentive plans are often classified in a manner that emphasizes their differences. One way of classifying incentive plans is by the source of the incentive. Usually an incentive is paid when quantity surpasses some standard, but sometimes the norm may be expressed in terms of quality or a combination of quantity and quality. Occasionally incentives are based on profits, but variations occur because the key profit figure may be gross profit, net profit, return on invested capital, or some other financial consideration. Other incentive plans stress cost savings instead of profit sharing. Within these plans financial incentives are based on the amount of money saved through employee suggestions, fewer accidents, less scrap and waste, and other items. Some plans share all cost savings with employees, while other incentive programs share only certain specific area cost reductions. Also, the percentage of savings shared varies from plan to plan. Occasionally all cost savings are shared with employees, but most cost reduction incentive plans split the extra money on a 50-50 (labor-management) basis. Still other incentive plans, instead of being based on profit sharing or cost saving, are geared to increases in productivity. Under productivity plans, incentives are paid according to some index of overall organizational productivity. Again many variations exist even within this type of incentive plan. Some productivity plans pay off only when "labor" productivity increases, others will pay even if the increase results from greater automation or technological advances. The percentage of financial sharing also varies considerably among productivity incentive plans. Furthermore, the exact definition of "productivity" varies from one incentive plan to the next. In addition to profit sharing, cost saving, and productivity incentive plans, various other hybrids exist, many of which feature a combination of profit sharing, cost saving, productivity increases, and other factors (Field).

Individual, Group, or Plant Wide

Incentive plans are often classified according to whom the incentive applies to or on what scope the incentive system is based. Scopewise, incentive plans may be either individual, group or plant (company) wide in dimension. Individual incentive plans pay individual employees based on their individual effort. Group incentive plans compensate groups based on group standards, and plant wide incentive plans reimburse all employees in accordance to total company payment criteria. These criteria may be profits, costs, productivity, sales, savings, or other factors as explained previously (Lawler and Hackman).

Direct or Indirect

Most incentive plans feature direct financial incentives. However, some incentive systems offer indirect or delayed rewards. An incentive may be in the form of a vacation, increased leisure time, a better pension, a gift, and so forth. The payoff may be immediate, at the end of the year, or deferred until retirement. As can be observed from the above discussion, the types and variations of incentive pay systems are so complex that it is impossible to mention all of the conceivable different combinations.

"Incentive" Definition

An incentive may be thought of as something that incites or has a tendency to incite action. Incentives are motives and inducements designed to enhance or improve production. Because all individuals are unique, they have different needs and different motives. What can serve as a motive or an incentive to one person may not incite action in someone else. The variety of incentive programs in existence organizationally today results from sincere attempts (often unique ones) by companies to appeal to the majority of workers within their particular employment setting.

F. INDIRECT COMPENSATION

Indirect compensations are reimbursements received by employees in forms other than direct wages or salary. Indirect compensation may be both financial or nonfinancial in nature. Various types of company benefits and services make up the concept of indirect compensation.

Indirect compensation is unrelated to the productive contributions of individual employees. Certain company benefits and services accrue to workers simply as a consequence of their participation in the enterprise. These supplemental benefits in essence are provided to workers not for their contributions but for their acceptance of the employee role.

Fringe Benefits

Indirect compensation is often mislabeled fringe benefits. Indirect benefits and services are not fringe because they are required and necessary today; they are not optional payments. In addition, the average total compensation package currently consists of approximately 30 percent in the form of company benefits and services. If 30 percent of a person's total compensation is in the form of benefits and services, such indirect remuneration is far from being fringe in nature and scope.

Controversies

Although there is some disagreement concerning matters relating to the determination and administration of direct wage and salary payments, indirect compensation contains even more elements of controversy. At least in the former there is usually agreement on what is being determined, the unit of measurement, and the objectives sought. In the latter, there is lack of agreement on what is or is not to be included as indirect compensation, the units in which the costs and values are to be measured, and the purposes to be served. There is also nonconsensus about who is ultimately responsible for indirect compensation programs, the financial cost and social value of such fringes, and the performance criteria on which to judge and assess the effectiveness and desirability of both the components within and the total constitution of these indirect compensation programs (Dunnette). However, in spite of all of this confusion and these complications, indirect compensation payments continue to expand. Indirect compensations will be discussed more thoroughly in the next chapter, which deals with employee "benefits and services."

G. PAY CONTROL

Once the previously discussed pay problems and issues have been settled, the question of pay control remains. Often information gathering and the decision making process will solve many pay problems such as pay level, pay structure, payment method, and other compensation issues. But the pay control consideration involves an ongoing continuous administrative question instead of a one-time decision or choice. The application and implications of direct and indirect financial company reimbursements form the heart of the pay control problem. Pay control involves the assessment of the sufficiency and efficiency of the solutions reached on other pay problems and issues. To a large extent, pay control is payroll control of direct and indirect labor costs. However, all pay programs and techniques call for regular appraisal to ensure that each is accomplishing its task. It is generally believed that pay control is the central problem of all wage and salary administration issues. If all other pay problems are solved, but the issue of pay control is not being effectively dealt with, then organizational compensation methodologies are not fulfilling their intended purposes and objectives.

Standards, Measurements, and Actions

Control requires a standard against which to compare practice. Pay control involves making certain that actual results conform to desired expectations. Because of the changing nature of compensation objectives, pay control problems are very complex in real world situations. The task of pay control is continually to (1) develop compensation standards and improve existing ones, (2) measure results against standards for consistency, and (3) take actions necessary to align changing remuneration standards and results. In summary, the pay control process involves assuring that compensation practices achieve their sought objectives.

Purposes

Pay control is needed for a number of reasons. All aspects and components of an organization's internal and external environments are constantly changing. Compensation programs must be continually evaluated to ensure that they adjust to changed conditions and still achieve pay objectives. Compensation objectives can easily change because of environmental pressures, and pay techniques and practices must then also be altered accordingly.

H. SPECIAL PROBLEMS

Special pay problems involve compensation issues related to exempt employees. In general, exempt workers are managers and professional employees who are paid on a salary instead of a wage basis. White collar workers represent a growing proportion of the entire work force in most organizations. The greater work interest, involvement, and commitment of this white collar group carried with it opportunities, challenges, and requirements to devise new pay arrangements that accord with both organizational and individual objectives.

Managers and Professionals

The pay problems of managers and professionals are often unique but not necessarily totally different from the compensation issues associated with other employees. Some personnel specialists believe that enough differences exist between exempt and nonexempt employees so that entirely unique compensation systems are needed for each group (Belcher). Just as the differences between a manager and a nonmanager or a professional and a nonprofessional are extremely difficult to discern, so too are the variations between exempt and nonexempt groups exceedingly ambiguous and nebulous in distinction. Even legislative statutes contain provisions when an exempt employee must be treated and paid as a nonexempt employee and vice versa.

Exempt and Nonexempt Employees

The Fair Labor Standards Act "exempts" certain employees from the requirements of premium pay for overtime. Hourly rated employees are nonexempt. Many salaried employees, including managers, supervisors, and outside salesmen are exempt. However, clerical employees and inside salesmen are often salaried employees, but are usually nonexempt according to the Fair Labor Standards Act. Included in the exempt category are numbers of people and groups whose work assignments vary greatly. First, there is the management group including everyone from first-line supervisors to top executives. Professional employees are also classified as exempt. Professional employees include scientists, mathematicians, engineers, economists, and lawyers. Nonsupervisory salesmen also are said to be exempt employees.

Problems, Issues and Considerations

Because of the diversity within the exempt classification, and because of the managerial and professional nature of the work involved, somewhat unique compensation problems, issues and considerations are associated with the remuneration practices applied to such groups. With such groups, it is possible to emphasize the motivation to produce over the motivation to join (participate) in the organization because of greater work commitment, interest, and involvement of these employees. However, more than simply different compensation philosophies apply to the exempt and nonexempt groups. At times even different pay techniques and procedures are utilized in determining exempt employee pay levels and structures. For example, maturity, progression, and career curves are frequently used to determine direct financial managerial or professional remunerations (Kassem). In addition, managers and professionals are often presented with unique indirect compensation programs such as those involving stock options, bonus plans, and special insurance and pension provisions. Although some exempt versus nonexempt legal, philosophical, and operational differences do exist, for the most part compensation theories, concepts, principles, practices, procedures, and methodologies do not vary much between various employee groups.

Overview

This concludes the discussion of principal wage and salary issues and problems. Figure 8-5 can be used to synthesize, integrate, and summarize the foregoing discussion. Figure 8-5 illustrates a composite pyramid labeled principal wage and salary issues and problems, consisting of subsets or

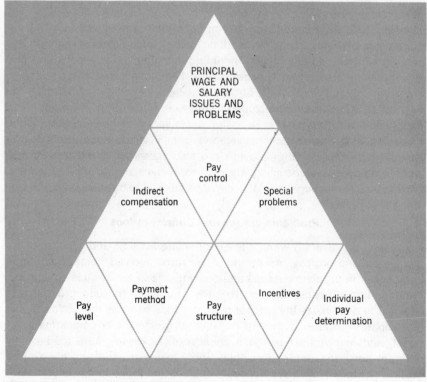

FIGURE 8-5 Principal wage and salary issues and problems.

elements of pay level, pay structure, individual pay determination, payment method, incentives, indirect compensation, pay control, and special problems. The dotted or broken triangle lines are meant to indicate that these eight pay issues and problems are best envisioned as partially interrelated and overlapping compensation concepts, instead of being conceived as totally distinct or completely synonymous wage and salary administration problems and issues. Most of these pay problems are dealt with simultaneously rather than at different times. Specific pay practices help to solve these problems collectively instead of being designed to treat these issues separately or in an isolated fashion.

3. Wage and Salary Criteria

The determination of pay for jobs and people has reached the stage where it is considered a logical, consistent, systematic, and explainable process. There are many factors, standards, or yardsticks used to help set pay rates in organizations, and they are designed to measure pay adequacy, equity, need, and contribution. The different parties applying these criteria emphasize certain yardsticks and place less importance on others. These factors do not operate alone but usually work together in determining pay rates. It also should be noted that pay criteria are partially economic, partially behavioral, and partially ethical in nature. In the hands of one party a given criterion may be ethical, but the same criterion applied by another may be economic in perspective. The most commonly used wage and salary criteria in this country are: (1) prevailing pay; (2) ability to pay; (3) union bargaining power; (4) cost of living; (5) living wage; (6) productivity; (7) job requirements; and (8) supply and demand market factors. These eight wage and salary criteria will now be discussed in greater detail.

A. PREVAILING PAY

The prevailing pay concept is sometimes identified as either the comparable wage or going wage construct. It is felt that the prevailing pay compensation criterion is the most influential of all remuneration factors or standards. Firms usually decide what pay rates they will offer by ascertaining what other firms are paying for the same type of work in the same labor market or sometimes in the same industry regardless of location. In the long-run, an organization must pay the same or about the same general level of wages and salaries to its employees as is paid by the organization's competitors, or else it will not be able to attract and maintain a sufficient quantity of proper quality manpower. The prevailing pay concept is, of course, an abstraction. Actually, a prevailing pay range exists. Some companies pay on the high side of the market in order to obtain goodwill or to insure an adequate supply of labor, while other organizations pay on the low side because economically they have to or, because by lowering hiring requirements they can keep jobs adequately manned (Belcher and Atchison).

B. ABILITY TO PAY

The ability of an employer to pay affects general organizational compensation levels and structures. The profitability of an organization is without question a consideration in wage and salary determination. This is even somewhat true of nonprofit, charity institutions. Almost all unions attempt to estimate an organization's ability to pay before making compensation demands. It is usually agreed that the ability to pay compensation criterion has some usefulness in setting wage and salary rates both at the bargaining table and when used unilaterally by the employer. The ability to pay remuneration criterion is in actuality a composite of the economic forces facing the company. Ability to pay seldom determines the precise wage or salary rate, instead it sets the range within which the actual pay level is fixed. Some observers have argued that this standard should properly be identified and labeled as inability to pay instead of as ability to pay in that it serves to set a limit to pay increases apparently justified on other grounds. When unions refer to this compensation criterion it becomes an ability to pay argument, but when management utilizes this concept it does so in an inability to pay fashion (Evan and Simmons).

C. UNION BARGAINING POWER

Often the arrived at pay rate depends somewhat on union bargaining power. This is true even in nonunion employer-employee relationships because of the effect unions have on the comparable or prevailing pay concept. Generally, the stronger and more powerful the union, the higher the final pay rate will be (Hammermesh). Union power or strength can best be measured in terms of the number of workers involved or the financial size of a union's strike fund. Key labor union personalities also affect union strength and power. The strike has long been the union's most powerful weapon, but in actuality it has not been used all that much. It is probably more accurate to say that the "threat" of a strike is in fact the strongest and most used union stratagem or tactic. Some observers have argued that unions force wages up faster than increases in productivity naturally allow and thus cause unemployment or higher prices and inflation (Bailey and Schwenk). However, for those remaining on the payrolls, a real gain is often achieved as a consequence of stronger bargaining power.

D. COST OF LIVING

This compensation criterion calls for pay adjustments based on increases or decreases in an acceptable cost of living index. In recognition of the influence of cost-of-living changes, "escalator clauses" have been written into labor contracts in recent years. A typical escalator clause provides a one-cent-per-hour change for each 0.5 change in the national Consumer Price Index, or a two-cent change for each 0.9 point change in the index. Usually adjustments are made at quarterly intervals. When the cost of living is rising, workers and unions demand adjusted wages to offset reductions in real wages. However, when living costs are stable or declining, management usually does not resort to this argument as a reason for wage reductions. Usually the cost of living compensation criterion is not a major force in setting or arriving at a final employer-employee pay rate. This standard is never employed as the sole consideration of pay adjustment. The cost of living pay criterion is usually regarded today as an automatic minimum equity pay correction (Lawson).

E. LIVING WAGE

The living wage compensation criterion concerns the question of "how much money does it cost a wage earner and his family to live per year at an adequate standard level of existence?" The living wage represents an "ideal" standard in the form of a "minimum budget." For example, in the early 1970s, the living wage for a family of four was estimated to be approximately $11,000. Minimum budgets involve numerous value judgments and estimates of sociological, psychological, and ethical phenomena. These budgets are not based as much on financial data as they are on subjective judgments. The actual use of minimum budgets in pay level determination of individual employing organizations is limited. Unions may present them as evidence of worker need. However, the living wage pay criterion is much more appropriately used as a guide for broad social policy instead of as a specific wage level determinant. For example, minimum budgets can provide a basis for changes in minimum wage laws. Generally employers do not favor using the concept of a living wage as a guide to pay determination, because they prefer to base wages on employee contribution rather than worker need. Also, they feel that minimum budgets are open to argument, since they are based on subjective matters of opinion (Rosen and Houff).

F. PRODUCTIVITY

Another compensation criterion is the productivity standard. Productivity is measured in terms of output per man-hour. There is currently a debate over whether or not there is actually a close long-run relationship between pay and productivity (Evans). Nor is there total agreement that a productivity standard is the best measure of pay determination. Pragmatically, the productivity criterion encounters the problems of definition and measurement. What is productivity? The usual measure is that of physical productivity arrived at by dividing units of output by man-hours worked. But this presumes that increases in productivity result solely from increases in labor productivity, that is, due only to better skill and effort on the part of the work force. Actually, physical productivity measures the contributions of all resource factors — men, machines, methods, materials, management, and the like (Rezler). No productivity index can be devised that will measure only the productivity of a specific factor of production. Another problem is that productivity can be measured at several levels — job, plant, industry, or national economy levels. Thus, although theoretically productivity is a sound compensation criterion, operationally many problems and complications exist because of definitional, measurement, and conceptual controversies (Schneider and Olsen).

G. JOB REQUIREMENTS

Of course, the requirements of a job are crucial factors in determining the wage or salary level of a person performing certain job responsibilities. Generally, the more difficult the job, the higher is its compensation rate (Hettenhouse). Measures of job difficulty are frequently used when ascertaining the relative value of one job to another within an organization (Penzer). This is the basis for the job evaluation and job analysis plans described in the "staffing and appraisal" chapter. Jobs are graded according to the relative amounts of skill, effort, responsibility, and job conditions required (Hinrichs). These factors will be discussed in the section on wage and salary administration systems.

H. SUPPLY AND DEMAND MARKET FACTORS

Wages and salaries are affected by supply and demand market conditions. If the supply of a particular labor skill becomes scarce, buyers (employers) may bid up the price in the labor market. If the supply of a labor talent is excessive, the price or wage per unit of labor decreases. Similarly, if a great demand for a labor expertise exists, prices rise, but if the demand for a manpower skill is minimal, then the wages of these skilled craftsmen will likewise be relatively small. The supply and demand compensation criterion is very closely related to the prevailing pay, comparable wage and on-going wage concepts since, in essence, all of these remuneration standards are determined by immediate market forces and factors (Mescon).

Overview

Figure 8-6 summarizes the discussion of wage and salary criteria. Figure 8-6 illustrates a composite portrayal identified and labeled as wage and salary criteria that is comprised of eight elements or subsets: namely; prevailing pay; the ability to pay; union bargaining power; cost of living; living wage; productivity; job requirements; and supply and demand market factors. The dotted or broken lines illustrate that these eight compensation criteria are best envisioned as partially interrelated and overlapping pay concepts instead of as totally distinct remuneration entities. Labor market conditions and the general state of the economy tie all of these compensation criteria together so that changes in one factor often are inseparable from alterations in other criteria, for example, costs of living determine living wages. Supply

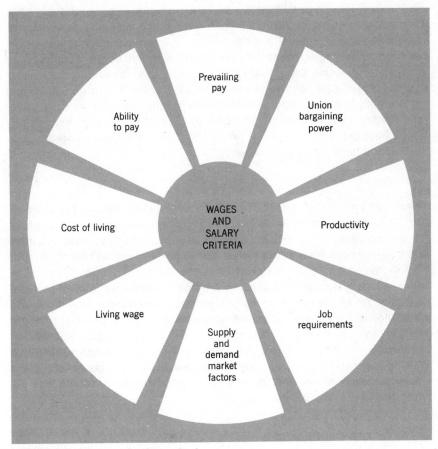

FIGURE 8-6   Wage and salary criteria.

and demand market factors result in prevailing wages and salaries. Productivity is the heart of the ability to pay remuneration criterion, and so forth.

4. Job Evaluation Systems

There are five main types of job evaluation systems used in organizations today: (1) ranking; (2) grade description; (3) point; (4) factor; and (5) time span of discretion. Each system will now be explained.

A. RANKING

Ranking is the simplest and easiest to explain job evaluation system. Jobs in an organization are merely ranked from highest to lowest in terms of whole job or overall task complexity and working conditions. This is a relatively easy thing to do if only a few jobs are involved, but it becomes very cumbersome when many organizational positions exist. The ranking method has other serious disadvantages that limit its usefulness. Different bases of comparison between raters occur because there is no standard(s) for whole job position analysis. Specific job requirements such as skill, effort, and responsibility are not normally analyzed separately under a simplified ranking method. Often rater judgments are strongly influenced by present wage rates. In addition, the ranking procedure does not provide any means for recording the substantiations for the ratings (Cangemi).

Nonquantitative

The ranking method is a nonquantitative job evaluation system featuring an ordinal numbering scale. As such, the ranking process does not tell one how far apart the jobs are in difficulty and content. For example, jobs one, two, and three may definitely be distinguishable in terms of overall complexity, but jobs six, seven, and eight may cluster together and be approximately equal in terms of job difficulty. The ranking method erroneously implies that the degree of difference between jobs one and two is the same in magnitude and proportion as the difference between jobs six and seven. This disadvantage is really inherent in the ranking method per se and is not a unique criticism that pertains only to the ranking job evaluation system. The principal virtue of the ranking wage and salary administration system is that it is easy to apply, but this advantage persists only as long as a limit of fifteen to twenty jobs are involved in the complete ranking system.

B. GRADE DESCRIPTION

The grade description wage and salary administration system also is referred to as the classification system. Essentially, grade description involves dividing the job hierarchy into a number of pay groups or grades, developing written definitions for each grade, and then assigning every organizational job to a particular grade classification. Grade descriptions are the result of basic job information usually derived from job analysis. After formulating and studying job descriptions and job specifications, jobs are then grouped into classes or grades that represent different pay levels ranging from low to high. Common types of tasks, skills, knowledge, responsibilities, and job conditions can be identified through the process of job analysis. Accordingly, certain jobs then become grouped together into a common grade or classification. Usually general grade (job) descriptions are then written for each job classification. After this has been accomplished for all grades, these grade descriptions can then be used as a standard for assigning all other jobs to a particular pay grade.

The grade description method is an extension of the ranking job evaluation system, only a larger number of jobs are involved. General job classifications and grades are first established and then are ranked in relationship to one another (grade I, grade II, grade III, etc.). Then specific jobs are placed within and assigned to the various grades and are usually ranked in relationship to other jobs within the same job classification. For example, Figure 8-7 illus-

GRADES OR CLASSIFICATIONS

RANKINGS	I	II	III	IV	V	VI	VII	VIII	IX	X
1	I - 1	II - 1	III - 1	IV - 1	V - 1	VI - 1	VII - 1	VIII - 1	IX - 1	X - 1
2	I - 2	II - 2	III - 2	IV - 2	V - 2	VI - 2	VII - 2	VIII - 2	IX - 2	X - 2
3	I - 3	II - 3	III - 3	IV - 3	V - 3	VI - 3	VII - 3	VIII - 3	IX - 3	X - 3
4	I - 4	II - 4	III - 4	IV - 4	V - 4	VI - 4	VII - 4	VIII - 4	IX - 4	X - 4
5	I - 5	II - 5	III - 5	IV - 5	V - 5	VI - 5	VII - 5	VIII - 5	IX - 5	X - 5
6	I - 6	II - 6	III - 6	IV - 6	V - 6	VI - 6	VII - 6	VIII - 6	IX - 6	X - 6
7	I - 7	II - 7	III - 7	IV - 7	V - 7	VI - 7	VII - 7	VIII - 7	IX - 7	X - 7
8	I - 8	II - 8	III - 8	IV - 8	V - 8	VI - 8	VII - 8	VIII - 8	IX - 8	X - 8
9	I - 9	II - 9	III - 9	IV - 9	V - 9	VI - 9	VII - 9	VIII - 9	IX - 9	X - 9
10	I-10	II-10	III-10	IV-10	V-10	VI-10	VII-10	VIII-10	IX-10	X-10

Matrix indicates specific jobs in different rankings and different grades (classifications).

FIGURE 8-7 Grade description system with "ranked" general classifications and "ranked" specific jobs.

trates a hypothetical grade description wage and salary administration system consisting of one hundred total jobs, ten general job grades, and an assumed ten specific jobs per job grade.

The grade description method is an improvement over the ranking job evaluation system because it requires a more thorough analysis of jobs. The classification method requires extensive job thinking and analysis, and when this is done, all the problems of wage and salary administration become easier to solve. Grade descriptions are used as fixed written statements against which to compare organizational jobs. The grouping of jobs into classifications makes pay determination problems administratively easier to handle. Pay grades are determined for and assigned to all job classifications. The grade description compensation system, however, does possess some serious drawbacks. Grade descriptions must of necessity be general and abstract in order to be applicable to a great variety of jobs. Also, like the ranking method, it features an ordinal scale and thus is nonquantitative in format. This means that there is not equal differences in job complexity between job grades or classifications. In addition, grade descriptions provide no way of weighting the compensable factors that make up jobs. To overcome such limitations, most organizations make use of point or factor job evaluation systems when determining company compensation structures.

C. POINT

The point system is, by a wide margin, the most commonly used wage and salary administration method in the United States. Point systems can follow a standard format or they can be uniquely tailor made. All point plans consist of various compensable job factors or characteristics. Standard point systems commonly utilize four main job-factor sets: skill, effort, responsibility, and job conditions. Each of these four job-factor sets contains numerous elements or subsets, for example, skill can be subdivided into judgment, adaptability, experience, and so forth; effort can be broken down into areas such as concentration, alertness, and physical demand; responsibility can be split into number of subordinates, total budget, and discretion time; and job conditions can be severed into hazards, accident frequency, and general working conditions. No single point system utilizes all of these factors, but instead each point plan picks eight to twelve of these characteristics that best apply to the job situation under analysis. Each factor is subdivided into degrees that define the relative extent and amount of that factor that is required for each of a series of jobs. For example, experience, which is one of the most commonly used job factors, could be subdivided into five degrees: first degree, three months or less; second degree, three to six months; third degree, six to twelve months; fourth degree, one to three years; and fifth degree, over three years. A precise set scale of points is assigned to the degrees of each factor. In summary, each point system consists of eight to

FACTORS	DEGREES				
	1	2	3	4	5
Skill:					
1. Judgment	X	X	X	X	X
2. Adaptability	X	X	X	X	X
3. Experience	X	X	X	X	X
Responsibility:					
4. Number of subordinates	X	X	X	X	X
5. Total budget	X	X	X	X	X
6. Discretion time	X	X	X	X	X
Effort:					
7. Concentration	X	X	X	X	X
8. Alertness	X	X	X	X	X
9. Physical demand	X	X	X	X	X
Job conditions:					
10. Hazards	X	X	X	X	X
11. Accident frequency	X	X	X	X	X
12. General working conditions	X	X	X	X	X

POINT MATRIX

Note. X's represent specific points per factor and per degree.

FIGURE 8-8   Point system.

twelve job factors with definitions for these factors, and each factor is broken down into degrees with written definitions for each degree. When evaluating a job, the proper degree for each and every factor is determined and the respective point values are added to obtain a final total job score. This total is associated with a certain pay level which, in turn, represents an exact wage or salary rate or range. Figure 8-8 summarizes the format used within a typical point wage and salary administration system. When point totals from the point matrix have been determined, a point conversion table as shown in Figure 8-9 is used to translate job points into job dollars.

POINT RANGE	HOURLY RATE RANGE
101 - 150	$1.60-$2.10
151 - 200	2.00 - 2.50
201 - 250	2.40 - 2.90
251 - 300	2.80 - 3.30
301 - 350	3.20 - 3.70
351 - 400	3.60 - 4.10
401 - 450	4.00 - 4.50
451 - 500	4.40 - 4.90

FIGURE 8-9   Point conversion table.

Eight to Twelve Factors

Whereas only one scale was needed with the grade description compensation system, numerous scales are needed for the point job evaluation system. A separate scale is required for each of the eight to twelve compensable factors used within any particular point plan. Job factors and factor degrees must be precisely defined and all such definitions must be constructed of words reflective of subjective human judgment. The point system gives one the impression of being objective, but on closer examination, the possible human errors that may be incorporated into the system can easily be found. In short, the point method is no more accurate than the rating scales (factors and degrees) developed and used. Reliable and valid rating scales can be formulated but not without considerable expenses of time, effort, and money.

Advantages and Disadvantages

The point compensation system features many advantages and disadvantages. One advantage of the point method is the stability of the rating scales. Once the scales are developed, they may be used for an extended time period. Usually such scales, if properly developed, are fairly reliable and valid. Worker acceptance of the point system is also favorable because it is more systematic and objective than other job evaluation methods. In addition, pay rates and ranges are easy to determine from total job point values and thus administrative problems are minimal when point pay plans are used. Furthermore, jobs are evaluated using several factors or criteria under a point system. Global, overview, subjective "whole job" evaluations are not utilized. Finally, permanent records and written substantiations are also part and parcel of point pay systems.

The greatest drawback of the point job evaluation method is the amount of money required to develop and install this system as compared with ranking and grade description compensation systems. The task of properly defining job factors and factor degrees is an immensely time-consuming and difficult aspect of point pay systems. Considerable clerical detail is involved in recording and summarizing the rating scales especially if many raters are used. In addition, the unique features of the point system are not easy to explain or understand. Often workers find it difficult to fully comprehend the meaning of concepts and terms such as factors, degrees, and points. In spite of these shortcomings, most organizations use point pay systems because the greater accuracy possible with this compensation method justifies the larger expenditures of time and effort. Some companies, however, prefer to use a factor comparison pay system that is a combination of the ranking and point job evaluation systems.

D. FACTOR

The factor comparison method of job evaluation compares jobs by making judgments concerning which jobs contain more of a certain compensable factors than others. Jobs are compared to each other factor by factor. Initially, key jobs are judged and rated, then, other jobs are compared to the key-job standards. The most commonly used compensable factors contained within this job evaluation system are: (1) mental requirements, (2) physical requirements, (3) skill requirements, (4) responsibility, and (5) working conditions. These factors are considered to be universal components of all jobs (Belcher, "book" reference citation).

The factor comparison system is the second most popular wage and salary administration system. It is usually, but not always, used for evaluating white-collar, professional, and managerial positions. As noted earlier, the factor method combines elements of the ranking and point compensation systems. Similar to the ranking method, jobs are rated by comparing them with one another. Similar to the point system, jobs are rated on several compensable factors to achieve a final total numerical rating (but now in terms of dollars and cents instead of points).

Key Jobs

In the factor pay system, key jobs serve as standards against which all other jobs are compared and contrasted. A key job is one whose content has become stabilized over time. Key jobs have pay rates that are agreed to be correct by both management and labor standards. In addition, key jobs are important pivotal positions within an organization. Key jobs usually are performed by a large number of people in an organization, but still they commonly involve a unique skill or expertise.

Five Factors

The process of job rating involves comparing the job description and the job specification for each job to be rated with all the job descriptions and the job specifications for the key jobs. The comparisons and contrasts must be performed by working one factor at a time until all five (or possibly more) of them have been analyzed. As a job is compared with all the other key jobs, one factor at a time, it is assigned a money value in cents-per-hour for each factor according to the point on the key-job scale at which this job best fits. This identical process and maneuver is repeated for all of the other factors (as identified, usually totalling five in number). The pay rate assigned to the job is obtained by adding the determined amounts as indicated by the money values shown within the five factor scales that individually set a job money

FACTORS

Cents Per Hour Per Factor	Mental Requirements	Skill Requirements	Physical Requirements	Responsibility	Working Conditions
100		Toolmaker[a]	(Laborer)		
90	Toolmaker[a]		Electrician[a]		
80			Toolmaker[a]	Inspector[a]	
70	Electrician[a]	(Machinist)		Toolmaker[a]	Toolmaker[a]
60	(Machinist)	Electrician[a]	(Machinist)		Inspector[a]
50	(Assembler)	(Assembler)	Inspector[a]	(Machinist)	Electrician[a]
40	Inspector[a]	Inspector[a]	(Assembler)	Electrician[a]	(Machinist)
30	(Laborer)			(Assembler)	(Assembler)
20		(Laborer)			(Laborer)
10				(Laborer)	

[a]indicates "key job"
( )indicates nonkey or unanalyzed job.

FIGURE 8-10 Factor system.

wise in relative comparison to fixed key jobs. The format used within a typical factor wage and salary administration system is shown in Figure 8-10.

Advantages

One advantage of the factor pay system is the requirement that a custom-built, tailor-made installation be constructed for each organization. No standard factor comparison formats exist because key jobs vary from organization to organization. The reliability and validity of uniquely designed job evaluation systems are greater than the same statistical measures obtained from group standardized job analysis plans and programs. Flexibility also results when fixed compensation procedures are not used. In addition, the factor comparison system tends to lead to favorable job description and specification procedures being utilized with a company. Furthermore, the limited number of factors (usually five instead of eight to twelve) tends to reduce the possibility of overlapping and overweighting of factors. Finally, the use of a monetary unit is considered by some to be an advantage in that this financial measure permits the pricing of a job as soon as its job level is established.

Disadvantages

There are some disadvantages or limitations associated with the use of factor compensation systems. The factor method assumes "universal" job factors (usually five in number) but many jobs differ so much that job comparisons based only on these criteria are misleading. The factor system also relies heavily on key jobs, but it is widely known that jobs change tremendously in content and importance over time. When monetary values of jobs are used in the development of the job comparison scale, another operational bias is introduced. Pay rates must be continually adjusted if they are to properly assess the monetary market value of key organizational jobs. Often the monetary measure arouses the emotions and anxieties of job raters who find it difficult to remain completely objective when actual dollar-and-cents units are involved in the job comparison process. Finally, the complexity of the factor pay system often makes it difficult to be explained to and understood by the common layman and the everyday nonsupervisory organizational employee.

E. TIME SPAN OF DISCRETION

The time span of discretion concept was constructed by Elliott Jaques after more than a decade of research in companies based in England. This idea has not been implemented widely in this country although it is, at least theoretically, a sound concept. By definition, the time span of discretion of each job is the maximum period of time during which the use of discretion is authorized and expected when performing a task without the review or supervision of a superior. According to Jaques, jobs at all organizational levels can be measured in discretion terms. In simple jobs, the time span for marginally substandard quality is considered. In more complicated jobs, discretion can be measured in terms of the pace and organization of the work. The Jaques pay determination system also features an equitable work-payment scale and standard earning progression curves along with the time span of discretion measure. The equitable work payment scale represents what an employer and the employees consider to be a fair and just wage payment for a particular job or type of work. Progression or maturity curves plot annual salary on a vertical axis and years since bachelor's degree on the horizontal axis and indicate the relationship between these two factors in the form of various curves. Different curves are needed for different degrees of evaluated performance. Figure 8-11 illustrates the progression or maturity curve concept.

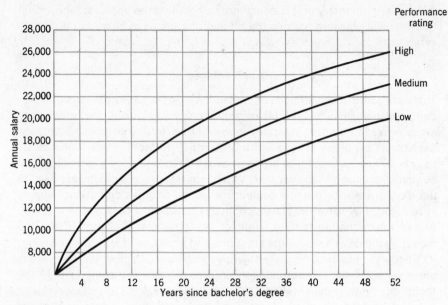

FIGURE 8-11 Progression or maturity curves.

One Factor Only

The time span of discretion concept is the only unique aspect of the Jaques pay determination system. The major criticism of this pay method is that it is a one factor job evaluation system. The one factor, time span of discretion, is the only major variable used to judge the complexity of a job. However, jobs are much too complex to be properly evaluated in terms of only one criterion (Charles). In addition, it is also shown that frequently the time span of discretion concept is similar to the responsibility variable used within most point and factor job evaluation systems. Because point and factor systems contain many other variables along with responsibility, they are considered to be better job evaluation systems than the Jaques method because they are more comprehensive and systematic in content and structure (Gordon).

Overview

Figure 8-12 summarizes the above discussion of job evaluation systems. A job evaluation "star" is shown as being comprised of five elements or subsets: ranking; grade description; point; factor and time span of discretion. Various other hybrid job evaluation systems have been devised and used over the years by some personnel practitioners and management consultants. But such hybrid pay systems are usually modifications of one or combinations of two or more of these five basic compensation systems described previously. The dotted or broken lines of the star-shaped subdivisions of Figure 8-12 indicate that even these five major job evaluation systems are best envisioned as partially interrelated and overlapping pay plans (instead of being thought of as totally distinct or completely synonymous pay system methodologies). This is because there are certain features and aspects that many of these pay plans have in common, for example, the "responsibility" factor is explicitly part of most point and factor job evaluation systems, and implicitly this variable is also part and parcel of the ranking, grade description, and time span of discretion remuneration plans as well.

5. Summary

In this chapter the subject matter of compensation: wage and salary administration was presented in area subdivisions concerned with: (1) principal

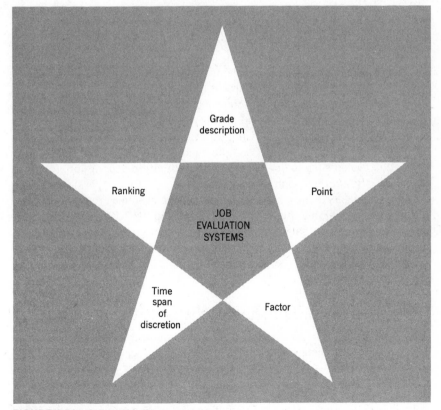

FIGURE 8-12 Job evaluation systems.

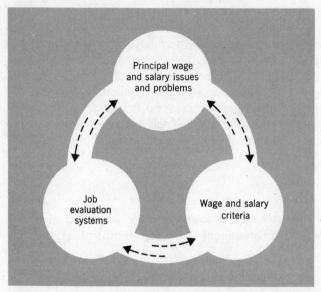

FIGURE 8-13 Compensation: wage and salary administration relationships.

wage and salary issues and problems [specifically, (a) pay level, (b) pay structure, (c) individual pay assignment, (d) payment method, (e) incentives, (f) indirect compensation, (g) pay control and (h) special problems]; (2) wage and salary criteria [specifically, (a) prevailing pay, (b) ability to pay, (c) union bargaining power, (d) cost of living, (e) living wage, (f) productivity, (g) job requirements, and (h) supply and demand market factors]; and (3) job evaluation systems [specifically, (a) ranking, (b) grade description, (c) point, (d) factor, and (e) time span of discretion].

Wage and salary issues, problems, criteria, and systems are compensation matters that are highly interrelated in nature. Figure 8-13 shows that compensation: wage and salary administration is best envisioned as a multiple interrelated network comprised of three main subsets or elements labeled principal wage and salary issues and problems, wage and salary criteria, and job evaluation systems.

DISCUSSION QUESTIONS AND ASSIGNMENTS

1. Identify and briefly explain the principal wage and salary administration issues and problems discussed in this chapter.
2. Identify and briefly explain the major wage and salary criteria discussed in this chapter.
3. Compare and contrast the point and factor job evaluation systems.
4. In your own words, present a definition of the term compensation.

5. Which wage and salary criterion do you feel is the most influential? Defend your choice.
6. Evaluate the merits of the time span of discretion concept.

REFERENCES

General Book References

Allen, Donna, *Fringe Benefits: Wages or Social Obligations,* 2nd ed. Ithaca, N. Y.: New York State School of Industrial and Labor Relations, Cornell University Press, 1969.

Belcher, David W., *Wage and Salary Administration,* 3rd ed. Englewood Cliffs, N. J.: Prentice-Hall, 1972.

Burgess, Leonard R., *Wage and Salary Administration in a Dynamic Economy.* New York: Harcourt, Brace & World, 1968.

Crystal, Graef S., *Financial Motivation for Executives.* New York: American Management Association, 1970.

Dunn, J. D., and Frank Rachel, *Wage and Salary Administration: Total Compensation Systems.* New York: McGraw-Hill, 1971.

Ferguson, H., *Wages, Earnings, and Incomes: Definitions of Terms and Sources of Data.* Ithaca, N. Y.: New York State School of Industrial and Labor Relations, Cornell University Press, 1971.

Lawler, Edward E., *Pay and Organizational Effectiveness: A Psychological View.* New York: McGraw-Hill, 1971.

Moore, Russel F. (ed.), *Compensating Executive Worth.* New York, American Management Association, 1968.

Zollitsch, Herbert G., and Adolph Langsner, *Wage and Salary Administration,* 2nd ed. Cincinnati: South-Western, 1970.

Specific Journal References

Bailey, W. R., and A. E. Schwenk, "Wage Differences Among Manufacturing Establishments," *Monthly Labor Review, 94* (5), 1971, pp. 16–19.

Bass, B. M., "Ability, Values, and Concepts of Equitable Salary Increases in Exercise Compensation," *Journal of Applied Psychology, 52* (4), 1968, pp. 299–303.

Belcher, David W., "The Changing Nature of Compensation Administration," *California Management Review, 11* (4), 1969, pp. 89–94.

Belcher, David W., and T. J. Atchison, "Equity Theory and Compensation Policy," *Personnel Administration, 33* (3), 1970, pp. 22–33.

Boynton, R. E., "How Employees Measure Their Pay," *Compensation Review, 2* (3), 1970, pp. 12–20.

Cangemi, Joseph P., "Personnel Evaluation Rating Scale," *Personnel Journal, 49* (8), 1970, pp. 665–667.

Charles, W. W., "Installing Single-factor Job Evaluation," *Compensation Review, 3* (1), 1971, pp. 9–21.

Dunnette, M. D., "Compensation: Some Obvious Answers to Unasked Questions," *Compensation Review, 1* (1), 1969, pp. 8–15.

Evan, William M., and Roberta G. Simmons, "Organizational Effects of Inequitable Rewards: Two Experiments on Status Inconsistency," *Administrative Science Quarterly, 14* (2), 1969, pp. 224–237.

Evans, W. A., "Pay for Performance: Fact or Fable," *Personnel Journal, 49* (6), 1971, pp. 726–731.

Field, Paul L., "Money Still Isn't Everything," *Business Management, 38* (4), 1970, pp. 18–19.

Gerwin, Donald, "Compensation Decisions in Public Organizations," *Industrial Relations: A Journal of Economy & Society, 8* (2), 1969, pp. 174–184.

Giles, B. A., and G. V. Barrett, "Utility of Merit Increases," *Journal of Applied Psychology, 55* (1), 1971, pp. 103–109.

Gordon, M. E., "An Evaluation of Jaques' Studies of Pay in the Light of Current Compensation Research," *Personnel Psychology, 22* (4), 1969, pp. 369–389.

Hammermesh, D. S., "White-collar Unions, Blue-collar Unions, and Wages in Manufacturing," *Industrial and Labor Relations Review, 24* (1), 1971, pp. 159–170.

Hettenhouse, G. W., "Compensation Criteria for Top Executives," *Harvard Business Review, 49* (5), 1971, pp. 113–119.

Hinrichs, J. R., "Correlates of Employee Evaluations of Pay Increases," *Journal of Applied Psychology, 53* (4), 1969, pp. 481–489.

Houff, James A., "Area Wages and Living Costs," *Monthly Labor Review, 92* (3), 1969, pp. 43–46.

Kassem, M. Sarni, "The Salary Compression Problem," *Personnel Management, 50* (4), 1971, pp. 313–317.

Kinyon, John, "Wage Developments in Manufacturing — 1969," *Monthly Labor Review, 93* (7), 1970, pp. 35–39.

Lawler, Edward E., and J. R. Hackman, "Impact of Employee Participation in the Development of Pay Incentive Plans: A Field Experiment," *Journal of Applied Psychology, 53* (4), 1969, pp. 467–471.

Lawson, H. G., "The Cost-of-Living Escalation Clause," *The Wall Street Journal, 46* (112), 1970, pp. 14–15.

Masters, S. H., "Wages and Plant Size: An Inter-industry Analysis," *Review of Economics and Statistics, 51* (2), 1969, pp. 341–345.

Mescon, Michael H., "Education, Compensation and Human Utilization," *Atlanta Economic Review 20,* (11), 1970, pp. 30–31.

Penzer, W. N., "Education Level and Satisfaction with Pay: An Attempted Replication," *Personnel Psychology, 22* (1), 1969, pp. 185–199.

Rezler, Julius, "Effects of Automation on Some Areas of Compensation," *Personnel Journal, 48* (4), 1969, pp. 282–285.

Rosen, Sherwin, "Unionism and the Occupational Wage Structure in the United States," *International Economic Review, 11* (2), 1970, pp. 269–286.

Sawhney, P. K., and I. L. Herrnstadt, "Interindustry Wage Structure Variation in Manufacturing," *Industrial and Labor Relations Review, 24* (3), 1971, pp. 407–419.

Schuster, J. R., and B. Clark, "Individual Differences Related to Feelings Toward Pay," *Personnel Psychology, 23* (4), 1970, pp. 591–604.

Schneider, Benjamin, and Loren K. Olsen, "Effort as a Correlate of Organizational Reward System and Individual Values," *Personnel Psychology, 23* (3), 1970, pp. 313–326.

Schweitzer, S. O., "Factors Determining the Interindustry Structure of Wages," *Industrial and Labor Relations Review, 22* (2), 1969, pp. 217–225.

contents

learning objectives

1. To understand the relationships between compensation, benefit, and service concepts.

2. To become familiar with the causes of benefits and services growth over the years.

3. To be knowledgeable about benefit program objectives, criteria, and problems.

4. To learn of the diversity in types or classifications of benefits and services.

Remuneration exists in many forms other than the pay check.

9

Compensation: Benefits and Services

1. Introduction

Direct wage and salary payments constitute only part of the total compensation package. Today a considerable portion of an employee's total remuneration is in the form of company benefits and services. Virtually all organizations in this country today provide their workers certain tangible benefits and services over and above the basic pay check. These financial supplements usually provide extra leisure, extra income, and a better work environment to the employees. Protection against accident, unemployment, illness, and loss of income also is provided through such company benefit plans. Other organizational service programs may be designed to fulfill social and recreational employee needs. Benefit and service programs are not directly related to the productive efforts of the employees, but instead are supplied to all company workers irrespective of the quantity or quality of their individual work outputs. Nevertheless, often many productive byproducts accrue to the organization that features progressive employee benefits and services programs. For example, easier recruitment, higher morale, greater loyalty, less absenteeism, and decreased theft may all be directly tied into employer efforts in these areas (Bureau of National Affairs).

Compensation Controversies

Although there are some controversies associated with the use of various direct wage and salary administration techniques and methodologies, a much greater degree of disagreement surrounds the issue of indirect employee compensation (Sloane and Hodges). Wage and salary matters involve precise questions, units of measurement, and objectives. Benefits and services, however, are controversial in both philosophy and format. No one agrees on what benefits or services should be "standard" for any or all organizations. The extent and cost of these programs also has not been generally agreed on. The purposes, responsibilities, measurement criteria, and evaluations of company programs in these areas are also matters of conjecture and controversy (Foegen).

Compensation Relationships

Compensation is the broadest employee remuneration concept of which both wage and salary administration and benefits and services are a part. Figure 9-1 shows compensation as the largest entity with subdivisions of wage and salary administration and benefits and services. Sometimes this same relationship is expressed by the following equation:

Compensation = wage and salary administration + benefits and services.

Generally, wage and salary administration refers to direct, financial remuneration matters, whereas benefits and services refer to indirect, financial, and nonfinancial compensation concerns. However, it is often difficult or impossible to tell a direct remuneration from an indirect one, or a financial payment from a nonfinancial recompense. For example, are expense accounts, bonuses, profit sharing, company cars, stock options, and the like direct or indirect, financial or nonfinancial? Because of such dilemmas and problems,

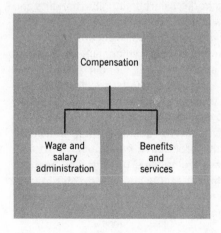

FIGURE 9-1 "Compensation," "wage and salary administration," and "benefits and services" relationships.

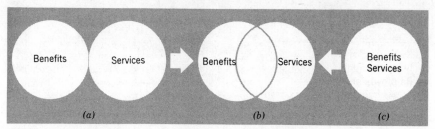

FIGURE 9-2 "Benefits" and "services" as distinct, interrelated, and synonymous set entities. (a) Distinct. (b) Interrelated. (c) Synonymous.

to envision direct versus indirect remuneration as totally distinct entities, or to picture financial versus nonfinancial payments as completely synonymous or indistinguishable activities, are both erroneous, extreme, and exaggerated viewpoints.

2. Semantic Problems and Definitional Difficulties

Often the terms benefits and services are considered synonymous. However, sometimes slight differences in meaning are associated with these two concepts. When a distinction is made between these terms, this variation usually claims that a benefit is an item for which a direct monetary value to the individual employee can be readily determined, while the term service is then reserved to be descriptive of any event, object, or thing for which a direct monetary value to the individual employee cannot be easily ascertained or established. Utilizing this distinction, a benefit would be company programs such as pensions, holiday pay, severance pay, health, or life insurance; while an organizational service would be things like a company newspaper, athletic field, Christmas party, or company purchasing service. Figure 9-2b illustrates that the terms benefits and services are best envisioned as partially interrelated and overlapping indirect compensation concepts, instead of their being visualized as totally distinct (Figure 9-2a) or completely synonymous (Figure 9-2c) set remuneration entities.

Interchangeable Phrases

Other phrases and terms also are used frequently to describe the benefits and services area of personnel management practice. Some of the more commonly used phrases include: fringe benefits; employee services; supplementary compensation; indirect compensation; supplemental pay; and nonwage remuneration. In general, these phrases individually and collectively are interchangeable and synonymous. Figure 9-3 lists some of the

BENEFITS AND SERVICES
(or)

---

1. Fringe benefits
2. Employee services
3. Supplementary compensation
4. Indirect compensation
5. Supplemental pay
6. Nonwage remuneration
Et al.

FIGURE 9-3   Interchangeable phrases.

phrases commonly seen or heard that are interchangeable and synonymous with the benefits and services concept. Of these substitute phrases, the fringe benefits term is the one most frequently heard today. But most personnel managers and practitioners object strongly to this expression because company benefits and services currently represent a very sizeable portion of the total labor cost for a firm, and thus they are not properly identified as fringe costs or items.

3. Causes for Growth

The number and extent of employee benefits and services have increased tremendously over the last several decades. There are a number of reasons for this rapid growth. This development is best understood if analyzed and approached historically.

Origin of Benefits

Although employee benefits and services have been provided by employers since the period of the guild system in medieval Europe, they began to be considered as a separate aspect of employee compensation during World War II. Originally, efforts to help those who could not adequately provide for themselves were made by the individual's immediate family, by churches, and by private charity. Later, beginning with the mercantile economy and the guild system, industry made its first effort to care for its own. During the 1920s and 1930s government began to involve itself in the problems of age, sickness, unemployment, and death. Among the many reasons for the shift in the sources of employee assistance were the growth of industrialization, increasingly heavy urbanization, and the growth of a capitalistic economy. These changes brought about shifts in public and political opinion.

Initial Industrial Reaction

The use of employee benefits and services began when the first retirement and death benefit plans were initiated by industry in the early 1900s. The next major step in the evolution of fringe benefits came in the 1930s when the federal government became concerned about the economic security of industrial workers. However, the greatest expansion of benefit programs occurred during World War II as a result of wage rates being frozen, because of the efforts of unions, and also resulting from managerial philosophies and practices that were competing for very scarce labor supplies (Davis, 1971).

Post World War II

When the war was over and companies wanted to return to basic wage plans, employees were unwilling to relinquish recently obtained benefit program gains. Strikes from 1945 to 1950 were often centered around fringe benefits. The emphasis during the 1950s was on some form of guaranteed employment or income. During the 1960s and 1970s, the battle cry has been for "shorter hours of work" (Foltman). The recent growth of fringe benefits has occurred during a period in the economic history of the United States when profits have been high and labor unions have been free to make fringe benefits a major bargaining issue. While pressure from organized labor is expected to continue, other trends and developments also are expected to have great impact on future employee benefit programs. Increased leisure time and flexible working hours are forces that will stimulate additional benefits with a leisure orientation. Higher levels of education and affluence, new medical advances, company-owned recreational facilities, increasing frustration and militancy among the blacks, and further social legislation by the government are other factors and forces that will share the development of future employee benefit and service packages. Although it is difficult to make specific predictions of what later employee benefits and services might develop, Figure 9-4, nevertheless, suggests some possible newer employee benefits and services, some of which are already being provided to the employees of a few companies (Foltman).

1. Company lunch programs
2. Complete dental care
3. Disability insurance
4. Discounted company products and services
5. Early retirement
6. Educational benefits for entire family
7. Flexible work day
8. Guaranteed annual wage
9. Guaranteed lifetime employment
10. Intra- and intercity pay differentials
11. Longer vacations
12. Maternity and paternity leaves of absence
13. Mental and emotional health care
14. Nursery and day care centers
15. Portable pensions
16. Sabbatical leaves
17. Severance pay
18. Shorter workweek
19. Sick leave with pay
20. Tailor-made compensation package
21. Total family medical and hospital coverage
22. Transportation pay or vehicle to and from work
23. Use of company-owned recreational facilities
24. Twelve to fifteen paid holidays

FIGURE 9-4   Newer employee benefits and services.

Reasons for Rapid Growth

Prior to the World War II period, only a few companies provided company benefits and services to their employees. From an initial zero percentage, indirect compensation has increased to the point where it now represents approximately 30 percent of the average worker's total compensation package. Several factors account for this significant increase in company benefits and services over the past thirty years. One of the most important reasons has been public policy or federal legislation. For example, the Social Security Act of 1935 requires employers to share equally with employees the cost of Old Age, Survivors and Disability Insurance, in addition to paying the full cost of unemployment insurance. The growth of unionism also has influenced the growth of company fringe benefits and services. National Labor Relations Board rulings and court interpretations of the Wagner and Taft-Hartley Acts also have given impetus to the expansion of pay supplements. Federal wage stabilization policies and corporate income tax requirements over the years also have encouraged managements to expand their company benefit programs. Labor scarcity and the competition for qualified personnel also were factors leading to the initiation and evolution of indirect compensation plans (Livernash).

Growing industrialization has changed and altered the basic nature of this country's economy. Productivity increases have led to increased employee remuneration alternatives, for example, part of this productivity increase has been distributed in the form of increased leisure time or shorter working hours. But advanced industrialization also means increased interdependence of people and more security risks per person. Today management allows some of the productivity increase resulting from increased industrialization to appear in the form of compensation in protecting employees from such insecurities as unemployment, sickness, injury, and old age. The general level of affluence and prosperity in this country has allowed management to become more concerned about employee needs for finding and keeping decent jobs or income sources. Company benefit and service programs are among the mechanisms managers use to supply these securities to their employees (Landay).

Three-Party Protection

Over the years, a tripartite concept of individual protection has developed. First, every individual is expected to be at least partially responsible for his own present and future well-being. Second, industry is now expected to help protect its workers from the hazards of life. In addition, government today is called on to support and finance worker assistance programs. The degree of contribution of these three parties of course varies depending on the nature and purpose of various employee benefit and service programs (Davis, 1969).

4. Benefit Program Objectives and Criteria

Objectives — Reduced Turnover

There are three main objectives of company benefit and service programs: (1) reduced turnover, (2) improved morale, and (3) enhanced security. Initially, reduced labor turnover was the major reason for employee benefit programs. During the World War II era, managers developed benefit packages so as to attract and maintain scarce labor supplies. However, over the years, labor turnover for production workers has decreased dramatically, although increased employee benefits are but one factor, perhaps not even the most important one, influencing this decreased mobility. On the other hand, although rank-and-file employees are tending to become more immobile, scientific, technical, managerial, and professional personnel are becoming more transient. Thus, in effect, the reduced turnover objective may be backfiring somewhat since least productive workers remain with a company, but the most highly trained manpower change jobs frequently.

Improved Morale

Improved morale is an objective of company benefit programs. This goal came somewhat after the initial benefit purpose of reduced turnover. After World War II, when company benefit programs became common, the major purpose of the programs was not to reduce turnover by giving a little something extra, but was to improve morale by remaining competitive with or better than other employers in terms of employee benefit packages. Employers, of course, believed that increased loyalty and morale on the part of the employees would lead to greater productivity. However, this belief is not as generally held now, since it is commonly felt that benefit programs have reached the point of diminishing returns as motivators and stimulants to productivity. A common opinion among employers is that paternalistic endeavors have led only to higher overhead, without commensurate increases in job satisfaction and productivity. Thus, even if benefits do *improve* employee morale, they do not necessarily raise worker productivity. Also it is questionable today whether benefit programs really serve to *improve* morale or simply to maintain it.

Enhanced Security

Today the major objective of company benefit programs has shifted from an employer-centered goal to an employee-oriented objective. Greater economic security for workers is now considered to be the major objective of benefit and service arrangements (Berkowitz and Burton). Unfortunately, this purpose is often self-defeating for employers, for often the greater the degree of security a worker has, the less productive he is. Nevertheless, the general trend in industry and government is towards enhanced worker protection and greater employment security. This trend is expected to increase instead of decrease in the foreseeable future.

Criteria

There are many factors that top management must weigh when deciding to establish a particular kind of employee benefit or service (Nielsen). Some of these benefit criteria are: (1) cost; (2) ability to pay; (3) needs; (4) union power; (5) tax considerations; (6) public relations; (7) social responsibility; and (8) workforce reactions. The total cost of a program to the company must be weighed against the ability of the company to financially afford the benefit package. The needs of individual employees for a particular program or service must be considered along with the collective strength of the union and the possibility of a strike or total work stoppage. Federal, state, and local tax laws often make or break many company benefit proposals. Public relations and consumer pressures often influence benefit decisions. The concept and practice of social responsibility, incorporating a true altruistic and humanitarian concern for the general well-being of employees, is often acknowledged by management as a major criterion for the adoption of new employee benefits and services. The anticipated general and specific reactions of the regular workforce also may have a bearing and impact on both the current composition and the future offerings of companies in terms of available employee benefit programs. The aforementioned are but some of the most important factors and criteria affecting and determining what forms of indirect compensation will be provided to employees by their employers. These benefit program criteria along with the previously discussed benefit program objectives are summarized in Figure 9-5.

BENEFIT PROGRAM

Objectives	Criteria
1. Reduced turnover	1. Cost
2. Improved morale	2. Ability to pay
3. Enhanced security	3. Need
	4. Union power
	5. Tax considerations
	6. Public relations
	7. Social responsibility
	8. Workforce reactions

FIGURE 9-5 Benefit program "objectives" and "criteria."

BENEFIT PROGRAM PROBLEMS

1. Charges of paternalism
2. Excessive expenses
3. Fads become fashion
4. Maintaining the least productive workers
5. Neglect of other personnel functions
6. New sources of grievances
7. Questionable relationships to motivation and productivity

FIGURE 9-6   Benefit program "problems."

5. Benefit Program Problems

There are many problems that result because of the existence of company benefit and service programs. Seven of the most frequently found benefit-related problems are summarized in Figure 9-6 and are explained in greater detail below.

Charges of Paternalism

Especially in the past but even today employers who provide an excessive degree of benefits and services to their workers are accused of playing a "father" or "ruler" role. Employees sometimes claim that they feel as if they are "children" being given handouts from a parent figure. Workers are generally glad to receive benefits and services from employers, but the atmosphere or climate of the work relationship also is important. Employees want to feel as if they have earned the benefits and are rightfully deserving of the services provided to them. Anything that smacks of a "freebie" or "handout" nature will not be accepted by employees without overtones of undesired paternalism.

Excessive Expenses

Fringe benefits and services also result in greater direct and indirect financial expenses. The cost of the program itself may be substantial, but the administrative detail and paperwork involved are often a burdensome expense factor. These expenses inevitably become fixed or overhead costs and, therefore, must be met regardless of worker production levels.

Fads Become Fashion

What may be considered a luxury at one time may be viewed later as a necessity. In addition, as soon as benefit patterns are set in one industry or company, they tend to spread to other industries or companies. What the newest fads are today often become the accepted fashions of tomorrow. This phenomenon is true of company benefit and service concepts as it is applicable to clothing apparel and hair coiffures (Houff). Credit unions and severance pay are examples of benefits that were once novel but are now commonplace.

Maintaining the Least Productive Workers

As mentioned earlier, company benefit and service programs also have a tendency to maintain rank-and-file workers, but they do not serve to decrease the mobility of more highly trained and talented personnel. In general, as fringe benefits increase, there is the tendency to freeze employees in their jobs since the benefits would be lost to them if they were to change employment. Top level workers can find comparable benefits in other employment situations, but the same is not usually true of lower level production workers (Petermann).

Neglect of Other Personnel Functions

With increasing attention being given to benefits and services by employees, there is the possibility that executives and personnel managers will focus their efforts on them and neglect other phases of the personnel program that may be equally or more important. Similarly, overemphasis on employee benefits and services may result in workers being more concerned about their future security than their present productivity (Shuster).

New Sources of Grievances

As additional benefits and services accrue to the employee, new potential problem areas are introduced into the company. In effect, any of the benefits and services that are provided by companies to workers may become the subject of criticism and formal grievance action. The administration of pension funds is an example of a benefit that now often involves labor grievances.

Questionable Relationships to Motivation and Productivity

Previously mentioned was the fact that increased benefits and services do not necessarily lead to greater employee motivation and productivity. In some situations there seem to be positive relationships among such factors, but in other circumstances, no significant relationships, or inverse relationships have been observed. If, in general, there is no significant relationship between company benefit and service programs and worker motivation and productivity, perhaps the entire rationale for and philosophy behind these programs need to be seriously reexamined by corporate administrators (Bauman).

INDUSTRY	PERCENTAGE
Banks, finance, and trust companies	34
Petroleum industry	32
Chemicals and allied products	32
Insurance companies	30
Stone, clay, and glass products	27
Printing and publishing	26
Pulp, paper, lumber, and furniture	24
Textile products and apparel industry	22
Mercantile trade	22

Source. Chamber of Commerce of the United States, *Employee Benefits 1971* (Washington, D.C., 1972), pp.25-30.

FIGURE 9-7   Benefits and services as a percentage of total compensation in various industries.

6. Cost of Benefit and Service Programs

Employee benefits and services now constitute from 25 to 35 percent of the total compensation package for most employees. During the 1930 to 1970 period, employee benefits have increased from around four percent of total wages and salaries to around 30 percent (Gordon and LeBleu). The precise percentage of total indirect compensation paid to workers varies from company to company and from industry to industry. For example, a recent Chamber of Commerce study reveals the data as shown in Figure 9-7 (Chamber of Commerce, book reference citation).

The results of this same 1971 Chamber of Commerce survey indicated that payments for employee benefits and services ranged from 14 to 60 percent of total payroll. The average for all companies (137 in total) included in the survey was 30.8 percent of payroll, 143.5 cents per payroll hour, or $2544 per year per employee (Chamber of Commerce, book reference citation). Figures 9-8 and 9-9 are based on costs reported by the 137 companies that have been included in all Chamber of Commerce surveys since 1951. Notice in Figure

INDUSTRY GROUP	1951	1961	1971
All industries (137 companies)	34.5	71.6	143.5
Manufacturing (56 companies)	31.0	69.1	143.2
Nonmanufacturing (81 companies)	36.9	73.4	143.7

Source. Chamber of Commerce of the United States, *Employee Benefits 1971* (Washington, D.C., 1972), p. 27.
Note: Statistics not adjusted for inflation.

FIGURE 9-8   Comparison of 1951-1971 employee benefits: Cents per payroll hour.

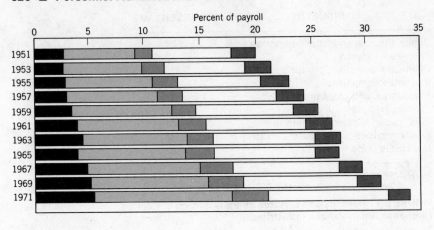

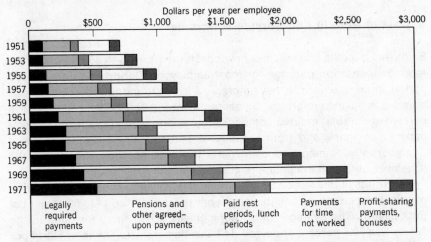

FIGURE 9-9 Comparison of 1951-1971 employee benefits for 137 companies. *Source:* **Chamber of Commerce of the United States, Employee Benefits 1971 (Washington, D.C., 1972), p. 28.**

9-8 that the average cents per payroll hour for all industries has increased from 34.5 in 1951 to 71.6 in 1961 to 143.5 in 1971. As shown in Figure 9-9, most of the increases took the form of pension and welfare benefits, and payments for time not worked, the two areas in which unions have been most active.

Legally Required Payments

Figure 9-9 also indicates 1951 to 1971 data for payments required of employers by state or federal law. These payments are made up of Social Security benefits at retirement, medical care for the elderly, compensation for injury on the job, and support for the unemployed. These expenses are payroll costs over which management has no direct control. In contrast to unemployment and workmen's compensation payments, which are paid for solely by employer contributions, benefits under the Social Security system are financed by a tax, half of which is paid by the employee and half by the employer. The amount of this tax has increased steadily over the years. In addition, another tax was assessed in 1966 to pay for health insurance (or Medicare) benefits for retired workers.

Increases in Other Employee Benefits

Along with increased legally required payments, Figure 9-9 indicates the 1951 to 1971 dollar increments for pension and other agreed on payments, paid rest periods and lunch periods, payments for time not worked, and profit-sharing payments and bonuses. Note that payments for pensions and for time not worked have increased proportionally much greater than have payments in the form of rest periods, lunch periods, profit sharing, or bonuses.

Administrative Costs

The above information and data relates basically to the direct costs of increased employee benefit and service programs. Increased indirect and administrative expenses also are involved although they are not commonly reported or accounted for in compensation surveys. Added personnel and administrative paperwork accompany enlarged company benefit programs. Productivity and morale adjustments, either upward or downward, are also indirect forms of either additional benefits or costs. In short, although everyone seems to be aware of the rising straight forward costs and percentages of employee benefits and services, intangible expenses and adjustments also should be measured in order to determine the accurate total cost of newly designed and recently augmented supplemental compensation or nonwage remuneration programs (Yount).

7. Types of Benefits and Services

There is no uniform method of classifying employee benefits and services. Various governmental agencies and management authors make use of different methods of grouping benefits for analytical purposes. One popular classification scheme is that followed by the Chamber of Commerce. As shown in Figure 9-9 and as illustrated in greater detail in Figure 9-10 the Chamber of Commerce benefit grouping system consists of five main categories.

CHAMBER OF COMMERCE
BENEFIT CLASSIFICATIONS

1. Legally required payments
2. Pensions and other agreed-on payments
3. Paid rest periods, lunch periods, wash-up time, travel time, clothes-change time, and get-ready time
4. Payments for time not worked
5. Other items including profit-sharing payments and bonuses

FIGURE 9-10 Chamber of Commerce benefit classification system.

It is, of course, impossible to identify all of the types of employee benefits and services. For benefit-identification purposes, I will use the following classification methodology to present a partial listing of such benefits and services to the reader: (1) employee security payments; (2) payments for time not worked; (3) bonuses and awards; and (4) service programs.

Employee Security Payments

Examples of employee security payments are listed below.

1. Legally required employer contributions: Old Age, Survivors, Disability, and Health Insurance; Unemployment Insurance; Workmen's Compensation; State Disability Insurance.
2. Supplemental unemployment benefits.
3. Accident insurance.
4. Disability insurance.
5. Hospitalization insurance.
6. Life insurance.
7. Medical insurance.
8. Surgical insurance.
9. Pensions.
10. Contributions to savings plans.
11. Contributions to stock purchase plans.
12. Home financing.
13. Payment of optical expenses.
14. Health and welfare funds.

Payments for Time Not Worked

Payments for time not worked include items such as:

1. Call-back and call-in pay.
2. Clean-up time.

3. Dental care time.
4. Death-in-the-family leave.
5. Down time.
6. Family allowances.
7. Holiday pay.
8. Jury duty time.
9. Lay-off pay.
10. Medical time.
11. Military service allowance.
12. National Guard duty.
13. Paid lunch periods.
14. Portal-to-portal pay.
15. Religious holidays.
16. Reporting pay.
17. Rest periods.
18. Room and board allowances.
19. Severance pay.
20. Sick leave.
21. Supper money.
22. Time spent on collective bargaining.
23. Time spent on grievances.
24. Vacation pay.
25. Voting time.
26. Witness time.

Bonuses and Awards

Bonuses and awards consist of financial amenities such as:

1. Holiday premiums.
2. Overtime premiums.
3. Shift premiums.
4. Weekend premiums.
5. Anniversary awards.
6. Attendance bonus.
7. Christmas bonus.
8. Quality bonus.
9. Safety awards.
10. Profit-sharing bonus.
11. Service bonus.
12. Suggestion awards.
13. Waste-elimination bonus.
14. Year-end bonus.

Service Programs

Service programs commonly provided by organizations to their employees might feature the following items:

1. Annual reports to employees.
2. Athletic teams.
3. Beauty parlors.
4. Cafeteria and canteen services.
5. Club membership payments.
6. Company housing.
7. Company newspaper.
8. Company stores.
9. Credit union.
10. Dances.
11. Dietetic advice.
12. Discount on company products.
13. Educational assistance.
14. Food subsidies.
15. Income tax service.
16. Legal aid.
17. Library and reading room facilities.
18. Loan funds.
19. Lunch period entertainment and music at work.
20. Magazine subscription payments.
21. Medical examinations.
22. Nursery.
23. Parking.
24. Parties and picnics.
25. Purchasing service.
26. Savings plans.

Of course, no one company provides all of these employee benefits and services. Employee needs and company preferences are the two most important factors affecting what combination of employee benefits and services a company will offer. Among the most significant and commonly found employee benefit and service programs are life insurance, health insurance, pensions, supplemental unemployment benefits, credit unions, social and recreational programs, holiday and vacation pay, and increased leisure time.

8. Legally Required versus Voluntary Programs

Legally Required Benefits

The following benefits are legally required by state and federal laws: (1) Old-Age, Survivors, and Disability Insurance (OASDI) and Hospital Insurance

(HI); (2) Unemployment Compensation; (3) Workmen's Compensation; and (4) State Disability Insurance. OASDI and HI, commonly called Social Security and Medicare, are financed jointly by the employer and the employee through payroll tax deductions imposed under the Federal Insurance Contributions Act and often called FICA taxes. The orginal Social Security Act of 1935 was amended quite drastically in 1965. Along with OASDI benefits and taxes being increased, two new benefits were made available for persons aged 65 and over. Medicare was introduced with its two components, namely, Hospital Insurance and Supplementary Medical Insurance (SMI). As of 1971, OASDI and HI were financed by a tax of 4.6 and 0.6 percent, respectively, of the first $7800 of an employee's annual earnings. The employer, who withholds these amounts from the workers' paychecks, is also obligated to match the contributions penny per penny. The total of 10.4 percent is paid to the government and goes into federal OASDI and HI Trust Funds. OASDI benefits when paid by the government go directly to eligible individuals, and HI payments go directly to the hospital, Blue Cross, or a private insurance company. SMI is a voluntary program that helps to pay doctor bills and provides numerous other health benefits and services. SMI participants pay $5.60 a month and the federal government pays an equal amount in yet another "matching" financial insurance arrangement.

Unemployment benefits are paid by each state to unemployed individuals who are willing and able to work and who meet certain specified conditions regarding their previous employment relationship. Such conditions pertain to length of service, reasons for dismissal, and other contingencies. The amount and duration of benefits vary from state to state and with each individual case. Unemployment compensation is financed by taxes paid only by the employer. The amount of tax varies according to each individual firm's experience rating. For example, in 1971 the maximum rate was 3.2 percent of the first $4200 paid in wages to each employee annually. This experience-rating factor, of course, encourages firms to be labor-turnover conscience. Workmen's compensation refers to the provisions in all states whereby firms must make plans for paying worker medical and hospital bills. In addition, workmen's compensation includes partial pay for wages lost by the employee due to industrial illness or work accidents. These costs are paid entirely by the employer through insurance companies, special firm funds, or mandatory state funds (Berkowitz and Burton). Some states also are requiring employers to pay the cost of state disability insurance for their employees.

Voluntary Programs

Voluntary programs include all benefits and services provided by employers to their workers other than those that are legally required. These additional benefits are usually granted unilaterally in nonunionized firms, but they are the result of labor-management collective bargaining in unionized work settings. Although classified as "voluntary," often the employer does not have total discretion as to whether or not he will offer these benefits to his workers. Strong unions, past practice, industry custom, and other environmental factors often make "voluntary" programs almost mandatory (Harrington). All of the benefits and services listed previously in this chapter, with the exception of those classified as "employee security payments — (1) legally required employer contributions," are examples of voluntary programs. Of the thirty-plus percent of benefits and services that make up the indirect compensation portion of total payroll for the typical manufacturing employee, approximately 25 percent of this 30 percent is in the form of voluntary programs, and a little over 6 percent is in the form of legally required payments (again see Figure 9-9).

9. Cafeteria Compensation Concept

Some companies today are experimenting with the smorgasbord or cafeteria compensation concept. Different employees, depending on their ages, educational and income levels, life-styles, and other forms of personal preference, demand and need different combinations of employee benefits and services (Trahair). For example, the typical young worker desires direct wages and educational assistance, whereas the greatest priorities often are for pension rights and health insurance for the older employee (Gallop). The cafeteria compensation concept basically involves the idea that each and every employee ought to design and tailor-make his own indirect compensation program by personally picking and choosing what benefits and services he desires from a collection of company provided alternatives. Choices and decisions made concerning benefit programs largely will depend on individual employee discretion, instead of on unilateral management fiat or centralized collective bargaining agreements (Greenberg). This benefit methodology has the major advantage of more adequately fulfilling the personal desires, needs, wants, and preferences of participating employees. The basic philosophy behind the cafeteria compensation concept is shown in Figure 9-11.

Drawbacks

The cafeteria compensation concept has been in existence now for over a decade, but it has not caught on rapidly or been adopted freely because of practical application problems. One major drawback is that the idea is not feasible for small organizations. This is because if only a limited number of employees desire a certain benefit, then low group rates cannot be provided by insurance companies to the employers directly or to the employees indirectly. Group rates mean lower costs; without group rates, the individually designed benefit program may actually dollar-wise be providing the

FIGURE 9-11   Cafeteria compensation concept.

worker with less than he would receive if he were under a group program. Increased administrative paperwork and expense on the part of both insurance companies and employers also are serious drawbacks of the cafeteria compensation concept. Tailor-made benefit programs require more staff and manpower in order to implement. Increased overhead costs are usually passed on to the employee partially in the form of lower benefit utility per dollar. Some individuals have argued that these administrative details can be handled efficiently by a properly programmed computer. However, examples of such efficiency are still relatively rare within industry today, and, as mentioned before, these conditions are found only in the largest of employment entities (Willis).

10. Summary

Today a considerable portion (around 30 percent) of an employee's total remuneration is in the form of company benefits and services. Compensation is the broadest employee remuneration concept of which both wage and salary administration and benefits and services are a part. The concepts of employee benefits and services are subject to numerous joint and individual semantic problems and definitional difficulties. The number and extent of employee benefits and servies have increased tremendously over the last several decades, especially since World War II, because of a number of interrelated federal, state, and local happenings.

There are three main objectives of company benefit and service programs: reduced turnover, improved morale, and enhanced security. Benefit decision-making factors and criteria considered by management include cost; ability to pay; need; union power; tax considerations; public relations; social responsibility; and workforce reactions. Some of the problems that result because of the existence of company benefit and service programs concern: charges of paternalism; excessive expenses; fads become fashion; maintaining the least productive workers; neglect of other personnel functions; new sources of grievances; and questionable relationships to motivation and productivity. The average cost of worker benefits and services for the typical employer is around $1.50 per payroll hour, or slightly over $2500 per year per employee.

There is no uniform way of classifying employee benefits and services, but in this chapter, benefits were categorized into four main groups: (1) employee security payments; (2) payments for time not worked; (3) bonuses and awards; and (4) service programs. Employee security payments include legally required employer contributions of OASDI, HI, unemployment compensation, workmen's compensation, and state disability insurance. All benefits and services provided by employers to their workers other than those that are legally required are said to be voluntary programs.

The cafeteria compensation concept basically involves the idea that each and every employee ought to design his own indirect compensation program by personally picking and choosing what benefits and services he desires from a collection of company provided alternatives.

DISCUSSION QUESTIONS AND ASSIGNMENTS

1. Explain the relationships between and among the compensation, benefit, and services concepts.
2. Identify the objectives of and the problems associated with company benefit and service programs.
3. What is the difference between legally required and voluntary benefit and service programs?
4. Research and provide the most recent data you can find indicating the cost of benefit and service programs for the typical employer.
5. What, in your view, are the major advantages and disadvantages of the cafeteria compensation concept?

6. Identify the benefits and services you would be most and least interested in receiving.

REFERENCES

General Book References

Allen, Donna, *Fringe Benefits: Wages or Social Obligation?* Ithaca, N.Y.: New York State School of Industrial and Labor Relations, Cornell University Press, 1969.

Becker, J. M., *Guaranteed Income for the Unemployed.* Baltimore: Johns Hopkins Press, 1968.

Bureau of National Affairs, Inc., *Basic Patterns in Union Contracts,* 7th ed. Washington, D.C.: BNA, Inc., 1971.

Chamber of Commerce of the United States, *Employee Benefits 1971.* Washington, D.C.: The Chamber, 1972.

Greene, M. R. et al, *Early Retirement: A Survey of Company Policies and Retirees' Experiences.* Eugene, Ore.: College of Business Administration, University of Oregon Press, 1969.

Poor, Riva (ed.), *4 Days, 40 Hours.* Cambridge, Mass.: Bursk & Poor, 1970.

Srb, J. H., *Communicating with Employees About Pension and Welfare Benefits.* Ithaca, N.Y.: New York State School of Industrial and Labor Relations, Cornell University Press, 1971.

Specific Journal References

Bauman, Alvin, "Measuring Employee Compensation in U.S. Industry," *Monthly Labor Review, 93* (10), 1970, pp. 17–24.

Berkowitz, Monroe, and John F. Burton, Jr., "The Income-Maintenance Objective in Workmen's Compensation," *Industrial and Labor Relations Review, 24* (1), 1970, pp. 14–31.

Bureau of National Affairs, Inc., "Trends in Holidays and Vacations," *Bulletin to Management,* (1100), March 11, 1971, pp. 4–6.

Davis, Harry E., "Negotiated Retirement Plans — A Decade of Benefit Improvements," *Monthly Labor Review, 92* (5), 1969, pp. 11–15.

Davis, Harry E., "The Growth of Benefits in a Cohort of Pension Plans," *Monthly Labor Review, 94* (5), 1971, pp. 46–50.

Foegen, Joseph H., "Fringe on the Fringe," *Personnel Administration, 35* (1), 1972, pp. 18–22.

Foltman, Felicia F., "Implications of Fringe Benefits in the 1970's," *Arizona Review, 17* (6–7), 1968, pp. 1–5.

Gallop, Gerald, "Retirement — Reward or Punishment," *Personnel Journal, 49* (4), 1970, pp. 338–340.

Gordon, T. J., and R. E. LeBleu, "Employee Benefits, 1970–1985," *Harvard Business Review, 48* (1), 1970, pp. 93–107.

Greenberg, David H., "Deviations from Wage-Fringe Standards," *Industrial and Labor Relations Review, 21* (2), 1968, pp. 197–209.

Harrington, David A., "How to Improve the Return from Your Fringe Benefit Program," *Personnel Journal, 49* (7), 1970, pp. 604–605.

Houff, James N., "Supplemental Wage Benefits in Metropolitan Areas," *Monthly Labor Review, 91* (6), 1968, pp. 44–48.

Landay, Donald M., "Trends in Negotiated Health Plans: Broader Coverage, Higher Quality Care," *Monthly Labor Review, 92* (5), 1969, pp. 3–10.

Livernash, E. R., "Wages and Benefits," *Review of Industrial Relations Research, 1* (1), 1970, pp. 79–144.

Nielsen, Niels H., "Organizing Benefits like a Business," *Conference Board Record, 7* (10), 1971, pp. 30–36.

Petermann, L. L., "Fringe Benefits of Urban Workers," *Monthly Labor Review, 94* (11), 1971, pp. 41–44.

Shuster, Jay R., "The Trouble with Employee Benefit Programs," *Business Management, 39* (6), 1971, pp. 34–37.

Sloane, Arthur A., and Edward W. Hodges, "What Workers Don't Know About Employee Benefits," *Personnel, 45* (6), 1968, pp. 27–34.

Trahair, R. C. S., "The Worker's Judgment of Pay and Additional Benefits: An Empirical Study," *Human Relations, 23* (3), 1970, pp. 201–223.

Willis, E. S., "Problems in Selecting Employee Benefits," *Monthly Labor Review, 92* (4), 1969, pp. 61–62.

Yount, H. H., "Total Compensation — Cost, Comparison and Control," *Compensation Review, 3* (4), 1971, pp. 9–18.

contents

learning objectives

1. To recognize the importance of and relationships among organizational health, safety, and plant security concerns.

2. To understand the differences in the conceptualizations and the analyses of occupational diseases and safety accidents.

3. To be able to comprehend the major features and requirements of the Occupational Safety and Health Act of 1970.

4. To envision employee and organizational health and safety matters from a "whole man" perspective.

A person's general health and safety is reflected in both his individual behaviors and his organizational activities.

10

Health and Safety

1. Introduction and Semantics

The topics of employee benefits and services and employee health and safety are presented in the same chapter in many personnel textbooks. However, in this book they are considered separately because, in my opinion, the main intent of employee benefits and services is to serve as supplemental, indirect remuneration, whereas the main intent of employee health and safety is to provide worker security. Of course, some types of employee benefits and services do, indeed, serve personal security needs. Examples include pensions, life insurance, hospitalization, accident insurance, supplemental unemployment benefits, and medical and surgical payments. In fact, all of those employee benefits and services listed in the previous chapter under the subheading of "employee security payments" can be properly considered as forms of personal, individual employee security. However, many other types of employee benefits and services are not security based but are intended simply as forms of indirect compensation. All of those employee benefits and services listed in the last chapter under the subheadings of "payments for time not worked," "bonuses and awards," and "service programs" are basically intended to be company compensation rather than security plans and features. Examples include holiday pay, vacation pay, anniversary awards, credit unions, company product discounts, and social and recreational programs. Actually, compensation in any form, direct or indirect, can be thought of as a means of providing security. Thus, although we will not consider further the security aspects of supplemental fringes in this present chapter, the dual nature of employee benefits and services must be kept in mind.

Individual and Organizational Perspectives

Although terms such as industrial health, industrial safety, occupational health, occupational safety, and plant security are commonly used, it is erroneous to think of health and safety matters from only a global company perspective. In the final analysis, employee health and safety is also an individual worker concern. Both organizational and individual employee perspectives are relevant in the study of health and safety management. In this chapter we discuss health and safety administration using three main personnel topic subareas: health, safety, and plant security.

2. Health

Definition

Health is a state or degree of bodily soundness. Often the term health is used to describe a universal good condition. Usually the total health concept is broken down into two subareas — physical health and mental health. Good physical health exists when all physiological, organic, and bodily features of living organisms are properly functioning — that is without pain, disease, or decay. Good mental health exists when a person or an organization is well adapted, has an accurate perception of reality, and can reasonably successfully adjust to the stresses and frustrations of life. We now discuss organizational health in greater detail using the following format: (1) occupational diseases; (2) hazardous hygienic conditions; (3) workmen's compensation; (4) "whole man" concept; (5) mental health; and (6) implementation.

A. OCCUPATIONAL DISEASES

One aspect of organizational health concerns industrial hygiene. Hygiene is the branch of medical science that relates to the preservation and improvement of health, both in individuals and communities. Anything that is described as hygienic is considered to be healthy, wholesome, and sanitary. The phrase, industrial hygiene has some historical and evolutionary basis, but today this area is better described as organizational instead of as industrial hygiene because its problems are common to all organzations whether they are business or nonbusiness, profit or nonprofit, or industrial or nonindustrial in character. Organizational hygiene is best considered as a subarea of organizational health. Health is the broader of the two concepts whether one is referring to personal or organizational physical well-being.

The objective of an organizational hygiene program is the prevention of occupational diseases. Such programs are designed to create and maintain a work environment that is conducive to good health, good morale, and high production. An occupational disease is not the same as an injury caused by an accident. Although human suffering may be involved in both instances, the legal distinction between an injury accident and an occupational disease is often important under state workmen's compensation laws. Many states provide only very limited coverages and benefits for occupational diseases. Usually accident injuries occur at a specific point in time and in a particular place and are unforeseen. In contrast, occupational diseases usually develop gradually over extended periods of time that often involve weeks, months, or years. Occupational diseases result from repeated or continuous exposures to toxic substances, microorganisms, airborne contaminants, or stress-producing elements.

B. HAZARDOUS HYGIENIC CONDITIONS

There are several problems and hazardous conditions that organizational hygienists seek to prevent. The most common causes of occupational diseases involve: (1) heat; (2) pressure; (3) vibration; (4) radiation; (5) noise; (6) contamination; and (7) skin irritants. It would be highly unlikely that an organization would encounter problems in all of these areas, but complications related to one or more of them are generally found in virtually all organizations at one time or another (Chase).

Heat

Hazardous conditions can result from either an abundance or a lack of heat, although the former is much more common. Especially during the summer months, employees may suffer from heat exhaustion, heat cramps, and heat strokes. Solutions to such problems are not as easy or practical as they might initially appear to be. For example, air conditioning or shorter work periods often result in tremendously increased company expenses.

Pressure

Pressure hazards may be due to either high or low extremes. However, unlike thermal (heat) hazards, those caused by pressure are relatively rare organizational complications. Divers, tunnel workers, fliers, and astronauts are workers who are subject to such hazards.

Vibration

Vibration hazards are also relatively rare but may be serious if they are experienced for extended periods of time. Vibrations are usually either directly or indirectly caused by mechanical operations. Long-distance truck drivers and workers who operate air hammers are examples of employees who experience vibration job hazards.

Radiation

Radiation is perhaps the rarest but most serious type of occupational disease. Relatively few workers are ever exposed to radioactive materials, but those who deal with or are surrounded by such materials usually must take numerous precautions to prevent overexposure. Both electromagnetic and ionizing radiation can quickly cause death if they are not handled properly. Most hospitals and chemical research centers must deal with radiation employment hazards.

Noise

The major occupational disease frontier is currently noise pollution. State and federal legislation now require noise levels to be reduced to ninety decibels or less. Ninety decibels is approximately the noise level produced by a fairly loud playing radio or television. Research has shown that repeated exposure to high frequency noise levels can cause human auditory damage and nervous tension. To eliminate these hazards and to comply in the long run with governmental regulations, organizations are redesigning various mechanical operations. Redesigned automobile engine testing operations are an example of such converted facilities. For the short-run, ear plugs, ear muffs, various hat styles, and other devices are used for noise protection purposes.

Contamination

Air pollution and water contamination can cause occupational diseases. Sanitary and construction workers sometimes must deal with water contamination problems. With respect to air pollution, inhalation is the most prevalent danger, but skin contact and ingestion also may cause considerable illness. Frequently experienced occupational hazards that are basically air contamination problems include gases, fumes, vapors, and airborne poisons. Painters, coal miners, and asbestos workers may suffer from illnesses caused by these contamination problems.

Skin Irritants

Various surveys indicate that skin ailments are the most frequently encountered forms of occupational disease. Skin diseases cause more suffering and account for the payment of more compensation dollars than any other type of occupational hazard. In the past, employers argued that skin diseases were due to employee allergies and thus were noncompensable. However, today this view has been largely displaced, since most skin diseases can be traced to occupational skin irritants such as solvents, acids, bases, and the like (Sternhagen).

Organizational Hygienist

The organizational hygienist deals with all of these forms of occupational disease and job hazards. To competently perform his job, the hygienist must have training in areas such as physiology, biochemistry, environmental engineering, toxicology, biophysics, and psychology. Unlike the safety engineer, who analyzes accidents through historical data and retrospection, the corporate hygienist must be able to spot and eliminate dangers before they become actual hazards or problems. In other words, industrial hygienists are trained to apply corrective measures before not after the fact.

C. WORKMEN'S COMPENSATION

Historical Framework

Before the twentieth century, organizations were liable for employee damages, accidents, injuries, and diseases only to the degree that their liability could be proved in court. The injured employee was required to sue the employer, but, since most employees did not have the financial wherewithal to do so, few won damage suits. Eventually, during the early part of the twentieth century, several state workmen's compensation laws were passed. In 1917 the United States Supreme Court approved the passage of these laws, and since then all states have passed workmen's compensation statutes.

Underlying Philosophy

The basic philosophy of workmen's compensation laws is that the employer is financially liable for all accidents arising out of, and in the course of, employment — regardless of whether the employee was specifically at fault. Most employers (about 80 percent) insure themselves against this risk with either a private or a state insurance agency, but some organizations are financially large enough so that they have the option of insuring (or not insuring) themselves. Benefits to injured employees under workmen's compensation laws are of two general types — substitute compensation for regular pay, and medical benefits. Percentages of wage and benefit payments vary from state to state. Payments in the various states also vary according to the duration of the disability, which is usually classified in one of four ways: temporary total; permanent total; permanent partial; or death.

Workmen's compensation laws are usually administered by a state industrial commission which investigates and makes injury awards. Although employees may appeal commission decisions to the judicial court system, the overwhelming majority of injured workers accept the commission's decision(s).

Workmen's compensation laws were originally intended to reimburse employees for industrially caused accidents and injuries. However, in many states the trend is for worker coverages in all employment settings and for all types of work related injuries, occupational diseases as well as industrial accidents, and even for the coverage of mental or emotional breakdowns that are related to job stresses.

Compulsory or Elective

Workmen's compensation laws are compulsory or elective. Under a compulsory law, every employer subject to it is required to comply with its provisions for the compensation of work injuries. These acts are compulsory for the employee also. An elective law is one in which the employer has the option of either accepting or rejecting the act. Although most employers elect to be covered by the act, some do not. In the latter case, employees may be unable to obtain compensation unless they sue for damages. The elective laws also permit the employee to reject coverage, but in practice this is rarely done. Of the state and territory workmen's compensation laws now in existence, thirty-one are compulsory and twenty-three are elective.

Varying Provisions

As is now provided by law in all states and for federal employees, workmen's compensation benefits for those injured are scaled to reflect weekly wages (but with a stated maximum). These benefits may also cover the costs of medical care and rehabilitation training. As one would expect, provisions vary from state to state and are subject to frequent change by state lesiglatures. Figure 10-1 summarizes the varying details of current state provisions.

Laws originally provided benefits for temporary total disability amounting to about two thirds of the average weekly wage. But these percentage maximums are restricted by dollar limits. These benefits are also limited by a specified maximum number of weeks for which they can be paid and by a maximum total payment. As a result, most of the actual benefit payments fall well below 50 percent of average weekly wages. Lastly, survivor's benefits are also provided within all state workmen's compensation provisions.

Trends in Workmen's Compensation

Workmen's compensation laws have gradually been extended in many areas to cover emotional impairments. Even emotional illnesses that occur before

Jurisdiction	Temporary Total Disability [1] Intended Benefit as % of Maximum Weekly Wage	Actual Maximum Weekly Benefit Allowed	Death Benefits Maximum Duration in Weeks	Maximum Total Payments	Maximum [2] Medical Care	Maintenance Benefits for Vocational Rehabilitation	Coverage of Occupational Disease
Alabama	55-65%	$44	400	$17,600 [11]	2 yrs.—$6,000	No	[3]
Alaska	65	100	W,C-18 [4]	20,000	2 yrs.[7]	Yes	Full
Arizona	65 [5]	150 [5]	W,C-18 [4]	....	....	Yes	Limited
Arkansas	65	38.50	450	14,500	6 mos.[7]	Yes	Full
California	61¾	70	250-293	17,500-20,500	F.P.	No	Full
Colorado	66⅔	54.25	312	16,980-20,501	6 mos.—$5,000 [21]	No	Limited
Connecticut	66⅔	74-111 [6]	W,C-18 [4]	....	F.P.	Yes	Full
Delaware	66⅔	50	400,C-18 [4]	....	F.P.	No	Full
District of Columbia	66⅔	70	W,C-18 [4]	....	F.P.	Yes	Full
Florida	60	49	350	15,000	F.P.	No	Full
Georgia	60	37	400	12,500	10 wks.—$2,000 [9]	No	Limited
Hawaii	66⅔	112.50	W,C-20 [4]	35,100 [10]	F.P.	Yes	Full
Idaho	55-60	37-63	400,C-18 [4]	16,000	F.P.	No	Limited
Illinois	65-80	62-76	W,C-18 [4]	15,000-21,000	....	No	Full
Indiana	60	51	450	25,000 [11]	[7]	No	Full
Iowa	66⅔	40-56	300	14,250	[7]	No	Limited
Kansas	60	49	W,C-18 [4]	16,500	$7,500	No	Limited
Kentucky	66⅔	47 [6]	400	16,000 [11]	$3,500 [7]	No	Limited
Louisiana	65	35	400	14,000	$2,500	Yes	Full
Maine	66⅔	62 [6]	W,C-18 [4]	....	F.P.	Yes	Full
Maryland	66⅔	55	500	27,500	F.P.	No	Full
Massachusetts	66⅔	62 [13]	400,C-18 [4]	16,000	F.P.	Yes	Full
Michigan	66⅔	64-93	500,C-21 [4]	....	F.P.	Yes	Full
Minnesota	66⅔	60	W,C-18 [4]	25,000 [11]	F.P.	No	Full
Mississippi	66⅔	35	450	12,500	F.P.	Yes	Not by Statute [22]
Missouri	66⅔	57	W,C-18 [4]	17,500	180 days [7]	Yes	Full
Montana	50-66⅔	37-60	600	22,200-36,000	36 mos.—$2,500 [14]	Yes	Limited
Nebraska	66⅔	45	325	14,625	F.P.	No	Full
Nevada	65-90	52.50-72.69	W,C-18 [4]	....	[20]	No	Full
New Hampshire	66⅔	58	341	19,778	[19]	No	Full
New Jersey	66⅔	83 [6]	W,C-18 [4]	....	[7]	No	Full
New Mexico	60	45	500	22,500	5 yrs.—$5,000 [7]	No	Limited
New York	66⅔	60	W,C-18 [4]	....	F.P.	Yes	Full
North Carolina	60	42	350	15,000	10 wks.[7]	No	Limited
North Dakota	80	50-75	W,C-18 [4]	....	F.P.	Yes	Full
Ohio	66⅔	63 [12]	....	17,000-20,000	F.P.	Yes	Full
Oklahoma	66⅔	40	....	13,500	60 days [7]	No	Limited
Oregon	50-75	39.23-73.85	W,C-18 [4]	....	F.P.	Yes	Full
Pennsylvania	66⅔	52.50	500,C-18 [4]	....	1 yr.[15]	No	Full
Puerto Rico	66⅔	35	W,C-18-25 [4]	....	F.P.	No	Full
Rhode Island	66⅔	50-62 [8]	500	....	600-1,200 [7]	No	Full
South Carolina	60	50	350	17,500	10 wks.[7]	No	Full
South Dakota	55	42	....	15,000-20,000	$1,700 [7]	No	Limited
Tennessee	65	42	W,C-18 [1]	16,000	2 yr.—$5,000	No	Limited
Texas	60	35	360	12,600	....	No	Limited
Utah	60	44-62	312	13,728-19,344	$1,283.38 [7]	No	Limited
Vermont	66⅔	52 [13]	W,C [1]	....	F.P.	No	Limited
Virginia	60	45	300	18,000	90 days [7]	No	Limited
Washington	....	42.69-81.23	W,C-18 [4]	....	....	No	Full
West Virginia	66⅔	47	W,C-18-22 [4]	....	$3,000 [17]	Yes	Full
Wisconsin	70	68	400	19,430 [18]	F.P.	Yes	Full
Wyoming	66⅔	44-64	W,C-18 [1]	13,000-23,000	[7]	No	Not by Statute [22]
Federal Employes	66⅔-75	331.92	W,C-18-22 [1]	....	F.P.	Yes	Full

[1] The lower figure represents the benefit for a single worker; the higher the maximum for workers with dependents.
[2] Benefits may not exceed period of time or amounts indicated. F. P. indicates full payment of all medical aid and hospitalization required.
[3] Covers only specified dust or pulmonary disease and/or diseases caused by the inhalation of poisonous gases or fumes, and radiation diseases.
[4] "W" means payment to widow until death or remarriage; "C" means payment to children until age specified. The higher figure represents age if child is attending approved educational institution. Vermont continues benefit to dependent children regardless of age while they are regularly attending school, and to widow until she is remarried, she is entitled to social security benefits, or death.
[5] Plus an additional $10.00 per month if there are total dependents.
[6] Maximum weekly benefit amount 55 percent of 85 percent of the average wage as computed by the Employment Security Commission in Kentucky, 50 percent of statewide average weekly wage as reported under the State Employment Insurance Act in Vermont, and 66⅔ percent in Maine and New Jersey, 60 percent of the statewide average weekly wages of production workers in Connecticut.
[7] May be extended by commission without limit, in Kentucky, justifiable need must be shown. The commission may authorize up to $25,000 in New Mexico, $21,000 in South Dakota, and extend benefits for three years in Virginia.
[8] If worker is receiving benefits under the State Temporary Disability Insurance Act, benefits under the Workmen's Compensation Act are limited to $45.00.
[9] An additional $500 may be allowed, plus unlimited time.
[10] Dollar maximum does not apply to children under 18 nor to unmarried children over 18 for 104 weeks beyond their 18th birthday.

if incapable of self-support, nor to widow physically or mentally incapable of self-support.
[11] Disability benefits already made are deducted from death benefits payable. Minnesota limits deduction to $17,500.
[12] During the first 12 weeks of disability the amount is $63.00, but thereafter, the maximum amount drops to $56.00.
[13] Massachusetts provides an additional $6.00 for each total dependent not to exceed the average weekly wage of the employe. Vermont provides an additional $3.50 for each dependent child under 21.
[14] In cases of occupational disease, no time limit is imposed. If employe with occupational disease is able to continue work, while undergoing medical treatment, medical benefit is limited to $1,000. In cases of total disability where the $2,500 is insufficient to meet all hospitalization expenses, additional benefits may be allowed.
[15] Medical and surgical cost during first 12 months; hospital treatment not to exceed prevailing charges for the same period; may be extended if employe's earning power would be substantially restored.
[16] Order of Commissioner required if aggregate exceeds $7,500.
[17] May be increased without limit, but no medical benefits are payable in silicosis cases.
[18] Additional death benefits payable from state fund for children.
[19] Reasonable medical and hospital services or other remedial care for 6 months and additional 6 month periods upon written request to the Commissioner may grant extension for aid.
[20] Reasonable medical, surgical, and hospital treatment and supplies, apparatus, artificial members for six months, which may be extended.
[21] Additional payments out of Medical Disaster Insurance Fund in excess of payments under Workmen's Compensation Act and Occupational Disease Act, maximum, $35,000.
[22] The one exception is radiation disease.

FIGURE 10-1 Major provisions of Workmen's Compensation benefits. (*Source.* For updating and more details, consult the labor reporting services and the Bulletin series prepared by the Bureau of Labor Standards, U.S. Department of Labor.)

they precipitate a physical injury have been found to be compensable. For example, courts in several states have held that job-induced strain, stress, anxiety, or pressure that leads to a heart attack is compensable. Even more recently, mental illness that can be linked to job conditions has also been found to be compensable.

Financing Workmen's Compensation

The workmen's compensation benefits prescribed by law in the various states generally are financed by employers. A few states require employees to make small contributions, but these funds meet only a small part of the expense involved in paying the benefits. While payment of the benefits is an operational expense for the employer, the customer ultimately pays the cost of benefits. Since the employer must be able to meet the prices of his competitors, however, he is encouraged to prevent accidents from occurring, thereby reducing the cost of operation.

Two methods of providing for workmen's compensation risks are commonly used. One method is for the state to operate an insurance system that employers may join or, in some states, are required to join. Another method is for the states to permit employers to insure with private companies, and in some states, employers may be certified by the commission handling workmen's compensation to handle their own risks without any type of insurance.

Under most state and private insurance plans the employer and the employee gain by maintaining good safety records. Employers are rated according to accident experience, and their casualty insurance costs are determined on this basis. Under many compensation plans, employees are encouraged to follow safe practices. In some states an employee's benefits under the law are reduced by a specified percentage if he is found to have willfully failed to use safety devices provided by the employer, willfully failed to obey safety rules, or if the injury resulted from intoxication of the employee. A method that provides the worker with reasonable compensation for injury but also penalizes him for being willfully negligent in the observance of safety practices should help to promote safe practices. Since the employer also loses in the event of an accident, his continuing attention to fostering safety likewise pays dividends to him.

D. "WHOLE MAN" CONCEPT

The "whole man" concept is the basic philosophy that management must or should be concerned about not only employee physical health but also employee mental health both on and off the job. To date, the whole man concept represents a theoretical goal that few companies, even the more progressive ones in terms of personnel policies, have been able to philosophically or financially achieve. The point has already been reached where occupational diseases, mental health problems and injuries due to accidents are being employer compensated for in many states. However, most of these illnesses and personal damages must be job related or tied into organizational stresses and conditions before companies are willing (or are forced) to pay the consequences. Off-the-job injuries and illnesses are still usually not employer compensable — nor should they be. Many observers of business today believe that the business sector is already doing more than its rightful share to alleviate most of society's social ills and problems. Organizations in general ought to be concerned about their employees both while they are on company grounds and when they are at home. But that concern should not and cannot always be in the form of financial reimbursement for all of life's complications. Governmental bodies and social agencies must help to alleviate off-the-job employee miseries. Individual initiative and self-help must also be encouraged and should not be totally replaced by organizational assistance (Forgrens).

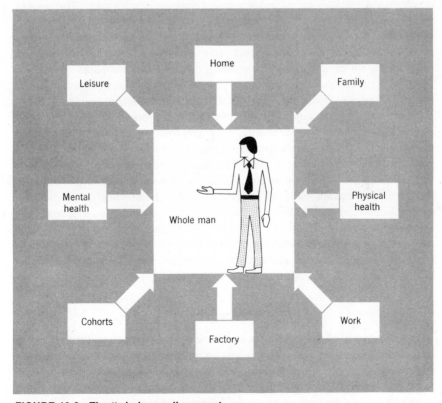

FIGURE 10-2 The "whole man" concept.

Mental health is not the only new area where organizations are being expected to help financially solve human and societal problems. Many private and public organizations also have special manpower programs (for alcoholics, drug addicts, ex-convicts, veterans, handicapped workers, and various hard-core minority and disadvantaged groups) to help mitigate many of society's cultural and social problems. Working sincerely with such global cultural concerns on a personalized, employer-employee, one-to-one basis is what the whole man security concept is all about. Although the whole man concept is an ideological goal that can never be completely achieved, more and more organizations are beginning to think that such an objective is worth striving for. Figure 10-2 summarizes the basic philosophy behind the "whole man" concept.

E. MENTAL HEALTH

Recently much attention has been given to organizational mental health. As noted previously, several state court decisions have assigned liability to employers for emotional stresses engendered by employment. The proper role of an organization to perform in the employee mental health area is a matter of heated controversy and ethical opinion. Proponents of an active organizational role have argued that the enterprise system in this country is responsible for creating and maintaining many of the pressures of modern life. These pressures can directly lead to mental breakdowns or can indirectly affect human emotional balances by being interrelated with employee problems of alcoholism, drug addiction, high accident rates, high tardiness and absenteeism, theft, and generally poor employer-employee relationships. Because of such problems and because of the recognized and accepted organizational role in the physical health area of employee welfare, many humanitarians and businessmen are calling for increased organizational concern and responsibility for employee mental health problems and programs. For decades physicians and psychiatrists have accepted the idea of the connection and interrelationship between mental and physical health, and many observers believe that it is now time for organizations to do likewise. It is known that a physical ailment can be aggravated because of anxiety, worry, or abnormal pressures related to employment factors.

Compensable

In the area of workmen's compensation, mental health is considered to be an expanding frontier. Organizations are being asked or forced to underwrite the costs of employee emotional breakdowns issuing from job stresses. Although such injuries and illnesses are not covered by existing federal legislation, workers and unions have taken such cases into state courts. In some instances the state courts have denied compensation; however, the trend is in the other direction. There is a progressive movement toward making an employer responsible for all human ills that may arise out of employment. Emotional disturbances can be caused by an employee's interaction with his work situation or by his relationship to his off-the-job personal environment. Unfortunately, many state court trials center around establishing the geographical location or cause of a worker's emotional condition. Many of these efforts are fruitless, however, because mental illness usually is caused by a combination of on-the-job and off-the-job factors (Cohen).

As noted earlier, good mental health can be described as a state wherein a person is well adapted, has an accurate perception of reality, and can reasonably successfully adjust to the stresses and frustrations of life. Mental health problems are best handled by professionally trained psychologists, psychiatrists, social workers, or personnel counselors. The majority of organizations do not employ such full-time specialists and, in fact, most organizations do not even employ or engage part-time workers or management consultants to help deal with and solve organizational mental health problems.

On an organizational rather than an individual basis, the major emphasis of any organizational mental health program should be on the creation of sound supervisor-subordinate relationships. The development of a favorable human relations climate often requires special management development programs designed to teach managers behavioral concepts and skills.

Alcoholism and Drugs

Perhaps the best specific example of what private firms can do in regard to mental health programs is in the area of the rehabilitation of alcoholic employees. Numerous companies have been conducting successful and worthwhile programs dealing with employee drinking problems. Work-related alcoholic counseling programs are usually much more effective than personal pleas from family and friends. Many companies rely heavily on Alcoholics Anonymous to assist them in the operation of their rehabilitation programs. Organizational supervisors are usually instructed to play a firm but sincere role when confidentially discussing an alcoholism problem with an employee. Although no state courts have yet required workmen's compensation awards for alcoholism induced by job-related pressures, more and more organizations have recognized the humanitarian reasons and the economic advantages of undertaking efforts in this regard. These same company and court actions and reactions to alcoholism are now recycling into the area of drug addiction. The treatment of drug-related employee problems is currently one of business's and society's most serious current and future health hazards.

F. IMPLEMENTATION

The implementation of a comprehensive organizational health program requires specialized manpower and resource facilities. A professional staff of physicians, nurses, psychologists, psychiatrists, and social workers must be maintained. Adequate facilities for emergency care of work injuries and for conducting preemployment and periodic medical examinations must exist. Provisions for proper first-aid treatment of occupational diseases and accident injuries must be available. A referral system for serious cases must be established between an organization and private-practice physicians and hospitals. A proper health program must also provide information to and educational services for company employees. In addition, consultation services must be part of the total health program. Written medical records and reports must be kept, and there must be cooperation with public health authorities to bring about the prevention of communicable diseases. Health personnel must also coordinate their efforts with the organization's safety programs and specialists. Furthermore, a pharmacy or medical dispensary is a necessary part of a comprehensive health program. Finally, serious mental health employee matters must be dealt with through psychiatric counseling, while less severe employer-employee emotional health concerns are alleviated through the development and maintenance of a proper internal human relations program. A comprehensive health program such as the one just described can only feasibly and financially be implemented by fairly large companies. Small organizations must carry out most of these elements and services by engaging the services of appropriate professional personnel on a retainer or consulting basis.

Organizational Design and Structure

In terms of organization structure, the health program can be tied into the overall design of an organization in several ways. However, two organizational patterns prevail in most large organizations. Figure 10-3 depicts the most common organizational health arrangement. A safety director, who is directly responsible to the personnel manager, supervises a safety department and a health and medical department. The safety department is largely made up of safety engineers, and the health and medical department is comprised mainly of physicains, nurses, social workers, and counselors.

Another increasingly popular format is illustrated in Figure 10-4, which shows an industrial hygienist, who reports directly to the personnel manager, as the director and coordinator of the safety and health and medical departments. This design structure is less frequently found, but it is preferred by some companies because of the preventative and forward-looking nature of industrial hygiene in relative comparison to the after-the-fact characteristic of organizational safety matters.

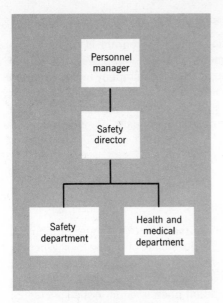

FIGURE 10-3 Organizational structure of health and safety services — alternative 1.

Of course, various other structural arrangements can be found relating company health and safety services to overall organizational activities. Unfortunately, the structural relationships just described exist only in large companies. Over two thirds of the companies in existence today have less than 500 employees, and organizations of this relatively small size typically do not have any formal arrangements for in-plant health services.

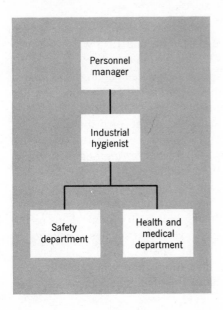

FIGURE 10-4 Organizational structure of health and safety services — alternative 2.

Health Responsibility

The implementation of an organizational health program is primarily the responsibility of corporate management. However, employee and union cooperation and responsibility are also needed if a company health program is to be totally effective. Although employees and employers may clash over economic matters, their objectives should be and usually are identical in the areas of personal injury prevention and personnel health administration.

3. Safety

Definition

Safety is a state of existence that involves freedom from danger or injury. A totally safe condition does not involve the possibility of risk or loss. Whereas organizational health basically concerns itself with occupational diseases, organizational safety largely involves injuries due to accidents. Although human beings often are part of the accident phenomenon, not all accidents directly involve human beings. Safety will be presented in greater detail in this chapter under five main subheadings: (1) historical background; (2) Occupational Safety and Health Act of 1970; (3) accidents; (4) implementation; and (5) contests. The majority of time and space, however, will be devoted to topics (2) and (3) since these areas form the heart of the current basic subject matter of safety management.

A. HISTORICAL BACKGROUND

Safety management is believed to have started around 1912 with the establishment of the First Cooperative Safety Congress and the organization of the National Safety Council. Prior to this time, a few states began the industrial safety movement by appointing safety officers to inspect industrial factories and workshops. A tremendous advancement in the introduction of health and safety programs throughout industry occurred because of the passage of workmen's compensation laws in the various states between 1910 and 1925. These laws hold employers financially responsible for injuries incurred by their workers on the job, regardless of the specific cause of the accident. The provisions of these laws require companies having high accident rates to pay higher insurance premiums than those having low accident rates. Along with state workmen's compensation laws, the work of such organizations as the National Safety Council and casualty insurance companies has done much to promote safety in employment. The National Safety Council's activities are primarily in research, education, and the compilation and publication of safety information. In addition, most states maintain safety inspection services within their departments of labor. In an effort to assist and encourage the states in their attempts to assure safe and healthful working conditions, the federal government recently enacted the Occupational Safety and Health Act of 1970. This Act authorizes the federal government to set and enforce occupational safety and health standards applicable to businesses affecting interstate commerce, and also provides for an Assistant Secretary of Labor for Occupational Safety and Health who has ultimate responsibility for setting safety and health guidelines related to specific industrial hazards. Traditionally, state laws have prescribed the safeguards that must be taken by employers, and state procedures and regulations have provided for the necessary inspections needed in order to determine compliance. Although the majority of health and safety laws are still state laws, a trend is beginning in which such matters may be superseded by federal authority (Pyle).

B. OCCUPATIONAL SAFETY AND HEALTH ACT OF 1970

New national policy was established on December 29, 1970, when President Richard M. Nixon signed the Williams-Steiger Occupational Safety and Health Act of 1970. At that time the President stated, "It is probably one of the most important pieces of legislation, from the standpoint of 55 million people who will be covered by it, ever passed by the Congress of the United States." The purpose of this landmark legislation, which became effective April 28, 1971, is to assure safe and healthful working conditions for the nation's wage earners. Secretary of Labor Hodgson called the Act a landmark piece of legislation that goes beyond the present workplace and considers the working environment of the future. The law provides that each employer has the basic duty to furnish his employees a place of employment that is free from recognized hazards that are causing or are likely to cause death or serious physical harm. Although this duty is one that employers have long accepted as a moral obligation inherent in the conduct of their business, the Williams-Steiger Act places specific responsibilities on each employer and subjects him to penalties if he fails to discharge them.

Occupational Safety and Health Standards

In general, job safety and health standards consist of rules for avoidance of hazards that have been proven by research and experience to be harmful to personal safety and health. They constitute an extensive compilation of wisdom that sometimes applies to all employees. An example of this would be fire protection standards. A great many standards, however, apply only to workers while engaged in specific types of work — such as handling compressed gases. It is the obligation of all employers and employees to familiarize themselves with the standards that apply to them and to observe them at all times. The Act authorizes the Secretary of Labor to promulgate as occupational safety and health standards the currently existing federal standards and any other national consensus standards. In addition, the Secretary of Labor may (on the basis of information submitted by the Secretary of Health, Education and Welfare, advisory committees, and others) revise, modify, or revoke existing standards and generate new ones. The creation of new standards involves various time limitations. Any person or company adversely affected by a standard issued by the Secretary may challenge its validity by petitioning the United States Court of Appeals within sixty days after its promulgation. The Act also provides for the establishment of emergency temporary standards, effective immediately on publication in the *Federal Register,* where it is found that employees are exposed to grave danger. The Secretary, after a hearing, is authorized to grant temporary variances from standards to give an employer sufficient time to comply, if he can show a need for the certain time extension and has a protection plan of action. Variance may also be granted without time limits if the Secretary finds that an employer is using safety measures that are as safe as those required in a standard.

Complaints of Violations

Any employee who believes that a violation of a job safety or health standard exists may request an inspection by sending a signed, written notice to the Department of Labor. This notice must mention specific grounds for the notice and a copy, without the identification of complainant, must be sent to the employer.

Enforcement

Enforcing the standards takes the form of on-site inspections by agents of the Secretary of Labor. These agents, who are usually safety engineers or industrial hygienists, can enter any area where work is performed at any reasonable time in order to inspect the premises. No advance notice of inspection is necessary. The inspector may also consult privately with employees, owners, and operators. The Act permits an employer or his representative to accompany the inspector during his examination of the workplace. When an investigation reveals an infraction, the employer is issued a written citation describing the specific nature of the violation. Citations must be publicly posted and must contain specific time limitations for the correction of infractions. Citations may be reviewed and time limitations may be extended by a cumbersome hearing request procedure.

Penalties for Violations

Figure 10-5 summarizes possible penalties under OSHA. These penalties are severe enough so that all employers have to give OSHA regulations serious attention and consideration.

INFRACTION	PENALTY
1. Citation for less serious violation	Discretionary up to $1,000
2. Citation for serious violation	$1,000 each
3. Failure to correct cited violation	$1,000 per day
4. Willful or repeated violations	$10,000 per violation
5. Willful violation causing death	$10,000 or up to six months in jail
6. Falsification of statements or records	Up to $10,000 and/or six months in jail

FIGURE 10-5 OSHA penalties.

Record-Keeping Requirements

In order to carry out the purposes of the Act employers are required to keep and make available to the Labor Secretary (and also the HEW Secretary) records on certain employer activities under the Act. Employers are also required to maintain accurate records of work-related deaths, injuries, and illnesses. Minor injuries requiring only first-aid treatment need not be recorded, but a record must be made if it involved medical treatment, loss of consciousness, restriction of work or motion, or transfer to another job. Employers can also be required to maintain accurate records of employee exposures to potentially toxic materials or harmful physical agents. In addition, an employer must promptly advise any employee of any excessive exposure and of the corrective action being undertaken.

The Secretary is directed to issue regulations requiring employers to keep their employees informed of their protections and obligations under the law through posting of notices or other appropriate means. The information that employers may be required to give their employees may also include the provisions of applicable standards.

Regulations issued under the OSHA of 1970 require all establishments subject to the Act to maintain records of recordable occupational injuries and illnesses occurring on or after July 1, 1971. Such records must consist of (1) a log of occupational injuries and illnesses (see Figure 10-6); (2) a supplementary record of each occupational injury and illness (see Figure 10-7); and (3) an annual summary of occupational injuries and illnesses (see Figure 10-8).

Protection Against Harassment

No employer can discharge or in any manner discriminate against any employee who exercises any right under the Act, files a complaint, testifies, or is about to testify in any proceeding under the Act. Any employee who believes that he has been discharged or otherwise discriminated against in violation of this provision may file a complaint with the Secretary of Labor.

OSHA NO. 100

LOG OF OCCUPATIONAL INJURIES AND ILLNESSES

Form Approved
OMB NUMBER 44R 145'

Case or file no.	Date of injury or initial diagnosis of illness. If diagnosis of illness was made after first day of absence enter first day of absence. (mo./day/yr.)	Employee's Name (First name, middle initial, last name)	Occupation of injured employee at time of injury or illness	Department to which employee was assigned at time of injury or illness	DESCRIPTION OF INJURY OR ILLNESS			EXTENT OF AND OUTCOME OF INJURY OR ILLNESS					
					Nature of injury or illness and part(s) of body affected (Typical entries for this column might be: Amputation of 1st joint right forefinger Strain of lower back Contact dermatitis on both hands Electrocution—body)	Injury or illness code. See codes at bottom of page.	Fatalities — Enter date of death (mo./day/yr.)	Lost Workday Cases			Nonfatal Cases Without Lost Workdays		
								Enter workdays lost due to injury or illness (see instructions on back.)	If, after lost workdays, the employee was permanently transferred to another job or was terminated, enter a check in column below	If no entry was made in columns 8 or 9, but the injury or illness did result in: Transfer to another job or termination, or: medical treatment, other than first aid, or: diagnosis of occupational illness, or: loss of consciousness, or: restriction of work or motion; Enter a check in the column below	If a check in column 11 represented a transfer or termination, enter another check in column 12	
1	2	3	4	5		6		7	8	9	10	11	12

Company Name _____

Establishment Name _____

Establishment Location _____

Injury Code

10 All occupational injuries

Illness Codes

21 Occupational skin diseases or disorders
22 Dust diseases of the lungs (pneumonioses)
23 Respiratory conditions due to toxic agents
24 Poisoning (Systemic effects of toxic materials)
25 Disorders due to physical agents (other than toxic materials)
26 Disorders due to repeated trauma
29 All other occupational illnesses

FIGURE 10-6 'Log of occupational injuries and illnesses. (Source. "Recordkeeping Requirements under the Williams-Steiger Occupational Safety and Health Act of 1970," U.S. Department of Labor, Occupational Safety and Health Administration, Washington, D.C.)

Form approved
OMB No. 44R 1453

Supplementary Record of Occupational Injuries and Illnesses

EMPLOYER

1. Name _____

2. Mail address _____
   (No. and street)   (City or town)   (State)

3. Location, if different from mail address _____

INJURED OR ILL EMPLOYEE

4. Name _____ Social Security No. _____
   (First name)   (Middle name)   (Last name)

5. Home address _____
   (No. and street)   (City or town)   (State)

6. Age _____   7. Sex: Male_____ Female_____ (Check one)

8. Occupation _____
   (Enter regular job title, *not* the specific activity he was performing at time of injury.)

9. Department _____
   (Enter name of department or division in which the injured person is regularly employed, even
   though he may have been temporarily working in another department at the time of injury.)

THE ACCIDENT OR EXPOSURE TO OCCUPATIONAL ILLNESS

10. Place of accident or exposure _____
    (No. and street)   (City or town)   (State)
    If accident or exposure occurred on employer's premises, give address of plant or establishment in which
    it occurred. Do not indicate department or division within the plant or establishment. If accident oc-
    curred outside employer's premises at an identifiable address, give that address. If it occurred on a pub-
    lic highway or at any other place which cannot be identified by number and street, please provide place
    references locating the place of injury as accurately as possible.

11. Was place of accident or exposure on employer's premises? _____ (Yes or No)

12. What was the employee doing when injured? _____
    (Be specific. If he was using tools or equipment or handling material,
    _____
    name them and tell what he was doing with them.)

13. How did the accident occur? _____
    (Describe fully the events which resulted in the injury or occupational illness. Tell what
    _____
    happened and how it happened. Name any objects or substances involved and tell how they were involved. Give
    _____
    full details on all factors which led or contributed to the accident. Use separate sheet for additional space.)

OCCUPATIONAL INJURY OR OCCUPATIONAL ILLNESS

14. Describe the injury or illness in detail and indicate the part of body affected. _____
    (e.g.: amputation of right index finger
    _____
    at second joint; fracture of ribs; lead poisoning; dermatitis of left hand, etc.)

15. Name the object or substance which directly injured the employee. (For example, the machine or thing
    he struck against or which struck him; the vapor or poison he inhaled or swallowed; the chemical or ra-
    diation which irritated his skin; or in cases of strains, hernias, etc., the thing he was lifting, pulling, etc.)
    _____
    _____

16. Date of injury or initial diagnosis of occupational illness _____
    (Date)

17. Did employee die? _____ (Yes or No)

OTHER

18. Name and address of physician _____

19. If hospitalized, name and address of hospital _____

_____

Date of report _____ Prepared by _____

Official position _____

FIGURE 10-7 Supplementary record of occupational injuries and illnesses. (*Source.* "Recordkeeping requirements under the Williams-Steiger Occupational Safety and Health Act of 1970," U.S. Department of Labor, Occupational Safety and Health Administration, Washington, D.C.)

Summary

Occupational Injuries and Illnesses

Establishment Name and Address:

Injury and Illness Category		Fatalities	Lost Workday Cases			Nonfatal Cases Without Lost Workdays*	
			Number of Cases	Number of Cases Involving Permanent Transfer to Another Job or Termination of Employment	Number of Lost Workdays	Number of Cases	Number of Cases Involving Transfer to Another Job or Termination of Employment
Code 1	Category 2	3	4	5	6	7	8
10	Occupational Injuries						
	Occupational Illnesses						
21	Occupational Skin Diseases or Disorders						
22	Dust diseases of the lungs (pneumoconioses)						
23	Respiratory conditions due to toxic agents						
24	Poisoning (systemic effects of toxic materials)						
25	Disorders due to physical agents (other than toxic materials)						
26	Disorders due to repeated trauma						
29	All other occupational illnesses						
	Total—occupational illnesses (21-29)						
	Total—occupational injuries and illnesses						

Nonfatal Cases Without Lost Workdays—Cases resulting in: Medical treatment beyond first aid, diagnosis of occupational illness, loss of consciousness, restriction of work or motion, or transfer to another job (without lost workdays).

FIGURE 10-8 Summary of occupational injuries and illnesses. *(Source.* "Record-keeping Requirements under the Williams-Steiger Occupational Safety and Health Act of 1970," U.S. Department of Labor, Occupational Safety and Health Administration, Washington, D.C.)

The Secretary is authorized to investigate the matter and to bring action in the United States district court for appropriate relief, including possible rehiring or reinstatement of the employee to his former job with back pay.

State Participation

OSHA includes provisions for permitting the states to take over the enforcement of safety and health standards where the state standards appear to be as effective in protecting the health and safety of employees as the federal standards.

Education and Training Programs

The Act provides for programs to be conducted by the Secretary of Labor, in consultation with the Department of Health, Education and Welfare, for the education and training of employers and employees in the recognition, avoidance, and prevention of unsafe and unhealthful working conditions and in the effective means for preventing occupational injuries and illnesses. The Act also provides for educational and training programs to supply adequate qualified personnel to carry out the law's purposes.

National Institute for Occupational Safety and Health

The Act establishes within HEW a new National Institute for Occupational Safety and Health primarily to carry out the research and education functions assigned to the HEW Secretary under the Act. In addition, the Institute is authorized to develop and establish recommended occupational safety and health standards; to conduct research and experimental programs determined by the Institute's Director to be necessary for developing criteria for new and improved job safety and health standards; and to make recommendations to the Secretaries of Labor and HEW concerning new and improved standards.

Assistance to Small Business

The law also includes amendments to the Small Business Act, which provides for financial assistance to small firms for alterations in its equipment, facilities, or methods of operation to comply with standards established by the Department of Labor or by any state if the Small Business Administration determines that such a firm is likely to suffer substantial economic injury without such assistance.

Other Provisions

OSHA also contains provisions pertaining to:

1. The creation of a twelve-member National Advisory Committee and the establishment of *ad hoc* advisory committees to advise, consult, and

make recommendations on matters relating to the administration of the Act.

2. A "nonobstruction requirement" so that information can be obtained with a minimum burden on employers, especially those operating small businesses.

3. The formation of an Occupational Safety and Health Review Commission whose functions are to hear and review cases of alleged violations and, where warranted, to issue corrective orders and to assess civil penalties.

4. A "trade secret" clause whereby data revealed to Labor Department personnel during the course of their duties under the Act will be considered confidential.

5. A "national defense tolerance" proviso that permits the Secretary of Labor to allow variations and exemptions from any or all of the Act's provisions, if he finds these necessary to avoid serious impairment of the national defense.

6. "Federal protection" for labor department inspectors. It now is a federal criminal offense to interfere with officials performing investigative, inspection, or law enforcement functions related to the Act.

7. The publishing of annual reports. Comprehensive annual reports on the Act must be prepared and submitted to the President for transmittal to the Congress by both the Secretary of Labor and the Secretary of HEW.

8. The establishment of a new Assistant Secretary of Labor post to head the new Occupational Safety and Health Organization within the Department.

9. Appropriations authority. Congress has authorized such funds to be appropriated to administer and enforce this law as Congress from time to time deems necessary.

10. Labor Department legal representation. The Solicitor of Labor is authorized to appear for and represent the Secretary in any civil litigation brought under the Act subject to the direction and control of the Attorney General.

OSHA Implementation

OSHA itself is only the first step. Getting it to work is the second and more difficult step. To help implement the Act, OSHA requires all employers to display the poster shown in Figure 10-9 in a prominent place in the employee work area.

To also aid OSHA implementation, the National Safety Council conducts free OSHA seminars and training programs for community businessmen. In addition, the National Safety Council provides voluminous materials dealing with OSHA compliance. Much of this NSC literature deals with self-evaluation industry checklists. These checklists aid a company in determining if it is in

SAFETY AND HEALTH PROTECTION ON THE JOB

The Williams-Steiger Occupational Safety and Health Act of 1970 provides job safety and health protection for workers. The purpose of the Federal law is to assure safe and healthful working conditions throughout the Nation.

The U.S. Department of Labor has primary responsibility for administering the Act. The Department issues job safety and health standards, and employers and employees are required to comply with these standards.

BY LAW: SAFETY ON THE JOB IS EVERYBODY'S RESPONSIBILITY!

EMPLOYERS: The Williams-Steiger Act requires that each employer furnish his employees a place of employment free from recognized hazards that might cause serious injury or death; and the Act further requires that employers comply with the specific safety and health standards issued by the Department of Labor.

EMPLOYEES: The Williams-Steiger Act also requires that each employee comply with safety and health standards, rules, regulations, and orders issued under the Act and applicable to his conduct.

COMPLIANCE WITH SAFETY AND HEALTH REQUIREMENTS

To ensure compliance with safety and health requirements, the U.S. Department of Labor conducts periodic job-site inspections. The inspections are conducted by trained safety and health compliance officers. The law requires that an authorized representative of the employer and a representative of the workers be given an opportunity to accompany the inspector for the purpose of aiding the inspection. Workers also have the right to notify the Department of Labor and request an inspection if they believe that unsafe and unhealthful conditions exist at their work-site. In addition, employees have the right to bring unsafe conditions to the attention of the safety and health compliance officer making the inspection. If upon inspection the Department of Labor believes that the Act has been violated, a citation of violation and a proposed penalty is issued to the employer.

Citations of violation issued by the Department of Labor must be prominently displayed at or near the place of violation.

The Act provides for mandatory penalties of up to $1,000 for each serious violation and for optional penalties of up to $1,000 for each non-serious violation. Penalties of up to $1,000 are required for each day during which an employer fails to correct a violation within the period set in the citation. Also, any employer who willfully or repeatedly violates the Act is to be assessed civil penalties of not more than $10,000 for each violation.

Criminal penalties are also provided for in the Act. Any willful violation resulting in death of an employee, upon conviction, is punishable by a fine of not more than $10,000 or by imprisonment for not more than six months, or by both. Conviction of an employer after a first conviction doubles these maximum penalties.

The Act provides that employees may not be discharged or discriminated against in any way for filing safety and health complaints or otherwise exercising their rights under the Act.

For assistance and information, including copies of the Act and of specific safety and health standards, contact the employer or the nearest office of the Department of Labor.

Secretary of Labor

FIGURE 10-9 OSHA poster. (*Source.* "Recordkeeping Requirements under the Williams-Steiger Occupational Safety and Health Act of 1970," U.S. Department of Labor, Occupational Safety and Health Administration, Washington, D.C.)

Vol. No.	Volume Title	Sub-part
	COMPLETE SIXTEEN-VOLUME SET OF CHECKLISTS	
1	General and administrative	
2	Walking and working surfaces	D
3	Means of egress	E
4	Platforms and manlifts	F
5	Health and environment	G
6	Hazardous materials	H
7	Personal protective equipment	I
8	General environment	J
9	Medical and first aid	K
10	Fire protection	L
11	Compressed gas and air	M
12	Materials handling and storage	N
13	Machinery and guarding	O
14	Hand and portable power tools	P
15	Welding, cutting, and brazing	Q
16	Electrical	S

FIGURE 10-10   Complete 16-volume set of National Safety Council's OSHA Checklists.

proper alignment with OSHA standards. As shown in Figure 10-10, the NSC actually has a complete sixteen-volume set of checklists. A specific example of a checklist worksheet from Volume 3, Subpart E, dealing with "means of egress," is shown in Figure 10-11.

OSHA Impact

Initially, major enforcement efforts under the Act were aimed at five target industries with the worst safety records. These industries were longshoring,

SUBPART E	SEC. 1910.36	TITLE	MEANS OF EGRESS—GENERAL REQUIREMENTS

AREA INSPECTED

INSPECTED BY		DATE

REQUIREMENT	EVAL	COMMENT

FUNDAMENTAL REQUIREMENTS—Continued
 	
(B) (5) Is every exit clearly visible, and the route to reach it clearly marked, so that everyone will be able to identify a safe means of escape to the outside?
 	
    ✓ Are all doorways or passageways which are not exits or routes to exits clearly marked to minimize possible confusion and prevent people from being directed to dead-end locations?
 	
Note. Requirements are more specific in § 1910.37, General Means of Egress.
 	
(6) Are all exit facilities provided with adequate and reliable artificial illumination?
 	
Note. (1) The Illuminating—Engineering Society makes these recommendations.
 	
INTERIOR AREAS
Office corridors, elevators, escalators, and stairways — 20 foot-candles, or not less than 1/5 the level in adjacent areas.
Storage rooms or warehouses—Active: rough bulky, 10 fc; medium, 20 fc; fine, 50 fc. Inactive: 5 fc.
Garages—Service, active traffic areas, 20 fc. Parking: entrance, 50 fc; Traffic lanes, 10 fc.
 	
EXTERIOR AREAS
Entrances
    Active (pedestrian and/or conveyance) — 50 foot-candles
    Inactive (normally locked, infrequently used) — 1.0 fc
Vital locations or structures — 5.0 fc.
Building surroundings — 1.0 fc
Active shipping area surroundings — 5.0 fc.
Storage areas—active — 20 fc.
Storage areas—inactive — 1 fc.
Loading and unloading platforms — 20 fc.
 	
(2) National Fire Protection Association Std. 101, "Life Safety Code," §5-10113, states, "The floors of means of egress shall be illuminated at all points . . . to values of not less than 1.0 foot-candle measured at the floor." §5-1021 covers emergency lighting.
 	
<center>(more)</center>		

These checklists present OSHA standards in such a manner as to enable employers to determine apparent compliance with them. Notes have been inserted to explain, illustrate or amplify the regulations.	EVALUATION KEY	YES—Apparently meets requirement NO—Apparently does not meet requirement NA—Not applicable U—Undetermined If NO, specify location, equipment, facility, other details under COMMENT

FIGURE 10-11 Specific checklist worksheet from Vol. 3, Subpart E dealing with "means of egress."

roofing and sheet metal, meat and meat products, miscellaneous transportation equipment, and lumber and wood products. However, the majority of employee complaints received during the first six months of the law's operation were concerned with health instead of safety hazards. The complaints dealt with things such as dust, fumes, and other environmental conditions.

About three fourths of all 29,255 workplaces inspected in the first year of OSHA operation were in violation of various standards. Penalties were proposed in 45 percent of the establishments. Employee complaints received the first year numbered 3421 and, in 1972 employers appealed 2418 job safety cases to the Occupational Safety and Health Review Commission.

One of the biggest obstacles to compliance with the law is the difficulty of changing the work habits of experienced employees. Other problems have also emerged from the setting of standards. Some regulations are already outdated, and many are expressed in highly technical terms.

Small businessmen especially claim that the strict application of OSHA standards could drive them out of business. They say it is unfair to firms lacking safety engineers and legal departments. Many businessmen claim that they do not understand the rules or believe them necessary. The National Federation of Independent Businessmen has used the term "Gestapo" to describe inspection procedures. Others complain about the high cost of compliance, but some feel it may be offset in the long run by a reduction in accidents and compensation expenses. Unions, on the other hand, charge the government with halfhearted enforcement.

The long-term effects of OSHA remain to be seen, and much depends on how much money and personnel the federal government earmarks for its enforcement. As a response to OSHA, many states have strengthened their safety laws, which apply to some enterprises not easily reached by the federal law. Provisions of the federal act at this point are likely to force a change in the operation of many businesses, and many concerned parties apparently agree with its provisions. However, the law is likely to be changed from time to time, and consequently personnel specialists must keep up to date on it.

C. ACCIDENTS

The literature of safety management is largely concerned either directly or indirectly with the occurrence of occupational accidents. Voluminous materials and data are available about both the theoretical and empirical foundations of the accident phenomenon. Most of this concern has been created and maintained only within the last half century. Today accident analysis has grown to the point where special educational university curriculums, occasionally even at the graduate level, have been designed to teach such methods to interested parties. Much conceptual and statistical accident information has become part of the safety management personnel subarea and academic discipline. Accidents will now be analyzed and discussed in this chapter under the following respective and sequential subtitles: (1) definition; (2) frequency and severity rates; (3) factors affecting accident ratios; (4) costs; (5) causes; and (6) accident proneness.

Definition

There is a difference in how a layman and a personnel specialist refer to and use the concept of an accident. Many people associate the occurrence of an accident with the happening of a personal injury. However, as the concept is used in the field of safety management, a personal injury need not necessarily result before an incident can be properly labeled as an accident. By definition, an accident is any unusual and unexpected occurrence that interrupts the regular progress of an activity. In addition, to the uninformed, accidents are often associated with chance and with unknown causes. Safety experts, however, try to find definite and precise reasons for and causes of accidents. The common man also tends to think of accidents in terms of severe unpleasantness, human suffering, or perhaps even personal death. Although most "unexpected occurrences" do involve some form of unfortunate loss, this privation need not necessarily be either human or grossly unpleasant. If an overhead crane is transporting some steel from one location to another in a plant and, if for some reason, a chain breaks and the load of steel crashes to the workshop floor, an accident has occurred. The steel does not have to injure a human being before this event can be classified as an accident. Nor does the steel have to damage or destroy shop machinery or other workshop equipment before this incident can be labeled as an accident. The fallen steel represents an "unual and unexpected occurrence," and thus it constitutes an accident. If personal injury or equipment damage also result, the accident is simply classified in a different way. Thus an accident may be a "first-aid injury" accident, a "disabling injury" accident, or a "lost time" accident. People must be aware that there is a distinction between an "accident" and an "accident injury." Many accidents take place without an injury resulting. Although injuries are normally thought of as direct human damages, direct and indirect injuries to mechanical equipment also can be accident consequences. The proper definition of general and specific accident classifications is necessary so that proper accident information, analysis, record keeping, and comparability can ensue.

Frequency and Severity Rates

A few decades ago it was impossible for management to keep accurate safety records that could be used to compare the working conditions in its plant to the working conditions in other firms and organizations. Before standard methods were used to compile accident information, at best, a company could only compare its own current safety records with its own past safety records. In so doing, a company might be able to tell only within its own confines whether accidents and safety conditions were getting worse or getting better. But, until recently, a firm could not compare and contrast its safety record with the accident information from other firms in the same industry or from other organizations in different industries. With the advent of standard record-keeping statistical methods, firms can now make both accurate internal and external safety record comparisons (Smith).

There are two main statistical ratios used in gathering accident information, the frequency rate and the severity rate. The formulas for these safety ratios are:

$$\frac{\text{Frequency}}{\text{Rate}} = \frac{\text{Number of lost-time accidents} \times 1{,}000{,}000}{\text{Total employee hours of exposure}}$$

$$\frac{\text{Severity}}{\text{Rate}} = \frac{\text{Number of days charged} \times 1{,}000{,}000}{\text{Total employee hours of exposure}}$$

The frequency and severity rates were established by the National Safety Council and today are almost universally recognized and accepted in all business and nonbusiness organizations. The frequency rate is the number of lost-time accidents per million manhours worked. Essentially, a "lost-time" accident is an accident in which some worker time is directly or indirectly lost. The denominator of "total employee hours of exposure" is used in order to make a proper distinction between firms that may have the same approximate number of accidents annually, but that vary considerably in terms of their total number of employees, number of days worked, and hours of overtime used. The 1 million figure in the numerator makes it possible to have a standard ratio of comparison among firms of all sizes in all industries, because it enables the frequency ratio to be expressed in terms of "per million manhours worked." Sometimes the term disabling injuries instead of lost-time accidents is used in the numerator of the frequency rate. Basically, a disabling injury is any accident that results in human suffering in the form of a total, partial, temporary, or permanent disablement. Often it is the number of disabling injuries in relation to the total manhours of exposure to possible injuries that provides the most meaningful measure of injury experience.

The severity rate is the number of days charged or lost because of accidents per million manhours worked. The number of days charged is computed by totaling all the days lost because of work injuries and adding in the standard time charges that have been agreed on for deaths, permanent total disabilities, and permanent partial disabilities. For example, the loss of an end of an index finger (distal phalange) would be counted as 100 days, but a death would result in a standard scheduled charge of 6000 days per case. Note that the 1 million figure in the numerators and that the denominators of the frequency and severity rates are identical.

Frequency versus Severity

Controversy exists as to which of these two rates is the better and more accurate measure of overall company safety. Most experts believe that the frequency rate is the more significant and sensitive indicator of global company safety performance, because the severity of a particular injury is largely a matter of change. In our previously used crane carrying steel example, whether or not the steel falls on a person is largely a chance factor. However, in industries where certain types of serious accidents are more common and frequent, such as coal mining, other experts have argued that the severity measure is better than the frequency rate as an index of global firm safety. Much, if not most, of this debate over which rate is the better measure is senseless. The two rates are uniquely designed to measure different accident and injury phenomena; one is designed to assess the frequency of accidents, while the other is intended to evaluate the severity of injuries. If one global index is desired, it can be obtained by combining the two rates instead of choosing between them. Many firms, accordingly, use the index of Frequency Rate/Severity Rate as their overall global measure of company safety conditions.

The main advantages now available to companies keeping their accident, injury, and safety records in terms of these ratios is that they not only can properly evaluate their own internal working-condition changes over the years but, perhaps more important, they can compare their safety records to those of other firms in the same industry and other organizations in the nearby community.

Factors Affecting Accident Ratios

INDUSTRY FACTOR

Three main factors directly affect the magnitude of company frequency and severity rates. These three factors are type of industry, company size, and management safety philosophy. Statistics for a representative year during the late 1960s and early 1970s are shown in Figure 10-12. The most interesting observation to note from these statistics is that many heavy industrial types of industries often have very low and respectable frequency and severity rates (e.g., automobile, aerospace, and electrical equipment). However, seemingly safe industries at times reveal hazardous working conditions both in terms of frequency and severity accident information (e.g., food, tobacco, and transit). Note the 1969 all-industries frequency rate of 8.80 and the all-industries severity rate of 640 in Figure 10-12. These injury rates should be contrasted to and compared with their respective rates during the last forty plus years, as shown in Figure 10-13. Progress showing a steady decline in the all-

Frequency rate
Disabling injuries per
1,000,000 man–hours

Severity rate
Time charges (days) per
1,000,000 man–hours

Industry	Frequency rate
Automobile	1.67
Aerospace	2.44
Electrical equipment	2.59
Steel	3.49
Chemical	4.02
Textile	4.17
Communications	4.31 Δ
Rubber and plastics	4.88
Machinery	4.88
Cement	5.44
Sheet metal products	5.53
Electric utilities	5.83
Shipbuilding	6.00
Gas	6.16
Fertilizer	6.22
Federal civilian employees	6.75 †
Petroleum	6.85
Glass	7.76
→ All industries	8.80
Storage and warehousing	8.33
Wholesale and retail trade	8.44
Marine transportation	8.56
Pulp and paper	8.85
Mining, surface	9.39
Nonferrous metals and products	9.42
Tobacco	10.56
Railroad equipment	10.66
Printing and publishing	10.93
Iron and steel products	11.37
Foundry	12.43
Clay and mineral products	12.83
Food	13.10
Construction	14.07
Wood products	14.31
Lumber	15.39
Quarry	16.33
Leather	17.02
Transit	23.35
Air transport	25.63
Meat packing	29.50
Mining, underground, except coal	31.47
Mining, underground coal	31.86

*Figures in parentheses show average days charged per case.

†Preliminary 1969.

‡1968.

Δ Not fully comparable to prior years due to change in exposure.

All rates compiled in accordance with the American National Standard Method of Recording and Measuring Work Injury Experience. ANSI Standard Z 16.1.

Severity rate	Industry
(55) 134 *	Aerospace
(75) 194	Electrical equipment
(29) 242	Storage and warehousing
(56) 243Δ	Communications
(153) 256	Automobile
(73) 354	Machinery
(34) 371	Printing and publishing
(45) 382	Wholesale and retail trade
(93) 387	Textile
(98) 384	Chemical
(30) 502	Leather
(107) 520	Rubber and plastics
(85) 525	Gas
(100) 555	Sheet metal products
(22) 567	Air transport
(80) 623	Glass
(91) 628 ‡	Federal civilian employees
(79) 640	All industries ←
(22) 653	Meat packing
(113) 376	Shipbuilding
(203) 707	Steel
(84) 717	Marine transportation
(69) 728	Tobacco
(31) 733	Transit
(65) 739	Iron and steel products
(57) 747	Food
(85) 756	Pulp and paper
(122) 838	Petroleum
(79) 839	Railroad equipment
(69) 861	Foundry
(141) 877	Fertilizer
(71) 911	Clay and mineral products
(70) 1,004	Wood products
(121) 1,140	Nonferrous metals and products
(204) 1,188	Electric utilities
(256) 1,395	Cement
(108) 1,667	Lumber
(122) 1,715	Construction
(228) 2,146	Mining, surface
(161) 2,626	Quarry
(154) 4,839	Mining, underground, except coal
(154) 4,902	Mining, underground coal

FIGURE 10-12 Frequency and severity rates, 1969, for firms reporting to the National Safety Council. (*Source.* Jennie Spadafora (ed.), *Accident Facts,* 1970 ed., National Safety Council, 1970, p. 26.)

industries frequency and severity of accidents has been achieved over the years, as indicated in Figure 10-13.

SIZE FACTOR

Company size is also related to accident statistics. Accident frequency information reveals that very small (under 20 persons) and very large (2500 or more persons) companies are the safest-size work organizations. The most

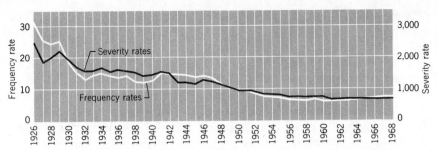

FIGURE 10-13 "All-industries" frequency and severity rates, 1926 to 1968. (*Source.* Jennie Spadafora (ed.), *Accident Facts,* 1969 ed., National Safety Council, 1969, p. 28.)

dangerous companies range from 50 to 1000 employees. The above statements are supported by the information provided in Figure 10-14. The fundamental reason for this is that owners and executives of small businesses are generally not as safety conscious and do not give as much effort to accident prevention as the managements of larger firms do. Thus the company size factor affecting accident ratios is intimately tied into the management safety philosophy variable influencing personal-injury occurrences.

PHILOSOPHY FACTOR

The accident and injury rates of a particular company or industry strongly reflect the amount of money, time, and effort that management devotes to accident prevention. Such factors easily override the effects of hazards

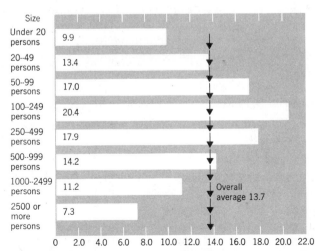

FIGURE 10-14 Injury frequency rates by company size. (*Source.* Plotted from data in *Injury Rates in Factories, New York State, 1966,* New York State Department of Labor, Division of Research and Statistics.)

inherent within the industries. As examples, the steel and atomic energy industries are hazardous, yet their accident rates are considerably below the all-industry averages because, in both these industries, top management long ago decided to carry on comprehensive safety programs that have resulted in very safe plants. Most work organizations, especially small business firms, that have bad accident records also have managers who have not been sufficiently motivated to take strong, corrective, safety-related actions. The typical small businessman does not even know what an accident or frequency rate is. The size of his workmen's compensation insurance payment is his only indication of company safety. This insurance premium is directly related to the number of injuries that happen within his firm annually. Most small employers cannot afford to hire a full-time safety director, and many may not even have a full-time personnel manager. The pressing problems of production, sales, and finance seem more important to the small businessman than the concerns and costs of accident prevention (Lyons).

Costs

HUMANITARIANISM AND ECONOMICS

There are two major incentives for an employer to attempt to reduce employee injuries and accidents. One is the humanitarian concern for the well-being of his workers. This is based on a genuine desire to prevent and eliminate, as much as possible, all human suffering. The other incentive is cost. Under normal conditions, it is much more economical to maintain a low accident-high attendance plant than it is to have extensive lost time caused by work-related injuries and sicknesses. The costs related to the payments of large medical expenses and high insurance premiums alone are often sufficient financial justification for the introduction of a comprehensive plant safety program. However, there are usually many hidden and commonly unrecognized costs also associated with the occurrence of an accident or injury.

DIRECT VERSUS INDIRECT OR INSURED VERSUS UNINSURED

Accident costs are usually classified as direct versus indirect or insured versus uninsured. Direct or insured costs are readily apparent and are covered by the insurance policy. Direct or insured costs include the money paid for doctor and hospital bills, payments to injured workers who are unable to return to work, and expenses because of death or accidental dismemberment. Indirect or uninsured costs are the hidden expenses associated with a job-related accident or injury. These costs are not covered by any insurance policy and thus must be borne by the company or organization. Usually indirect costs are not apparent to executive-managers unless someone specifically calls such matters to the attention of the corporate officers. Often detailed study, research, and analysis are needed before such expenses can be isolated and identified properly. When an accident or injury occurs, indirect or uninsured costs often exist in the forms of lost time of the injured worker; lost time of the fellow employees who aid or observe the injured person; supervisory time spent assisting the injured worker; administrative expenses to process paperwork connected with the accident; research time spent investigating the accident; lost production; damaged material and equipment; and retraining costs associated with bringing in a new worker or a temporary employee replacement along with quantity and quality adjustments associated with the new man's work. Such indirect and uninsured costs mount up quickly and often become a large, collective, annual employer expense.

ICEBERG RELATIONSHIP

Currently there is a heated controversy about the magnitude of the relationship between the direct and the indirect costs of an accident. Obviously, this relationship would vary greatly from one accident or injury to another. Almost everyone, however, agrees that indirect or uninsured costs are almost always greater than the direct or insured expenses involved. In fact, research has indicated that, on an average, indirect costs are about four times greater than direct accident expenses. In other words, the insured or direct costs represent only about 20 percent of the total costs of an accident. Part of the controversy over the ratio of indirect to direct costs is due to the difficulty of defining these terms precisely. Direct costs are those covered by the insurance policy; indirect costs are all other accident expenses for which the company will not be reimbursed. Because insurance payment or nonpayment is a clear-cut distinction, the costs associated with an accident or injury are best described as insured versus uninsured instead of direct versus indirect. The insured-uninsured cost relationship is often described in terms of an iceberg, as shown in Figure 10-15, since only a relatively small portion of the total cost is readily apparent and most of the expenses are below or underneath surface appearances.

HUMAN COSTS

In addition to the financial burden imposed by accidents on a company or organization, the individual employees who are injured bear a substantial cost, also. In addition to the anguish and suffering, most state workmen's compensation laws specify a waiting period of at least one week before an injured worker can collect weekly benefits to make up for his lost wages. If a worker loses only one to seven days of work, he normally receives no wage compensation whatsoever. When weekly benefits are paid, they are com-

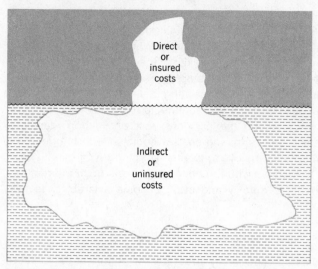

FIGURE 10-15   Iceberg relationship of accident costs.

monly limited in duration and amount. Weekly benefits usually are two thirds of the worker's normal pay up to a certain maximum.

Causes

Most people recognize that accidents do not just happen; they are caused. People who believe that most accidents are due to luck, chance, fate, or happenstance simply are informally and unconsciously admitting that they have not analyzed the event in question enough to associate it with tangible facts or causes. There are causes or motives of all behaviors and events; they are human or nonhuman, accident involving or nonaccident involving.

TECHNICAL CAUSES

Accidents are caused by a number of interacting variables or factors. The causes of accidents can be grouped and classified into three general areas: technical, human, and environmental. Technical accident causes involve unsafe chemical, physical, or mechanical conditions. Common examples of unsafe technical conditions include improper personal protective equipment; unsafe mechanical design or construction; defective condition of tools and equipment; and inadequate mechanical guarding. At the beginning of the Industrial Revolution in this country, most of the accidents occurring at work sites were thought to be largely due to such technical conditions or factors. Recent studies, however, indicate that now it appears that only 10 to 15 percent of all accidents are caused by unsafe technical work considerations. As I will explain later, these statistics are misleading. Nevertheless, it is unquestionably true that past accidents mainly attributable to unsafe physical and mechanical conditions are much less prevalent in the many companies and organizations that exist today. Much of this change has been due to technological innovation and improved injury research and accident analysis.

HUMAN CAUSES

Human accident causes include unsafe personal acts, such as removing safety devices or making them inoperative; assuming an unsafe position or location; failing to follow established safe working procedures; and horseplay or fighting. Whereas technical accident causes are connected with deficiences in plant, equipment, tools, and materials, human accident causes are connected with deficiencies within the individual, such as improper attitudes, carelessness, recklessness, inability to do the job, and daydreaming. There is an increasing appreciation in industry of the importance of the human factor in accidents. It is impossible to create a completely safe work environment where no one could possibly injure himself. However, most technical accident causes can be and often today have been largely eliminated. Thus many modern companies are concentrating now on the human or personal causes of accidents in an effort to improve their accident statistics even further (Vilardo).

ENVIRONMENTAL CAUSES

Environmental accident causes involve unsafe situational and climatic variables, such as improper lighting; excessive noise; disorderly housekeeping; poor ventilation; and undue job-related stress or tension. Environmental accident causes may be physical, psychological, or organizational. For example, improper lighting and poor ventilation are physical and perhaps could have been classified as a technical cause of accidents. Employee stress and worker tension, similarly, are at least partially human or personal reasons for accidents. General working conditions and plant housekeeping are global organizational factors that can directly or indirectly lead to personal accidents and injuries.

COMBINATION OF CAUSES

The most recent analyses of accident statistics reveal that the vast majority of all accidents are due to a combination of causes (McBain). An accident is not caused by a technical, human, or environmental condition acting solely and independently. Even if an unsafe technical condition exists, a human being could not be hurt unless he is somehow involved with the work situation. Conversely, if a technical hazard were not present in the first place, a

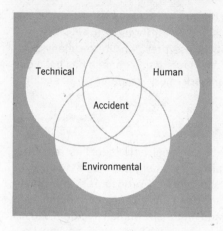

FIGURE 10-16 An accident is the result of a combination of causes.

personal injury could not have occurred. Or, perhaps, technical and human work conditions were safe, but environmental factors presented some danger. But this environmental condition is a contingent danger only if certain human and technical factors also appear at a certain place and time. Today there is a movement away from the "culprit" or "villain" approach to a situational approach in the analysis of accident causes. Technical, human, or environmental factors cannot and should not be blamed in an isolated manner for the occurrence of an accident. Combinations of people, factors, and conditions cause accidents. Accidents do not have a cause; they have causes. Such causes are highly interrelated and must be dealt with as a comprehensive unit, not in an individualized or isolated fashion. Figure 10-16 illustrates that certain technical, human, and environmental conditions must all be present at the same time and place in order for an accident to occur.

There are other causes, factors, and conditions that are sometimes related to the occurrence of accidents and injuries. Some researchers have discovered a direct relationship between accident frequency and seniority; longer-service personnel have fewer accidents. Others have discovered a relationship between the type of motivation employed by management and the frequency of accidents; the tensions caused by aggressive, negative supervisors tend to increase the likelihood of accidents. Available research evidence shows conclusively that young workers, untrained workers, and workers who are new on the job have substantially higher frequencies of work injuries than older workers, trained workers, and more experienced workers (Greenberg). Other accidents have been known to be caused by alcoholism, boredom, drug addiction, fatigue, and exhibitionism. It is impossible to identify all of the plausible factors or conditions that interrelate to cause an accident. The main point to remember is that an accident or an injury is caused by a combination of conditions, the most influential of which vary from one situation to another (Kirkpatrick).

Accident Proneness

Especially in the past, but even to some extent presently, many observers have claimed (claim) that accident proneness is a major cause of personal injuries. Accident proneness is a state in which a human being is mentally inclined, strongly disposed, attitudinally addicted, or personally destined to become continually involved in an ongoing and never-ending series of accidents or injuries. Accident proneness is seen by many as a human cause of accidents about which little, if anything, can be done. It has always been an observed fact that certain individuals have more accidents than allegedly can be expected on the basis of pure chance. Many earlier writers in the field of safety management attributed these phenomena to employee accident proneness. As the field of safety matured and advanced, the lessening role and importance of the accident proneness concept could be and has been observed within the safety management literature. To say specifically that an accident is due to employee accident proneness is as much of a cop-out as to state generally that personnel administration is nothing but common sense. Such statements are made by people who do not know any better. Closer examinations from recent accident research studies have shown that the abstract concept of accident proneness empirically can be broken down into many tangible subunits. Accident proneness is a catchall phrase that laymen use to describe injury causes that they are not capable of comprehending intuitively or as yet have not been exposed to. In actuality, accident proneness consists of human motor skills, emotional stability, muscular coordination, visual ability, manual dexterity, and perceptual capacity. Research has shown that there are definite relationships between such factors and accident rates.

Unsubstantiated Accident Proneness Concept

Just because a small percentage of workers have a high percentage of accidents is not proof of the existence of employee accident proneness. According to the laws of probability, some workers will have more accidents than others. During any given time period, some employees can be expected, by chance, to have several accidents, while other workers will have none. People who allegedly are accident prone simply have a temporary tendency toward frequent accidents. This tendency is explainable, after closer examination, in terms of human traits, qualities, and characteristics, such as those mentioned above (dexterity, coordination, etc.). The accident proneness concept also breaks down after closer scrutiny and analysis, because it is a temporary, not a permanent human state. Research has shown that employees who have the most accidents in one year are different from those who have the most accidents or injuries during the next year. This rationale or argument assumes that the true physical or human causes of previous accidents and injuries have been discovered, and that adequate provisions and needed human-technical corrections have been implemented. Although the theory of accident proneness seemed to be a promising alternative explanation of work injuries for many years, when put into proper perspective, this concept actually contributed nothing to, but instead retarded the progress being made in, the systematic analysis of accidents.

Accident Repeater

Today the concept of accident proneness is being replaced by the concept of the "accident repeater." These terms are the same except for variances in connotation. An accident repeater repeatedly has more than his expected share of accidents during a certain time period. The accident repeater concept takes the mystical, witchcraft, supernatural, and enchantment connotations away from the reoccurring-injury phenomenon. Repeated accidents are not due to sorcery or soothsayers. Human differences in terms of personality, emotional makeup, family background, physical conditions, and so forth, in the context of specific job demands and general employment conditions, account for the occurrence of human accidents and injuries. Age, training, experience, supervision, placement, and other factors are also related to the sometimes reoccurring nature of job accidents and human injuries.

D. IMPLEMENTATION

There are many steps involved with the implementation of a safety program within an organization. These steps may vary from one company to another, and their sequence or order also can change among institutions. Nevertheless, there are certain major actions and activities that most organizations follow when first setting up and then implementing a companywide safety program. Such steps usually involve: (1) establishing safety objectives and policies; (2) gaining top management support; (3) appointing a safety director; (4) designing the total safety function into the overall corporate structure; (5) engineering a safe plant and operation; (6) establishing job safety analysis methods; (7) gathering and analyzing accident and injury information; (8) educating all employees to act safely; (9) enforcing safety rules through disciplinary action; (10) treating on-the-job injuries; (11) supervising safety contests; and (12) providing for employee rehabilitation. Although these steps have a tendency to appear in the above order, most of these actions are often going on simultaneously within a well-planned safety program. All of these steps involve ongoing processes. They cannot be done "once and for all," and then forgotten. Each of these twelve activities needs constant revision and monitoring to remain effective. This is even true of the initial steps of establishing safety objectives and policies and gaining top management support. Safety objectives can, should, and must change over time, and executive support must be reaffirmed frequently so that remaining safety implementation steps can be properly directed.

Structural Arrangements

In the implementation portion of the health section of this chapter, the organizational structure of the personnel health and safety subareas was briefly discussed. Figures 10-3 and 10-4 illustrated two common design relationships often appearing structurally within organizations. In order to properly establish safety and health responsibilities, such organizational relationships are needed (Stewart). All medium- and large-sized companies should have a full-time safety director. In fact, most big corporations employ a number of safety analysts, engineers, inspectors, and industrial hygienists. A rough rule sometimes used is that there should be one full-time safety specialist employed for every 2000 employees. As shown previously in Figure 10-3, most commonly the safety director reports to the personnel manager (or to the director of industrial relations).

Safety Responsibility

Many companies also use safety committees to help implement safety programs. The union collectively and workers individually often play key roles in the establishment and maintenance of an organizational safety program. Safety is the ultimate, manifest, or operational responsibility of first-line supervision. This responsibility is, however, shared with the workers, staff personnel, and upper-level line executives. Usually, a safety director serves only as an innovator, organizer, creator, advisor, teacher, analyzer, investigator, stimulator, and prodder of organizational safety concerns and matters (Lippert).

E. CONTESTS

Safety contests are a specific technique or method of implementing safety objectives and policies. In addition, safety contests can be considered a form of employee safety education. However, there is much current controversy over the possible merits of safety contests. Unfortunately, past company experiences with safety contests often reveal that accidents decline during the period of the contest only to rise again after it has ended. Nevertheless, safety contest prizes and awards often do serve to stimulate efforts in the direction of accident prevention. It is usually assumed that the habit of acting safely during the contest period will become part of worker habits after the contest is over. Indeed, often the newly established accident level, although higher than during the contest, is lower than the precontest accident level.

Awards and Prizes

Safety awards and prizes appear in various forms. Money, dinners, plaques, watches, cigarette lighters, dances, and recreational outings often serve as contest giveaways. Unfortunately, the incentives provided by some safety contests have led to abuses. Contests have their place as a means of arousing employee interest in safety, but some safety directors lose sight of safety fundamentals and place too much emphasis on safety gimmicks and awards. During safety contests, in an effort to win a prize, a worker sometimes will not report an accident. Consequently, inadequate medical attention and often more serious complications result. While the contest prevails, the accident record becomes all important, and actual events often become misrepresented so that they show up favorably on the record. Often serious accidents, but especially minor injuries, are not reported in any form. The main trouble with safety contests and award programs is that they avoid the central safety problems and issues. If a safety director places most of his faith in contests and attention-getting gimmicks, he often tends to neglect grossly the fundamentals of hazard elimination, accident analysis, injury prevention, health training, and safety enforcement (Hampton).

4. Plant Security

Definition

Security is a state of being secured from danger or poverty. A secured object is guaranteed against, unexposed to, and freed from the fear of danger. Security includes the confidence of safety and the certainty or assurance of proper physical or financial defense. As an area of personnel management, security includes the concerns of health, safety, and plant security. Many personnel authors might also include employee benefits and services under the label of security systems since, very often, on a personal, individual basis, security is synonymous with financial security. The general concept of security has often been used in reference to physical security and social security. Physical security is basically what is meant by the phrase "plant security." Plant security involves the protection of company buildings, equipment, materials, and other tangible resources from physical dangers such as theft, sabotage, fire, flood, and windstorm. Social security involves the protection of company personnel from monetary or financial dangers. Company efforts to bring about financial personnel security is largely the subject matter of employee benefits and services that were discussed in the previous chapter. Pension plans, life and health insurance, accident and surgical insurance, supplementary unemployment benefits, and the like are examples of specific organizational attempts to bring about personnel financial security.

Plant Security versus Personnel Security

Plant security and personnel security are not totally and separately existing phenomena. Employee or personnel security involves freedom from physical danger as well as freedom from financial hardship. The health and safety major sections of this chapter basically concern the matter of protecting workers from physical harm. On the other hand, plant security involves protecting all company assets from physical danger, and these assets include human beings as well as machines, buildings, and materials. Figure 10-17b reveals that plant security and personnel security are best envisioned as partially interrelated and overlapping protection concepts instead of as totally distinct (Figure 10-17a) or completely synonymous (Figure 10-17c) set entities.

Physical Protection

In general, plant security involves the protection of a company's physical facilities from human dangers and natural disasters. Theft and sabotage are the principal human dangers encountered by most organizations. Various methods can be used to prevent human theft and sabotage. A fence six feet high, topped with barbed wire, is a primary measure used to discourage trespassers. The number of company gates can be kept to a minimum, unused gates should be locked, and all locks should be changed from time to time. Fenced areas, dark corners, and especially parking lots should be well lighted. Delivery trucks should be checked. Visitors should not be permitted to park their cars within the regular parking area, and all guests should be

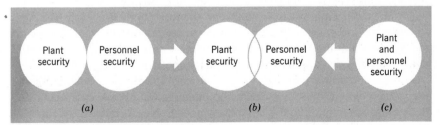

FIGURE 10-17 Plant security and personnel security as distinct, interrelated, and synonymous set entities. (a) Distinct. (b) Interrelated. (c) Synonymous.

required to sign a registration book. Guards (sometimes armed) are the principal means of insuring plant security. Guards should inspect briefcases, tool kits, and packages of anyone coming into and departing from company premises. These measures pertain to only industrial companies. Public organizations housed in public buildings often cannot implement such plant security precautions.

Engineering and Insurance Solutions

Security from and protection against natural disasters often take the form of proper engineering, design, and construction plus adequate insurance coverage. Fires, windstorms, floods, and other forms of nature-related catastrophes, contrary to common belief, can be at least partially prevented and controlled. Proper physical design and construction can prevent or control excessive damages caused by floods, fires, or windstorms. Automatic sprinklers, iron doors, emergency exists, reinforced concrete, fire extinguishers, sump pumps, and other control devices are specific examples of catastrophe prevention techniques. Indirect plant security from natural disasters also can be provided by insurance coverage and protection.

Security Structure

In smaller organizations, the safety director is usually responsible for plant security. In larger companies, a fire chief and plant security chief often will report directly to the safety manager. In the largest institutions, plant security is often a separate department from safety and on a par with it and the organizational health function.

5. Summary

This chapter has dealt with health, safety, and plant security. Organizational health concerns itself with the analysis of occupational diseases and other hazardous hygienic conditions. The whole man concept is emerging in that organizations are becoming concerned with both the physical and the mental health of their employees in both on-the-job and off-the-job settings. Workmen's compensation laws at the state level and the Occupational Health and Safety Act at the federal level are helping to bring about this expanded whole man organizational health and safety concept.

Organizational and employee safety concerns itself most with problems and issues related to job accidents and personal injuries. Accident analysis involves issues relating to the definition, measurement, costs, and causes of job accidents. The implementation of organizational safety programs, similar to the application of company health plans, involves shared administrative responsibilities among top executive line personnel, staff specialists, first line supervisors, and organizational employees.

Plant security involves the protection of a company's physical facilities from human dangers and natural disasters. Plant security and personnel security are closely related personnel concepts. However, personnel security often concerns human beings and financial protections in the form of compensation benefits and services, while plant security emphasizes physical facilities and guarantees against organic and natural phenomena.

DISCUSSION QUESTIONS AND ASSIGNMENTS

1. What is an occupational disease? Give some examples of occupational diseases.
2. Present a definition for the term "accident."
3. Explain the whole man concept of employee health and organizational safety.
4. Interview an industrial first-line supervisor and ask him what impact OSHA is having on work operations in his plant.
5. What role do you personally feel organizations should have when dealing with an individual worker's mental health problems?
6. Design a plant security system for the organization in which you were last employed.

REFERENCES

General Book References

Bureau of National Affairs, Inc., *The Job Safety and Health Act of 1970.* Washington, D.C.: BNA, Inc., 1971.

Department of Labor, *Recordkeeping Requirements under the Williams-Steiger Occupational Safety and Health Act of 1970.* Washington, D.C.: U.S. Department of Labor, Occupational Safety and Health Administration, 1973.

Dunnette, Marvin D. (ed.), *Handbook of Industrial and Organizational Psychology.* Chicago: Rand McNally & Co., 1973.

National Safety Council, *Fundamentals of Industrial Hygiene.* Chicago: National Safety Council, 1968.

Simonds, Rollin H., and John V. Grimaldi, *Safety Management.* Homewood, Ill.: Richard D. Irwin, 1963.

Spadafora, Jennie (ed.), *Accident Facts, 1969.* Chicago: National Safety Council, 1969.

Specific Journal References

Chase, Richard B., "Work Physiology: A New Selection Tool," *Personnel Administration, 32* (6), 1969, pp. 47–53.

Cohen, Wilbur J., "Revolution in Mental Health," *Personnel Administration, 32* (2), 1969, pp. 5–8.

Forgrens, Roderick A., "A Model of Supportive Work Conditions Through Safety Management," *Personnel Journal, 48* (5), 1969, pp. 351–358.

Greenberg, L., "Learning as a Factor in Accident Experience," *Personnel Psychology,* *24* (1), 1971, pp. 71–76.

Hampton, D. R., "Contests Have Side Effects Too," *California Management Review, 12* (4), 1970, pp. 86–94.

Kirkpatrick, Donald L., "Supervisory Inventory on Safety," *Personnel Administrator, 8* (4), 1968, pp. 32–34.

Lippert, F. G., "Role Conflict and Ambiguity in Enforcing Safe Work Practice," *Journal of American Society of Safety Engineers, 20* (5), 1968, pp. 12–14.

Lyons, J. M., "Safety: The Company, the Committee and the Committed," *Personnel Journal, 51* (2), 1972, pp. 95–98 and 137.

McBain, W. N., "Arousal, Monotony, and Accidents in Line Driving," *Journal of Applied Psychology, 54* (8), 1970, pp. 509–519.

Pyle, Howard, "On the Proposed Occupational Safety and Health Legislation," *National Safety News, 100* (6), 1969, p. 41.

Smith, Sidney, "Accident Report for 1969," *National Safety News, 101* (3), 1970, pp. 174–175.

Sternhagen, Charles J., "Medicine's Role in Reducing Absenteeism," *Personnel, 46* (4), 1969, pp. 28–35.

Stewart, R. D., "How to Manage Your Injury Problem," *Personnel Journal, 49* (8), 1970, pp. 590–592.

Vilardo, Frank, "Human Factors Engineering: What Research Found for Safetymen in Pandora's Box," *National Safety News, 98* (2), 1968, pp. 35–41.

contents

learning objectives

1. To envision the past, present, and future perspectives of the labor relations-collective bargaining process.

2. To understand the stages, subject matters, pressures, and ritualisms of the contract negotiation process.

3. To become knowledgeable about disciplinary and grievance procedures in various types of organizations.

4. To comprehend the similarities and differences between the concepts of labor relations, collective bargaining, contract negotiation, and contract administration.

11

Labor Relations-
Collective Bargaining

1. Definitions and Semantics

Collective bargaining involes the formation of the terms and methods of a mutual contract, agreement, or understanding between two or more persons, pertaining to something that is to be done, such as the performance of work. The two main parties involved are labor and management, each of which represents a larger number of constituents. The term collective bargaining is normally used only to designate two party contract negotiation, and usually a third party such as the government is not included in true or "free" collective bargaining situations. Although the labor party or entity usually is unionized, unionization technically is not a prerequisite for labor-management arrangements. Labor-management relationships occur in both unionized and nonunionized work settings, but many authors prefer to reserve the collective bargaining concept to associate only with formally organized (unionized) labor activities, while others use the terms "labor relations" and "collective bargaining" synonymously. Of course, labor relations is really labor-management relations since it involves a two-way instead of a one-way arrangement and, in addition, labor relations does not necessarily presume an industrial setting. These are the semantic problems related to the labor relations and collective bargaining concepts. Some personnel practitioners prefer the terms "industrial relations" or "employee relations" to describe this area of personnel concern (Prasow and Peters). However, for the purpose of this chapter, labor relations and collective bargaining should be thought of as interchangeable concepts.

2. Labor Relations-Collective Bargaining Perspective

The perspective of labor relations-collective bargaining will be presented using the format of (1) types of unions, (2) current status of labor unions, (3) labor legislation, and (4) forms of union security. Such historical and evolutionary subject matter will help set the stage for a more thorough discussion of present and future labor relations or collective bargaining issues.

A. TYPES OF UNIONS

Industrial Union

There are two main types of labor unions, the industrial or vertical, and the craft or horizontal. The industrial union is vertical in that it includes all the workers in a particular company or industry regardless of their occupational skill level. This concept represents the mass production worker or common man approach to labor organization. This theory was pioneered by the CIO (Congress of Industrial Organizations) movement in 1936 and is currently evidenced within the unions of the United Automobile Workers and United Steel Workers.

Craft Union

The horizontal or craft union cuts across many companies and industries. Members of craft unions belong to a common trade or to a closely related group of occupations. The craft union concept is the underlying philosophy of the AFL (American Federation of Labor) movement and can be illustrated currently by reference to the organized union structures of carpenters and printers.

Craft or Industrial?

The industrial (craft) union is not without its craft (industrial) problems. In practice, these two union philosophies have many similar characteristics and, although they may appear to be distinct, pragmatic applications of these divergent philosophical approaches reveal similar and interrelated work issues and concerns (Garbarino). Recognizing these application dilemmas, the AFL and the CIO merged in 1955. In reality, many industrial unions contain skilled craftsmen, and many craft unions contain a heterogeneous membership.

Public Unions

The growing emergence of public worker unionization is further evidence of the blending of the industrial and craft unionization concepts. Both horizontal and vertical organization efforts are involved when teachers, sanitary workers, firemen, policemen, or transit workers unite. Many observers see public unions as such a growing force that these organizations should be considered a separate type of unionism instead of a craft-industrial hybrid. The public employee situation will be discussed in more detail later in this chapter under the heading of "future labor relations-collective bargaining issues."

B. CURRENT STATUS OF LABOR UNIONS

It can be argued that the history of the labor movement in this country began in 1776 with the initial step eventually leading to the present system of labor relationships and collective bargaining. However, organized labor and industrial rather than craft unionization made relatively little progress until the 1920s and the 1930s at which time various federal acts were passed that encouraged the unionization process. Before World War I, total union membership in this country was only around 2½ million workers. In 1920, aided by war prosperity and favorable governmental (federal) directives, union membership increased to over 5 million persons. This led to managements developing a "paternalistic" philosophy in order to prevent their workers from organizing. The labor movement suffered as a result of the Great Depression and experienced an actual decline in numerical strength to a level of less than 3 million members in 1933. However, with the passage of the Wagner Act in 1935, the union movement in this country again surged forward. From 1933 to 1945 union membership grew from less than 3 million to almost 15 million workers. Growth has continued over the last few decades so that currently over 20 million workers in this country belong to a union of some sort. This figure represents aproximately 25 percent of all the workers in this country (Sherman). Figure 11-1 traces the growth (and decline) of total union membership over the past forty years.

Growth Trends

Although absolute and relative proportions of unionized to nonunionized workers have increased in size in this country over the years, controversy

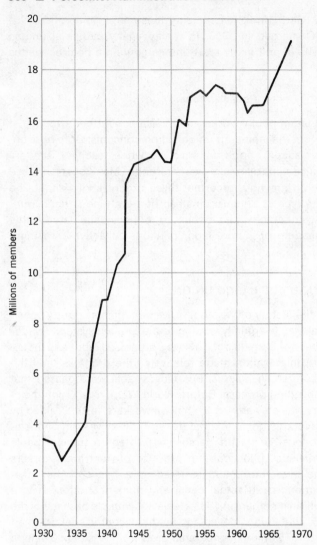

FIGURE 11-1 Total union membership. Excludes Canadian membership but includes members in other areas outside the United States. Members of AFL-CIO directly affiliated local unions are also included. For the years 1948-52, midpoints of membership estimates, which were expressed as ranges, were used. (*Source. Directory of National and International Unions,* Bureau of Labor Statistics, Bulletin No. 1665, 1970, p. 68.)

surrounds the issue of the current vitality of the American labor movement. Data are available that have been interpreted in opposite fashions and directions. A few current experts see the labor movement dying out in this country as a result of more white collar jobs, more women employees, more part-time workers, more employee mobility, aging labor leaders, corrupt handling of union pension funds, better management personnel practices, a higher general standard of living, more highly educated workers, and the like (Marcus). However, most current alleged and acknowledged experts see the American labor movement on the verge of another tremendous leap forward as policemen, firemen, teachers, government employees, nurses, and other professionals and paraprofessionals begin to organize (Tyler). Because of these different expert interpretations of standard Bureau of Labor Statistics data, the current and future strength of the union movement in this country is difficult to state with precision (Raskin). Figure 11-2 indicates union mem-

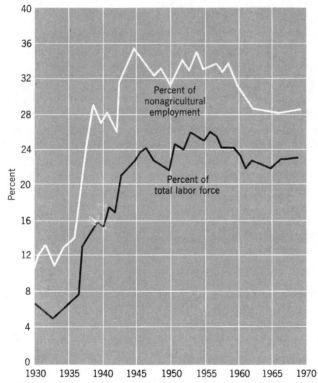

FIGURE 11-2   Union membership as a percent of the total labor force and a percent of nonagricultural employment. Excludes Canadian membership. Total labor force includes employed and unemployed workers, self-employed, members of the Armed Forces, etc. Employment in nonagricultural establishments excludes the Armed Forces, self-employed, as well as the unemployed, agricultural workers, proprietors, unpaid family workers, and domestic servants. (*Source. Directory of National and International Unions,* Bureau of Labor Statistics, Bulletin No. 1665, 1970, p. 67.)

bership as a percent of the total labor force and as a percent of employees in nonagricultural establishments.

AFL-CIO

Of the total 20 million unionized workers in this country, AFL-CIO affiliates claim approximately 75 percent. This represents a relatively recent decline in strength due to the withdrawal of the UAW in 1968 with its 1.5 million members. The United Auto Workers joined with another major independent union, the Teamsters Union, which contains nearly 2 million members, to form the Alliance for Labor Action in 1969. The Alliance for Labor Action was formed to play a more active role than the AFL-CIO in various social and political matters. Although the UAW and the Teamsters are the two largest unions in the United States, the AFL-CIO is the core of the union movement in this country. Actually, the AFL-CIO is not a union, but a collection or federation of over 100 national and international unions. The major source of power in the AFL-CIO exists at the international union level. It exercises general control over these international unions by establishing criteria for membership. An international union is composed of a number of local unions and may contain anywhere from 10 to 2000 local unions.

In addition to the unionized workers, it is estimated that approximately another ½ million unionized employees deal with single employers in one location. Also there are a number of other major independents such as the United Mine Workers and the railway brotherhoods, and many smaller unaffiliated independents. Potential white collar unionization may in the future add significantly to these totals (Kleingartner and Vogel). The unionization of women employees on a large scale may also increase these amounts tremendously (Dewey, 1971A).

C. LABOR LEGISLATION

As stated previously, federal legislation has had a significant effect on the growth of American unionism, and applies only to those firms engaged in interstate commerce. Although state laws regulate companies involved solely with intrastate activities, such enterprises are usually small in size and such laws are relatively insignificant in impact compared to federal statutes directing large corporate dealings. Labor legislation in general indicates the tremendous importance of the role that government plays in the collective bargaining process.

Early significant federal labor legislation concerned the operation of the railroads. As early as 1898, Congress passed the Erdman Act, which prohibited discrimination against railroad workers because of union membership. The Act was later declared unconstitutional, but still later it was reinstituted in 1926 with the passage of the Railway Labor Act. One of the main provisions of this Act was to forbid any denial of the right of employees to join a labor organization.

There are five monumental acts that have drastically affected the growth of American unionism. These acts include: (1) the Norris-LaGuardia Act of 1932; (2) the Wagner Act of 1935; (3) the Taft-Hartley Act of 1947; (4) the Landrum-Griffin Act of 1959; and (5) the Kennedy Executive Order 10988 of 1962. The major provisions of these acts will be briefly identified and explained.

1. *The Norris-LaGuardia Act of 1932.* This Act presents the first major statement of general public policy concerning labor unionization. The Norris-LaGuardia Act stated that workers should have the right to organize into unions of their own choosing if they so desire. It also outlawed yellow-dog contracts and restricted an employer's freedom to use labor injunctions to halt work stoppages.

2. *The Wagner Act of 1935.* The Wagner Act is the main federal law protecting unionized workers. This Act guarantees the right of employees to organize by forbidding an employer to: (1) interfere or restrain employees in the exercise of this right; (2) interfere or restrain any labor union; (3) discriminate against anyone for union activity; (4) discriminate against anyone who gave testimony under the Act, and (5) refuse to bargain collectively with chosen employee representatives. In addition, the National Labor Relations Board was established by the edict of this Act and it has two main functions: (1) to prevent or correct any of the five unfair labor practices listed above; and (2) to establish the appropriate bargaining units and specific representative organizations for the employees. In effect, the Wagner Act, which also is called the National Labor Relations Act, allowed unions to gain employer recognition via an orderly process of democratic elections instead of by means of the strike mechanism.

3. *The Taft-Hartley Act of 1947.* This Act, which is also known as the Labor-Management Relations Act, attempted to correct certain union abuses. Some labor union officials have argued that this Act represents a step backward for the labor movement in this country. This perspective sometimes exists because the Taft-Hartley Act identified the following as unfair practices of labor unions: (1) to restrain or coerce an employee into joining or not joining a labor union; (2) to cause an employer to discriminate against an employee because of nonmembership in the union resulting from any action other than nonpayment of union dues; (3) to refuse to bargain collectively with the employer; (4) to engage in secondary boycotts and jurisdictional strikes; (5) to require workers to pay exorbitant fees; and (6) to require an employer to pay for services not rendered (a practice known as featherbedding). Also, the Taft-Hartley Act outlawed the closed shop and made it illegal for supervisors to join employee unions.

Employers also were given the right to sue unions for contract breaches, and managements were designated to deduct employee union dues from paychecks (the "checkoff") only when so authorized by an individual employee in writing. The Labor-Management Relations Act also required union leaders to file union financial reports and permitted the President of the United States to terminate excessively long strikes in basic industries that affected or endangered the national economy and that could lead to national emergency situations.

4. *The Landrum-Griffin Act of 1959.* The Landrum-Griffin Act, also known as the Labor-Management Reporting and Disclosure Act, was designed to curb both improper labor and unfair management practices such as: (1) the infiltration of labor unions by gangster elements; (2) collusion between labor and management in the signing of "sweetheart" contracts; (3) a lack of democratic union procedures; (4) the abuse of international union power to place selected local unions under protective custody or trusteeship; (5) widespread misuse of union funds such as interest free loans to union officials and poor audits of union ledgers; (6) the use of labor spies by management, and (7) union picketing of organizations whose employees have no desire to join the union. In addition, other provisions of this Act require both labor and management officials to provide a series of reports to be filed with the Secretary of Labor. Constitutions, bylaws, annual reports, contracts, policy statements, and the like must be "reported" and "disclosed" by both labor and management executives. Furthermore, the Landrum-Griffin Act establishes a "bill of rights" for union members, which includes: freedoms of speech and assembly; secret-ballot guarantees; the right to sue the union; safeguards against improper union disciplinary action; and, equal rights to nominate and vote for candidates for union office.

5. *The Kennedy Executive Order 10988 of 1962.* Executive Order 10988, which was issued by President John F. Kennedy in 1962, was a major stimulus to the growth of collective bargaining in the public sector of the economy. Executive Order 10988, which is also entitled "Employee Management Cooperation in the Federal Service," requires federal agencies to recognize, as exclusive bargaining agents, unions that represent the majority of employees as determined by a vote of those in the bargaining unit (Curtin). This Order represents a major advance for the aspirations and interests of government employees. The Wagner Act of 1935, which granted collective bargaining rights to employees in private industry specifically excluded public employees. In addition to having a great impact on federal governmental employees, Executive Order 10988 also encouraged many states to pass laws that granted to state and local employees the rights: (1) to form unions; (2) to have these unions recog-

nized as bargaining agents by the appropriate governmental unit; and (3) to negotiate contracts and process grievances (Cohany and Dewey).

D. FORMS OF UNION SECURITY

The phrase "union security" refers to both the right of a union to exist as an organization and its right to continued existence in a particular company. The first right is guaranteed by the labor laws previously discussed in this chapter. However, the second right is much more controversial. Traditionally, employers oppose labor unionization and, because of this, many unions have attempted to negotiate union security clauses into their labor contracts. These provisions insure a union of continued presence in a company. Union security provisions appear in a variety of forms: (1) closed shop; (2) union shop; (3) maintenance of membership shop; (4) modified union shop; (5) preferential shop; (6) agency shop; (7) simple-recognition shop; (8) open shop; and the (9) restricted shop. In general, this list moves from the most to the least secure form of union security.

1. *Closed shop.* This form of union security was outlawed under the Taft-Hartley Act. It requires that an employee be a union member at the time of hiring. Under such an arrangement, the union becomes the only source of labor to the employer. Although this setup is technically illegal, in practice it appears in many work industries such as construction, maritime, and printing due to custom and management's willingness to use a union hiring hall procedure.

2. *Union shop.* The union shop agreement allows an employer to hire nonunion workers, but all employees must eventually join the union within a stipulated period of time or else they will automatically lose their jobs. With a union shop in existence, all workers who remain with a company must pay union dues. Most of the labor-management contracts in this country provide for this form of union security.

3. *Maintenance of membership shop.* This form of union security is a compromise between freedom to join or not join a union and compulsory unionism. An employee is not required to join the union. If he does join, however, he is compelled to remain in the union for the life of the labor-management agreement. After the contract expires, a short escape period is provided for the employee who wishes to withdraw his union membership.

4. *Modified union shop.* Under this form of union security, present employees who do not belong to the union are not required to join; but those who already belong must continue their membership as a condition of employment; and, all new hires must also join the union within a specified number of days.

5. *Preferential shop.* Under this arrangement, the union is recognized and union members are given preference in certain areas of employment such as hiring, layoff, transfer, and promotion. The employer goes to the union first when trying to fill a position.

6. *Agency shop.* In an agency shop employees are not required to join the union, but they must pay a fee to the union for the bargaining services and benefits that the union provides for everyone in the bargaining unit. All employees pay union dues whether or not they are actually union members.

7. *Simple-recognition shop.* This form of union security is one in which management has recognized a union as the official and exclusive bargaining agent of all employees in its area of jurisdiction. Under this arrangement, the union may have only one more than half of the total workers as dues-paying members; yet it still is authorized to bargain for 100 percent of all the employees. Thus, "free riders" may exist. "Free riders" are employees who get the benefits and services provided through union bargaining and negotiation but who pay no union dues.

8. *Open shop.* In a true open shop there is neither a union present nor a management program to promote or keep out a union. Employees are free to decide whether or not to join a union. Usually some do, but the majority do not join the union under this labor-management arrangement.

9. *Restricted shop.* Restricted shops prevent the hiring and employment of any union members. A restricted shop may be legal or illegal. Management may try to keep a union out with employee persuasion — which is legal; or it may utilize yellow dog contracts, employee threats, reprisals against those interested in unionism, bribes to workers who vote against unionization, and so forth — all of which are illegal.

3. Contract Negotiation

Any present day labor-management collective bargaining arrangement involves two main sets of activities; contract negotiation and contract administration. Contract negotiation is the process by which employers and employees deliberate, persuade, influence, argue, and haggle with one another in order to settle their differences concerning wages, hours of work, and other conditions of employment. Eventually an agreement in the form of a labor-management contract is reached. There are considerable differences between an employee-employer contract and a commercial contract such as the buying or selling of a commodity. Human beings are not physical goods. Social, political, psychological, and emotional as well as economic and technological issues are involved. In addition, once a labor-management contract is signed, both parties must agree to bargain in good faith in the future. Because dealings cannot arbitrarily be broken off, the union and management must learn to live with one another whether they like it or not.

The contract negotiation process will be discussed later in this chapter under the subheadings of: (1) stages; (2) subject matter; (3) union and management pressures; and (4) ritualism versus reality.

A. STAGES

It is hard to describe a general model that is descriptive of all labor-management contract negotiation processes. However, despite the variety and disparity of such negotiations, all employer-employee agreements tend to progress through the following stages: (1) prenegotiation; (2) selection of union and management representatives; (3) formation of a negotiation strategy; (4) implementation of negotiation tactics; and (5) the final labor-management contract or agreement.

When the employer-employee agreement has been signed for one term, the prenegotiation stage usually begins for the next contract period. Facts and figures concerning wages, hours, pensions, vacations, and the like must be gathered, analyzed, and interpreted by both parties. Not only must organizational entities be analyzed, but also the backgrounds and personalities of particular negotiators must be studied. The actual negotiators themselves may be any of a number of persons. Management often is represented by the industrial relations director, the personnel manager, the head of production, an executive vice-president, the company lawyer, or a committee of such individuals. On the union side, a team approach is often used. The chief labor spokesman customarily is a representative of the international union; while other union team members might be business agents, shop stewards, and the president(s) of the local union(s). Both labor and management negotiators plan negotiation strategem and tactics. Strategy is concerned with mapping out the basic plan and policies to be followed in the negotiating process. Tactics are the particular actions taken at the bargaining table in order to accomplish the overall strategy plan. Strategies and tactics may be either overt actions and activities; or they can involve attitudes, emotions, true or purposively contrived opinions, gestures, and other indirect forms of expression. After labor and management negotiating interaction occurs, eventually an agreement or contract is reached that stipulates in formal terms the nature of the relationship between the employer and the employees for the upcoming contract period that normally will run for two or three years (Kelley).

B. SUBJECT MATTER

There are numerous subjects about which labor and management negotiate when they meet at the bargaining table. Although any individual agreement would contain special items of interest particular to that situation, the following topics commonly appear within all labor-management contracts.

1. Union recognition and scope of the bargaining unit.
2. Union security.
3. Union activities and responsibilities.
4. Strikes and lockouts.
5. Working time and time-off policies.
6. Discipline, suspension, and discharge.
7. Grievance handling and arbitration.
8. Job rights and seniority.
9. Wages.
10. Health and safety.
11. Insurance and benefit programs.
12. Management rights.

Many of these items have already been or will be discussed in this or other chapters. Only two of these items, job rights and seniority and management rights, will be discussed further now.

Job Rights and Seniority

Job rights concern key issues such as seniority regulations, transfers, promotions, layoffs and recalls, and job posting or bidding. Unions try to furnish as much job security to their members as possible by seeking to have all job changes decided on the basis of company seniority. Labor feels that this is a fair and objective criterion that prevents favoritism and discrimination. Management, however, desires to make personnel changes on the basis of economics and merit (ability) (Mills). The net result is usually a compromise in which job changes are based on a combination of seniority and ability.

Management Rights

Management rights or management prerogatives concern the issue of whether an employer can make his own business decisions free from union interference. Historically and traditionally, managers were given the almost unilateral "right" to make work-related decisions because of the concepts of "property rights" and "stockholder representatives." Today, however, unions often are consulted or even help to make many employment decisions. In essence, the management rights issue is the counterpart of the union security concern. Managers believe that they should have the final say over operating conditions. On the other hand, unions believe that labor should have a voice in all those things and matters that affect work relationships. There are many subject areas over which labor and management differ sharply concerning the matter of who should ultimately control such issues of employment. Some examples of these issues include: subcontracting of work outside the plant; scheduling of work; discontinuing certain types of work; setting production standards; determining disciplinary penalties; and assigning duties to jobs. Unless there is specific mention of employment or work factors in the agreement, residual job-related issues not covered in the contract are assumed to be areas of management responsibility. A statement to this effect, normally called a "management rights clause," is part and parcel of almost all labor-management contracts today. However, there is a trend today for residual and noncontract-covered employment factors to be negotiable items not belonging ultimately to either labor or management; but this trend is just now gaining impetus, and to a large extent, in most employment situations, contract residuals are still considered to be management rights.

C. UNION AND MANAGEMENT PRESSURES

Management Tactics

Although management may use many forms of informal threats, sanctions, and punishments in an attempt to persuade employees, the only major direct forms of management pressure are the lockout and the shutdown. A lockout is usually a temporary closing of a plant or place of business by management in the course of a labor dispute with its employees. This action is taken by management in an attempt to force workers into accepting management contract offerings. Some employers have turned temporary lockouts into permanent shutdowns instead of being forced into operating under conditions demanded by the union. The lockout is increasingly being used today as a management pressure technique especially by companies that belong to an employer association (Wingo).

Union Pressures

Unions have more of a variety of pressure tactics at their disposal than managements do (Miles and Ritchie). Strikes, picketing, and boycotts are, however, the most frequently used union pressure mechanisms. Picketing involves the patrolling of workers or employees, usually stationed at the outside of a plant affected by a strike, for the purpose of publicizing (through the use of signs, posters, and pickets) alleged company malpractices and grievances. On rare occasions, picketing may occur without a strike being in process. Picketing is legal so long as: pickets are bonafide employees instead of strangers; the picketing takes place near but off actual company premises; a limitation to the total number of pickets is maintained; and, it remains a peaceful demonstration. Normally, the picket line is a very powerful union pressure device since it is usually respected by members of most other unions in addition to many members of the general public.

Boycotts

A boycott is a refusal to buy or use a company's product(s) or service(s). Boycotts can be undertaken by employees or the general public. When people combine together in refusing to deal or associate with some enterprise, a boycott exists. Boycotts may be primary or secondary in nature and scope. A primary boycott exists when employees of a company or members of society refuse to buy or use the products or services of a particular enterprise. A secondary boycott exists when a union, which is seeking concessions from employer X, places pressure on employer Y to influence exployer X to grant the concession. In addition, the union may also attempt to make employers U, V, W, and Z refuse to deal with employer X until he falls in line with union demands. Depending on the situation and the industry, some secondary boycotts are legal while others are clearly illegal. In the early 1970s successful boycotts were evidenced when farm workers boycotted the purchase of lettuce and grapes.

Strikes

A strike is a concerted withholding of labor supply in order to bring economic pressure to bear on an employer to cause him to grant worker or union demands (Kennedy). The strike mechanism is usually considered to be the ultimate and most powerful form of union pressure. Strikes come in a variety

Issue	Percent of Strikes
General wage changes	49.6
Supplementary benefits	1.2
Wage adjustments	5.1
Hours of work	.1
Other contractual matters	1.5
Union organization and security	10.4
Job security	3.3
Plant administration	15.5
Other working conditions	4.0
Interunion or intraunion matters	8.8
Not reported	.4

Source. Bureau of Labor Statistics, U.S. Department of Labor, *Analysis of Work Stoppages, 1969,* Bulletin 1687 (Washington, D.C., 1971), p. 19.

FIGURE 11-3 Strikes by major issues during 1969.

UNION DEVELOPMENT	STRIKE ISSUE
Formative years	Recognition and jurisdiction
Early years	Wages and hours
Growing union	Seniority, job security, working conditions, and fringe benefits
Mature union	Organizational goals

FIGURE 11-4   Strike causes vary depending upon union growth and development.

of forms, the most common of which include the: (1) economic strike; (2) jurisdictional strike; (3) recognition strike; (4) sit-down strike; (5) sympathy strike; and (6) wildcat strike. The economic strike is a strike that is based on an employee demand for better wages, hours, and working conditions than the employer is willing to grant. When two unions argue about which of them has jurisdiction or authority over a particular type of work, and when these two unions exert pressure on an employer to allocate this work to one or the other of these unions, a jurisdictional strike exists. These strikes are illegal. Recognition strikes exist when employees attempt to force an employer into recognizing and dealing with a union. Sit-down strikes, which are also illegal, occur when workers strike but remain at their job locations in the plant. Another unlawful strike form is the sympathy strike, which occurs when unions, who are not a party to the original strike, consent to strike in "sympathy" with the original union. The final strike form, which also is illegitimate, is the wildcat strike. Wildcat strikes are sudden, unannounced, and unauthorized work stoppages. They are not approved by the union leadership and are in violation of the labor-management agreement (Eisele).

As shown in Figure 11-3 most strikes (about one half) are over general wage changes. Strike issues, however, change over time and, as shown in Figure 11-4, they tend to depend on the stage of union growth and development.

Although other forms of labor and management pressure techniques may be used, the above devices are the most commonly utilized and frequently observed methods of employer or employee force (Dewey, 1971B).

D. RITUALISM VERSUS REALITY

Contract negotiations involve both serious concerns and showmanship. The serious concerns are the subject matter areas mentioned previously. The showmanship relates to the role playing and theatrical performances often put on by both labor and management negotiators. Management officials have to appear to be representing the corporate stockholders well, and union officers have to give the impression of doing everything they can in order to best serve employee wants, needs, and desires. Because top corporate and union positions are elected political posts, this showmanship is necessary for publicity purposes. It is a matter of debate and a consequence of unique contract negotiating sessions as to just how much of the contract negotiation process is for real, and how much of it is ritualistic (Peterson). Some research studies have shown that a much larger portion of this process is showmanship than is commonly believed. Both labor and management representatives have been asked, before negotiating sessions have begun, as to what they expect will be the final contract outcome, and after days, weeks, or even months of haggling, the final agreement often is extremely close to positions hypothesized even before the bargaining ensued (O'Neal). This phenomenon is especially apparent in the large private business industries such as autos, steel, chemicals, and rubber where price leadership and pattern bargaining are generally followed. Figure 11-5 illustrates that contract negotiation is best envisioned as a composite set consisting of ritualism and reality subsets or components (Bok and Dunlop).

The "reality" portion of contract negotiation involves factual economic and technological issues. The "ritualism" aspect of contract negotiating centers around political and social concerns. Saving face and putting on a show are as much of the negotiation process as are hard facts and figures. The formation of a labor-management contract cannot be properly understood unless analyzed from both a reality (economic) and a ritualistic (political) perspective.

The portion of this chapter dealing with "contract negotiation" is summarized in Figure 11-6. The topics of stages, subject matter, union and management pressures, and ritualism versus reality and their respective subdivisions are shown in Figure 11-6.

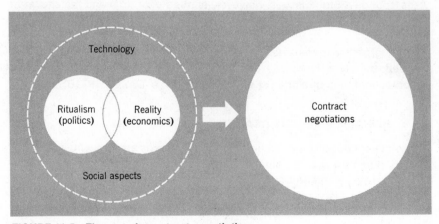

FIGURE 11-5 Elements in contract negotiation.

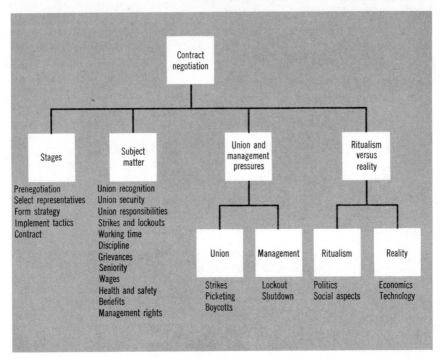

FIGURE 11-6   Contract negotiation.

4. Contract Administration

The second major portion of labor relations-collective bargaining is contract administration. Contract negotiation and contract administration together constitute labor relations-collective bargaining. Sometimes a third subset of contract interpretation is identified as a component of labor relations-collective bargaining (Allen). I will assume, however, that contract interpretation is part of the contract administration process. Contract interpretation matters are relatively rare in occurrence and legalistic instead of personnel or manpower related in scope and nature.

   The administration of a labor-management agreement involves applying and putting into practice all of the subject matters contained within the negotiated contract. As mentioned previously, such subject matters and topics include: (1) union recognition and scope of the bargaining unit; (2) union security; (3) union activities and responsibilities; (4) strikes and lockouts; (5) working time and time-off policies; (6) discipline, suspension, and discharge; (7) grievance handling and arbitration; (8) job rights and seniority; (9) wages; (10) health and safety; (11) insurance and benefit programs; and (12) management rights. Many of these topics have already been discussed.

However, two of these subjects, (1) discipline and (2) grievances, will now be presented in greater depth, since they have not been discussed at length yet, and because these two areas are especially crucial to an understanding of the contract administration process as viewed from a personnel or manpower perspective.

A. DISCIPLINE

The topic of personnel or manpower discipline will be presented utilizing the following format: (1) semantic issues; (2) approaches; (3) progressive penalty system; (4) burden of proof; (5) due process, reasonableness, consistency, and flexibility; (6) offenses and penalties; and (7) right of appeal.

Semantic Issues

Discipline involves the conditioning or molding of behavior by applying rewards and punishment. It is a form of control gained by enforcing obedience or by training that corrects, molds, strengthens, or perfects undesirable individual human behaviors. Many authors try to distinguish between the concepts of "discipline" and "disciplinary action." If this is attempted, discipline is explained as a controlled state or condition brought about through the use of disciplinary actions or procedures. Disciplinary actions include both positive motivational activities such as praise, participation, and incentive pay, as well as negative motivational techniques such as reprimand, layoff, and fines. Both types of disciplinary actions and activities seek to condition employee behavior in order to achieve "controlled discipline" in an organization. Although disciplinary action may be either positive or negative in nature, the state or condition of "discipline" is best thought of as a neutral concept. If discipline within an organization is described as "good" or "bad," this means that either the situation is under control or it is not under control. Used in this context, "good" or "bad" does not refer to whether or not positive or negative methods of disciplinary action are being utilized. According to some authors, discipline is an end-state, goal, or objective, while disciplinary actions are the instrumental means, procedures, techniques, and methodologies used to bring about this controlled state of affairs.

Approaches

Normally approaches to personnel discipline are described in terms of dichotomies, such as positive versus negative, constructive versus punitive, formal versus informal, clinical versus legalistic, and so forth. Of these dichotomies, the positive versus negative classification scheme is the one most frequently used. A negative disciplinary approach is confined to the application of penalties in an attempt to inhibit undesired behavior and to keep people in line. Positive discipline takes the form of rewards, constructive support, and reinforcement of approved personnel actions and behaviors. In addition, positive discipline emphasizes the concepts of self-discipline and self-control. Of course, no organization in reality practices only one or the other of these two approaches. Organizational discipline is always a combination of positive and negative elements. There is much individual talk but little organizational action stressing the merits of positive discipline instead of the negative form. Negative discipline usually achieves only the minimum performance necessary to avoid punishment. Also punishment has never been demonstrated to be an effective permanent deterrent of undesired behavior. Nevertheless, many organizations not only utilize, but they also emphasize negative stimuli generated by penalties. All organizations are required on occasion to use some form of negative discipline. There are certain tactics, procedures, or guides that should be followed when implementing and applying any type of negative disciplinary action. Some of the most commonly cited guides include the following.

1. Disciplinary action should be administered privately.
2. The application of a penalty should be handled in a constructive manner.
3. Disciplinary action should be applied by the immediate supervisor.
4. Disciplinary action, when called for, should be administered promptly.
5. Disciplinary actions for similar offenses must be administered consistently.
6. After a disciplinary action has been applied, the supervisor should then attempt to assume and reestablish a normal attitude toward the disciplined employee.

Progressive Penalty System

Most organizational disciplinary actions and procedures have become fairly well standardized as a result of practice and custom. Usually a system of penalties in a progressively severe sequence is administered. This sytem is identified as a "progressive penalty system." It is labeled as progressive not because it is liberal or avant in nature, but becaue it progresses sequentially, chronologically, and systematically through a prescribed series of steps or events. Commonly a progressive penalty system will have five steps, such as (1) oral reprimand; (2) written warning; (3) second written warning; (4) temporary suspension; and (5) permanent discharge. Some organizations, especially those that are nonunionized, will have no such formal system or will have a prescribed penalty procedure with but only one, two, or three steps. Discipline within smaller and nonunionized plants often is only informal and in the form of oral reprimands; and then if these vocal warnings do not correct the unwanted behavior, a worker may be discharged without any preliminary or previous type of formal warning. In larger, unionized organizations, often more than five formal steps may be involved in the penalty system. If additional steps are added, they usually appear in the form of written warnings and suspensions. For example, three different and separate written warnings may be required, or a series of suspensions such as one day, three days, one week, and so forth may be provided before an employee can be formally discharged. Also, other types of penalties may be introduced or substituted into such a system. For example, fines, loss of privileges, or demotion can serve as steps within the formal progressive penalty system.

FOR MINOR OFFENSES ONLY

Progressive penalty systems are only used for minor employee offenses. If a worker physically assaults his boss, he is not normally given only an oral reprimand, even if it is his first offense. Serious offenses bring immediate discharge. Employee offenses and penalties will be discussed in greater detail in a later section of this chapter. Only one other point should be made at this time: an employee's slate or record is normally wiped clean at the end of one or two years when using a progressive penalty system. This is done because there is no reason or justification for holding against a man, in perpetuity, his indiscretions of past years if he has reformed himself in the meantime.

Burden of Proof

Within both formal progressive penalty systems and grievance procedures, the burden of proof is on the employer to show that a worker is guilty of an alleged offense. This location of the burden of proof is a relatively recent phenomenon. In the past, especially during the beginning of the Industrial Revolution, if an employee was accused of a crime or rule infraction, it was his responsibility to prove to management that he was innocent of this misbehavior if he expected not to be punished accordingly. Only within the last few decades have business and nonbusiness organizations in this country come to accept this shifted burden of proof. The principle underlying industrial relations jurisprudence systems in this country is the same as the main concept on which both the English and United States legal court systems are constructed: an individual is presumed innocent until proven guilty. Normally, the degree of proof varies with the seriousness of the charge; the more severe the charge against the employee, the more proof will be needed by the employer to establish the guilt of the employee. More and more, penalty and grievance systems used by organizations to control their employees are taking on the semblance of judicial courtroom situations. This is especially true of grievance procedures instead of progressive penalty systems. This shifted burden of proof is largely due to the fact that arbitration rather than mediation is the most commonly found final step within an organization grievance procedure. A very small percentage of cases actually progress through a grievance system to the final step of arbitration. But if a case advances this far, arbitrators, although not legally bound to do so, tend to act like judges, and if there is some doubt as to an employee's guilt or innocence, some observers have noted that arbitrators tend to give the worker the benefit of the doubt. This trend is especially noticeable when looking at the number of arbitration cases today being decided in favor of labor. Labor, contrary to what has been the experience in past decades, wins considerably more than half of all labor-management cases that are decided by an arbitrator (Kilberg). Grievance handling and arbitration will be discussed in greater detail later in this chapter.

Due Process, Reasonableness, Consistency, and Flexibility

Contract administration in general and employee disciplining in particular must attempt to follow certain guidelines or objectives. The main mission should be dual in nature and perspective. This mission is to preserve the interests of the organization as a whole and to protect the rights of individual employees.

DUE PROCESS

One of the main criteria used in administering disciplinary action is the concept of due process or just cause. In determining whether or not an employee has been disciplined for just cause, an investigator should consider three main factors. First, "Did the employee in fact commit the improper act?" If management can prove that he did, then the second consideration is, "Should the employee be punished for his behavior?" Just because the employee committed an infraction does not necessarily mean that he should automatically be punished. If industry custom, company tradition, past practice, or some other rationale can be given as support for why such an individual behavior ensued, then no penalty may be judged to properly accompany the rule infraction. However, even if the employee violation does warrant punishment, the third step of the just cause process requires that the penalty assigned by management fit the nature of the offense. This requirement prevents severe penalties being given for minor infractions such as an employee being fired for coming to work late or leaving the plant early. This third provision is sometimes referred to as a reasonableness criterion.

CONSISTENCY AND FLEXIBILITY

Consistency and flexibility must also be observed and practiced when administering disciplinary action. These criteria seem to be contradictory but in fact they are only paradoxical. Penalties must be given out consistently, that is, in a nondiscriminatory manner. In general, two employees should receive the same penalty for the same offense, although this is not always true. Often a range of penalties for the same offense may help provide and introduce flexibility into a disciplinary system. This flexibility is both needed and justifiable. For example, two men arrive late for work, one may be orally reprimanded and the other may be fired. This could be justifiable if the orally reprimanded employee had never been late for work before, whereas the fired employee was formerly and formally warned repeatedly and had even previously been suspended recently for a similar offense. Normally, penalty ranges do not fluctuate between such dire extremes; but they do, nevertheless, strive to help institute flexibility within corporate disciplinary systems.

Offenses and Penalties

Rule infractions are grouped into two broad categories: minor (or moderate) and serious (or major) offenses. Although no such classification could apply to all organizations and all situations, examples of representative minor and major offenses are indicated in Figure 11-7.

Often what is a minor offense in one company may be a major infraction in a different siuation and vice versa. For example, smoking in a chemical plant may be grounds for immediate employee dismissal. Stealing may be minor offense if the item stolen is not of significant value. In any unique set of

MINOR OFFENSES

Loafing	Selling or canvassing on company property
Sleeping on the job	Failure to obey safety rules
Unexcused absence	Failure to report accidental injury
Gambling	Leaving the work area without authorization
Horseplay	Smoking in a prohibited area
Habitual tardiness	Excessive scrap and waste
Excessive defective work	Clock-punching another's time card

MAJOR OFFENSES

Malicious destruction of company property
Deliberate falsification of company records
Fighting with a supervisor
Carrying concealed weapons
Stealing
Gross immoral, indecent, or disgraceful conduct
Failure to obey safety rules

FIGURE 11-7   Examples of "minor" and "major" disciplinary offenses.

circumstances each major offense might be minor and every moderate infraction could be serious.

PENALTIES

The seven main forms of organizational penalties, in the general order of their severity from mild to harsh, are:

1. Oral reprimand.
2. Written warning.
3. Loss of privileges.
4. Fines.
5. Temporary suspension.
6. Demotion.
7. Permanent discharge.

Ordinarily there are varying penalties for first, second, and third offenses of the same rule. Violations of minor offenses are subject to a progressive penalty system. However, the first offense of a major infraction can bring immediate suspension or discharge. Loss of privileges, fines, and demotions are not commonly used forms of organizational penalties especially within the private business sector of our economy.

Right of Appeal

Usually whether a person has actually committed an infraction of the rules is a matter of opinion. Because of this, an accused employee should always have the right to appeal to a higher authority. Often if an individual is again found guilty as charged, it is best to have a full hearing before higher authorities to demonstrate to all parties that the person has been justly treated. The appeal system is needed, however, for cases in which lower authorities have not properly judged the merits or severity of an employee case.

INDUSTRIAL VERSUS JUDICIAL SYSTEMS

In the judicial court system it is a well-established principle of law that a person must not be judged by his accuser. However, in industrial relations jurisprudence systems, in both profit and nonprofit organizations, this separation of prosecution and judicial functions does not normally take place — especially during preliminary and initial steps within organizational disciplinary and grievance systems. Managers usually determine whether a rule violation has occurred, decide its severity and invoke a penalty against the involved employee. If the employee wishes to contest such a penalty, he must make use of the company's grievance procedure. But a grievance procedure has only one genuinely neutral review step, that being arbitration — a step at which typically only about one percent of all grievances arrive because they are usually settled before this point. Nonunionized plants may not even have any formal grievance handling procedure. In these instances, the idea that a judge should not be a party to the dispute or issue is especially violated. Ideally, the concepts of appeal and impartial judgment cannot be flouted. Pragmatically and economically, however, these rights cannot be completely guaranteed to all organizational employees in all discipline and grievance situations. A distinct separation of judicial review from the management function within organizations would require wholly different enterprise arrangements than currently exist within most business firms. Now let us discuss the handling of grievances.

B. GRIEVANCES

As mentioned previously, discipline and grievances are only two of many subject matter areas of the contract administration process. Discipline and grievances, however, are not unrelated contract administration issues. Disciplinary issues constitute the largest single category of complaint cases at all grievance levels. Research studies are available to indicate that about 25 percent of all organizational grievances involve disciplinary issues. Seniority, job evaluation, and work assignment matters constitute most of the remaining grievances.

Grievances will now be discussed under the following four subheadings: (1) semantic issues, (2) purposes, (3) typical grievance procedure, and (4) mediation versus arbitration.

Semantic Issues

Much definitional difficulty is experienced when trying to distinguish among concepts such as dissatisfaction, complaint, and grievance. Personnel authors usually attempt to make clear-cut distinctions among these concepts of discontent; however, different authors make different distinctions. Generally, dissatisfaction is any state or feeling of discontent, whether it be innate and unexpressed or externally and explicitly stated. A dissatisfaction that is orally made known by an employee to another employee is called a complaint. A complaint becomes a grievance when this dissatisfaction, which must be work-related instead of a personal nature, is brought to the attention of a management representative. Thus, by definition, a grievance is any dissatisfaction or feeling of injustice in connection with one's employment situation that is brought to the attention of management.

GRIEVANCE DEFINITION

Many individuals, however, prefer a much narrower definition of the grievance concept. Some organizations require that a complaint be in written

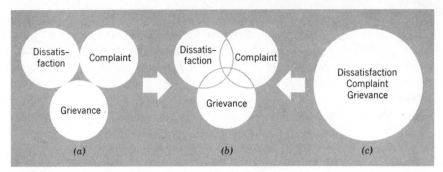

FIGURE 11-8 Dissatisfaction, complaint, and grievance as distinct, interrelated, and synonymous set entities. (a) Distinct. (b) Interrelated. (c) Synonymous.

instead of oral format before it can properly be called a grievance. Other companies require a complaint to begin to be processed through normal grievance procedure channels before it can be labeled as a grievance. In addition, some strongly unionized companies have even narrower definitions of the grievance concept. One such definition is that a grievance exists only when and if there has been some alleged violation of the labor agreement. With such a narrow definition, employees have a right to complain to management only about those specific issues involved with either the application or the interpretation of the union-management agreement. Instead of being seen as totally distinct (Figure 11-8a) or completely synonymous (Figure 11-8c) set entities, Figure 11-8b illustrates that the discontent concepts of dissatisfaction, complaint, and grievance are best envisioned as partially interrelated and overlapping displeasure constructs.

Purposes

Many employers, especially those in nonunion companies, believe that there is no real need for an organization to have a formal grievance procedure. These employers believe that well-trained first-line supervisors should be able to handle most forms of employee dissatisfaction. Whatever these managers cannot handle may be solved through enlightened general personnel policies and practices. This thinking is overly optimistic and is not characteristic of normal conditions and circumstances existing within a typical employment situation.

There are several sound reasons for establishing a company grievance handling system. It is impossible for all employee complaints and dissatisfactions to be settled satisfactorily at the first-line level of supervision. This may be due to improper training, lack of authority, discrimination, personality conflicts, and other causes. In addition, a grievance procedure reduces the likelihood of arbitrary action by first-line managers since these supervisors know that unjust deals will be referred to and reviewed by higher management. As mentioned before, an employee must have the right to appeal his case to some higher official. Such appeals bring employee problems to the attention of higher management, and thus a grievance procedure also can function as a medium of upward communication. Top corporate executives can become sensitive to employee needs by being subjected to employee frustrations, problems, and expectations.

An employee grievance handling system also serves as an outlet for worker frustrations, discontents, and gripes (Bloch). This system permits employees to release work-related pressures and anxieties in a legitimate, officially approved manner. Finally, a grievance system serves as an aid to company morale. The mere act of listening to employee complaints can improve employee morale. Even if a worker loses his case, the simple fact that one or more management representatives have listened attentively to his story serves to demonstrate to the employee that he is important to management and that somebody cares about him.

Typical Grievance Procedure

There probably is no such thing as a "typical grievance procedure" because such formal complaint systems vary from company to company due to variations in organizational size, union strength, management philosophy, company custom, industry practice, and other factors. Realizing these constraints and limitations, nevertheless, a commonly found five-step grievance procedure system used within many medium- and large-sized unionized companies is presented in Figure 11-9.

Step	Labor Representative	Management Representative
1	Employee or union steward	Employee's immediate supervisor
2	Chief steward or business agent	Superintendent or industrial relations office
3	Company grievance committee	Industrial relations director or plant manager
4	Regional or district representatives of the international union	Top corporate management
5	Arbitration by an impartial third party	

FIVE STEPS

FIGURE 11-9   A typical five-step grievance procedure.

PERCENTAGE OF GRIEVANCES SOLVED IN VARIOUS STEPS

The following grievance procedure is frequently found in larger, unionized, industrial business organizations. When a grievance procedure is operating properly, the vast majority of worker complaints, usually ranging from 70 to 90 percent or more, are handled and solved at step 1 (Yaffe). A very small percentage (usually less than 1 percent) of cases ever reaches arbitration. By the time a case has reached arbitration, it already represents an investment of several hundreds of dollars in terms of union and management research, investigation, and administrative time. The cost factor alone prohibits an abundance of labor-management disagreements from reaching this point. In addition, management knows that if a case progresses this far, historical data supports the fact that labor has a greater than fifty-fifty chance of winning the contest. Because of these and other reasons, managers try to solve employee grievances in the beginning grievance stages (Ash).

TIME LIMITATIONS

There are always time limitations between grievance steps. Additional grievance stages are used within a grievance system only when labor remains unsatisfied with the management solution suggested at lower complaint decision points (Shea). Both labor and management must make grievance decisions within certain stated time periods. Typically, the time allowed for a foreman to answer a grievance is one or two days. At the higher steps, labor must appeal and management must answer grievance matters generally within one to two weeks. An arbitrator is given two to four weeks to make his final decision. Although time limits are set between grievance steps, such time limits can be and frequently are extended by mutual consent.

NUMBER OF STEPS

There are not always five steps in a grievance system. Smaller organizations with fewer company levels typically have less steps. Larger companies may have additional grievance stages corresponding to set labor and management levels or echelons within the overall corporate hierarchy. It should also be noted that special grievances may not be processed through normal grievance channels. Although all grievances must be processed step by step through a stated grievance format, on rare occasions a special grievance case may be given unique attention. This unique attention usually is in the form of skipping a few formal grievance steps in order to arrive at a quicker decision because the grievance matter may be crucial to current operating and working conditions. In addition, the handling of special grievances may involve special steps as well as, or in the place of, skipping certain steps within normal grievance channels (Pettefer).

Step	Labor Representative	Management Representative
1	Steward and aggrieved employee	Foreman
2	Shop committee	General manager
3	Arbitration by an impartial third party	

THREE STEPS

Step	Labor Representative	Management Representative
1	Steward and aggrieved employee	Foreman
2	Shop committee	Personnel manager
3	Local union officers	President
4	Arbitration by an impartial third party	

FOUR STEPS

FIGURE 11-10   Typical three-step and four-step grievance procedures.

Most grievance procedurres (at least nine out of every ten) contain either three, four, or five steps. Figure 11-9 shows a typical five-step grievance procedure. Figure 11-10 shows both a typical three-step and a four-step grievance system. Small plants usually use a three-step procedure while many medium-sized plants prefer a four-step system.

Grievance procedure systems are used to handle fairly serious employee matters. For example, recall that minor or moderate worker offenses are handled through a progressive disciplinary system. Major disciplinary problems, as well as other serious types of work-related issues and phenomena when challenged or contested by labor, are handled through the formal grievance procedure mechanism. It also should be mentioned that the grievance techniques described above are almost always associated with only unionized work settings.

NONUNION GRIEVANCES

Grievance settlements for nonunion employees can occur in a number of ways. Here are some of the grievance approaches used in nonunion situations:

1. Personnel counseling.
2. Open-door policy.

   3. Inspector-general method.
   4. Ombudsman.
   5. Formal shop committee.
   6. Floating committee.
   7. Periodic employee meetings.
   8. Board of neutrals.
   9. Company grievance committee.
   10. Suggestion system.
   11. Multistep grievance procedure.
   12. Effective personnel department.

Most of these grievance approaches are explained sufficiently by their titles so they will not be discussed further.

EFFECTIVE GRIEVANCE HANDLING

It is commonly believed and generally accepted that the best way to handle grievances in a unionized setting is to have competent, well-trained, sensitive, and human-relations-oriented foremen or first-line supervisors (in other words, handling worker complaints in step one of the formal grievance procedure). Equally known and established is the idea that an effective personnel department is the best method of handling employee grievances within nonunionized situations.

Mediation versus Arbitration

Over 95 percent of all formal grievance procedure systems today contain arbitration as the final step (Kilberg). An arbitrator is an impartial third party who makes a final and binding decision on labor-management disputes to which both parties have voluntarily agreed to abide. The key aspects of the arbitration process are that it is impartial, it is voluntary, and the decision that is made is final and binding (Rime).

At one time mediation instead of arbitration was found as the final step within most formalized grievance procedures. A mediator also is an impartial third party who labor and management voluntarily accept, but a mediator cannot and does not make final and binding decisions. A mediator serves only as a linking pin between employee and employer representatives. The concept of conciliation is closely related to mediation. Today the concepts of mediation and conciliation are generally considered to by synonymous and interchangeable. In the past, however, mediation was used to describe a "friendly" labor-management situation in which the third party played a very "active" role in terms of making suggestions to and trying to secure compromises from employee and employer representatives. Concilation used to be the label used to describe "hostile" collective bargaining negotiations in which the third party played a very "passive" role, that is, he only served as a messenger boy between labor and management officials who were not speaking to each other, and the conciliator did not try to make alternative proposals, recommendations, or suggestions to the negotiating parties.

CHOICE INSTEAD OF COMPROMISE

Arbitration has replaced mediation as the final step in most formal grievance systems for a number of reasons. One of the main reasons is because both labor and management have historically been unhappy with "compromise" outcomes. Win or lose situations at least make one party happy, and this can be achieved through arbitration. A third party who plays an active negotiating role also makes collective bargaining situations more complex than before since now three, instead of two different entities and viewpoints are involved.

ARBITRATOR QUALIFICATIONS

Anyone can be an arbitrator as long as labor and management agree to accept a person's decision as binding in a grievance matter. Formerly, many clergymen served as arbitrators, but today lawyers and business professors perform this service part time. If a company needs an arbitrator and does not know how to find one, the Federal Mediation and Conciliation Service, the American Arbitration Association, and other organizations will supply a list of names to any institution requesting this information. The list contains names of local residents who are willing to perform this function for a fee ($100 to $300 a day plus expenses). Labor and management officials review the list and mutually decide on an arbitrator based on a candidate's reputation and decision record, hearsay information, and other factors. An arbitrator's fee normally will be paid half by labor and half by management.

ARBITRATION PROCESS

Arbitrators are not judges and are not bound to follow legal precedent. Arbitration hearings may be formal, similar to a courtroom setting, but more often they are much more relaxed and informal. An arbitrator is supposed to be concerned with one thing: interpret the labor-management contract. Some arbitrators, however, are beginning to make value judgments concerning clauses within the employee-employer agreement, but such arbitrator behavior is rare and usually very much unwanted by both labor and management representatives. Arbitrators are not bound by past legal precedent established through decisions made about similar issues in different situations. Nevertheless, as the arbitration process has matured, as records of arbitration decisions have been increasingly recorded, and with the growing sophistication and training of arbitrators, it is now common for arbitrators to consult past cases to serve as reference for current decisions.

AD HOC OR PERMANENT ARBITRATOR

Most arbitrators are used on an ad hoc instead of a permanent basis; that is, they are individually called in on special occasions to decide unique cases. Because only a small percentage of cases ever reach arbitration, a company would have to be very large in order to justify the expense of a full-time, permanent arbitrator. Some companies prefer that the same arbitrator, be he full- or part-time, judge all company cases because he will be familiar with company and union policies, procedures, and the like, while other organizations prefer to get new ideas and fresh decisions from a variety of different arbitrators.

NLRB AND JUDICIAL COURT ROLES

Arbitration is supposed to be the final grievance and appeal step, but sometimes labor or management, although initially agreeing voluntarily to abide by an arbitrator's decision, refuse to go along with the judgment made. These cases then must go into NLRB (National Labor Relations Board) hearings or into the judicial court system. In the majority of cases, judges in judicial court systems support arbitrator decisions since both parties did agree in advance to follow this decision and procedure. Often judicial courts refuse to reevaluate arbitrated cases. An increasing number of arbitrated cases are being appealed to the judicial court system, but of those that are, they usually are refused court time or are decided in favor of the original arbitrator's decision (McKelvey).

VOLUNTARY AND INVOLUNTARY ARBITRATION

The arbitration process is voluntary in nature, that is, labor and management mutually agree without outside intervention to abide by an impartial third party's decision. On rare occasions, however, involuntary or compulsory arbitration results when labor and management are forced to act according to a third party's recommendation. This occurs when the federal government intervenes in those collective bargaining negotiations that affect the well-being, safety, and security of the entire country. These national emergency situations can occur in key industries that involve or deal with automobiles, rails, shipping, steel, air transportation, and the like.

FACT FINDING

Along with arbitration and mediation, fact-finding boards are sometimes used as a step in trying to decide work-related grievances. A fact-finding board is appointed by either the federal or a state government to conduct a complete investigation into the facts, issues, and opposing positions in a labor dispute. Sometimes this board has the power to recommend a particular settlement. The board's statement of the complete facts and recommendations is almost always made available to the general public. The theory is that public opinion will force the parties to reach an agreement once the issues and positions of the two sides, along with any board recommendations are made public. Presumably, if one side has been holding to a position that is unreasonable, it will be forced to become more conciliatory when exposed to the glare and wrath of public opinion and pressure (Kilberg).

5. Future Labor Relations-Collective Bargaining Issues

This chapter has dealt only with past and present labor relations-collective bargaining issues, problems, and phenomena. However, there are a number of crucial matters in the labor-management arena that largely concern the future status and strength of the labor relations-collective bargaining concept (Brown). As times change, so do the dominant issues in labor relations and collective bargaining (McLaughlin). For example, the past issue of union recognition has been largely replaced by economic issues of wages, hours, and working conditions. In addition, with the advent of mechanization and automation, job security and supplemental employee benefits and services have assumed greater importance. Currently some of the newer issues of labor relations and collective bargaining concern include: (1) noninflationary wage settlements; (2) protection against the effects of technology; (3) guaranteed annual wages; (4) early retirement; (5) subcontracting; (6) plant relocation; (7) the use of new methods and equipment; (8) the establishment of production standards; (9) work rules governing the creation of job crews; and (10) the shorter workweek and the quality of work life. These issues and concerns are already the subject matter of some labor relations-collective bargaining agreements, but they are most significant as areas of future labor-management debate and reconciliation (Bakke). Although issues as those just identified will be of major concern in the years to come, two additional matters warrant even more serious attention: public employee strikes and coalition bargaining.

Public Employee Strikes

The right to strike in the past has traditionally been withheld from public employee unions because these strikes are against employers who have been elected by society and who obtain their funds through taxation. The correctness of this prohibition is most widely recognized in the cases of fire and police protection. But the strike is the only really forceful and powerful technique that a union possesses to gain what it wants, and public employers can make decisions that are just as unfair as the decisions of private companies. Consequently, public employees have used semistrike techniques such as slowdowns, sick calls, threatened mass resignations, reduced work time, and other devices in an endeavor to achieve their objectives. In addition, actual work stoppages and strikes have even been used illegally by many public employee unions. Many observers believe that we are approaching an era when public employees will collectively be accorded substantially the same status and role as private employees. Federal and state laws must and will be changed eventually to accommodate this movement. However, because the public welfare or emergency issue still remains, public collective bargaining will in the future probably differ from private collective bargaining in that constant mediation and continual information to the public will characterize these negotiations. Even with constant mediation and continual information to the public, however, all strike situations will not be totally averted or completely avoided. It is increasingly common for teachers, letter carriers, nurses, transit workers, sanitation employees, penitentiary guards, and others to strike for better employment conditions; and even firemen and policemen are beginning to jump on the public employee strike bandwagon.

Coalition Bargaining

Coalition bargaining is also a major future labor relations-collective bargaining issue and movement (Nelson). By definition, a coalition is an alliance or fusion together of several persons or parties into one mass. Coalition bargaining occurs when several smaller unions join together in a united front to collectively confront an employer or a group of employers. Although the coalition is formed among union parties, it also may be representative of joint management endeavors. Coalition bargaining is especially popular among cooperating unions because it enhances union bargaining power. Company managements are fearful that such industry-wide bargaining will result in greater government interference and pressures leading to political decisions in public interest strikes. However, all employers are not against coalition bargaining and, in fact, some seek to encourage it in order to reduce the degree and number of inconsistencies and complications in dealing with multiple unions. In most instances, employers who desire coalition bargaining operate in a single location. Large, integrated employers with widely separated sites and different technologies generally desire contract flexibility and, therefore, are opposed to any form of coalition bargaining. It appears very likely that the movement toward coalition bargaining will continue to gain added impetus during the upcoming decades (Oswald).

6. Summary

This chapter has discussed the topic of labor relations-collective bargaining from past, present, and future perspectives. An overview of labor relations-collective bargaining can be gained through knowledge concerning types of unions, the current status of labor unions, labor legislation, and the forms of union security. Future labor relations and collective bargaining issues are many, but among the most important concerns are the topics of public employee strikes and coalition bargaining.

Present or current labor relations-collective bargaining matters can be separated into two main activities: contract negotiation and contract administration. The contract negotiation process exists in several stages and covers a wide range of subject matters. Although both labor and management have their respective forms of pressure, conflict resolution is often as much a matter of ritualism as it is realism.

Contract administration concerns the interpretation and application of the labor-management agreement. All subject matters contained within the employee-employer contract are subareas or subsets of the total contract administration process. Discipline and grievances are two of these subsets that have been discussed. Corporate discipline is typically administered through a progressive penalty system when rule infractions are of a minor nature. Employee discipline cases and other work-related issues can be appealed formally usually through a stated company grievance procedure system. The final step within the vast majority of organizational jurisprudence systems is arbitration that involves a final and binding decision made by an impartial third party.

Figure 11-11 illustrates that contract negotiation and contract administration are best envisioned as partially interrelated and overlapping labor-management processes, instead of being thought of as totally distinct or completely synonymous set labor relations entities. In reality, it is hard to tell where contract negotiation ends and contract administration begins. The distinction of before and after the signing of the labor-management contract or agreement is an overly simplistic notion. All aspects of contract negotiation and contract administration are intimately interwoven together, and

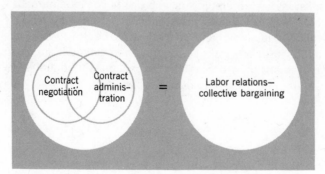

FIGURE 11-11 Labor relations-collective bargaining.

collectively they constitute the activity usually called either labor relations or collective bargaining as shown in Figure 11-11.

DISCUSSION QUESTIONS AND ASSIGNMENTS

1. Identify and briefly explain the different types of unions and the various forms of union security.
2. Describe a typical organizational progressive penalty system and a typical organization grievance procedure system.
3. Point out the similarities and differences between labor relations, collective bargaining, contract negotiation, and contract administration.
4. Interview two current labor officials and ask them to comment on the expected future growth of the labor movement in the United States during the next five years.
5. Read and analyze in the newspapers a recent contract negotiation process. How much of this interaction was ritualism and how much was reality in your opinion?
6. Predict what future issues will become common labor relations-collective bargaining subject matters within the next 10 to 15 years.

REFERENCES

General Book References

Baer, Walter E., *Grievance Handling.* New York: American Management Association, 1970.

Beirne, Joseph A., *Challenge to Labor: New Roles for American Trade Unions.* Englewood Cliffs, N.J.: Prentice-Hall, 1969.

Black, James M., *Positive Discipline.* New York: American Management Association, 1970.

Blum, Albert A., et al., *White-collar Workers.* New York: Random House, 1971.

Kassalow, Everett M., *Trade Unions and Industrial Relations: An International Comparison.* New York: Random House, 1969.

Murphy, Richard J., and Morris Sachman, *The Crisis in Public Employee Relations in the Decade of the Seventies.* Washington, D.C.: Bureau of National Affairs, 1970.

Prasow, Paul, and Edward Peters, *Arbitration and Collective Bargaining.* New York: McGraw-Hill, 1970.

Roberts, Harold S., *Labor Management Relations in the Public Service.* Honolulu, Ha.: University of Hawaii Press, 1969.

Roberts, Harold S., *Roberts' Dictionary of Industrial Relations.* Washington, D.C.: Bureau of National Affairs, 1971.

Schwarz, P. J., *Coalition Bargaining.* Ithaca, New York: New York State School of Industrial and Labor Relations, Cornell University Press, 1970.

U.S. Department of Labor, Bureau of Labor Statistics, *A Brief History of the American Labor Movement.* Bulletin 1000, Washington, D.C.: Superintendent of Documents, 1970.

U.S. Department of Labor, Bureau of Labor Statistics, *Directory of National and International Unions.* Bulletin 1665, Washington, D.C.: U.S. Government Printing Office, 1970.

Van DeVall, Mark, *Labor Organizations*. Cambridge, Massachusetts: Harvard University Press, 1970.

Woodworth, Robert T., and Richard B. Peterson, *Collective Negotiation for Public and Professional Employees*. Glenview, Ill.: Scott, Foresman and Company, 1969.

Specific Journal References

Allen, Dale A., Jr., "A Systems View of Labor Negotiations," *Personnel Journal, 50* (2), 1971, pp. 103–114.

Ash, Philip, "The Parties to the Grievance," *Personnel Psychology, 23* (1), 1970, pp. 14–18.

Bakke, E. Wight, "Reflections on the Future of Bargaining in the Public Sector," *Monthly Labor Review, 93* (7), 1970, pp. 21–25.

Bloch, Richard I., "Race Discrimination in Industry and the Grievance Process," *Labor Law Journal, 21* (10), 1970, pp. 627–644.

Bok, Derek C., and John T. Dunlop, "How Trade Union Policy Is Made," *Monthly Labor Review, 93* (2), 1970, pp. 12–20.

Brown, Martha A., "Collective Bargaining on the Campus: Professors, Associations, and Unions," *Labor Law Journal, 21* (3), 1970, pp. 167–181.

Cohany, Harry P., and Lucretia M. Dewey, "Union Membership Among Government Employees," *Monthly Labor Review, 93* (7), 1970, pp. 15–20.

Curtin, E. R., "The Facts About White Collar Unionization," *The Conference Board Record, 6* (6), 1969, pp. 11–13.

Dewey, Lucretia M., "Women in Labor Unions," *Monthly Labor Review, 94* (2), 1971A, pp. 42–48.

Dewey, Lucretia M., "Union Merger Pace Quickens," *Monthly Labor Review, 94* (6), 1971B, pp. 63–70.

Eisele, C. F., "Plant Size and Frequency of Strikes," *Labor Law Journal, 21* (8), 1970, pp. 779–786.

Garbarino, Joseph W., "Precarious Professors: New Patterns of Representation," *Industrial Relations, 10* (1), 1971, pp. 1–20.

Kelley, Matthew A., "The Contract Rejection Problem — A Positive Labor-Management Approach," *Labor Law Journal, 20* (7), 1969, pp. 404–415.

Kennedy, T., "Freedom to Strike Is in the Public Interest," *Harvard Business Review, 48* (4), 1970, pp. 45–57.

Kilberg, William J., "The FMCS and Arbitration: Problems and Prospects," *Monthly Labor Review, 94* (4), 1971, pp. 40–45.

Kleingartner, Archie, "Professionalism and Engineering Unionism," *Industrial Relations, 8* (3), 1969, pp. 224–227.

Marcus, Robert J., "The Changing Workforce: Implications for Companies and Unions," *Personnel, 48* (1), 1971, pp. 8–15.

McKelvey, Jean T., "Sex and the Single Arbitrator," *Industrial and Labor Relations Review, 24* (3), 1971, pp. 335–353.

McLaughlin, Richard P., "Collective Bargaining Suggestions for the Public Sector," *Labor Law Journal, 20* (3), 1969, pp. 131–137.

Miles, Raymond E., and J. B. Ritchie, "Leadership Attitudes Among Union Officials," *Industrial Relations, 8* (1), 1968, pp. 110–118.

Mills, D. Q., "Wage Determination in Contract Construction," *Industrial Relations, 10* (1), 1971, pp. 72–85.

Nelson, Wallace B., "Coercion on Collective Bargaining," *Labor Law Review, 21* (1), 1970, pp. 43–45.

O'Neal, Frederick, "The Role of the Black Trade Unionist," *American Federationist, 77* (7), 1970, pp. 7–12.

Oswald, Rudolph A., "Union Bargaining Goals in the 1970's," *Monthly Labor Review, 93* (3), 1970, pp. 40–42.

Peterson, D. J., "Why Unions Go to Arbitration: Politics and Strategy vs. Merit," *Personnel, 48* (4), 1971, pp. 44–49.

Pettefer, J. C., "Effective Grievance Arbitration," *California Management Review, 13* (2), 1970, pp. 12–18.

Prasow, Paul, and Edward Peters, "The Semantic Aspects of Collective Bargaining," *Review of General Semantics, 25* (3), 1968, pp. 292-293.

Raskin, A. H., "The Labor Movement Must Start Moving," *Harvard Business Review, 48* (1), 1970, pp. 105–113.

Rime, J. Thomas, Jr., "Arbitration: How to Avoid It," *Personnel, 47* (3), 1970, pp. 26–30.

Shea, John, "Would Foremen Unionize?" *Personnel Journal, 49* (11), 1970, pp. 926–931.

Sherman, V. Clayton, "Unionism and the Nonunion Company," *Personnel Journal, 48* (6), 1969, pp. 413–422.

Tyler, Gus, "Labor in the 1970's: A New Era," *American Federationist, 77* (1), 1970, pp. 1–5.

Vogel, Alfred, "Your Clerical Workers Are Ripe for Unionism," *Harvard Business Review, 49* (2), 1971, pp. 48–54.

Wingo, Walter, "How to Win at the Bargaining Table," *Nation's Business, 58* (2), 1970, pp. 38–42.

Yaffe, B., "The Protected Rights of the Union Steward," *Industrial and Labor Relations Review, 23* (4), 1970, pp. 483–499.

contents

learning objectives

1. To know the definition of research and to recognize the need for personnel research.

2. To understand the relationship of personnel research to the other sub-areas or subsets of personnel administration.

3. To become acquainted with personnel research tools and the sources of personnel research information.

4. To be able to recognize the limitations of personnel research endeavors.

The future of the future is the present.

12
Personnel Research

1. Research Definition and Semantics

Research is the systematic and purposive investigation of facts and their relationships among objects, events, attitudes, values and opinions. It establishes cause-and-effect relationships between two or more phenomena and expands the frontiers of knowledge through systematic investigation. Methodologically, this systematic investigation often exists in the form of carefully considered hypotheses and thoughtful questions.

The word "research" implies repeated searching, investigations, reexaminations, assessments, and reevaluations, and it is undertaken as a shortcut to knowledge and understanding. It replaces trial and error with systematic, purposive investigation and seeks solutions to problems that are often expressed in terms of null hypotheses.

Pure versus Applied Research

Pure research (also called *basic* or *exploratory* research) is designed to provide knowledge or understanding for its own sake, and is not concerned with immediately practical applications or uses. *Applied* or *operational*

423

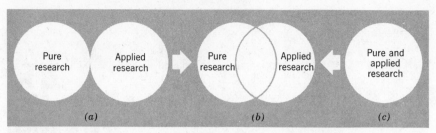

FIGURE 12-1 Pure research and applied research as distinct, interrelated, and synonymous set entities. (a) Distinct. (b) Interrelated. (c) Synonymous.

research attempts to find answers for specific, current problems. Most of the research undertaken by business and public agencies is applied research. However, any research project is to some degree, both "pure" and "applied" in nature. Figure 12-1b illustrates that pure and applied research are best envisioned as partially interrelated research concepts, instead of totally distinct (Figure 12-1a) or completely synonymous (Figure 12-1c) set entities.

Characteristics of Research

Occasionally semantic and definitional disputes arise over the essentials and characteristics of research. Sometimes the claim is made that descriptive studies or library investigations are not "real" research. Critics raise questions as to how penetrating a study must be to justify its designation as research. Whether replication studies, library research, descriptive explanations, and the like are real research studies is not discussed here. The different labels of "pure," "basic," "exploratory," "operational," and "applied" have been coined by some authors to differentiate between the various types and levels of research (Hinrichs, 1969).

Research should not be confused with casual observation, because it uses systematic investigation and objective analysis instead of casual and informal means. True research takes place when interpretations of data and information occur after rather than before the fact(s). The essential characteristic of research is its method or point of view. This viewpoint is *purposive, objective,* and *systematic.* Good research begins with specific questions and a comprehensive plan that tries to answer the questions. Subjective bias is recognized and eliminated as much as possible throughout every step of the total research process.

Research Analysis

Research studies vary widely in the amount of emphasis given to the analysis of information and data. Some studies are basically descriptive; that is, they report on what *was* or *is,* rather than on *why.* Pure or basic research is most likely to emphasize complex interrelationships and empirical analysis. Applied or operational research stresses practical explanations and common understanding. Research analysis provides the basis for research generalizations and conclusions. These abstractions are desirable so that research findings can extend beyond the limits of the specific data examined in a particular study. Analytical research is needed to provide the theoretical framework and background on which total knowledge and operational practice can be based.

Research analysis involves the careful statement of hypotheses that are tested in order to verify or disprove them. Research studies seek to identify variables and factors affecting some happening, and then to hypothesize tentative relationships between these variables, factors, and outcomes. Relationships can be stated in a variety of formats ranging from simple, direct cause-and-effect relationships to exceedingly complex, indirect, and intervening relationships among numerous variables. The varying degree of complexity of these relationships makes it more difficult to define the research concept. Levels, types, complexity, methodology, sophistication, nature, and intent of research studies vary considerably, and these differences all involve semantic and definitional (as well as methodological and operational) research problems.

2. Need for Personnel Research

There is no aspect of management and administration that cannot benefit from systematic and purposeful research. This is true of personnel administration as well as of general management. Manpower or personnel research like all facets of organizational research is currently in vogue. Executives today are "R & D" minded because they are well aware of the usefulness of the research tool. Today, research is being used to solve problems in every major area of human activity and interest, and it often leads directly to increased understanding and improved practices whenever it is undertaken seriously and systematically.

Human Research

Although research has long been recognized as a means of improving products and production processes, human resources research is just now being envisioned as a vital aspect of a well managed organization. Today, all aspects of administration are being studied, and much of this research effort has focused on the human organizational element. One of the reasons for the slow acceptance of the human resources research function is the fact that the human factor is extremely difficult to study in controlled experiments.

Unlike the physical sciences, human beings and the social sciences are so complex that human behavior can never be completely predictable. Behavioral studies may lead to predictions of human activity, but because of the complexity of intervening variables, these predictions always contain some element of risk or uncertainty.

Research Pressures

Several pressures and developments explain the growing use of research in management. Research has often made direct contributions to corporate growth and earnings. The rapid growth of management consulting has popularized the research emphasis. Expanding educational programs for managers often stress research methodology and findings. Evaluations of top collegiate management education programs have led to massive university commitments and endeavors in this regard. Improved information technology together with the possibility of relatively inexpensive statistical analysis has resulted in the growth and advancement of research. In addition, the trend toward increased professionalization of management also exerts pressure for increasing amounts of manpower research. These and other factors point toward the increasing need for the use of management and personnel research.

Research Purposes

Research is performed today so that an organization can keep abreast with or ahead of its competitors. Newer products, techniques, and organizational practices must be found to replace outdated former procedures. Because times change, research efforts must continually search for newer and better ways of doing things. To grow, or sometimes even to survive, an institution must be able to insure its continued existence. To a large extent, research helps to fulfill this necessity, since it serves as a hedge against obsolescence.

Research is a multipurpose tool that is used to help solve a variety of organizational problems. In this chapter we are concerned only with manpower or personnel research, but it must be recognized that the major research contributions to date have been in organizational aspects and areas that only indirectly involve human activities. The concept of research can apply to all organizational studies, be they large or small, descriptive or analytical, major or minor, human or nonhuman, and broad or narrow in perspective, dimensions, and scope (Block).

Today, research is envisioned as the key to organizational progress and has achieved increasing recognition as a way of life in modern societies. Various organizations now spend considerable sums on research studies aimed at improving organizational effectiveness. In many organizations research appears to be the spot where the action is and where it will continue to be in the decades ahead. Not only is research growing, but manpower and personnel research is advancing disproportionately in many companies because some of the technical problems of the world have been solved, but human-relations advancements are still in their rudimentary stages. It seems ludicrous to many that we are able to place men on the moon but unable to have peace on earth. Increased people-oriented research efforts are also a part of the general societal movements toward humanitarianism, social responsibility, enlightened self-interest, and the way on poverty. This increased emphasis on behavioral and manpower research is expected to continue during the next several decades (Patterson; Liebtag).

Personnel Research as an Enterprise Function

Not all organizations will identify personnel research as an official area of job responsibility. Many organizations do not have separate departments, divisions, or even certain persons assigned to carry out these work assignments. Especially in smaller companies, personnel research, at best, will be only a small part-time portion of the job duties of a personnel officer. Larger organizations will be more likely to have a clearly defined personnel research program. But even within larger enterprises, the top management attitude concerning the importance of personnel research varies tremendously from one extreme to the other. Although my opinion is not shared by everyone, I believe strongly that personnel research is or should be important enough to be considered as a separate and distinct enterprise function. Exactly what specific duties and responsibilities are or should be involved in the personnel research function will depend on company size, top management support, enterprise profitability, organizational operations and procedures, and other factors. In addition, the specific subject-matter areas of personnel research cannot be properly comprehended without an understanding of the relationship of personnel research to other subject-matter personnel administration subsets.

3. Relationship to Other Personnel Administration Subsets

Past, Present, and Future Perspectives

The employee research function always has been identified as a part of personnel administration, but it is a segment that is often slighted or given very low priority in comparison to other employee-personnel duties. The traditional personnel administrator did sometimes identify the employee research function, but identification only, instead of implementation, was the extent of what many companies actually did in reference to this manpower concern. The modern human resource manager gives (or should give) the

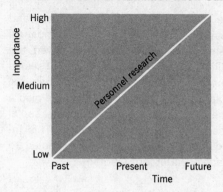

FIGURE 12-2 The projected growing importance of personnel research.

personnel research function much more emphasis than did his organizational predecessor. Today, employee research is viewed as an essential component of a well-rounded, total personnel program (Pyle). Contrary to what was often done in the past, human resources research is not the last duty or responsibility to arrive within or the first to depart from the scope of a personnel administrator's job. Figure 12-2 hypothetically indicates the growing importance of personnel research over the years. Although the viewpoint is not universally shared, I see the role of personnel research expanding in the future. Human resources research, in a variety of forms, is taking on added emphasis and many observers expect this trend to continue and enlarge in the future.

Variety of Research Areas

There is no end to the number of things that need to be researched in the field of personnel administration. The previous chapters dealt with motivation and communication; organizational climate and leadership; human resource planning; staffing and appraisal; training and development; compensation: wage and salary administration; compensation: benefits and services; health and safety; and labor relations-collective bargaining, all containing perplexing problems of varying human complexity. The relationship of the personnel research function to the other subject-matter areas of personnel administration is shown in Figure 12-3. In essence, all topics that are part of the global personnel administration concept contain or should contain a personnel research component. However, studies are available to show that within these personnel administration subareas, some topics and types of research are more common than others (Block). The following section discusses some of these specific personnel research areas in greater detail.

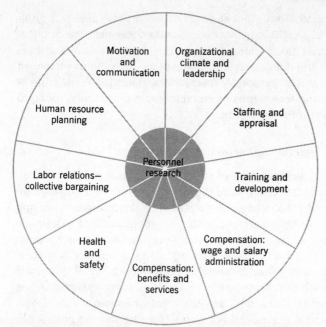

FIGURE 12-3 Personnel research relationship to other personnel administration subsets.

4. Personnel Research Areas

Academic Ties

Personnel and human resources research finds its roots in a number of academic disciplines. Psychological research can be generally applied to employee relations problems, and the specific discipline of industrial psychology has contributed the most worthwhile research to the personnel area. Sociological studies also have been of use to the modern human resources manager as have the findings of economists who have made major research contributions, particularly, in the personnel subfunction and area of compensation. Other social science research studies have dealt with human resource topics, but in terms of relevance and numbers, psychological studies dominate.

Academic Training

Many major firms hire personnel researchers to investigate human resource problems and issues. Studies are available that show that most of these personnel researchers are trained psychologists with either a Ph.D. or a master's degree in psychology (Block). Most organizational research projects involve aspects of psychology, sociology, and economics. The application of these disciplines takes place in a real business environment; thus organization and personnel research tends to be of the operational instead of the pure variety. In practice, personnel researchers utilize the knowledge of many disciplines and the techniques of multiple approaches when trying to solve specific organizational problems.

Improving Personnel Practices

In identifying research as a function of personnel administration or human resources management, it is recognized that the human element (in addition to other organizational resources such as materials, land, equipment, and capital), also must be analyzed and studied in an economic and systematic manner. Objective decisions need to be made concerning hiring, training, compensating, and maintaining employees within the corporate structure. Personnel and human resources research is performed to more efficiently bring about these conditions. As shown in Figure 12-4, personnel research is the "means" of bringing about the "end-state" of improved performance. The fundamental purpose of employee research is to improve the philosophy and the practice of personnel administration and manpower management. Also, the behavioral research performed by organizations attempts to discover ways to maintain abilities and attitudes of employees at good or high levels on a continuing basis. Organizational research is intended to be productive in that it tries to raise the level of employee performance or, at least, attempts to maintain the current level of personnel management effectiveness.

Specific Topics

Applied personnel research is directed toward the solution of particular organizational problems. Usually the payoff of such employee research is immediate, substantial, and tangible. The scope of such research can vary from very simple to extremely elaborate, or from short and inexpensive to

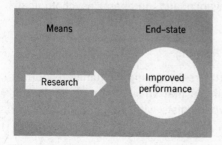

Means   End–state

Research → Improved performance

FIGURE 12-4 Research is a "means" of bringing about improved performance.

long and costly. The personnel researcher seeks to discover basic relationships that can lead to improved personnel decision making in such areas as turnover, absenteeism, compensation levels and structure, job satisfaction, employee morale, assessing managerial potential, training effectiveness, grievance handling, and the like. In terms of their frequency (and probably their importance), the following personnel research areas are frequently identified in terms of their high to low appearance: selection, opinion measurement, training and development, appraisal, motivation, organizational effectiveness, managerial obsolescence, counseling, and retirement (Lake, Ritvo, and O'Brien). Most studies reveal that the four most dominant personnel research areas are selection, training and development, attitudes and leadership, and measurement devices (Block). In terms of the greatest future personnel research needs, *managerial* selection and development along with general employee motivation are constantly identified by surveyed personnel administrators as the two human resource areas in greatest need for additional research.

5. A Research Method and Personnel Research Tools

There are various techniques that can be used in the investigation of personnel research problems. One of the first steps in research involves the careful consideration of choices among research designs. The general procedure is choosing the mechanism that promises adequate quality at a minimum of difficulty, effort, and cost. Several types of research studies or methodologies have achieved wide recognition, and these include or are an extension of the "scientific method." In this section, the scientific method and the personnel research tools of historical studies, case studies, surveys, statistical studies, mathematical models, simulation, field research, and controlled experimental studies will be briefly discussed.

A. SCIENTIFIC METHOD

All research involves the application of the scientific method, which starts with a problem, goes through a rigid and systematic sequence of activities that stress rationality and inference and arrives at a conclusion. It is formal, procedural, and emphasizes objectivity, and normally includes the following steps: (1) define the problem; (2) state objectives; (3) formulate hypotheses; (4) collect data (empirical observation and verification); (5) classify, analyze, and interpret data; and (6) draw conclusions, generalize, restate, or develop new hypotheses.

Physical and Social Sciences

The scientific method has been utilized with tremendous success within the physical sciences for many years, and social scientists only now are beginning to fully realize the applications of this technique as a methodology for studying and analyzing human groups and organizational phenomena. Many personnel administrators and human resource managers are attempting to apply this methodology to help them solve institutional employee problems.

Mental and Physical Activities

The scientific method is a combination of mental and physical activities throughout its various stages. All of the six steps emphasize mental activities, with the exception of step four: collecting data. However, these mental activities are systematically and rigidly controlled and directed within the scientific method. In addition, the implementation of these mental processes requires overt human physical actions, activities, movements, and behaviors (Dale).

Defining the Problem

One mistake commonly made by researchers who attempt to adhere to the scientific method is to underestimate the importance of the first step in the process; defining the problem. The importance of properly defining the problem cannot be overemphasized, since the entire scientific method is useless unless step one is adequately performed. Individuals take for granted or assume that their initial identification of a problem is in fact the real problem. Actually, many people cannot properly distinguish between a problem and a symptom of a problem. An individual may have a headache, but a headache is a symptom not a problem. Similarly, organizational inefficiency or ineffectiveness is a symptom of a more basic problem or series of interrelated problems. Another error is to think that only one problem exists. Usually organizational inefficiency and other undesirable institutional phenomena are a result of a number of interrelated problems. Often a combination of solutions is needed in order to solve a combination of problems.

Figure 12-5 summarizes the preceding discussion of the scientific method. The scientific method consists of six systematic, sequential steps that may either be conceptually envisioned as distinct entities as shown in Area A or as interrelated activities as shown in Area B. The general consensus is that the integrated interpretation is more realistic, but the exact degree of overlap between the six steps in the scientific method remains a matter of personal conjecture. As also shown in Area B of Figure 12-5, the scientific method is realistically best envisioned as containing various feedback loops that emerge from and are contained within each of the six states that collectively constitute this methodology.

The remaining research tools to be discussed also make use of the scientific method, which is the underlying rationale behind all systematic hybrid operational research forms, techniques, and procedures.

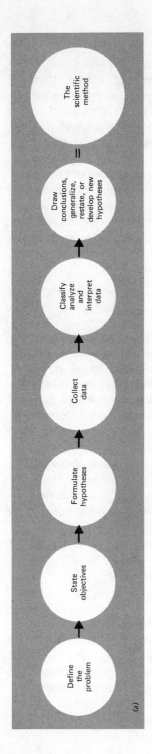
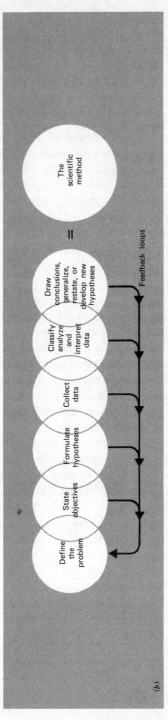

FIGURE 12-5 The scientific method. (a) Distinct steps. (b) Interrelated steps with feedback loops.

B. HISTORICAL STUDIES

Historical studies systematically investigate past records and documents, and also can include interviews with former employees. The essential feature of the historical method is its systematic investigation utilizing an extended time-span or longitudinal dimension. Most organizations keep on file a wealth of useful information, much of which contains valuable records about personnel. For example, absenteeism, accident rates, and turnover are types of personnel records kept by almost all firms, and they can provide useful data and information to a personnel researcher. Historical studies attempt to determine fundamental factors that affect an organizational problem, and they collect evidence about these factors from historical company records. This assumes, of course, that the organization has on file the appropriate records needed for such a research investigation. These studies are considered "historical" because they make use only of past or dated information that may range from being several years to several hours old.

C. CASE STUDIES

Case studies allow the analytical investigation of relationships that have been significant during a single situation or set of circumstances. Although the precise meaning of findings in a case study is limited to the unique past situation, careful analysis and thoughtful generalization may permit broader significance and application. Individual case studies can lead to general hypotheses that can be of value in laying the foundation for additional, broader, or more intensive future research. Conclusions drawn from a relatively limited number of case studies, of course, are of a highly tentative nature. The main advantage of case study research and analysis is that it permits the thorough, in depth investigation of a few key incidents. The main drawbacks of case study analysis and research are that it is historical in nature, and that it is not necessarily representative of general conditions either historically, currently, or futurally. Because the future will never be identical with the past, case study research and analysis can only be of limited informational usefulness.

D. SURVEYS

The distinctive aspect of a survey is its concentration on the collection of original data and information. The survey method is one of the most commonly used business research methods, and usually appears in the form of a questionnaire or a structured interview. Like all other research methods, surveys incorporate the scientific method as they attempt to determine present practices and relate them to particular causes and certain results. Usually certain research hypotheses are established and survey questions are designed to gather information related to these hypotheses. Data are gathered and then correlations among observed phenomena, possible causes, and related effects are computed, after which certain generalizations deducible from the survey studies can be made. These generalizations can be of value in suggesting to management what might be done in reference to a particular problem. Surveys may be intra- or interorganizational in nature, dimension, and scope. The key to success in the survey method of research is the ability to ask the right questions. The disadvantages of the survey method are that it may be time-consuming and costly. In addition, the survey method is sometimes criticized because applications of the method may emphasize the collection of empirical data with little attention to analysis or theory (Hayes).

E. STATISTICAL STUDIES

Many research studies concentrate on the collection, analysis, classification, and interpretation of mathematical data and quantitative information (Mitzner). These studies emphasize quantification, mathematical manipulation, and statistical inference. Some of the terminology involved within statistical studies includes the concepts of averages, means, medians, modes, measures of dispersion, trends, regressions, correlations, samples, probabilities, distributions, expected value, and the like. Statistical studies are increasing in frequency because of the development of high speed, modern electronic data-processing equipment. Computer improvements have made it possible to use more sophisticated techniques and more complicated models that include a larger number of complex interrelated variables. The more complex models are usually more realistic, and, therefore, they represent an improvement in the quality and usefulness of statistical research study findings (Hinrichs, 1970).

F. MATHEMATICAL MODELS

Mathematical models are closely related to statistical studies; the only distinction is that mathematical models involve further quantification. Most research makes use of models that attempt to explain the relationships among variables that are, have been, or will be examined. Statistical studies measure the variables involved and infer patterns of interaction. Mathematical models often begin where statistical studies end. They seek to develop and test designs and sequences of equations that tentatively describe the behavior of interacting variables in terms of mathematical notation. Dependent and independent variables within such mathematical equations are identified. Mathematical models have been used in various disciplines for decades, but their extended application and enhanced acceptance into management and personnel research are of comparatively recent vintage.

Much of this expanded usage is due to recent computer capability advancements that enable formerly time-consuming calculations to be made within seconds.

G. SIMULATION

Currently, simulation is perhaps the most popular form of management and personnel research. A simulation is a lifelike model that takes on the form and aspects of the real world as nearly as possible. Simulations attempt to reproduce artificial environments that approximate real-life situations so as to serve as training circumstances and analytical frameworks. Management simulations of organizational environments are used for studying problems of production control, inventory control, purchasing, marketing, and various aspects of personnel administration, such as collective bargaining, training and hiring. Often role playing is a specific type of performance simulation that can be used to research human behavior (Miller). Computers also have stimulated and popularized research designs involving simulation (MacGuffie). So-called "business games," which are now commonly used within colleges of business curriculums and within various management development programs, are a development of the simulation research method. Business games as simulations are, however, more popular and useful as training techniques instead of as research methods. Just as mathematical models were an extension of statistical studies, so also are simulations more advanced and more highly sophisticated representations of mathematical models (Teach).

H. FIELD RESEARCH

Field research, also called action research, is a global phrase used to describe studies in which the researchers sometimes directly involve themselves in the behavior to be studied. Field research has been used most successfully in understanding group behavior in working organizations and in communities. Occasionally, field research studies are similar in format and analysis to what also has been called group dynamics, sensitivity training, and laboratory training. Action research design-wise suffers from the complication that the observer becomes a variable in the process under observation. This self-involvement by the researcher, however, also may be an advantage in that new insights can be gained from active interaction that could not be possible from passive observation (Kelly and Denney).

I. CONTROLLED EXPERIMENTAL STUDIES

Controlled experiments are the most sophisticated but the least used organizational research tool. Controlled personnel research experiments have not been attempted frequently, because it is impossible to keep all other factors constant and then isolate them one at a time when human beings are involved. Methodologically, a controlled experiment is one that usually has two groups of participants; an "experimental" group, which is subjected to research variables under consideration, and a "control" group, which is not given exposure to the factors being analyzed. At best, management and personnel research can only approximate valid controlled experimental conditions. For example, one group of employees may be given training of a certain type while an untrained worker segment makes up the control group. Although all environmental conditions cannot be kept constant or controlled completely, certain tentative conclusions can be drawn at the end of the study concerning the value of the training given. The distinctive feature of the experimental method is the investigator's control of the variables involved. The researcher atempts to make observations and factor manipulations under conditions assumed to be controlled. Although in real-life experiments, true and complete control is not possible; nevertheless, the personnel researcher, through statistical analyses and simulation, can hold the influence of one or several variables constant while spotlighting variations in others.

Pilot Studies

Pilot studies are ministudies performed on a reduced sample size. They are "experimental," but they are not often "controlled," at least not to the extent that specific variables can be manipulated. Pilot studies are usually performed on small reduced populations to gauge the tentative reactions of a larger group to some proposed organizational change. In essence, they are small-scale concrete, research implementations of large-scale tentative, pragmatic proposals. Product testing and minority hiring are organizational activities often introduced initially on a pilot-study basis.

Overview

Figure 12-6 summarizes the previously discussed personnel research techniques. A set diagram is shown as comprised of nine interrelated subsets: scientific method; historical studies; case studies; surveys; statistical studies; mathematical models; simulation; field research, and controlled experimental studies. It also illustrates that these nine management research techniques are best envisioned as partially interrelated and overlapping research concepts instead of as totally distinct or completely synonymous set entities. The main thread connecting all of these research methods is the underlying rationale of the scientific method that is shown as the central set circle in Figure 12-6.

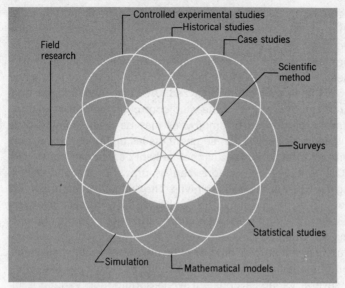

FIGURE 12-6   A research method and personnel research tools.

6. Personnel Researchers

If we are to talk about personnel and human resource research, it is imperative that the main researchers in this area be identified. Numerous bodies and entities conduct research pertaining to employee relations, but the following classifications cover much of this on-going research effort. Five agencies or group entities that perform a considerable amount of personnel and human resource research are: (1) colleges and universities; (2) government; (3) private consultants; (4) personnel departments; and (5) line departments.

A. COLLEGES AND UNIVERSITIES

It has been estimated that colleges and universities do about one third of the personnel research performed annually (Block). This research is both pure and applied. Within larger universities, it is very common to find "bureaus of business research," which engage in personnel projects as well as investigations into other aspects of organizational management. In addition to bureaus of business research, many of the most prestigious universities in this country also maintain "survey research centers" or "social research institutes." The most famous and productive of these university research entities has been the Institute for Social Research at the University of Michigan. The funds for such research agencies come from the university, business firms, and from foundations of various types, such as the Ford Foundation.

B. GOVERNMENT

Numerous local, state, and federal governmental agencies conduct both basic and applied personnel research. The federal Department of Labor is especially involved in human resource investigations. The United States Employment Service and the Department of Defense also conduct numerous research projects dealing with personnel problems and issues. State and local governments frequently engage in similar types of personnel research activities, but only on a much smaller scale. State and local governments often utilize the services of private consultants for human resource research purposes.

C. PRIVATE CONSULTANTS

Private consultants perform about 40 percent of all research that is done in the personnel-manpower area (Block). In terms of funds, the federal government supplies about two thirds of all the dollars spent on research studies carried out by private consultants. Private consultants may be individual management consultants doing and selling operational research designed for a particular company, but more commonly the private consultants are part of a larger, more sophisticated research organization, some of the more famous of which include the National Industrial Conference Board, the Brookings Institute, the RAND Corporation, and the Stanford Research Institute.

D. PERSONNEL DEPARTMENTS

Of course, personnel departments within individual companies also conduct human resource research projects. Studies indicate that about 3 percent of the total expenditures made by personnel departments were spent on research (Block). This research tends to be of the applied instead of the pure variety. In general, most companies are allocating increasing amounts of money for personnel research expenditures and endeavors.

E. LINE DEPARTMENTS

Departments other than personnel also conduct human resource studies within their own divisions. These studies may be done in conjunction with the personnel department or independently. Trial and error is a crude form of operational research, but a most expensive type when used exclusively. The line manager must not conclude that all personnel research be done only by a staff personnel department because many important facts and relationships are available only to the immediate first line supervisor.

7. Sources of Personnel Research Information

Personnel and human resource research information and data can come from a variety of sources. All of it initially comes from original research techniques such as the scientific method, historical studies; case studies; surveys; statistical studies; mathematical modes; simulations; field research; and controlled experimental studies, which were all explained previously in this chapter. These research mechanisms are employed by personnel and human resource researchers (colleges and universities, government, private consultants, personnel departments, and line departments) who also can be identified as sources of research information.

Usually personnel research techniques and their results are reported in written format in books, monographs, conference proceedings, and journals, and these recorded forms serve as the major sources of personnel research information. In addition, many university centers and institutes maintain research series that include reprints, bulletins, newsletters, and other releases. Periodicals and journals are probably the best and most widely used sources of personnel and human resource research information. Although it would be impossible to present a totally comprehensive listing, the periodicals and journals listed in Figure 12-7 are among those that directly or indirectly pertain to and report personnel and human resource research data and information.

In addition to periodical literature, numerous excellent special personnel and human resource research reports are issued on an irregular basis from organizations such as the American Management Association, the National Industrial Conference Board, the American Society for Personnel Administration, the International Personnel Management Association, and others. Several other professional associations, in addition to those just mentioned, often conduct special conferences and seminars dealing with personnel and human resource issues, problems, and concerns. The American Society for Training and Development, the Administrative Management Society, the National Academy of Management, the Industrial Relations Research Association, the Society for the Advancement of Management, and the International Industrial Relations Association are examples of organizations that provide additional sources of personnel research information. Along with these national and international professional associations, scores of local personnel and industrial relations groups exist. Several hundred local associations, usually city-wide in scope, offer membership to personnel practitioners in

Academy of Management Journal	Labour Gazette
Administrative Science Quarterly	Management Abstracts
Advanced Management Journal	Management of Personnel Quarterly
American Behavioral Scientist	Management Research
British Journal of Industrial Relations	Manpower
California Management Review	Manpower and Applied Psychology
Creativity Review	Monthly Labor Review
Harvard Business Review	Occupational Psychology
Human Organization	Pension and Welfare News
Human Relations	Personnel
Industrial Engineering	Personnel Administration
Industrial and Labor Relations Review	Personnel Administrator
Industrial Management Review	Personnel and Guidance Journal
Industrial Medicine and Surgery	Personnel Journal
Industrial Relations	Personnel Management
Industrial Relations News	Personnel Management Abstracts
Industrial Relations Quarterly Review	Personnel Practice Bulletin
International Labour Review	Personnel Psychology
Journal of Applied Behavioral Science	Poverty and Human Resources Abstracts
Journal of Business	Public Personnel Review
Journal of Creative Behavior	Supervision
Journal of Human Resources	Training and Development Journal
Labor Law Journal	Unemployment Insurance Review

FIGURE 12-7   Sources of personnel research information: selected periodicals and journals.

most of the larger metropolitan areas. These local associations commonly meet once a month and occasionally publish newsletters reporting recent personnel and human resource research findings.

8. Personnel Research Limitations

In spite of the growing personnel and human resource research emphasis, there are many shortcomings and limitations associated with behavioral research in general and with personnel research in particular. There are numerous critics who question both the quantity and quality relevancy of current human resource investigations. Many past personnel research studies have been merely descriptive instead of analytical. These studies concentrate on reporting what *is* rather than *why* it is that way, and consequently, they are only journalistic summaries of formerly existing personnel practices and procedures. In addition, many employee relations research studies are too narrow in scope, attempting only to explain personnel behavior in terms of economic or psychological factors. Multidisciplinary approaches utilizing integrated, systems frameworks are now just starting to arrive on the scene, and the "systems" and "whole man" approaches need to be emphasized. Another drawback of personnel research has been its proprietary nature. Often companies coming up with relevant manpower research findings have been reluctant to share these insights with other companies and with the general public. Furthermore, many studies are poorly designed and lack a theoretical or conceptual base, and this lack often results in contaminated findings that are insufficient in validity and reliability. Poor research design and the lack of appropriate conceptual models are interrelated problems that jointly form the greatest shortcoming of personnel research efforts to date.

Human Complexity

Another major dilemma is that personnel research involves persons and human behaviors that remain as mysterious phenomena not totally explained by any theory or combination of theories. Human behavior and motivation are of such complexity that precise and accurate predictions of past, present, and future human activities never have been and never will be totally possible The uniqueness of individuals and the inability to control environmental variables when studying human behavior are two inevitable problems and limitations of all personnel research endeavors (Lake, Ritvo, and O'Brien).

Improving Designs, Practices, and Communications

Several steps have been taken to overcome some of these limitations, such as more analytical studies and improved research designs. The quality of research seems to be improving, but much remains to be done. Improvements continually need to be made because personnel practitioners are increasingly being faced with numerous personnel research responsibilities. The modern human resources manager must keep informed of relevant studies and their findings. Personnel practices must be kept in tune with changing individual, organizational, and societal needs. The gap between personnel theory and practice must be lessened through properly designed and controlled employee studies. In addition, the findings from relevant experiments need to be reported so that the personnel field as a whole can progress and improve. These increased responsibilities require the improved quality as well as the enhanced quantity of relevant human resource research.

All of the benefits of additional research studies can become fully available only as the personnel field develops generally accepted concepts. Along with standard terminology, the need for increased communication and circulation of research findings must be dealt with. Researchers undertaking investigations must have access to thorough, reliable, up-to-date reports on earlier relevant studies. This can be possible only to the extent that all researchers are both willing and able to share their findings with others, even their competitors. The professionalization of personnel administration suggests an ethical responsibility of investigators to report their significant research contributions.

Although personnel and research conditions are improving in most organizations, institutional personnel research records leave much to be desired. Much remains to be done, and this residual is both challenging in nature and formidable in scope and dimension.

9. Summary

Research is the systematic and purposive investigation of facts and the relationships among facts, objects, events, attitudes, values, and opinions. The need for personnel research stems from the requirement and goal of finding the most efficient manner of handling people-related employment concerns. Manpower and human resource research, although not a totally new personnel function, is often considered to be a component of the modern personnel manager's job responsibilities. Specific areas of employee or personnel research include all of the personnel administration subareas as discussed in Parts II and III of this text.

Various management and personnel research tools and techniques exist, but all of them are based on modifications of the scientific method. Commonly used manpower research tools include historical studies; case studies; surveys; statistical studies; mathematical models; simulation; field research; and controlled experimental studies. The main personnel researchers who utilize these research tools include colleges and universities, government, private consultants, personnel departments, and line departments. Personnel research techniques and researchers also serve as "sources of personnel research information" as do various professional associations, journals and periodicals in the personnel-manpower area. There are many limitations to personnel and human resource research, but two of the most formidable are the inevitable uniqueness of individuals and the inherent inability to control environmental variables when studying human behavior.

A summary of the outline overview of this personnel research chapter is shown in Figure 12-8, and both major and minor topic breakdowns are indicated in the summary figure.

DISCUSSION QUESTIONS AND ASSIGNMENTS

1. Why is there a need for personnel and human resource research?
2. What is the difference between "pure" and "applied" research?
3. Identify some of the most commonly used personnel research tools.
4. Go to the nearest college or university library and find out what personnel, manpower, and human resource journals are part of the regular subscription listing.

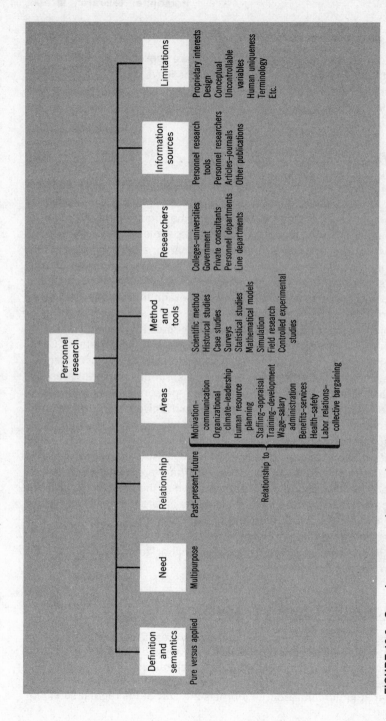

FIGURE 12-8 Overview personnel research outline and summary.

5. What, in your opinion, are the major shortcomings or limitations of the personnel research function?
6. Comment on the significance of the personnel research function in an organization with which you are familiar.

REFERENCES

General Book References

Byham, William C., *The Uses of Personnel Research.* New York: American Management Association, Research Study 91, 1968.

Heneman, H. G., Jr., *Contributions of Industrial Relations Research.* Minneapolis: Industrial Relations Center, University of Minnesota Press, Reprint 62, 1969.

Kolstoe, Ralph H., *Introduction to Statistics for the Behavioral Sciences.* Homewood, Ill.: Dorsey Press, 1969.

Morrison, Edward J., *Developing Computer-Based Employee Information Systems.* New York: American Management Association, Research Study 99, 1969.

Vichnevetsky, Robert, *Simulation in Research and Development.* New York: American Management Association, Management Bulletin No. 125, 1969.

Specific Journal References

Block, Carl E., "Industrial Relations Research: Needs and Suggestions," *Personnel Journal, 47* (4), 1968, pp. 237–241.

Dale, Ernest, "A Plea for Coalition of the Quantifiable and Non-quantifiable Approaches to Management," *Academy of Management Journal, 12* (1), 1969, pp. 15–20.

Hayes, Robert O., "Qualitative Insights from Quantitative Methods," *Harvard Business Review, 47* (4), 1969, pp. 108–117.

Hinrichs, John R., "Characteristics of the Personnel Research Function," *Personnel Journal, 48* (8), 1969, pp. 597–604.

Hinrichs, John R., "The Computer in Manpower Research," *Personnel Administration, 33* (2), 1970, pp. 37–44.

Kelly, Horace O., and H. Joe Denney, "The Purposes of Pilot Studies," *Personnel Journal, 48* (1), 1969, pp. 48–51.

Lake, Dale G., Miriam R. Ritvo, and Gregory M. St. L. O'Brien, "Applying Behavioral Science: Current Projects," *Journal of Applied Behavioral Science, 5* (3), 1969, pp. 367–389.

Liebtag, Wesley R., "How EDP Personnel Data Systems Work for Corporate Growth," *Personnel, 47* (4), 1970, pp. 15–21.

MacGuffie, John V., "Computer Programs for People," *Personnel Journal, 48* (4), 1969, pp. 250–258.

Miller, James R., III, "Micro-simulation as an Aid to Managing Human Resources," *Industrial Management Review, 11* (2), 1970, pp. 24–30.

Mitzner, Paul L., "Statistics and Quantitative Measurements in Personnel Administration," *Best's Insurance News, Fire and Casualty Edition, 68* (1), 1968, pp. 77–78.

Patterson, Eldon R., "The Computer Helps in Hiring and Keeping 'Top' Personnel," *Personnel Journal, 50* (2), 1971, pp. 141–143.

Pyle, William C., "Monitoring Human Resources — On Line," *Michigan Business Review, 22* (14), 1970, pp. 19–32.

Teach, Leon, et al., "Simulating the Employment Environment," *Management of Personnel Quarterly, 7* (1), 1968, pp. 15–18.

Index